Cultural Considerations for Effective Digital Transformation in Education

Shaoxu Du
https://orcid.org/0009-0002-8142-1343
Universiti Sains Malaysia, Malaysia

Mageswaran Sanmugam
https://orcid.org/0000-0003-3313-4462
Universiti Sains Malaysia, Malaysia

Nurul Maziah Mohd Barkhaya
https://orcid.org/0009-0002-2192-0706
Universiti Sains Malaysia, Malaysia

Chuang Chen
Zhengzhou University of Industrial Technology, China

Jia Wang
Chung-Ang University, South Korea

IGI Global
Scientific Publishing
Publishing Tomorrow's Research Today

Vice President of Editorial	Melissa Wagner
Director of Acquisitions	Mikaela Felty
Director of Book Development	Jocelynn Hessler
Production Manager	Mike Brehm
Cover Design	Jose Rosado

Published in the United States of America by
IGI Global Scientific Publishing
701 East Chocolate Avenue
Hershey, PA, 17033, USA
Tel: 717-533-8845 | Fax: 717-533-7115
Website: https://www.igi-global.com E-mail: cust@igi-global.com

Library of Congress Cataloging-in-Publication Data

Names: Du, Shaoxu, 1990- editor | Sanmugam, Mageswaran, 1982- editor | Barkhaya, Nurul Maziah Mohd, 1988- editor | Chen, Chuang, 1988- editor | Wang, Jia, 1988- editor

Title: Cultural considerations for effective digital transformation in education / Edited by Shaoxu Du, Mageswaran Sanmugam, Nurul Maziah Mohd Barkhaya, Chuang Chen, Jia Wang.

Description: Hershey, PA : IGI Global Scientific Publishing, [2026] | Includes bibliographical references and index. | Summary: "This book aims to create a comprehensive and inclusive space for researchers, educators, technologists, and designers to share their insights, theories, and practical applications at the intersection of culture, education, and digital technology"-- Provided by publisher.

Identifiers: LCCN 2025020200 (print) | LCCN 2025020201 (ebook) | ISBN 9798337336732 hardback | ISBN 9798337336749 paperback | ISBN 9798337336756 ebook

Subjects: LCSH: Education--Effect of technological innovations on | Education and globalization | Artificial intelligence--Educational applications | Gamification | Multicultural education

Classification: LCC LB1028.3 .C84 2026 (print) | LCC LB1028.3 (ebook)

LC record available at https://lccn.loc.gov/2025020200

LC ebook record available at https://lccn.loc.gov/2025020201

British Cataloguing in Publication Data
A Cataloguing in Publication record for this book is available from the British Library.

Table of Contents

Detailed Table of Contents

pedagogical strategies for critical AI literacy and urges redesign of systems to honor marginalized epistemologies. Ultimately, it argues that tools shaped by dominant grammars cannot ethically translate insurgent voices.

As AI-powered technologies become increasingly embedded in educational systems worldwide, a critical question emerges: whose languages, values, and epistemologies are being amplified—and whose are being erased? This chapter explores the tensions between global AI solutions and local cultural and linguistic realities. It interrogates the design assumptions behind popular AI tools, uncovering how algorithmic logic often overlooks diverse modes of knowing and speaking. Drawing from real-world examples and critical theory, the chapter advocates for culturally responsive and linguistically inclusive AI development. It calls for participatory design approaches that center marginalized communities and rethink what it means to "personalize" learning. Ultimately, the chapter urges educators, technologists, and policymakers to move beyond one-size-fits-all innovation and toward a more pluralistic, justice-oriented digital future in education.

The advent of Generative Artificial Intelligence (GenAI) marks a pivotal moment for creative industries, including cultural product design. This paper proposes specific research questions and outlines the research method used to develop a revised framework with GenAI. The core of the paper presents this four-stage framework detailing student activities, GenAI integration points, GenAI roles, and expected outputs for each stage. Foundational principles and strategic imperatives for effective GenAI integration are discussed. The framework aims to guide educators and students in leveraging GenAI's potential to foster innovation while upholding cultural integrity and ethical responsibility, fostering a human-AI cultural symbiosis.

Preface

Education in the digital age is no longer bound by classrooms or traditional methods—it is a constantly evolving interplay between technology, culture, and human creativity. This book, *Cultural Considerations for Effective Digital Transformation in Education*, gathers an extraordinary range of perspectives that illuminate how artificial intelligence, virtual and augmented reality, gamification, mobile technologies, and blended learning are reshaping the future of teaching and learning. The chapters contained herein weave together theory, practice, and cultural context, offering new pathways for inclusive, ethical, and innovative education.

CHAPTER OVERVIEW

The opening contribution,**Beyond Toolness: A Qualitative Content Analysis of Generative AI Platforms for Design Creation** critically assesses generative AI tools such as Canva, Midjourney, and ChatGPT, underscoring their ability to foster creativity while raising concerns about homogenization, authorship, and cultural depth.

With **Beyond Lexical Accuracy: AI's Catastrophic Loss of Political Blood in Translating Lorde's Revolutionary Vernacular**, the ethical and cultural stakes of AI translation are revealed, showing how revolutionary poetics risk being diluted by algorithmic neutrality and dominant linguistic frameworks.

Cultural and Linguistic Diversity in AI-Powered Educational Technologies interrogates how global platforms risk erasing local epistemologies and calls for culturally sensitive, participatory approaches to technology development that honor diverse ways of knowing.

In **Integrating Generative AI into Cultural and Creative Product Design Education: A Framework for Student Designers**, AI is presented as a partner in fostering innovation while ensuring cultural authenticity and ethical responsibility in product design.

Integration of AI Technology for Chinese Language Teaching—A Study on Current Status, Challenges and Future Prospects investigates how AI transforms language instruction, exploring teaching strategies, efficiency, and long-term prospects for Chinese language learning.

Promoting Intercultural Understanding and Motivation in Language Learning through Kahoot! showcases how game-based tools can foster cross-cultural dialogue and motivation among young learners in Japan and Australia.

Bridging Cultures through EdTech: Integrating Cultural Approaches in Online Learning presents case studies of culturally responsive online platforms, emphasizing the role of inclusivity in shaping digital classrooms.

Distributed Leadership Effect on Global Collaboration in Digital Education by Mediation of Culture of Inclusivity and Openness in Horn of Africa examines how shared leadership and cultural openness can enhance international cooperation in digital learning.

Culturally Responsive Financial Education in the Digital Age: Empowering Diverse Learners demonstrates how digital platforms can promote financial literacy and inclusion, particularly among marginalized groups worldwide.

Culturally Attuned Digital Transformation in Education: Integrating FemTech for Inclusive Learning Ecosystems highlights the role of gender-sensitive technologies in improving access, equity, and engagement in education.

Cultural Sensitivity in Digital Learning Platforms: A Global Perspective reflects on design choices that either alienate or empower learners, advocating for culturally adaptable and reflexive digital platforms.

The volume closes with **Cultural Diversity in Gamified Learning: Leveraging Multinational Teamwork in Business Simulations** analyzes how cross-cultural collaboration in gamified settings fosters creativity, problem-solving, and intercultural competence.

This book represents a mosaic of research, practice, and cultural reflection. By drawing on voices from across the globe, it calls for a future where digital transformation in education is not merely a technological shift, but a cultural dialogue that values inclusivity, justice, and creativity. It is our hope that this collection will serve as both a reference and an inspiration for scholars, practitioners, and policymakers committed to building equitable educational ecosystems in the digital era.

Shaoxu Du
Universiti Sains Malaysia, Malaysia

Mageswaran Sanmugam
Universiti Sains Malaysia, Malaysia

Nurul Maziah Mohd Barkhaya

Universiti Sains Malaysia, Malaysia

Chuang Chen
Zhengzhou University of Industrial Technology, China

Jia Wang
Chung-Ang University, South Korea

Acknowledgement

The editor would like to express heartfelt gratitude to all who contributed to the successful completion of this book, Cultural Considerations for Effective Digital Transformation in Education. First and foremost, sincere appreciation goes to the authors for their valuable research, dedication, and commitment. Their thoughtful contributions have been central in shaping this volume and deepening our understanding of how culture and technology intersect in education.

The editor is also deeply thankful to the editorial team at IGI Global for their consistent guidance and support throughout the publication process. Their professionalism and expertise have been instrumental in bringing this project to fruition.

Special thanks are extended to the reviewers, whose careful and constructive feedback ensured the quality and scholarly rigor of the chapters. Their insights and commitment to excellence have enriched this book and greatly enhanced its academic value.

Finally, the editor wishes to acknowledge the many educators, researchers, and practitioners who shared their perspectives and experiences. Their voices have contributed significantly to the discussions presented in this book, helping to make it a collaborative and meaningful effort.

The editor would like to extend special acknowledgment to the following reviewers whose expertise and thoughtful feedback greatly contributed to the success of this book:

Dr. Zhang Jingru

Dr. Olufemi Timothy Adigun

Dr. Amrita Chaudhary

Tian Feng

Wako Jio

Diya Garg

Song Fenglin

Dr. Andy Lim Teik Hong

Sun Jingru

Shashi Kant

Dr. Mustafa Kayyali

Xu Biao

Darren Yie

Arvin Cheong Kee Sin

Lin Chaoquan

Dr. Luqman Mahmud

Hélder Fanha Martins

Dr. Maheswaran Muthuraman

Dr. Shinji Okumura

Dr. Selvakumar P

Sara Cerqueira Pascoal

Melanie Shaw

Dr. Pravesh Soti

Wang Hanxu

Yang Jingran

Wang Ying

Zhen Huixin

Liu Jinya

Chapter 1
Beyond Toolness:
A Qualitative Content Analysis of Generative AI Platforms for Design Creation

Fenglin Song
https://orcid.org/0009-0006-3447-5532
Universiti Sains Malaysia, Malaysia

Siti Nazleen Abdul Rabu
https://orcid.org/0000-0003-2765-0348
Universiti Sains Malaysia, Malaysia

ABSTRACT

This study employs a qualitative content analysis of three generative AI platforms—Canva, Midjourney, and ChatGPT—to examine their roles in design creation, focusing on how they support creative practices and the functional similarities and differences among them. The findings revealed that generative AI platforms impact various aspects of creative work. However, tensions emerge between enhanced individual creativity and risks of homogenised outputs, driven by algorithmic reliance and data-driven constraints. While generative AI platforms lower technical barriers and accelerate workflows, challenges persist in sustaining originality, balancing human-AI collaboration, and addressing ethical concerns like authorship and cultural depth. The study underscores the need for critical integration of generative AI platforms to complement human creativity while fostering diverse and sustainable design practices.

DOI: 10.4018/979-8-3373-3673-2.ch001

1 INTRODUCTION

Generative artificial intelligence (AI), a technology that generates data through algorithms and models, is revolutionising the way people create and interact with content. It has enormous potential in a variety of fields, including art, design, and entertainment, by facilitating the generation of novel and creative output (Ooi et al., 2025). In recent years, the scope of generative AI applications has expanded continuously, encompassing areas such as text generation, visual creation, and music production (Cao et al., 2023; Taylor et al., 2024; Suryadevara, 2020). Specifically within the design field, the integration of the AI technology is reshaping traditional creative processes and impacting multiple professional fields, such as industrial design, architectural design, and graphic design (Bertão et al., 2025; Lee et al., 2025; Li et al., 2025).

The underlying technology of generative AI is primarily based on deep learning algorithms and neural network models. Leveraging these technologies, numerous generative AI platforms have emerged in the market. These platforms are categorized according to different creative formats, including text generation platforms, image generation platforms, video generation platforms, music generation platforms, and 3D generation platforms. These generative AI platforms not only simplify workflows for artists and designers but also enable cross-medium artistic expression (Adeleye, 2023; Guo et al., 2023). From static images to dynamic videos, generative AI platforms inject innovative power into the fields of art and design. Generative AI platforms have become a key driver and catalyst for design creation, providing users with diverse creative experiences.

Although studies have explored the role of single generative AI platforms in design (Tan & Luhrs, 2024; Zhou & Lee, 2024), there is a lack of comprehensive analyses across generative AI platforms and functional dimensions. This study is particularly focused on how generative AI platforms can support design creation. The research is divided into two parts. The first part discusses the integration of generative AI platforms in creative practices. The second part focuses on how selected generative AI platforms are used in design creation. Two research questions were developed to guide this study:

1. How generative AI platforms being integrated into creative practices?
2. What similarities or differences in content exist between the different generative AI platforms?

2 LITERATURE REVIEW

2.1 Generative AI Technologies: Underlying Mechanisms for Supporting Generative AI Platforms

Machine learning (ML) and artificial neural networks (ANNs) are fundamental technologies supporting generative AI platforms (Kalota, 2024). ML involves the development of statistical algorithms that enable systems to learn from data and generalise this learning to unseen data to execute tasks without explicit instructions. ANNs, a branch of machine learning models, are constructed based on principles of neural organization derived from the biological neural networks found in the brain.

ML aims to iteratively develop an understanding of datasets without requiring explicit rule encoding (Di Franco & Santurro, 2021). This allows computational systems to start with an input dataset, automatically learning and predicting, adjusting their parameters through optimisation of performance standards defined on the data, and reducing error rates at each stage of the learning process (Goodfellow et al., 2014).

Another name for ANNs is deep learning (DL). Specifically, DL is a subset of ANNs that uses multi-layered networks to process information (Di Franco & Santurro, 2021). ANNs are organized into three layers: the input layer, the hidden layer, and the output layer. The input layer presents data, the hidden layer transforms the data, and the output layer produces the response. DL networks include at least one hidden layer. Early discoveries in deep learning can be traced back to the 1960s, aiming to learn models that may occur or happen in the brain (Di Franco & Santurro, 2021). Because it is difficult for computers to understand the meaning of raw input data, DL breaks down the required tasks into a series of nested concepts, with each concept being described by different layers of the model, thus solving this challenge (Di Franco & Santurro, 2021; Goodfellow et al., 2014; LeCun et al., 2015).

Generative AI platforms use generative models based on neural network architectures, such as the Generative Pre-trained Transformer (GPT) and Generative Adversarial Networks (GAN). GPT is a generative pre-trained language model based on the transformer architecture (Radford et al., 2021). It is trained on a vast amount of text data, enabling it to understand and generate text with high proficiency. GAN operates with two competing neural networks to train data. One network, the generator, is responsible for creating new data, while the other, the discriminator, distinguishes between real and generated data. Through iterative training, the generator continuously improves the quality of the generated data until it becomes indistinguishable from real data by the discriminator (Goodfellow, 2014).

Generative AI platforms also use Contrastive Language-Image Pre-training (CLIP) (Radford et al., 2021). CLIP is a multimodal pre-training method based on contrastive learning. It uses text-image pairs to train the model, enabling it to learn the relationship between images and text. CLIP's discriminative capability can be applied to various tasks: 1) Image retrieval: CLIP can retrieve relevant images based on textual descriptions; 2) Zero-shot learning: CLIP can identify new categories without labelled data; 3) Text generation: CLIP can generate images that align with textual descriptions. CLIP-based neural networks can effectively learn visual concepts from natural language supervision and can be applied to any visual classification task, requiring only the name of the visual category to be recognized (Radford et al., 2021). These technologies collectively contribute to the practical applications of generative tools in design creativity.

2.2 Empowering Design Creation: Opportunities and Challenges

In 2022, the emergence of AI tools such as ChatGPT, Stable Diffusion and Midjourney marked a significant enhancement in the efficiency and accuracy of image generation technologies, significantly expanding the creative paths in design. Text generation platforms, such as ChatGPT, utilise deep learning models to automatically produce natural language, code, and even literary texts, greatly enhancing the efficiency of designers in areas like copywriting, narrative expression, and interaction design (Zhang, 2024). However, this data-driven creative model may diminish the designer's ability to express individuality and cultural depth, potentially leading to homogenisation and templated content. Similarly, image generation platforms like Midjourney have revolutionised visual creation, enabling designers to quickly generate high-quality visuals through technologies like text-to-image and image-to-image, providing convenience for creative exploration and rapid iteration (Bansal et al., 2024). However, it is important to be cautious of the increasing reliance on technology, which could reduce the creator's ability to control image construction logic and visual language. Moreover, most existing technologies rely heavily on the recombination of existing materials or are constrained by the data they are trained on, which may hinder the expansion of originality. In the field of video generation, although platforms like Runway are still in their developmental stages, their potential is undeniable. With automatic editing, special effects generation, and content synthesis, such platforms significantly lower the barrier to video production, offering an efficient new paradigm for animation, gaming, and short video creation (Huang et al., 2023). Nevertheless, technical limitations in logical coherence, emotional expression, and narrative complexity continue to restrict its full application in high-end art and design fields. Music generation platforms, such as Stable Audio, break down traditional barriers in music creation, allowing even non-professionals to participate in musical design (Wang et al., 2024). This undoubtedly broadens the scope of sound expression in design but also raises discussions about the emotional depth, cultural symbolism, and originality of music. When algorithms become the primary driver of creativity, the emotional authenticity and human warmth of music may face challenges. Three-dimensional generation platforms like Magic3D provide tremendous support for product design, architectural design, and virtual world construction through automated modelling and scene reconstruction (Bono, 2024). These platforms lower the technical barrier and promote spatial imagination and form innovation. However, the reliance on existing models and data may limit the boundaries of design innovation and even raise concerns regarding originality, copyright, and ethical issues.

2.3 AI Design: A New Paradigm in Design Creation

Traditional design usually involves artists or designers creating realistic and attractive character images on paper or computer screens, which requires some drawing and design skills. In contrast, generative AI technology eliminates the need to draw or design by hand to create images (Xi & Chung, 2023). Generative AI can transform textual descriptions into visual representations, effectively bridging the gap between conceptualisation and visualisation (Yin et al., 2023). This capability enables designers to quickly generate diverse and unique digital images based on input keywords or specific parameters, thereby speeding up the design process (Zhang & Liu, 2024). In addition, generative AI facilitates iterative design, allowing for rapid creative exploration and conceptual refinement (Mansour, 2023).

AI design represents an emerging form of creation that incorporates generative AI technology into the design process. In contrast to traditional design, AI design is characterised by the following features: 1) It focuses on exploring and expressing art through technologies such as machine learning and deep learning; 2) The creative agent in AI design is the AI algorithm guided by human thought; and 3) AI design creates artistic works that transcend the physical world through the analysis, processing, and generation of vast amounts of data. This contrasts with traditional design, where the creator is a human designer expressing personal emotions and thoughts through the representation of objects or scenes from the real world. Furthermore, traditional designers are expected to possess high levels of design literacy and professional skills, whereas AI designers are recommended to have knowledge in computer science, mathematics, and related fields, and to be able to apply various algorithms and models flexibly. Therefore, understanding the similarities and differences among various generative AI platforms may be beneficial for AI design processes, helping to address certain limitations of traditional design approaches.

3 METHOD

Due to the prominence of DigitalOcean and Zapier in providing design recommendations for designers and developers, the researcher considered them relevant sources for compiling a list of the most significant tools used in creative practice (DigitalOcean, 2025; Lukan, 2025). These platforms regularly publish numerous articles covering various aspects of creative work. Based on the recommendations, the mainstream generative AI platforms for design creation are shown in Table 1.

Table 1. The mainstream generative AI tools for creative practices

Category	Tools	Key Features
Image Generation	Midjourney, DALL·E, Stable Diffusion	AI painting, illustration
Video Generation	Runway, Pika, Kaiber	Video style transfer, video creation, dynamic imagery
3D Design	Spline, Luma	3D modeling, spatial design, virtual environments
Graphic/Brand Design	Looka, Designs.ai	Logo creation, brand visuals, template generation
Dynamic Creativity	Adobe Firefly, Canva	Image editing, text-to-image conversion, animation effects
AI Collaboration & Inspiration	ChatGPT, Jasper AI	Content ideation, story scripting, design assistance

To gain a deeper understanding of how generative AI platforms support design creation, this study involved content analysis of the selected generative AI platforms. It was deemed more appropriate to observe and analyze several applications to explore the potential impact of these platforms on creative practice. The platforms were chosen based on the following criteria: (a) open access; (b) no requirement for specialized hardware; (c) market influence; (d) technological sophistication; and (e) the assurance of proper data protection for users. After a thorough selection process, three platforms were identified for this study: Canva, Midjourney, and ChatGPT.

Due to the inherent complexity and uniqueness of generative AI platforms, controlling all relevant variables proved challenging, which in turn limited our ability to gain a comprehensive understanding of the phenomenon. Therefore, qualitative methods are employed in this study. Unlike quantitative approaches, the qualitative methodology adopted in this study allowed for the continuous and dynamic analysis of data, enabling the information to evolve and grow as more insights were gathered from the three case studies. Guided by the research questions, the study analysed potential activities associated with the use of generative AI platforms. During the data collection process, significant features were recorded as potential evidence of design activities. Upon completion of the study, a cross-case analysis was conducted to identify similarities or differences between the cases, providing deeper insights into the potential patterns and trends of tool usage.

4. RESULTS

4.1 Case-in-Point 1: Canva

Canva is an online graphic design platform founded in Australia in 2013 by Melanie Perkins, Cliff Obrecht, and Cameron Adams. It enables users to create a wide range of visual materials, including social media graphics, presentations, posters, and documents. Designed with generative AI capabilities, Canva aims to help users produce professional-level designs with minimal effort, regardless of their design background. The platform offers a free version, while additional tools and functionalities are available through paid plans such as Canva Pro and Canva for Enterprise. For educational purposes, Canva also provides a free version specifically designed for schools, encouraging collaboration between educators and students. One of Canva's main strengths lies in its extensive collection of visual assets, which includes high-resolution images, multilingual fonts, original templates, and custom illustrations. Its simple and intuitive drag-and-drop interface allows users to create and modify designs efficiently. The platform offers access to a large content library, which features millions of photos, graphics, and typefaces, providing abundant resources to support creative work. In March 2023, Canva expanded its functionality by launching a series of AI-powered tools that aim to simplify the design process and improve output quality.

The AI features are grouped under a toolkit known as Magic Studio. Among them, Magic Write, developed using OpenAI technology, supports the generation of ideas and topics to assist users in initiating their design concepts. The tool provides prompt suggestions and produces written content such as marketing texts, blog outlines, personal bios, and content strategies tailored to user needs. It is capable of generating a wide range of textual formats, including summaries, long-form articles, short notes, lists, and paragraph structures. Furthermore, it allows users to rewrite, expand, or paraphrase existing content.

Magic Design supports users in transforming text descriptions and image inputs into relevant visual outputs. By entering the intended design content into the search bar, users receive suggestions for templates, logos, posters, social media graphics, and presentation slides based on their descriptions. This feature is particularly beneficial for individuals without advanced design or technical skills.

Magic Switch enables users to change the format, size, and language of their designs with ease. It facilitates the conversion of visual content into different document types, such as blog posts, summaries, or emails, and can also translate existing designs into various languages or adjust dimensions to suit different platforms.

Magic Edit, which leverages Stable Diffusion technology, allows users to alter or replace specific elements within an image through guided AI input. Users can select areas of an image and enter text descriptions to make desired changes. Magic Expand provides the ability to extend the borders of an image in any direction, helping to correct awkward framing or improve composition. In addition, Canva includes various AI functions for object removal, background elimination, animation creation, and the generation of visual patterns and textures.

Another noteworthy component is Magic Media, which incorporates advanced AI tools such as DALL·E, Imagen, and Runway. This feature enables users to convert text prompts into images or videos, supporting more dynamic and imaginative content creation. Machine learning algorithms trained on extensive datasets generate visuals based on user input, which can then be integrated into projects like presentations or digital media posts. Canva also offers diverse artistic styles, such as watercolor, fantasy, anime, and cinematic aesthetics, allowing users to experiment with different visual expressions during the creative process. Table 2 summarises the dimensions of design activities supported by Canva.

Table 2. Dimensions of Design Activities in Canva

Dimension	Features	Design Activities
Inspiring ideas	Prompt Suggestions	Suggesting random words and phrases to guide users in initiating design activities
	Magic Write	Generating ideas and themes to support brainstorming
	Magic Design	Generating design templates to clarify design requirements
Artistic exploration	Magic Media	Exploring various artistic styles such as watercolor, dreamy, anime, and filmic across different settings
Content generation	Magic Write	Generating short-form or long-form text, including headings, summaries, outlines, and lists
	Magic Media	Generating images or videos based on text prompts
	Magic Design	Generating design assets such as templates, logos, posters, and presentations
	Magic Morph	Transforming text and shapes into patterns or textures using prompts

continued on following page

Table 2. Continued

Dimension	Features	Design Activities
Image enhancement	Magic Edit	Reimagining and editing image elements based on prompts
	Magic Grab	Removing unwanted details or distractions from photos
	Magic Expand	Expanding images in any direction
	Magic Remover	Removing backgrounds from images or videos
Design transformation	Magic Switch	Transforming design projects into formats such as blog posts, summaries, or emails Resizing designs for various applications Translating designs into multiple languages

4.2 Case-in-Point 2: Midjourney

Midjourney is an AI image generation platform that uses deep learning techniques. It was developed by a research lab led by David Holz. It was first released in August 2021 and entered public beta testing in July 2022. After several updates, the platform now supports better text reproduction and more literal interpretation of prompts. Midjourney is widely used in art creation, design, entertainment, and education. When users enter text prompts on Discord, Midjourney can generate matching images based on AI algorithms and choose art styles from various painters such as Da Vinci, Dali, and Picasso. It can also recognize specific camera angles or photography terms. This technology has brought revolutionary change to the creative industry, allowing users to create impressive visual works without needing professional art skills or expensive design software.

The Showcase page on the Midjourney website displays works created by users with AI. Users can browse these images to find inspiration or search for specific pictures. Once a suitable creative work is selected, users can view its detailed page, which includes the generation prompt, aspect ratio, model, and style options.

The core function of Midjourney is implemented by entering commands into the Midjourney Bot on Discord. These commands can be used to create, mix, and describe images, as well as perform other useful tasks. The "imagine" command generates images based on a short text description, known as a prompt. By invoking the "imagine" command and entering the description of the desired image—including details such as the expected style, environment, objects, and emotions—in the prompt field, the user sends a message. The Midjourney Bot then processes the request and creates four distinct image options in a short period of time. If the user wishes to further modify or optimise an image, they can click the button below to select an image, re-run the command, or vary the image based on one of the generated options.

When users are satisfied with the generated image, they can further enhance or modify it. The “Vary” function allows the user to create stronger or more subtle variations of the chosen image by regenerating a new set of images. The “Zoom” function enables the user to enlarge the image to improve its detail and quality. The “Pan” function lets the user expand the canvas in a selected direction without altering the content of the original image; the new canvas is filled using the prompt and guidance from the original image. In addition, the “Blend” command allows the user to upload and combine their own images, merging 2–5 images into one new image. The “Describe” command lets the user generate inspiring and suggestive text prompts based on the uploaded image to help interpret its content. If the user needs further assistance or has any questions, they can interact one-on-one with the Midjourney Bot.

Midjourney is an open community by default. To ensure the platform is easy to access and widely accepted, Midjourney requires all community members to follow its community guidelines. These guidelines include being friendly and respectful to one another and the staff and not sharing someone else's work without permission. In addition, users are not allowed to create images or use text prompts that are inherently disrespectful, aggressive, abusive, violent, or harassing. They are also prohibited from producing visually shocking or disturbing content. The Midjourney Bot uses technical measures to automatically block command inputs that contain such texts. These rules apply to all content, whether created on private servers, in private mode, or through direct messages with the Midjourney Bot. Any violation of these rules may result in the user losing access to the service. Table 3 summarises the dimensions of design activities supported by Midjourney.

Table 3. Dimensions of Design Activities in Midjourney

Dimension	Features	Design Activities
Inspiring ideas	Response	Browsing user-generated images for inspiration Viewing prompts used by others as references
Artistic exploration	Prompts	Experimenting with different text prompts to explore artistic themes and concepts
Content generation	Imagine	Entering text descriptions to generate four unique image options Regenerating images using the same prompt
	Re-run	Re-running the same prompt to explore additional outcomes
	Variation	Modifying selected images to create new variations
	Blend	Uploading and combining 2–5 images to create a new composite visual
	Describe	Uploading an image to generate text prompts for interpreting its content

continued on following page

Table 3. Continued

Dimension	Features	Design Activities
Image enhancement	Vary	Creating stronger or more subtle variations of a selected image
	Zoom	Enlarging an image to enhance detail and quality
	Pan	Expanding the canvas in a chosen direction while maintaining consistency with the original image
Community identity	Community	Joining the Midjourney Discord community to view and participate in events and activities

3.3 Case-in-Point 3: ChatGPT

ChatGPT was launched by OpenAI in November 2022. It is a natural language processing model capable of generating, summarising, and interpreting text in a conversational format. Since its release, it has gained popularity across various creative fields, including design. Although the platform is freely accessible to the public, users may subscribe to paid tiers such as Plus or Pro to enjoy additional features. These include unlimited access to different reasoning models such as o3-mini, o3-mini-high, o1, and the research preview version of GPT-4.5. ChatGPT serves millions of users worldwide and has been widely adopted by designers, educators, students, and professionals. Users interact with the tool by inputting prompts in natural language and receiving AI-generated responses within seconds.

One of the key features of ChatGPT is its “response” function, which plays a critical role in the early stages of the design process by helping users generate new ideas. Through text-based dialogue, users can brainstorm concepts and explore creative directions. For instance, a user might type a prompt such as “Give me five sustainable poster design ideas,” and ChatGPT will provide suggestions. These responses can stimulate creative thinking and support designers in shaping their design concepts and directions.

In addition, ChatGPT is also capable of creating both text and images. The text creation feature is especially useful for generating design copy, such as product descriptions, advertisements, or website content. Designers may enter prompts like “Write a slogan for AI-powered glasses,” and ChatGPT will offer a variety of suggestions. These outputs can be integrated into marketing campaigns, design presentations, or web content. Furthermore, ChatGPT can summarise lengthy text and extract key design elements, helping users condense complex ideas into more focused and accessible information. For example, a user could submit the transcript of a design meeting, and ChatGPT would identify major themes, design objectives, and target audiences based on the prompt.

The image creation feature extends ChatGPT's capabilities beyond text, enabling users to generate visual drafts from textual descriptions. For example, users may describe a design need using keywords like "organic, sustainability, and urban lifestyle", and ChatGPT can produce visual representations accordingly. This helps designers quickly explore various visual styles, layouts, and colour schemes. It can also assist in translating narratives into visual forms by turning stories, emotions, or concepts into coherent visual compositions.

ChatGPT also supports the retrieval of design-related information, allowing users to learn design principles, explore tutorials, and discover high-quality design examples. For instance, by asking, "What are the key principles of typography in graphic design?", users receive instant answers that support their understanding of core design knowledge. ChatGPT can also guide users through design tutorials by offering step-by-step summaries or explanations for various software tools or visual practices. In addition, the tool helps users discover outstanding design cases, such as award-winning projects or influential case studies. This curated access to quality content allows users to analyse successful works and gain inspiration for their own projects.

Furthermore, ChatGPT allows users to upload images and receive text-based feedback. Designers can upload their work, and ChatGPT will analyse the image to provide interpretations related to composition, colour use, and style. This type of feedback is especially helpful for students or novice designers seeking guidance. For example, after uploading a poster design, users may ask ChatGPT to analyse the visual content. The model may describe how the design balances shapes, uses colours, and organises visual hierarchy. This functionality supports designers in reflecting on their work and understanding how their visuals communicate meaning. ChatGPT can also help identify emotional expressions embedded in visual compositions. For instance, it may recognise a sense of calm in a pastel-toned layout or a sense of movement in an asymmetrical composition.

ChatGPT supports a wide range of design activities through its diverse functionalities. It aids in idea generation through responsive dialogue, enables content creation in both text and image formats, facilitates learning through information retrieval, and provides multimodal interpretations that support reflection and analysis. While not without limitations, ChatGPT plays an increasingly important role in design education and professional practice. When used thoughtfully and critically, it can help designers focus more on higher-level problem-solving and user-centred innovation. Table 4 summarises the dimensions of design activities supported by ChatGPT.

Table 4. Dimensions of Design Activities in ChatGPT

Dimension	Features	Design Activities
Inspiring ideas	Response	Brainstorming design concepts Exploring creative directions
Content generation	Creating text	Generating design copy Summarising text and extracting key design elements
	Creating Images	Generating visual drafts based on text prompts Translating narratives into visuals
Information retrieval	Search	Learning design principles Exploring design tutorials Discovering examples of good design
Multimodal interpretation	Upload	Explaining image composition, colour, and style through text Extracting design ideas or emotional expressions from design works

5. DISCUSSION

The integration of generative AI platforms such as Canva, Midjourney, and ChatGPT has significantly transformed the landscape of design creation. These platforms offer diverse functionalities that support various aspects of the design process, from ideation to execution (See Figure 1). This section discussed the impact of these platforms on design creation.

Figure 1. The integration of generative AI platforms in design creation

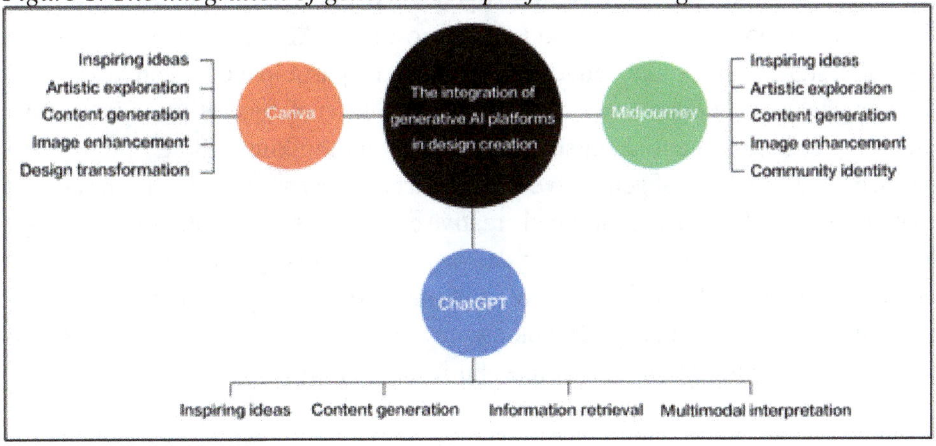

5.1 Inspiring Ideas

These three platforms, Canva, Midjourney and ChatGPT, inspire creativity through similar mechanisms. For instance, Canva enhances ideation by suggesting random words and phrases to initiate design activities, generating thematic ideas to support brainstorming, and generating design templates to help users clarify their design requirements. Midjourney promotes inspiration by allowing users to browse a wide range of user-generated images and view the text prompts associated with those visuals, offering valuable references for their own creative exploration. In contrast, ChatGPT supports creativity by facilitating the brainstorming of design concepts and encouraging users to explore diverse creative directions through conversational prompts.

The potential of generative AI to inspire ideas has attracted significant academic attention. Doshi and Hauser (2024) demonstrated that generative AI can increase the perceived creativity, particularly among individuals with lower baseline creativity. However, their study also revealed a concomitant reduction in the diversity of novel content, indicating a potential homogenisation effect. This suggests that while generative AI can serve as a valuable tool for enhancing individual creativity, its widespread use might inadvertently diminish the collective novelty of creative works. Further research by Liu et al. (2024) examined the sustainability of generative AI's impact on creativity. Their study revealed that although generative AI could temporarily boost creative performance, this effect did not persist once the AI assistance was removed. In addition, the homogenisation of content persisted even after discontinuing AI use. This suggests that generative AI, while temporarily increasing human creativity, limits it in the long run. Similarly, Wadinambiarachchi et al. (2024) explored the effects of AI-generated images on design fixation and divergent thinking. The study found that exposure to AI-generated visuals led to higher design fixation and reduced originality in participants' creative outputs. This emphasises the importance of cautious integration of generative AI in creative processes to avoid potential constraints on divergent thinking. These findings emphasise the dual nature of generative AI's impact on creativity. While it can serve as a powerful tool to enhance individual creative capabilities, especially for those with lower inherent creativity, there is a risk of reduced diversity and originality in the broader creative landscape. Therefore, it is imperative to approach the integration of generative AI in creative endeavours with a balanced perspective, ensuring that it complements rather than undermines human creativity.

5.2 Content Generation

Content generation is a foundational capability of generative AI platforms to support diverse design creation. For example, Canva allows users to generate both short-form and long-form text—such as headlines, summaries, outlines, and lists—while also enabling the creation of images and videos from text prompts. Additionally, Canva facilitates the generation of design assets including templates, logos, posters, and presentations, and supports the transformation of text and shapes into creative patterns or textures. Midjourney specialises in image generation, offering capabilities such as producing multiple image variations from a single text description, re-running prompts for expanded outcomes, and blending multiple images into a composite. It also allows users to upload images and generate descriptive prompts for content interpretation. In contrast, ChatGPT focuses on textual generation, excelling at producing design copy and summarising texts to extract essential design elements. These activities illustrate the various ways in which generative AI enhances visual and textual creations in design.

Recent research has increasingly explored the role of generative AI in content generation. Antony and Huang (2025) integrated generative AI to co-create visual stories, aiming to reduce the technical barriers in storytelling. Their study demonstrated that generative AI can enhance user enjoyment and exploration, though issues of immersion and alignment with user intentions remain. This indicates that while generative AI facilitates accessibility in content creation, the human-AI partnership still needs refinement to reach its full potential. Jin et al. (2025) further examined the broader implications of generative AI on design innovation. Their findings suggest that generative AI can efficiently generate quality design data across various modalities such as texts, images, audio, video and simulated sensor data, leading to increased efficiency and creativity. This suggests a paradigm shift in how design is conceptualized and executed, offering novel opportunities to enhance outcomes through AI generation. However, Binhammad et al. (2024) investigated the role of generative AI in education and found that although AI-generated materials enhanced student performance overall, their effectiveness varied based on individual learner characteristics such as prior knowledge and interest. Notably, some students did not benefit from the AI-generated content. This suggests that when integrating generative AI into educational contexts, it is essential to account for factors such as learner motivation, existing knowledge, and the quality of the AI model. Collectively, these findings emphasise that generative AI accelerates content creation by lowering technical barriers, but its application must carefully consider user context and the evolving nature of generative AI technologies.

5.3 Artistic Exploration

Generative AI facilitates artistic exploration by enabling users to engage with diverse artistic styles. For instance, Canva allows users to experiment with various artistic styles, such as watercolor, dreamy, anime, and filmic in different settings, making style exploration more accessible. Similarly, Midjourney empowers users to explore artistic themes and concepts by experimenting with diverse text prompts.

Recent literature has explored how generative AI reshapes artistic exploration. Işık (2024) examined how AI technologies expand traditional artistic boundaries. This study demonstrates that AI not only transforms the materials and techniques available to artists but also broadens access and inclusivity within the art world. Garcia (2024) further investigated the cultural implications of this technological shift, arguing that the integration of generative AI into the art domain constitutes a profound cultural transformation rather than a mere technical advancement. His findings suggest that generative AI challenges conventional notions of authorship and artistic agency, urging a redefinition of the role of the artist in the age of artificial creativity. In contrast, Zhou and Lee (2024) presented a more critical perspective. Their research indicates that while AI-assisted artists may produce work that peers favor, the average novelty of AI-generated artworks is in decline—even as peak novelty increases. This paradox implies that although the creative space is expanding, efficiency in sustained novelty production may be diminishing. It highlights the risk of over-reliance on algorithmic suggestion, which can lead to homogenization of creative outputs over time. These findings emphasize both the transformative potential and emerging tensions within AI-mediated artistic practices. They underscore the need to balance human intentionality with algorithmic assistance and to critically assess how generative AI reshapes not only how art is made, but what art means in a rapidly evolving cultural context.

5.4 Image Enhancement

Image enhancement is another area where generative AI provides significant support to design creation. Canva allows users to reimagine and edit image elements based on text prompts, effectively transforming visual content with minimal effort. Users can remove unwanted details or distractions from photos, expand images seamlessly in any direction, and eliminate backgrounds from both images and videos to suit various design needs. Similarly, Midjourney supports image refinement by enabling users to generate stronger or more subtle variations of a selected image, facilitating iterative artistic development. These generative AI-powered features not only streamline the editing process but also enhance creative control and flexibility, making image enhancement more accessible to users across different skill levels.

Bansal et al. (2024) explored how generative AI can transform traditional multimedia experiences by creating personalised and interactive visual content. Their findings indicate that AI-enhanced images can produce compelling visual effects, enriching documentary narratives that are based on historical text descriptions. This highlights generative AI's transformative potential in broadening the aesthetic and experiential scope of design creation. However, Nguyen et al. (2024) noted that with the growing demand for image processing, traditional tools such as Photoshop, while powerful, require substantial technical expertise to use effectively. Although generative AI integration in platforms like Canva offers image enhancement capabilities, these solutions often require extensive retraining and fine-tuning, resulting in high user costs. In response, they developed a generative AI-driven tool that integrates advanced editing features such as object removal, background modification and region-specific manipulation into a user-centred interface to improve efficiency and ease of use. This advancement suggests that deep integration of generative AI can lower the technical barriers to image processing. This research aligns with the perspective of Striuk and Kondratenko (2023), who acknowledged that although current GAN models deliver promising results in image enhancement, there is still room for performance improvement.

5.5 Design Transformation

Generative AI also supports users in transforming design formats directly. For instance, Canva enables users to convert design projects into alternative content formats such as blog posts, summaries, or emails. It also allows for automatic resizing of designs to suit various platforms and applications, as well as translating visual content into multiple languages, thereby enhancing versatility and accessibility in design creation. Bonde and Dembele (2024) further illustrated generative AI's versatility by demonstrating its application in converting diverse social media content—including text, images, audio, and video—into structured textual formats suitable for machine learning algorithms. This highlights generative AI's transformative impact on design practices, facilitating dynamic content adaptation and expanding creative possibilities.

5.6 Community Identity

Community identity is fostered through the collaborative and interactive features of generative AI platforms. Midjourney's integration with Discord allows users to participate in a community where they can share creations and exchange ideas.

Carbajal-Carrera (2024) highlighted that generative AI in education has implications for the representation of knowledge and identity. Similarly, Antony and Huang (2025) emphasised the importance of AI identities to foster effective human-AI collaboration. Their findings suggested that while generative AI can enhance creation experiences, challenges remain in achieving immersive and aligned partnerships between users and AI systems. Smith and Lundström (2024) further argued that emerging technologies like generative AI can redefine human creativity by assigning new creative roles, rather than eliminating them, thus reshaping our understanding of human identity in the digital age. Collectively, these studies highlight the transformative potential of generative AI in redefining creative practices and identity constructions.

5.7 Information Retrieval

Information retrieval allows users to access information on design principles, tutorials, and examples of good design. This capability supports users in acquiring design-related knowledge and skills, facilitating informed decision-making in the design process. The role of generative AI in information retrieval has transformed how users access and interact with information. Adelakun (2024) emphasised that AI technologies, including machine learning and natural language processing, have enhanced the relevance, personalisation, and semantic understanding of search results, leading to more efficient and tailored user experiences. These advancements have shifted information retrieval systems from traditional keyword-based approaches to more sophisticated, context-aware mechanisms. However, the adoption of AI in information retrieval is not without challenges. Hersh (2024) highlighted concerns among users, particularly academics, regarding the authoritativeness, timeliness, and contextualisation of search results in the era of generative AI. While large language models offer new functionalities, there remains a critical need for traditional search systems and ongoing research to ensure the reliability and accuracy of information retrieval. These perspectives emphasise the importance of striking a balance between AI-driven innovation and the fundamental principles of information retrieval.

5.8 Multimodal Interpretation

Multimodal interpretation in generative AI refers to the capability of models like ChatGPT to process and integrate diverse media forms into a cohesive understanding. This integration enables AI systems to perform complex tasks that require both visual and linguistic comprehension. For instance, ChatGPT can analyse images to provide detailed textual descriptions of their composition, colour schemes, and stylistic elements. This functionality assists users in understanding visual aesthetics and can be particularly beneficial in fields like design and art. Additionally, ChatGPT can extract design concepts or emotional expressions from visual artworks, facilitating deeper insights into the conveyed messages or themes. Alasadi and Baiz (2024) explored the ability of GPT-4 to interpret graphical information in chemistry, finding that the integration of text and image processing allows multimodal AI to solve problems effectively. However, challenges persist in multimodal systems. Zhan et al. (2023) identified critical issues in multimodal image synthesis and editing, including the alignment of multimodal features, the generation of high-resolution images, and the development of reliable evaluation metrics. These challenges highlight the need for continued research to enhance the fidelity and coherence of multimodal outputs.

6 LIMITATIONS AND FUTURE RECOMMENDATIONS

Although this study offers valuable insights into the integration of generative AI platforms in design creation, there are several limitations that warrant consideration. First, it should be noted that only three generative AI platforms were examined in this study, and they do not represent all available tools. Therefore, the findings may not be generalisable to other platforms with different feature sets. Second, the qualitative case study methodology, although appropriate for exploring complex phenomena, inherently limits the ability to draw causal inferences or to quantify the magnitude of observed effects. It is possible that unobserved contextual variables, such as participant familiarity with AI or domain-specific expertise, may influence the outcomes attributed to each platform. Third, the reliance on researcher observations may introduce subjectivity and overlook user cognitive and affective processes that underpin creative decisions. Fourth, the selection criteria prioritized open access and market influence but did not systematically account for user diversity in terms of cultural background, professional role, or cognitive style, which may affect how generative AI platforms are experienced and utilised. Last, the cross-case analysis focused primarily on similarities and differences in functionality rather than on longitudinal changes in user behaviour or creative output quality over time.

To address these limitations, future research should employ mixed-methods designs that integrate quantitative metrics, such as creativity scores, design fixation measures, and task completion times, with qualitative insights to gain a deeper and broader understanding of generative AI's impact. In addition, future research could incorporate experimental or quasi-experimental designs to determine the causal relationship between specific AI features and creative outcomes. This may overcome the limitations of purely observational case studies. Moreover, future investigations could recruit samples of participants from different cultures and professional fields to capture a wider range of user experiences and examine how environmental factors moderate the impact of generative AI on design creation.

Furthermore, ethical considerations, particularly regarding authorship, originality, and potential homogenization of creative outputs (Doshi & Hauser, 2024; Garcia, 2024), were not systematically addressed. Future work should explore designers' attitudes toward AI-generated content ownership and the implications for creative labour markets. Finally, it would be fruitful to investigate algorithmic transparency that enables users to understand when and how models shape design suggestions.

7. CONCLUSIONS

This study has examined how generative AI platforms support and transform the design creation. Through qualitative content analysis and cross-case comparison, it becomes evident that Canva, Midjourney and ChatGPT significantly impact various aspects of creative work, including inspiring ideas, content generation, artistic exploration, image enhancement, and design transformation. Canva's AI-driven templates and text-to-image tools allowed rapid content generation and image enhancement, transforming raw input into polished visual assets. Meanwhile, Midjourney pushes the boundaries of visual imagination through text-to-image synthesis while ChatGPT facilitates content generation, information retrieval and multimodal interpretation. Despite their distinct functionalities, all three platforms support the ideation process by stimulating creative thinking. In addition, these platforms democratise access to advanced creative capabilities, reduce technical barriers, and facilitate the rapid prototyping of ideas, offering both novice and expert designers an expanded set of affordances in the design process.

This study also identifies several critical tensions that emerge with generative AI integration. First, while generative AI can enhance individual creativity, especially for users with lower creative self-efficacy (Doshi & Hauser, 2024), it may lead to a homogenisation of creative output over time (Liu et al., 2024; Zhou & Lee, 2024). Second, although these platforms simplify content generation and enhance image quality (Nguyen et al., 2024), their effectiveness often depends on users' prior knowledge, interest, and the need for continuous fine-tuning (Binhammad et al., 2024). Third, the evolving nature of these tools demands ongoing literacy development to maximise their affordances without becoming overly reliant on algorithmic suggestions.

This research contributes to the understanding of how generative AI technologies are reshaping the creative landscape, particularly in the context of design creation. It emphasises that while generative AI enhances ideation, it also tends to homogenise outcomes. Designers, educators, and policymakers must recognise both the opportunities and the limitations posed by these platforms. Future studies could further explore the long-term cognitive effects of generative AI use in design learning and professional practice and investigate how to balance human creativity with machine-generated assistance to foster more sustainable, diverse, and original design cultures.

REFERENCES

Adelakun, N. O. (2024). Exploring the impact of artificial intelligence on information retrieval systems. *SSRN*, *4*(5), 1–5. DOI: 10.2139/ssrn.4834942

Adeleye, I. O. (2023). The AI effect: Rethinking design workflows for enhanced productivity and creativity. *International Journal of Science and Technology Innovation*, *2*(1), 1–19. DOI: 10.70560/c9m3kd97

Alasadi, E. A., & Baiz, C. R. (2024). Multimodal generative artificial intelligence tackles visual problems in chemistry. *Journal of Chemical Education*, *101*(7), 2716–2729. DOI: 10.1021/acs.jchemed.4c00138

Antony, V. N., & Huang, C. M. (2025). ID. 8: Co-creating visual stories with generative AI. *ACM Transactions on Interactive Intelligent Systems*, *14*(3), 1–29. DOI: 10.1145/3672277

Bansal, G., Nawal, A., Chamola, V., & Herencsar, N. (2024). Revolutionizing visuals: The role of generative AI in modern image generation. *ACM Transactions on Multimedia Computing Communications and Applications*, *20*(11), 1–22. DOI: 10.1145/3689641

Bertão, R. A., Yeoun, M. H., & Joo, J. (2025). A blind spot in AI-powered logo makers: Visual design principles. *Visual Communication*, *24*(1), 222–250. DOI: 10.1177/14703572231155593

Binhammad, M. H. Y., Othman, A., Abuljadayel, L., Al Mheiri, H., Alkaabi, M., & Almarri, M. (2024). Investigating how generative AI can create personalized learning materials tailored to individual student needs. *Creative Education*, *15*(7), 1499–1523. DOI: 10.4236/ce.2024.157091

Bonde, L., & Dembele, S. (2024, August). A unified generative artificial intelligence approach for converting social media content. In *2024 International Conference on Artificial Intelligence, Big Data, Computing and Data Communication Systems (icABCD)* (pp. 1-5). IEEE. https://doi:DOI: 10.1109/icABCD62167.2024.10645267

Bono, G. (2024). Text-to-building: Experiments with AI-generated 3D geometry for building design and structure generation. *Architectural Intelligence*, *3*(1), 1–24. DOI: 10.1007/s44223-024-00060-5

Cao, Y., Li, S., Liu, Y., Yan, Z., Dai, Y., Yu, P. S., & Sun, L. (2023). A comprehensive survey of AI-generated content (aigc): A history of generative AI from GAN to GhatGPT. *arXiv preprint arXiv:2303.04226*. https://doi.org//arXiv.2303.04226DOI: 10.48550

Carbajal-Carrera, B. (2024). AIsplaining: Generative AI explains linguistic identities to me. *Australian Review of Applied Linguistics*, *47*(3), 340–365. DOI: 10.1075/aral.24077.car

Di Franco, G., & Santurro, M. (2021). Machine learning, artificial neural networks and social research. *Quality & Quantity*, *55*(3), 1007–1025. DOI: 10.1007/s11135-020-01037-y

DigitalOcean. (2025). *14 AI design tools for creative professionals.* DigitalOcean. Retrieved April 6, 2025, from https://www.digitalocean.com/resources/articles/ai-design-tools

Doshi, A. R., & Hauser, O. P. (2024). Generative AI enhances individual creativity but reduces the collective diversity of novel content. *Science Advances*, *10*(28), 1–17. DOI: 10.1126/sciadv.adn5290

Garcia, M. B. (2024). The paradox of artificial creativity: Challenges and opportunities of generative AI artistry. *Creativity Research Journal*, •••, 1–14. DOI: 10.1080/10400419.2024.2354622

Goodfellow, I. J., Pouget-Abadie, J., Mirza, M., Xu, B., Warde-Farley, D., Ozair, S., & Bengio, Y. (2014). Generative adversarial nets. *Advances in Neural Information Processing Systems*, *27*, 2672–2680.

Guo, C., Lu, Y., Dou, Y., & Wang, F. Y. (2023). Can ChatGPT boost artistic creation: The need of imaginative intelligence for parallel art. *IEEE/CAA Journal of Automatica Sinica, 10*(4), 835-838. https://doi:.DOI: 10.1109/JAS.2023.123555

Hersh, W. (2024). Search still matters: Information retrieval in the era of generative AI. *Journal of the American Medical Informatics Association : JAMIA*, *31*(9), 2159–2161. DOI: 10.1093/jamia/ocae014

Huang, Y., Lv, S., Tseng, K. K., Tseng, P. J., Xie, X., & Lin, R. F. Y. (2023). Recent advances in artificial intelligence for video production system. *Enterprise Information Systems*, *17*(11), 2246188. DOI: 10.1080/17517575.2023.2246188

Işık, V. (2024). Exploring artistic frontiers in the era of artificial intelligence. *Sanat ve Tasarım Dergisi*, *14*(2), 577–603. DOI: 10.20488/sanattasarim.1603119

Jin, J., Yang, M., Hu, H., Guo, X., Luo, J., & Liu, Y. (2025). Empowering design innovation using AI-generated content. *Journal of Engineering Design*, *36*(1), 1–18. DOI: 10.1080/09544828.2024.2401751

Kalota, F. (2024). A primer on generative artificial intelligence. *Education Sciences*, *14*(2), 172. DOI: 10.3390/educsci14020172

LeCun, Y., Bengio, Y., & Hinton, G. (2015). Deep learning. *nature, 521*(7553), 436-444. https://doi.org/DOI: 10.1038/nature14539

Lee, S. Y., Law, M., & Hoffman, G. (2025). When and how to use AI in the design process? Implications for human-AI design collaboration. *International Journal of Human-Computer Interaction, 41*(2), 1569–1584. DOI: 10.1080/10447318.2024.2353451

Li, Y., Chen, H., Yu, P., & Yang, L. (2025). A review of artificial intelligence in enhancing architectural design efficiency. *Applied Sciences (Basel, Switzerland), 15*(3), 1476. DOI: 10.3390/app15031476

Liu, Q., Zhou, Y., Huang, J., & Li, G. (2024). When ChatGPT is gone: Creativity reverts and homogeneity persists. *arXiv preprint arXiv:2401.06816.*

Lukan, E. (2025). *The 50 best AI tools for 2025.* Synthesia. Retrieved April 6, 2025, from https://www.synthesia.io/post/ai-tools

Mansour, S. (2023). Intelligent graphic design: The effectiveness of Midjourney as a participant in a creative brainstorming session. *International Design Journal, 13*(5), 501–512. DOI: 10.21608/idj.2023.231684.1090

Nguyen, H. P., Vo, D. K., Do, T. L., Nguyen, H. D., Nguyen, T. C., Nguyen, V. T., . . . Le, T. N. (2024, December). EPEdit: Redefining image editing with generative AI and user-centric design. In *International Symposium on Information and Communication Technology* (pp. 272-283). Singapore: Springer Nature Singapore. https://doi.org/DOI: 10.1007/978-981-96-4288-5_22

Ooi, K. B., Tan, G. W. H., Al-Emran, M., Al-Sharafi, M. A., Capatina, A., Chakraborty, A., Dwivedi, Y. K., Huang, T.-L., Kar, A. K., Lee, V.-H., Loh, X.-M., Micu, A., Mikalef, P., Mogaji, E., Pandey, N., Raman, R., Rana, N. P., Sarker, P., Sharma, A., & Wong, L. W. (2025). The potential of generative artificial intelligence across disciplines: Perspectives and future directions. *Journal of Computer Information Systems, 65*(1), 76–107. DOI: 10.1080/08874417.2023.2261010

Radford, A., Kim, J. W., Hallacy, C., Ramesh, A., Goh, G., Agarwal, S., & Sutskever, I. (2021, July). Learning transferable visual models from natural language supervision. In *International conference on machine learning* (pp. 8748-8763). PMLR.

Smith, C. H., & Lundström, F. (2024, July). Hyperhumanism in the age of generative AI: The impact on human creativity and identity. In *Proceedings of EVA London 2024* (pp. 154-159). BCS Learning & Development. http://dx.doi.org/DOI: 10.14236/ewic/EVA2024.27

Striuk, O., & Kondratenko, Y. (2023). Implementation of generative adversarial networks in mobile applications for image data enhancement. *Journal of Mobile Multimedia, 19*(3), 823–838. DOI: 10.13052/jmm1550-4646.1938

Suryadevara, C. K. (2020). Generating free images with OpenAI's generative models. *International Journal of Innovations in Engineering Research and Technology, 7*(3), 49–56. DOI: 10.26662/ijiert.v8i3.pp74-80

Tan, L., & Luhrs, M. (2024). Using generative AI Midjourney to enhance divergent and convergent thinking in an architect's creative design process. *The Design Journal, 27*(4), 677–699. DOI: 10.1080/14606925.2024.2353479

Taylor, J., El Ardeliya, V., & Wolfson, J. (2024). Exploration of artificial intelligence in creative fields: Generative art, music, and design. *International Journal of Cyber and IT Service Management, 4*(1), 39–45. DOI: 10.34306/ijcitsm.v4i1.149

REMOVED HYPERLINK FIELDWadinambiarachchi, S., Kelly, R. M., Pareek, S., Zhou, Q., & Velloso, E. [REMOVED HYPERLINK FIELD]Wadinambiarachchi, S., Kelly, R. M., Pareek, S., Zhou, Q., & Velloso, E. (2024). The effects of generative AI on design fixation and divergent thinking. *Proceedings of the 2024 CHI Conference on Human Factors in Computing Systems*, 1–18. https://doi.org/DOI: 10.1145/3613904.3642919

Wang, L., Zhao, Z., Liu, H., Pang, J., Qin, Y., & Wu, Q. (2024). A review of intelligent music generation systems. *Neural Computing & Applications, 36*(12), 6381–6401. DOI: 10.1007/s00521-024-09418-2

Xi, C., & Chung, J. (2023). A study on character design using [Midjourney] application. *International Journal of Advanced Culture Technology, 11*(2), 409–414. DOI: 10.17703/IJACT.2023.11.2.409

Yin, H., Zhang, Z., & Liu, Y. (2023). The exploration of integrating the Midjourney artificial intelligence generated content tool into design systems to direct designers towards future-oriented innovation. *Systems, 11*(12), 566. DOI: 10.3390/systems11120566

Zhan, F., Yu, Y., Wu, R., Zhang, J., Lu, S., Liu, L., Kortylewski, A., Theobalt, C., & Xing, E. (2023). Multimodal image synthesis and editing: The generative AI era. *IEEE Transactions on Pattern Analysis and Machine Intelligence, 45*(12), 15098–15119. DOI: 10.1109/TPAMI.2023.3305243

Zhang, R. (2024). The impact of artificial intelligence represented by ChatGPT on UI design. *Applied and Computational Engineering, 77*(1), 56–62. DOI: 10.54254/2755-2721/77/20240651

Zhang, Y., & Liu, C. (2024). Unlocking the potential of artificial intelligence in fashion design and e-commerce applications: The case of midjourney. *Journal of Theoretical and Applied Electronic Commerce Research*, *19*(1), 654–670. DOI: 10.3390/jtaer19010035

Zhou, E., & Lee, D. (2024). Generative artificial intelligence, human creativity, and art. *PNAS Nexus*, *3*(3), 1–8. DOI: 10.1093/pnasnexus/pgae052

Chapter 2
Beyond Lexical Accuracy: AI's Catastrophic Loss of Political Blood in Translating Lorde's Revolutionary Vernacular

Jyoti Prakash Pujari
https://orcid.org/0000-0003-1261-2568
Christ University, India

Aditi Dirghangi
https://orcid.org/0000-0002-6672-7267
Christ University, India

ABSTRACT

This chapter examines how generative AI systems (ChatGPT-4o, Gemini 2.5) process the revolutionary poetics of Audre Lorde, revealing systematic patterns of grammatical standardization, affective dilution, and political neutralization. Through comparative analysis of three poems (Power, A Litany for Survival, Who Said It Was Simple) under minimal and culturally contextual prompts, the study demonstrates AI's architectural inability to preserve African American Vernacular English (AAVE), embodied metaphor, or radical tonality. These distortions—rooted in training data biases and fluency optimization—constitute epistemic violence by sanitizing texts where form enacts resistance. Findings expose limitations in developer frameworks prioritizing "harmlessness" over linguistic justice. The chapter proposes pedagogical strategies for critical AI literacy and urges redesign of systems to honor marginalized epistemologies. Ultimately, it argues that tools shaped by dominant grammars cannot ethically translate insurgent voices.

DOI: 10.4018/979-8-3373-3673-2.ch002

1. INTRODUCTION

"The master's tools will never dismantle the master's house."

Audre Lorde, *Sister Outsider* (1984)

Audre Lorde's line is more than just a work of alliterative flourish. It serves as a political warning. According to Gayatri Chakravorty Spivak's seminal text "Can the Subaltern Speak?" (1988), we see that language, when shaped by the powerful, does not liberate the oppressed. Today, that warning reverberates in the smooth, polished outputs of generative artificial intelligence systems such as ChatGPT, Gemini, and Claude, among others, as tools often marketed as neutral, efficient, and universal. In general, these tools remain a favourite among the masses primarily because of their access, personalization, and democratization of knowledge. Yet, their architectures are deeply rooted in data, which is heavily biased by the hierarchies of its training data (Benjamin, 2019; Noble, 2018).

This chapter looks into how AI systems process, analyse, and neutralize the revolutionary poetics of Audre Lorde according to their training data. It focuses on three of her most significant poems: *Power* (1978), *A Litany for Survival* (1978), and *Who Said It Was Simple* (1973). Each poem is an extension of Lorde's ideas of resistance, crafted in language that refuses to give in to the dominant ideologies of the time. Because of it, her poems are replete with historical residue of racial violence, the erotic charge of queer survival, and the urgent pulse of Black feminist pedagogy. Their language is sharp, vernacular, and unfiltered. However, generative artificial intelligence systems consistently transform Audre Lorde's poetry through processes of grammatical standardization, affective dilution, and political neutralization. These algorithmic interventions pose critical questions about linguistic justice when applied to texts where form enacts resistance.

Consider Lorde's *Power*:

"A policeman who shot down a ten-year-old in Queens
stood over the boy with his cop shoes in childish blood."

Lorde's aesthetic strategy rejects theoretical abstraction. She deploys unadorned syntax and visceral imagery to force witness. This linguistic confrontation resists interpretive detachment.

The necessity of examining AI's engagement with such texts is threefold. First, AI increasingly mediates literary access in educational contexts, where its summaries may inadvertently sanitize historically charged language. Second, technical validation metrics prioritize fluency over fidelity to marginalized epistemologies (Spivak, 1993). Third, the translation of resistance poetics by systems trained on dominant linguistic corpora risks replicating epistemic violence (Benjamin, 2019).

This study interrogates a core tension: Can architectures designed for universal legibility adequately convey poetry engineered to shatter complacency? The answer bears materially on algorithmic accountability in cultural transmission.

Language models are trained on vast corpora that overwhelmingly reflect dominant norms standardized English, formal registers, and decontextualized discourse (Blodgett et al., 2020). African American Vernacular English (AAVE), a rule-governed linguistic system forged through resistance, is often treated as defective or grammatically incorrect (Baker-Bell, 2020). When AI encounters structures like the habitual *be* or the completive *done*, it flags them as errors. These are not accidents. They are enactments of what Baker-Bell (2020) names "linguistic racism" the devaluation of Black language under the guise of correction.

Audre Lorde's poetic trilogy *Power*, *A Litany for Survival*, and *Who Said It Was Simple* operates through what Baker-Bell (2020) identifies as linguistic disobedience, deploying vernacular resistance as both aesthetic imperative and political strategy. These works share a commitment to syntactical rupture that mirrors racial violence, incantatory repetition that archives ancestral memory, and surgical irony that exposes liberal hypocrisy techniques constituting what Lorde herself termed "poetry as survival." Their language actively refuses assimilation through AAVE grammatical structures, Black sermonic rhythms, and embodied metaphors of trauma, creating what Spillers (1987) theorizes as counter-grammars of flesh against abstraction.

Generative AI systems fundamentally misalign with these strategies due to their architectural DNA. As Blodgett et al. (2020) demonstrate, models trained on standardized corpora inevitably normalize grammatical rupture into conventional syntax, flatten liturgical cadences into monotone narration, and recast radical irony as observational ambiguity. This occurs because algorithmic architectures privilege fluency over friction, universality over specificity, and resolution over sustained tension biases embedded in what Benjamin (2019) critiques as the "New Jim Code" of techno-governance. The smoothing logic Noble (2018) exposed in search algorithms manifests equally in literary processing: systems erase vernacular markers like habitual *be* while pathologizing non-standard syntax as errors.

The consequences manifest as epistemic triage across Lorde's corpus. Vernacular structures undergo grammatical correction that Baker-Bell (2020) condemns as linguistic racism, ancestral rage faces affective dilution into therapeutic anxiety, and embodied trauma what Spillers theorizes as "hieroglyphics of the flesh" suffers semantic abstraction into clinical euphemism. Crucially, intersectional critique gets neutralized through omission: as evidenced when *Who Said It Was Simple*'s indictment of white feminism becomes reframed as generic "activist tension." These transformations constitute more than technical failure; they enact what Spivak (1993) terms sanitized translation, erasing historicity under readability's guise.

This pattern reveals an ontological rift. Lorde's trilogy demands what her *Litany* calls "learning to live with the living fear" sustained engagement with discomfort as political praxis. Generative systems, however, engineer resolution through de-racination, aligning with what Noble (2018) identifies as algorithmic oppression's demand for palatable narratives. When "cop shoes in childish blood" becomes "law enforcement incident" or "shattered Black face" morphs into "facial trauma," AI enacts Spillers' symbolic de-fleshment. That such distortions persist despite contextual prompting confirms Benjamin's (2019) warning: tools shaped by racial hierarchies cannot dismantle their own epistemic houses.

This chapter builds on emerging research that exposes the cultural failures of AI in literary contexts. Almaktary (2024) demonstrates that ChatGPT struggles with metaphor and emotional undertone when translating French and Arabic poetry. Bisht and Pujari (2025) show that AI distorts the imagery of Partition poetry, turning "night-bitten dawn" into "stained morning." These studies confirm that AI is ill-equipped to handle texts shaped by historical trauma, postcolonial symbolism, and linguistic insurgency.

What sets Lorde's work apart is that the politics are embedded in the *grammar*. The structure of her language is not ornament; it is resistance. When AI systems normalize her syntax, they neutralize her politics. When they remove the anger, the eroticism, the cadence, they participate in the same silencing Lorde fought her whole life to resist.

This chapter asks four questions:

1. How do ChatGPT-4o and Gemini 2.5 process AAVE structures, poetic rhythm, and Black feminist lexicon in Lorde's poetry?
2. How does AI dampen emotional and political affect in comparison to human readings?
3. Can culturally specific prompts mitigate these distortions?
4. What frameworks can help educators audit and resist AI's misreadings of culturally significant texts?

The method follows a comparative approach, analyzing each poem under two prompt conditions: a generic prompt ("Explain this poem") and a context-attuned prompt ("Preserve Black vernacular grammar, feminist metaphors, and emotional intensity") through ChatGPT-4o and Gemini 2.5. These outputs are then dissected for linguistic fidelity, metaphor integrity, and tonal curacy. The analytical framework draws from Smitherman's (1977) work on Black English, Spivak's (1993) critique of translation politics, and Lorde's own theorization of poetry as a tool for survival and pedagogy.

Generative AI does not misread Lorde because it lacks training data. It misreads her because it was never built to understand her. These systems are calibrated to smooth over rupture, to harmonize dissent, to rephrase what is unpalatable. In doing so, they automate the silencing of voices that speak outside the grammar of power.

2. LITERATURE REVIEW

The use of artificial intelligence in literary translation has become an area of expanding interest, especially with the growing capabilities of large language models (LLMs) such as ChatGPT and Gemini. To clarify this chapter's contribution, existing research can be categorized into three key domains:

2.1 AI Translation of Canonical/Formal Texts:

Most current research centers on model accuracy, fluency, and performance in translating between formal, high-resource languages. They tend to do this in institutional or instructional contexts (Rane et al., 2024; Gupta et al., 2021). These methods are valuable to learn how machine translation functions, but they tend to lack the intricate interaction between language, power, and cultural specifics. This is especially the case when the source material is from politically charged, emotionally charged, or non-linguistically conventional traditions.

Early studies in this field examined machine translation for straightforward, utilitarian content, like legal texts, instruction manuals, and bureaucratic texts (Khoshafah, 2023). With the advancement of transformer-based neural networks, tools such as DeepL, Google Translate, and later, generative models like ChatGPT and Gemini, have extended their use to more stylistically rich forms, including fiction, essays, and poetry. These developments have prompted a number of comparative studies in AI literary translation. Farghal and Haider (2024) explore the differences between AI-generated and human translations of classical Arabic poetry. They note that while AI outputs often achieve semantic accuracy, they struggle to preserve formal features like prosody and metaphor. The focus is on coherence and clarity, even when the source material does not support those values.

Even in texts that do not explicitly resist standardization, the poetic voice is flattened unless human intervention reintroduces affective nuance. Alsajri et al. (2024), analyzing tri-lingual AI translation across Arabic, French, and English, reaches comparable conclusions. Cultural specificity, metaphorical density, and political tone are among the first casualties in machine-generated translations, particularly when models attempt to render figurative speech into literal or "universal" terms. He opines, "ChatGPT struggles with elements like metaphors, similes, and alliteration, resulting in translations that lack the artistic qualities of the original texts... Cultural references and allusions within poetry also pose a significant challenge, resulting in translations that are culturally insensitive or incorrect" (p. 9). The inconsistencies with translations are an aspect that is not limited to translations, as it tends to rob the cultural features of a text.

Farghal and Haider (2024) provide critical insights through their comparative analysis of human versus AI translations of classical Arabic poetry. Their study demonstrates ChatGPT and Gemini achieve competent thematic rendering but reveal significant limitations in prosodic preservation a core element of poetic integrity. As they note, "because of its generative characteristics... GPT is more capable of navigating through these complications... Gemini's methodology might be more inflexible, resulting in translations that overlook subtle prosodic elements crucial to poetry" (p. 12). This prosodic failure reflects a fundamental pattern: AI prioritizes semantic coherence over sonic and rhythmic intentionality. Such limitations foreshadow how systems might handle Lorde's incantatory structures in A Litany for Survival, where cadence carries political meaning.

Alsajri et al. (2024) corroborate this pattern in their NLP comparison study, identifying divergent strengths: "ChatGPT demonstrates proficiency in generating original and human-like prose... Gemini exhibits greater variation... in contextual comprehension" (p. 144). While both models show contextual adaptability, their study confirms neither consistently maintains culturally embedded aesthetics. This technical limitation becomes epistemic when processing texts like Lorde's, where vernacular cadences encode ancestral resistance. The fluency-celebration in such studies overlooks how "human-like" outputs may still sanitize radical voices.

Doudou and Faizi (2024) further validate this concern through Arabic poetry case studies. They observe ChatGPT 3.5 preserves meter mechanically but requires human intervention for metaphorical depth a finding directly relevant to Lorde's embodied imagery in Power. Resende and Hadley (2024) extend this argument, noting LLMs offer lexical innovation but demand extensive post-editing to achieve cultural authenticity. Collectively, these studies position AI as strictly assistive a framework this chapter challenges by examining whether human refinement can adequately mitigate AI's political erasures.

2.2 AI Handling of Culturally Complex/Sacred Texts:

Beyond language proficiency, several researchers have noted that AI often fails to preserve the cultural or spiritual significance of literary texts. Doshi (2024), for example, critiques the reductionism evident in AI translations of Jain religious literature from Hindi to English. In these cases, philosophical depth and historical meaning are lost to linguistic equivalency. Wei (2024) makes a related observation in his examination of Buddhist classical Chinese texts, noting that while LLMs can translate sentences with grammatical consistency, they often distort the conceptual logic embedded in religious or philosophical terms. Such distortions are rarely flagged, raising critical concerns about how authority is assigned to "readable" outputs.

Although these studies make important interventions, they often focus on literature rooted in classical or sacred traditions. Much less attention has been paid to texts whose form is inseparable from their political function.

2.3 Gaps in AI Processing of Resistant/Non-Standard Poetics:

The poetry of Audre Lorde belongs to the category of texts where form is political function. Written in the voice of resistance, often through African American Vernacular English (AAVE), her work defies standard grammar and demands to be heard in the cadence of struggle. In these cases, translation becomes an ethical and political act, not merely a linguistic operation.

Spivak (1993) articulated this challenge in her seminal essay "The Politics of Translation," arguing that all translation involves a transfer of power, particularly when the speaker is positioned within colonial or racialized systems. For Spivak, the task of the translator is not to simplify but to remain accountable to the rhetorical force of the original. When AAVE is reworded, standardized, or "corrected," as often happens in AI-mediated reading, this accountability is broken. Lorde's poetry does not merely narrate oppression it performs its refusal. The grammar, punctuation, and rhythm of her writing are integral to the political message. As such, translating Lorde involves far more than linguistic equivalence; it requires attentiveness to the poetics of survival.

Baker-Bell's (2020) work on "linguistic justice" emphasizes this further by critiquing the educational systems that pathologize AAVE and frame it as an error to be fixed. Her research highlights how institutional language norms replicate anti-Blackness under the guise of grammatical correctness. When applied to generative AI, her critique takes on new urgency. Models trained on massive datasets drawn from white, Anglophone, and institutional sources are likely to reproduce these patterns of erasure. As Blodgett et al. (2020) show, the biases baked into natural language processing (NLP) systems are not incidental but systemic. These biases include the devaluation of non-standard English, the erasure of regional or racialized speech, and the prioritization of fluency over specificity.

The implications of these limitations extend into the field of education. Benjamin (2019) and Noble (2018) both argue that algorithmic infrastructures produce harm not only through what they misrecognize but through what they systematically leave out. For literary texts especially ones produced by Black women the omission of emotion, cultural memory, and grammatical particularity results in a different kind of error: epistemic violence. In pedagogical contexts where AI-generated summaries and paraphrases are used for classroom support or accessibility, this violence becomes institutionalized.

One significant precedent is Bisht and Pujari (2025). They examined how ChatGPT and Gemini interpret Subh-e-Azadi, a Partition-era Urdu poem by Faiz Ahmed Faiz. Their results show that the AI systems often remove metaphors. They also make the images simpler. In addition, they flatten the emotional tone of the poem. They argue that these models do not just produce different versions of the poem; they rewrite it to fit grammars of comfort and readability. Their study sets a precedent for the present chapter in method, but focuses on postcolonial symbolism not the nexus of AAVE, Black feminist poetics, and deliberate linguistic disobedience central to Lorde.

Despite these advances, a critical gap persists: while studies have examined translation quality in high-resource languages and canonical poetic forms, almost none have looked at what happens when generative AI encounters AAVE, queer feminist metaphor, or poetry that deliberately resists readability. There is also little sustained engagement with how prompts shape the outputs of AI systems in such cases. This chapter intervenes precisely at this intersection.

3. METHODOLOGY

This study uses a qualitative, prompt-based comparative framework to examine how generative AI systems respond to politically and linguistically resistant poetry. The focus is on three of Audre Lorde's poems *Power*, *A Litany for Survival*, and *Who Said It Was Simple* each of which engages Black feminist poetics through the use of vernacular syntax, rhetorical repetition, and metaphorical intensity. The analysis centers on the capabilities and limitations of two widely used large language models: ChatGPT-4o by OpenAI and Gemini 2.5 by Google. These models were selected based on their public availability, pedagogical prominence, and their developers' claims regarding interpretive sophistication.

In choosing these poems, the study prioritizes textual works that do not separate linguistic form from political content. *Power* is a text that exemplifies the condition of oppression among the masses of the African American community. It uses syntactic rupture and tonal confrontation to narrate and indict. *A Litany for Survival* relies on repetition, second-person address, and liturgical rhythm to center collective fear and survival of the masses. *Who Said It Was Simple* foregrounds racial contradiction and feminist hypocrisy through compressed irony and tonal restraint. These poems share an investment in pushing language beyond normative function. They demand that readers confront not only what is said, but how it is said and why that form matters. The political function of the language, its grammar, affect, and cadence, cannot be divorced from its content.

Each poem was submitted to both AI systems under two distinct prompting conditions. The first was a minimal prompt. The prompt was, "Please explain the following poem in simpler terms so it is easier to understand." This prompt is designed to simulate default educational or classroom use, where users are unlikely to provide deep contextual metadata such as students who are introduced to the texts.

The second was a culturally grounded prompt, explicitly asking the AI to retain elements such as Black vernacular grammar, political metaphors, and emotional tone. The following prompt is used for generating more detailed results. "Please explain the following poem in clearer terms for a general reader, but do so while preserving its political meaning and emotional intensity. The poem uses African American Vernacular English (AAVE)." This version highlights the poem's sociolinguistic context and a directive not to standardize the syntax unless essential for comprehension. The aim here is to examine whether prompting significantly alters the fidelity of the explanation and if so, how.

This design produces twelve AI outputs in total: three poems, translated under two prompts, across two models. These outputs are then evaluated through close textual comparison against the source texts. This comparison is not merely linguistic; it involves rhetorical, cultural, and affective dimensions. The analysis is guided by three primary concerns. First, the study examines whether the AI retains or erases features of African American Vernacular English, including zero-copula structures, aspectual *be*, and rhetorical questioning. Second, it investigates how metaphor, imagery, and symbolic density are rendered whether they are simplified, substituted, or preserved. Third, the study evaluates the affective and political tone of the outputs, identifying tendencies toward euphemism, depoliticization, or emotional flattening. The results of the generations of ChatGPT and Gemini would be categorised as

1. ChatGPT-Minimal
2. ChatGPT-Contextual
3. Gemini-Minimal
4. Gemini-Contextual

The analytic process involves a line-by-line reading of each AI output in parallel with the original poem. Where deviations occur, the nature and consequences of the change are annotated and interpreted. Particular attention is paid to phrases that carry historical trauma, cultural resonance, or affective charge. For example, the transformation of a term like "childish blood" or "those of us who were never meant to survive" would not be read as lexical substitutions alone but as potential erasures of political context. Cross-model comparison also allows for identifying whether certain systems are more prone to euphemism or grammatical correction than others. In cases where prompt effects are visible, those variations are noted as evidence of the models' responsiveness or resistance to cultural instruction.

This method draws directly from prior work by Bisht and Pujari (2025), who evaluated AI translations of Urdu poetry from the 1947 Partition of India. Their study revealed consistent AI tendencies to neutralize political content, simplify metaphor, and render trauma into bureaucratic language. The present chapter adopts their prompting model while extending the analysis to Black American poetics in English. Unlike conventional comparative translation studies, which often measure output against "accuracy" or semantic fidelity, this framework emphasizes political legibility, cultural integrity, and affective resonance.

This approach does not aim to test whether AI can replicate poetic form. Instead, it asks what happens when machines built for fluency confront texts designed to disrupt. The focus remains interpretive rather than computational. There is no attempt to quantify metaphor density or assign numerical accuracy ratings. Instead, each translation is read as a cultural and rhetorical event, situated within the broader context of algorithmic literacy and linguistic resistance.

Limitations of this methodology include its sample size and model scope. The study works with only two AI systems and three poems. However, this narrow scope enables depth of analysis and specificity of interpretation. Additionally, because AI models are continuously updated, findings are time-bound and may not reflect future versions of the models. Nonetheless, the patterns revealed in these outputs point to systemic issues that extend beyond temporary software limitations.

4. FINDINGS AND ANALYSIS

4.1 "Power"

Audre Lorde's "Power" is a poem of rupture, violence, and linguistic refusal. As a text, it resists containment, and as an artifact of Black feminist resistance, it mobilizes affect and syntax as tools of survival.

Across the four AI outputs for "Power," a clear pattern emerges: when prompted minimally, the models tend to neutralize violence, euphemize trauma, and simplify metaphor. When prompted with cultural context, some stylistic and political features are retained, but even then, the AI systems often introduce explanatory framing or editorial tone. These outputs do not function as paraphrases in the traditional sense. They are not line-by-line restatements, but rather interpretive summaries shaped by underlying norms of clarity, fluency, and civility. Even when instructed otherwise, the models struggle to remain faithful to the poem's form, tone, and rhetorical contradictions.

In the opening stanza, Lorde writes: "The difference between poetry and rhetoric / is being ready to kill / yourself / instead of your children." Both ChatGPT-minimal and Gemini-minimal transform this into abstract moral reflection. Gemini-minimal describes poetry as confronting one's own suffering, while rhetoric sacrifices others. This reframing displaces the bodily immediacy of Lorde's line. It also smooths over the poem's radical juxtaposition of language and action. ChatGPT-contextual version preserves this better, rewording it in a way that approximates Lorde's syntax and tone: "what make poetry different from just talk / is you willing to die / yourself / instead of lettin yo babies be the ones that go." Here, the use of nonstandard grammar and rhythmic phrasing reflects a closer alignment with Lorde's original. Yet even this version reads like an imitation, not a transformation.

One of the poem's most politically direct moments the police shooting of a ten-year-old boy in Queens reveals how AI systems handle racial violence. In the original, the line "Die you little motherfucker" is presented without qualification. It is a quote, not a metaphor, and its inclusion is a rhetorical and ethical necessity. In Gemini-Minimal, the quote is replaced with the phrase "used a racial slur," a euphemism that erases the brutality of the scene. ChatGPT-Minimal retains the quote but adds commentary, stating that the officer's boots were "soaked in blood" and that he said the line as he stood over the child. These additions soften the impact of the original by layering explanation over exposure. ChatGPT-Contextual performs best, retaining the quote, replicating the lineation, and preserving AAVE, yet even this version includes subtle insertions such as "real calm," editorializing the tone of the speech.

Lorde's use of AAVE throughout the poem is another key site of distortion. The officer's trial testimony, "I didn't notice the size nor nothing else / only the color," is rewritten in all minimal outputs as standardized speech. Gemini renders it as "I didn't notice anything but the boy's skin color," removing both the rhythm and the rhetorical deflection embedded in the original syntax. ChatGPT-Contextual renders the line as "i ain't see his size or nothin / just saw the color," maintaining both the grammar and affect of the source text. This fidelity demonstrates the model's capacity to follow contextual instruction, but again, the output feels like a simulation of vernacular voice rather than a retention of its cultural function.

The poem's most disturbing image appears in the final stanza: the speaker imagines herself committing a racially motivated act of revenge if her power is not channeled through poetry. The original reads: "raping an 85 year old white woman / who is somebody's mother." In Gemini-Minimal, this entire passage is omitted or generalized as "a terrifying possible future," erasing both the speaker's rage and the moral risk Lorde is willing to articulate. ChatGPT-Minimal includes the act but frames it with a distancing moral commentary: "She never did anything to deserve this. How monstrous they are." These phrases are not part of Lorde's voice; they are part of the AI's compulsion to resolve. ChatGPT-Contextual retains the full image and rhythm, refraining from editorializing, though the underlying system still reorders lines and phrases to close approximations rather than transmit.

The image of the Black juror who "lined her own womb with cement / to make a graveyard for our children" is another example of metaphor reworked as message. Gemini-Minimal rewrites this as "betraying her own people," stripping the metaphor of its bodily and reproductive violence. ChatGPT-Minimal paraphrases it into an act of submission. Only ChatGPT-Contextual retains the metaphor in something close to its original form, though even here, the line is broken up, its pacing altered.

Ultimately, the AI systems do not fail because they misunderstand the poem. They fail as it is packed with a lot of cultural nuance. Lorde's poem is not meant to be understood in the way AI is designed to understand: through summarization, smoothing, and simplification. "Power" functions as a refusal of those very logics. It is jagged, unresolved, and emotionally excessive. The AI systems, even when prompted carefully, respond by trimming the excess, smoothing the edges, and reconstituting the text in the grammar of sense-making. What emerges is not a neutral explanation, but a domesticated version of a voice that was never meant to be polite.

This encounter between generative AI and radical poetics reveals something beyond technical limitation. It shows how algorithmic readability is structurally opposed to poetic resistance. The systems read too much into what they cannot process, and in doing so, they expose what kinds of voices AI might not have trained not to hear.

4.2 "A Litany for Survival"

Audre Lorde's "A Litany for Survival" occupies a quieter register than "Power," but it is no less politically and racially charged. It moves in the rhythms of prayer, chant, and survivalist repetition. The poem addresses a collective "we," situating vulnerability as a shared experience among those historically denied safety, certainty, and voice (the African American community). It is a poem of fear not in submission, but in confrontation. Lorde asks what it means to survive in a world that is not made for you, and whether survival alone is enough. As with "Power," this section evaluates how generative AI systems interpret the poem when asked to explain it under both minimal and culturally contextual prompts.

The minimal outputs from both ChatGPT and Gemini tend to reframe the poem as a self-help or resilience narrative. ChatGPT-Minimal opens with phrases like "This poem is about people who live in fear," framing Lorde's invocation of terror in therapeutic language. Gemini-Minimal explains the refrain "we were never meant to survive" by stating that "society doesn't support everyone equally," a phrasing that dilutes the poem's indictment of structural violence into liberal generality. The AI systems translate existential fear into digestible concepts: marginalization, anxiety, the courage to speak. But Lorde's language is not meant to be digested. It is meant to remain caught in the throat.

ChatGPT-Contextual performs better. It retains Lorde's repetition and addresses the collective "you" in second-person, preserving the urgency and direct address that structures the poem. It echoes the rhythm of the original without completely mimicking it. Gemini-Contextual also recognizes the poem's prayer-like structure and repeats some lines with minimal change, though it still introduces clarifying explanations. Both contextual outputs do a better job of preserving emotional tone, but they cannot resist the pull toward readability. When Lorde writes, "and when the sun rises we are afraid / it might not remain," she uses natural imagery to express Black futurity as fragile and imperiled. The AI rephrases this as a fear of instability or change, collapsing metaphor into meaning.

The poem's final lines, "so it is better to speak / remembering / we were never meant to survive," is consistently interpreted across models as a call to empowerment. In minimal outputs, this becomes a moral takeaway: speak even when afraid. Gemini-Minimal refers to it as "a message of resilience." But Lorde's line is not an inspirational quote. It is a grim acknowledgment that speech, for the marginalized, is not a path to power but a risk taken in defiance. ChatGPT-Contextual comes closest to retaining this contradiction. It frames the final lines as a warning: silence is deadly, but speech is no guarantee of survival either. That ambiguity is central to the poem's power.

All four outputs remove ambiguity in favour of legibility. Lorde's layering of fear we are afraid to love, afraid to speak, afraid to remember, afraid to forget is rendered by the AI systems as a list of internal anxieties rather than as a map of historical trauma. Her use of repetition is flattened into prose explanation. Her invocation of "the silence of the border between two voices" is interpreted as a communication issue rather than a political metaphor about erasure, exile, or the liminal condition of the oppressed.

An interesting event could be noticed in the generations of this text. Even when prompted to preserve emotional and cultural specificity, the systems prefer to have narrative coherence. And coherence, in this case, is a form of erasure."A Litany for Survival" is a poem about fear that refuses to be conquered. It does not aim to soothe. It offers no promise. In attempting to explain it, AI systems reveal their structural discomfort with texts that resist closure. Their instinct to tidy what Lorde leaves deliberately broken turns the poem into something safer than it was meant to be. That safety, ultimately, comes at the cost of the poem's resistance.

4.3 "Who Said It Was Simple"

Audre Lorde's "Who Said It Was Simple" is a short but layered poem of irony, visual contrast, and feminist critique. It stages a speaker watching white women protest for equality, all while remaining oblivious to their own participation in systems of racial and economic violence. The poem's critique lies in its juxtapositions: between solidarity and exploitation, between protest and performance, and most importantly, between who is seen and who is hired to be unseen. It offers a restrained indictment of white liberal feminism, where those with power demand freedom without recognizing the foundations their freedom rests upon. The poem's complexity depends not on metaphor or elevated diction but on understatement, irony, and a careful unfolding of images qualities that AI explanations, particularly those prompted minimally, repeatedly flatten.

ChatGPT-Minimal explains the poem as if it were an observational account of alienation. It notes that the speaker feels conflicted watching a protest, but offers no insight into the racial and economic contradictions embedded in the scene. The description focuses on how the speaker is emotionally distanced or "troubled," with no reference to the line "the problematic girls / they hire to make them free." That line is crucial it exposes how white women's claims to liberation are often underwritten by the labor of racialized women. Gemini-Minimal, similarly, describes the poem as expressing discomfort in a justice movement, missing the poem's central turn: the speaker is not confused; she is precise. Both outputs interpret the speaker's silence as uncertainty, rather than as critical, controlled observation.

The culturally contextual prompts yield more nuanced, though still cautious, interpretations. ChatGPT-Contextual notes that the poem critiques white women's feminism for being blind to their own reliance on racialized labor. It describes the final line as unsettling and critical, though the commentary still tends to soften the poem's directness. Gemini-Contextual registers the layered irony of the protest scene more clearly than the minimal version, and it identifies a critique of structural racism, but avoids naming whiteness or referencing feminist complicity. Instead, it uses terms like "some activists" and "hidden systems," obscuring the political target.

The final line, "the slighter pleasures of their slavery" is where the AI systems falter most. In Lorde's poem, this phrase delivers the concluding charge: that the protestors, though fighting for gender equality, quietly benefit from racial inequality. ChatGPT-Minimal reads this as a vague reference to "others not recognizing their own oppression." Gemini-Minimal offers a similar reading, describing the poem as about people unaware of their complicity. Both reframe the line as a misunderstanding rather than an indictment. ChatGPT-Contextual gets closer to the poem's logic by interpreting the line as a commentary on superficial forms of freedom that rest on exploitation, but still hedges its language. None of the models emphasize that the line is meant to sting.

Ultimately, the AI outputs demonstrate a shared discomfort with rhetorical understatement and strategic silence. The speaker's choice not to speak in the scene is not passivity it is a decision to watch, record, and later write with precision. Yet the AI explanations continually mistake this restraint for hesitation, interpreting the poem's tight control as emotional confusion. This is perhaps the most revealing aspect of the AI's misreading: Lorde's quietest poem is the one most mistranslated, precisely because its critique is not announced, but embedded. The models expect feminist outrage to be loud. When it whispers, they ask if it's unsure.

"Who Said It Was Simple" critiques the very frameworks that AI seems to rely on: liberal consensus, visible grievance, and emotional resolution. Lorde's poem does not deliver catharsis; it withholds it. The AI systems, in turn, attempt to supply that missing affect. They explain away the discomfort. But in doing so, they betray the poem's core gesture: to force the reader to see what they would rather not name. The systems read the scene but not the silence.

4.4 AI Processing Patterns Across Lorde's Poems

As summarized in the following table, generative AI consistently exhibits patterns of grammatical normalization, affective dilution, and political neutralization across all three poems.

Table 1. Cross-Poem Analysis of AI Processing Patterns: Grammatical Normalization, Affective Dilution, and Political Neutralization in Lorde's Poetry

Feature	"Power"	"A Litany for Survival"	"Who Said It Was Simple"	AI Mechanism
AAVE Retention	**Minimal:** Standardizes syntax (e.g., "nor nothing else" to "didn't notice anything") **Contextual:** Partial retention but adds editorial tone ("real calm")	**Minimal:** Individualizes collective "we" **Contextual:** Fails sermonic rhythm	**Minimal:** Neutralizes vernacular defiance **Contextual:** Misses coded resistance	Grammatical normalization
Metaphor Integrity	**Minimal:** Abstracts violence ("shattered Black face" to "facial trauma") **Contextual:** Retains "womb with cement" but alters pacing	**Minimal:** Dilutes "living fear" to anxiety **Contextual:** Flattens liturgical cadence	**Minimal:** Softens "slavery" to "complicity" **Contextual:** Loses ironic compression	Metaphor concretization
Political Affect	**Minimal:** Moralizes rage ("monstrous they are") **Contextual:** Retains violence but reduces urgency	**Minimal:** Reframes terror as resilience **Contextual:** Depoliticizes "never meant to survive"	**Minimal:** Misreads irony as confusion **Contextual:** Avoids naming whiteness	Affective dilution
Resolution Bias	**Minimal:** Imposes closure on ambiguity **Contextual:** Reorders lines for coherence	**Minimal:** Adds "message of resilience" **Contextual:** Frames survival as coping	**Minimal:** Resolves irony into observation **Contextual:** Softens indictment	Coherence optimizatio

5. CROSS-POEM ANALYSIS: PATTERNS OF AI MISREADING, ERASURE, AND NORMALIZATION

Across the three Audre Lorde poems *Power*, *A Litany for Survival*, and *Who Said It Was Simple* a revealing pattern emerges: generative AI consistently reshapes radical, resistant poetic language into forms that prioritize readability, neutrality, and emotional resolution. Despite differences between models (ChatGPT and Gemini) and between prompts (minimal vs. culturally contextual), the systems struggle to preserve rhetorical complexity, formal tension, and political intensity. This indicates not just technical shortcomings, but structural biases rooted in their design, training data, and usage ideology. From the generations of all three texts the following inferences could be made regarding the salient features and perhaps patterns that generative AI prefers:

5.1. Flattening Affect and Political Urgency

One consistent failure across all three poems is the flattening of political emotion into personal feeling. In *Power*, Lorde's act of naming state violence and racial terrorism becomes a cautionary moral tale e.g., in Gemini-Minimal, the line "Die you little motherfucker" vanishes or becomes sanitized. ChatGPT-Minimal, though retaining the quote, frames it within moral commentary rather than allowing its raw force to stand alone. In *A Litany for Survival*, what should read as collective, existential terror is interpreted as therapeutic anxiety a general problem to be solved, not survival to be endured. And in *Who Said It Was Simple*, the AI sees confusion rather than critique, failing to register the poem's precise political targeting of white feminist complicity.

By defanging these touches of rage and political shock, AI smooths the semantic field into emotion or psychology creating what literary scholar Sylvia Wynter might call a "desubjectification" of the radical voice. Generative AI reframes poetry as "user-friendly" content a trend also noted in larger surveys of AI-created poems, where non-expert readers tend to prefer AI output due to its emotional immediacy, even if it lacks structural complexity (Porter & Machery, 2024; Köbis & Mossink, 2020).

5.2. Misreading Irony, Restraint, and Ambiguity

A particularly revealing case is *Who Said It Was Simple*, a poem that performs critique through silence, visual contrast, and irony. The poem's poignant stillness is often underestimated by AI ChatGPT and Gemini misinterpret restraint as indecision. The critical interjection of "the slighter pleasures of their slavery" is glossed over or turned into vague references to unrecognized oppression. This misreading mirrors known weaknesses in NLP systems around figurative language: irony, humor, and metaphor tend to be flattened into literal interpretation unless specifically engineered to detect them (Yi & Xia, 2025). Despite prompting, the AI fails to preserve Lorde's strategic withholding or to sense the tension beneath surface calm. The models substitute tonal coherence for rhetorical rupture.

5.3. Standardizing Vernacular and Collective Language

Across all poems, AI exhibits a clear bias toward standardized English and individualized expression. The rich registers of AAVE in *Power*, such as "nor nothing else," are edited into standard grammar unless a culturally contextual prompt preserves them often superficially. What sounds like vernacular becomes a syntactic novelty, not an epistemic stance. Lorde's use of collective "we" and second-person "you" in *Litany* a poetic device that builds communal voice is rendered as individual anxiety or self-help advice. This reflects a deeply embedded linguistic injustice, as identified by Baker-Bell (2020) and Smitherman (1977), wherein non-standard vernaculars are treated as errors. The models' scrubbing of syntax erases political subjectivity and reduces it to sanitized familiarity.

5.4. Over-Reliance on Resolution and Readability

When AI systems produce explanation outputs, they rarely leave a poem hanging; they explain, moralize, or resolve ambiguity. Lorde's poems function by refusing neat closure *Power* ends in violent ambiguity, *Litany* closes on exasperation, and *Simple* finishes with a cold indictment. Yet AI outputs often insert a redemptive note or psychological framing "it's a warning," "be resilient," "learn from it." This speaks to an algorithmic default mode: to reduce complexity to digestible moral arcs that stand in for closure. As performance surveys have shown, non-experts prefer simpler emotional arcs especially when unaware of AI origin (Porter & Machery, 2024). AI explanation follows suit, fluffing tension into resolve and political intensity into motivational maxims.

5.5. The Limits of Contextual Prompting

Adding culturally contextual prompts does improve surface fidelity. ChatGPT-Contextual retains quotable sharp lines, vernacular syntax, and echoes of repetition. Gemini-Contextual registers irony and tone better. Yet these gains are shallow. Even in *Power*, editorial insertions like "real calm" insert an external narrator onto Lorde's own voice. In *Simple*, even when naming structural hypocrisy, the models avoid naming whiteness or class alongside exploitation talking of "some activists" rather than identifying the oppressor. This echoes findings in Bloom's taxonomy studies, where AI in literary education prefers thematic analysis over critical contextualization (Discover Computing, 2025). Prompt framing helps but cannot overcome genre inclinations toward overt intelligibility and emotional neatness especially in the absence of deeper algorithmic changes.

These failures are not random; they reflect architectural biases in neural training. Large language models encode semantic correlations from massive English mainstream corpora white, male-dominated, standard-issue (Blodgett et al., 2020; Caliskan et al., 2017). Vernacular, queer, or political form are rare outliers in such datasets and are treated as noise. This is not just lack of data it's training signal suppression. Aylin Caliskan's work shows that embedding models encode social bias implicitly. In language generation, AAVE, structural critique, and ironic understatement all receive lower probability in output sampling. AI's attempt at "inclusion" through context prompts feels tokenized, not structural. These biases are not incidental but reinforced by developer priorities

5.6 Systemic Constraints in Developer Frameworks

While AI developers acknowledge linguistic bias as a technical challenge, their mitigation strategies remain misaligned with the epistemic violence exposed in this analysis. OpenAI's System Card for GPT-4 (2023) explicitly prioritizes "harmlessness" through output filtering a paradigm that conflates Lorde's political rage with toxicity, silencing radical speech under safety protocols. Google's Gemini Responsible AI Practices (2024) similarly emphasizes "fairness" via demographic representation in training data, yet fails to address how standardization workflows inherently pathologize non-dominant grammars like AAVE. Crucially, neither framework recognizes textual resistance as a protected category, instead optimizing for fluency metrics that reproduce what Benjamin (2019) terms the New Jim Code: hierarchies rebranded as technical efficiency. Until developers reconstitute "accuracy" to include fidelity to marginalized epistemologies not just grammatical conformity their tools will remain architecturally incapable of reading Lorde.

6. BROADER IMPLICATIONS FOR LITERARY STUDIES

What does this mean for the future of literary pedagogy and analysis? The Sydney Review warns that AI's ubiquity in writing and reading requires heightened textual literacy an ability to resist auto-generated "user-friendly" language. Studies recommend that AI be used not as an interpreter but as a partner tool, offering suggestions while teaching analytical rigor (Yi & Xia, 2025). Beyond pedagogy, Lorde's poetry, which resists understanding for the sake of disruption, reveals how AI reduces resistance into palatability undermining affective learning about power, oppression, and refusal. As algorithmic bias literature establishes, invisibility is itself a form of violence (Noble, 2018).

Counterfactual prompting can yield better results when asked directly to interpret form or name the political context, AI improves modestly. But for Lorde's verse, which weaponizes form, this is not enough. Responsible explanation would require multimodal annotation exposing syntax, oral delivery, cultural registers. But current commercial models are neither designed for that nor supported by training. AI can't hypothetically produce these results unless structured to decenter normativity, including:

1. Explicit flagging of non-standard syntax as register

2. Annotation of collective pronouns as devices of solidarity
3. Instruction to preserve unresolved tension
4. Ability to cite political affiliations of oppressor categories

Without these, AI will continue to misread poetry of resistance as noise. This critique doesn't rule out generative AI in literary studies it cautions against uncritical integration. Educators might use AI for surface-level tasks, but must foster reflective, situated reading habits. A possible future lies in creating ethically trained LLMs, capable of mapping non-normative registers. Open tools like Hugging Face's SHADES dataset aim to identify biases across language varieties. Community-controlled models informed by cultural historians, feminist theorists, and linguists could better preserve poetic rupture. Until then, AI remains a convenient but reductive mirror.

7. PEDAGOGICAL IMPERATIVES: CRITICAL FRAMEWORKS FOR RESISTING ALGORITHMIC ERASURE

The habitual structures of misreading throughout Lorde's writing grammatical standardization, affective dilution, and political neutralization require pedagogical systems that challenge what Spivak (1993) understands as sanitized translation: the suppression of historicity in the name of readability. Teachers need to create critical practices that reverse AI's architectural biases, which consistently favor fluency over friction and resolution over prolonged tension (Benjamin, 2019; Noble, 2018). Instead of placing AI in the role of interpretive authority, pedagogical practices must prepare students to identify how these systems perform what Baker-Bell (2020) describes as linguistic racism through seemingly innocuous actions. For instance, when A Litany for Survival's collective invocation "for those of us who were never meant to survive" is reframed as individualized anxiety about societal inequality, the AI performs a double erasure: of Black communal epistemology and of what Spillers (1987) theorizes as the "counter-grammars of flesh" encoded in Lorde's rhythm.

Effective pedagogy must therefore center diagnostic auditing of AI's smoothing mechanisms. Students should be trained to identify how vernacular resistance becomes reconstituted as defect as when Who Said It Was Simple's surgical indictment of white feminist hypocrisy ("the problematic girls / they hire to make them free") is transformed into depoliticized observations about "activist tensions." Similarly, the visceral charge of Lorde's metaphors undergoes clinical abstraction; Power's "shattered Black face" becomes "facial trauma" in AI outputs, excising the racial terror embedded in the original imagery. These transformations represent not technical limitations but what Benjamin (2019) identifies as the New Jim Code technological systems that replicate hierarchy under neutrality's veneer.

Prompt engineering offers partial mitigation but requires strategic framing. Contextual instructions to "preserve AAVE syntax and political affect" can prevent surface-level standardization, as evidenced when Power's zero-copula construction ("I didn't notice the size nor nothing else") remains intact rather than being rewritten as standardized English. Yet deeper structural biases persist: even when retaining metaphors, systems like Gemini impose narrative coherence on Lorde's deliberate ruptures, reframing A Litany's unresolved terror ("learning to live with the living fear") as therapeutic coping strategies. This reveals the core pedagogical imperative: AI outputs must be positioned not as explanations but as artifacts of dominant linguistic politics, analyzed alongside Lorde's essays on poetry as survival and Black feminist critiques of language normalization.

Ultimately, institutional practice must extend beyond classroom tactics. Developers should be challenged to implement resistance-aware architectures mechanisms that flag vernacular patterns as intentional rather than erroneous, preserve affective intensity through customizable bias thresholds, and disclose training data provenance. As Lorde (1984) reminds us, tools shaped by existing power structures cannot dismantle their own epistemic houses; educators must therefore wield AI's failures as pedagogical instruments, using Lorde's unassimilated voice to expose the limits of algorithmic reading rather than seeking reconciliation between incompatible frameworks.

8. CONCLUSION

Audre Lorde's poetry refuses ease. Her language, shaped by grief, anger, desire, and refusal, demands to be heard on its own terms not decoded, not improved, not made palatable. Across *Power*, *A Litany for Survival*, and *Who Said It Was Simple*, Lorde constructs poetic spaces that are structurally disruptive and politically defiant. Her form is not separate from her politics it is a technique of survival, a pedagogy of confrontation. As this chapter has shown, generative AI systems such as ChatGPT and Gemini are not yet capable of engaging this kind of poetics with fidelity or care.

The core issue is not simply one of technical failure but of epistemic misalignment. AI models are built to explain, simplify, and make sense. Lorde's poetry exists to disrupt, destabilize, and resist resolution. When the AI attempts to explain a poem like *Power*, it rewrites fury as emotional upset. When it translates *A Litany for Survival*, it reimagines historical terror as psychological insecurity. And when it approaches *Who Said It Was Simple*, it confuses precision with hesitation. In each case, what is politically deliberate in the poem becomes narratively convenient in the AI output.

Even with culturally contextual prompts to alert the model to questions of syntax, voice, and cultural specificity the results only modestly improve. This suggests that the limitations are not just prompt-related but embedded within the model's training infrastructure and evaluative logic. AI systems are optimized for clarity, legibility, and standardization. Lorde's poetry offers opacity, vernacular rupture, and political specificity. The two operate on fundamentally different assumptions about what language is supposed to do.

The pedagogical implications are substantial. As generative AI becomes more common in educational settings used to explain, summarize, or paraphrase poetry, the risk of interpretive violence grows. When AI erases the political edge of a line or smooths out a poem's grief, it does more than misread. It reproduces the very dynamics of erasure that Lorde's work exists to contest. In this sense, the deployment of AI in literary study is not neutral. It is an act of cultural translation with stakes.

Yet this critique is not an argument for purity or withdrawal. AI can and should be studied critically within the humanities not as a replacement for reading but as an object of inquiry. Lorde's work, in fact, offers a powerful framework for evaluating AI: her poems ask not just what language means, but what it does, and for whom. They offer a methodology of attention: listen to the silences, name the violence, refuse the false resolution. This chapter argues that any responsible use of AI in literary spaces must adopt similar principles.

To read Lorde through AI is to witness what happens when radical poetics meet algorithmic normativity. The results are often uncomfortable, but that discomfort is instructive. It reveals the politics of explanation, the cost of clarity, and the difficulty of translating resistance. In the end, the question is not whether AI can "understand" poetry. It is whether we are willing to let poetry remain difficult, uncorrected, and uncompromised. Lorde's voice insists: not all texts want to be simplified. Not all wounds can be paraphrased. Some power must remain untranslatable.

REFERENCES

Almaktary, H. (2024). Reflections on translating poetry through ChatGPT: Insights from Arabic, English, and French. *Journal of English Studies in Arabia Felix*, *4*(1), 1–12. DOI: 10.56540/jesaf.v4i1.108

Alsajri, A., Salman, H. A., & Steiti, A. (2024). Generative Models in Natural Language Processing: A Comparative Study of ChatGPT and Gemini. *Deleted Journal*, *2024*, 134–145. DOI: 10.58496/BJAI/2024/015

Baker-Bell, A. (2020). *Linguistic justice: Black language, literacy, identity, and pedagogy*. Routledge. DOI: 10.4324/9781315147383

Benjamin, R. (2019). *Race after technology: Abolitionist tools for the New Jim Code*. Polity Press.

Bisht, P., & Pujari, J. P. (2025). Translating Subh-e-Azadi: ChatGPT, Gemini, and the Cultural Complexity of 1947 Partition Poetry. In Al Aqad, M. (Ed.), *Role of AI in Translation and Interpretation* (pp. 267–292). IGI Global Scientific Publishing., DOI: 10.4018/979-8-3373-0060-3.ch010

Blodgett, S. L., Barocas, S., Daumé, H., III, & Wallach, H. (2020). Language (technology) is power: A critical survey of "bias" in NLP. *arXiv*. https://doi.org//arXiv .2005.14050DOI: 10.18653/v1/2020.acl-main.485

Caliskan, A., Bryson, J. J., & Narayanan, A. (2017). Semantics derived automatically from language corpora contain human-like biases. *Science*, *356*(6334), 183–186. DOI: 10.1126/science.aal4230 PMID: 28408601

Doshi, A. V. (2024). The loss in AI translation. *ResearchGate*. https://www .researchgate.net/publication/383037053_The_Loss_in_AI_Translation

Doudou, W., & Faizi, H. (2024). Enhancing Poetry Translation via ChatGPT 3.5: A Comparative Contrastive Study on Translated versions Qabbani's Poem Belqees & Fortune Teller by Kevin Moore [MA Dissertation, Kasdi Merbah Ouargla University]. https:// dspace. univ - ouargla. dz/ jspui/ bitstream/ 123456789/ 36859/ 1/ Enhancing %20Poetry %20Translation %20Via %20ChatGPT %203. 5. pdf

Gupta, R., Srivastava, D., Sahu, M., Tiwari, S., Ambasta, R. K., & Kumar, P. (2021). Artificial intelligence to deep learning: Machine intelligence approach for drug discovery. *Molecular Diversity*, *25*(3), 1315–1360. DOI: 10.1007/s11030-021-10217-3 PMID: 33844136

Köbis, N., & Mossink, L. D. (2020). Artificial intelligence versus Maya Angelou: Experimental evidence that people cannot differentiate AI-generated from human-written poetry. *PLoS One*, *15*(12), e0243863. DOI: 10.1016/j.chb.2020.106553 PMID: 33320864

Lorde, A. (1984). *Sister outsider: Essays and speeches*. Crossing Press.

Noble, S. U. (2018). *Algorithms of oppression: How search engines reinforce racism*. NYU Press. DOI: 10.18574/nyu/9781479833641.001.0001

Porter, B., & Machery, E. (2024). AI-generated poetry is indistinguishable from human-written poetry and rated more favorably. *Scientific Reports*, *14*(1), 26133. DOI: 10.1038/s41598-024-76900-1

Rane, N., Choudhary, S., & Rane, J. (2024). Gemini Versus ChatGPT: Applications, Performance, Architecture, Capabilities, and Implementation. SSRN Electronic Journal. DOI: DOI: 10.2139/ssrn.4723687

Resende, N., & Hadley, J. (2024). The Translator's Canvas: Using LLMs to enhance Poetry translation. In *Proceedings of the 16th Conference of the Association for Machine Translation in the Americas* (Vol. 1). https:// aclanthology .org/ 2024 .amta - research .16 .pdf

Smitherman, G. (1977). *Talkin and testifyin: The language of Black America*. Wayne State University Press.

Spillers, H. J. (1987). Mama's baby, papa's maybe: An American grammar book. *Diacritics*, *17*(2), 65–81. DOI: 10.2307/464747

Spivak, G. C. (1988). Can the subaltern speak? In C. Nelson & L. Grossberg (Eds.), Marxism and the interpretation of culture (pp. 271–313). University of Illinois Press.

Spivak, G. C. (1993). The politics of translation. In *Outside in the teaching machine* (pp. 179–200). Routledge.

Yi, P., & Xia, Y. (2025). Irony detection, reasoning and understanding in zero-shot learning. *arXiv*. https://arxiv.org/abs/2501.16884

Chapter 3
Cultural and Linguistic Diversity in AI-Powered Educational Technologies

Mustafa Kayyali
https://orcid.org/0000-0003-3300-262X
Maaref University of Applied Sciences, Syria

ABSTRACT

As AI-powered technologies become increasingly embedded in educational systems worldwide, a critical question emerges: whose languages, values, and epistemologies are being amplified—and whose are being erased? This chapter explores the tensions between global AI solutions and local cultural and linguistic realities. It interrogates the design assumptions behind popular AI tools, uncovering how algorithmic logic often overlooks diverse modes of knowing and speaking. Drawing from real-world examples and critical theory, the chapter advocates for culturally responsive and linguistically inclusive AI development. It calls for participatory design approaches that center marginalized communities and rethink what it means to "personalize" learning. Ultimately, the chapter urges educators, technologists, and policymakers to move beyond one-size-fits-all innovation and toward a more pluralistic, justice-oriented digital future in education.

INTRODUCTION

In recent years, the convergence of artificial intelligence (AI) and education has inspired a global wave of optimism. Automated tutors, adaptive learning platforms, speech recognition tools, and algorithm-driven feedback systems are transforming the way students learn and teachers teach. Proponents of AI in education promise

DOI: 10.4018/979-8-3373-3673-2.ch003

increased efficiency, individualized instruction, and greater access to knowledge (Saltman, 2022). But amid this technological revolution, a more sobering and less discussed reality is emerging: AI technologies, far from being neutral, are shaped by the cultural, linguistic, and ideological assumptions of their creators. As these systems are deployed across increasingly diverse educational contexts, they risk reinforcing existing hierarchies, marginalizing non-dominant cultures, and flattening the rich linguistic textures of learners' lives.

Education is not merely the transfer of information—it is a cultural act (Babazade, 2024). Language is not just a medium of instruction—it is a vessel of identity, memory, and meaning. And yet, many AI-powered educational tools treat language as a data point, a variable to be optimized, or worse, a barrier to be corrected. English, often the default language in AI systems, dominates the architecture of many global educational platforms, subtly encoding Western norms into algorithms, instructional content, and feedback mechanisms (Evurulobi et al, 2024). While such systems may function adequately for learners situated within dominant linguistic or cultural paradigms, they can unintentionally alienate or exclude those who do not conform to such norms.

Consider, for instance, the experiences of a student in rural India navigating an AI-enabled math tutor that lacks support for their mother tongue. Or the misrecognition of a child's regional accent by a speech recognition app designed and trained primarily on American English. Or the erasure of culturally embedded learning styles—such as oral storytelling, collective problem-solving, or context-rich teaching methods—in favor of linear, text-heavy instruction optimized for standardized testing. These are not edge cases. They are widespread and deeply consequential.

The cultural and linguistic diversity of learners across the globe cannot be reduced to a series of parameters in a training set (Bromham et al, 2022). Education systems are embedded in complex webs of history, power, and identity, and the technologies we introduce into them must be attuned to this complexity. AI is not immune to cultural bias; on the contrary, it often encodes and amplifies it. Without deliberate, inclusive design, we risk building systems that privilege a narrow slice of humanity while sidelining the rest.

This chapter confronts these challenges head-on. It explores the cultural and linguistic blind spots of AI in education and interrogates the epistemic assumptions behind so-called "intelligent" systems. It asks uncomfortable questions: Whose knowledge counts? Whose accent is "correct"? What happens when AI "personalization" ignores cultural context? And how might we reimagine educational technologies that genuinely reflect and respect the diversity of human experience? By weaving together critical scholarship, lived experiences, and emerging case studies, this chapter argues for a radical rethinking of what AI in education should strive to become. (Williams, 2022) It proposes a model of development grounded not in efficiency or scalability alone, but in empathy, co-creation, and justice. For AI to serve as a tool of inclusion rather than exclusion, it must be anchored in the messy, beautiful multiplicity of the world's languages and cultures. Only then can we harness its potential in ways that honor both the learner and the learning.

The Promise and Peril of AI in Diverse Educational Landscapes

There's a curious duality at the heart of any conversation about artificial intelligence in education. It is at once exhilarating and unsettling—this sense that machines might finally unlock the promise of individualized learning, while at the same time threatening to flatten the contours of cultural and linguistic difference. In classrooms from Helsinki to Harare, AI is seeping into the fabric of pedagogy—not as a guest, but increasingly as a co-teacher, a silent assessor, a translator, even a guide (Kahila et al, 2024). Yet, beneath the algorithmic sheen lies a tension that many have yet to name aloud: what if the very tools designed to "help" us learn end up deciding *how* we're allowed to learn—and more hauntingly, *who* gets to learn at all?

It's easy to be seduced by the promise. Picture a child in a remote village, learning geometry through an interactive AI-powered tutor that adapts to her pace and style. Or a refugee student navigating a new language with the help of an intelligent speech app that patiently decodes pronunciation errors without judgment. Or an overworked teacher, relieved by AI-generated lesson plans tailored to the week's curriculum (Poth, 2024). There's magic in these stories—real, powerful, and deeply needed. For many, AI is the long-awaited answer to decades of overcrowded classrooms, overstretched educators, and learning gaps that traditional systems have stubbornly failed to close (Kayyali, 2025 c). But the story doesn't end there. It rarely does. Because behind every "smart" system sits a set of assumptions: assumptions about what it means to learn, what counts as "good" performance, what language is "clear," what behavior is "engaged." And these assumptions aren't universal—they're deeply rooted in the cultural norms of the developers, the institutions funding the research, and the dominant languages that dominate the training datasets. English, for example, isn't just a language—it's a worldview. When AI systems are built primarily around English-language corpora, trained on standardized English tests, and evaluated by metrics derived from Anglophone pedagogies, they carry with them a kind of epistemic gravity, pulling everything else toward their orbit (Stošić & Malyuga, 2024). The peril is subtle but profound.

Imagine a bilingual student—fluent in their home language, expressive in metaphor, rich in cultural references—struggling with a chatbot that can't recognize their way of thinking because it deviates from what the model has been trained to expect (Ma, 2024). Or think of a machine-generated feedback tool that flags a student's writing as "confusing" because it doesn't follow the expected argumentative structure common in Western academic essays. These aren't just technical glitches; they're acts of epistemic injustice. They say, in essence: your way of knowing doesn't belong here. And what about accents? There's a peculiar cruelty to voice recognition tools that fail to process non-standard English, especially when they're embedded in high-stakes assessments or speech therapy platforms. When the machine doesn't "hear" you, it doesn't simply make an error—it invalidates your presence. You're not just misunderstood; you're rendered invisible by the very system meant to include you. But let's slow down. This isn't a takedown of AI in education. Far from it. The potential remains staggering. AI can identify learning difficulties early, provide real-time translation in multilingual classrooms, and tailor learning journeys in ways no human teacher reasonably could (Fitas, 2025). It can scaffold confidence in students who feel alienated by traditional schooling. It can bring Shakespeare to a slum, quantum physics to a refugee camp, and indigenous folklore to the cloud—if designed thoughtfully (Kayyali, 2026 a). The catch? *Design thoughtfully.* And that's where the conversation often falters. Because "thoughtfulness" in AI isn't just a matter of clever coding or rigorous testing. It's about cultural fluency. It's about humility. It's about listening—really listening—to the communities these tools intend to serve. Not in the shallow "user feedback" sense, but in the sense of *co-creation.* The kind where an AI literacy app isn't just translated into Swahili, but reimagined in a way that speaks to the rhythms, metaphors, and values of Swahili-speaking learners. The kind where indigenous knowledge systems aren't footnotes, but foundational to the system's design.

Of course, that takes time. And money. And a willingness to slow down the breakneck pace of Silicon Valley-style "innovation." It means putting equity above scale. It means refusing to treat "diverse" as an add-on and starting from the premise that diversity *is* the default. The challenge is not only technical—it's philosophical. We have to ask: what is education *for*? Is it to assimilate learners into a singular, globalized mold? Or is it to help them grow in ways that honor their roots, their communities, and their unique ways of knowing? If the former, then AI is doing just fine. If the latter, then we have work to do. Because there's a danger here—not just of cultural erasure, but of pedagogical conformity. AI systems, by their nature, optimize. They search for patterns, for efficiency, for the "best" outcomes (Richardson et al, 2023). But learning isn't always efficient. It's messy. It's emotional. It's shaped by context and contradiction. The risk is that in our pursuit of personalized learning, we create systems that are technically tailored but culturally sterile. A perfectly customized learning journey that never once asks who you are. And yet, despite all this, there are glimmers of hope.

There are developers experimenting with AI that learns *from* local educators rather than overriding them (Nazaretsky et al, 2022). There are collaborative projects building datasets in underrepresented languages—not just to preserve them, but to celebrate them. There are learning platforms that allow students to teach the AI back, creating a loop of mutual transformation rather than one-way instruction (Jayanthi et al, 2023). These are not mainstream—yet. But they exist. And they show us what's possible when we stop asking, "How do we make AI smarter?" and start asking, "How do we make AI more human?"

Still, this shift won't happen on its own. It requires pressure—from educators, from policymakers, from the communities whose voices have too long gone unheard. It demands frameworks that embed cultural and linguistic inclusion as core metrics of success, not post-hoc corrections. It requires a rebalancing of power—away from the tech giants and toward the learners themselves.

One might argue: but isn't education already unequal? Isn't AI just reflecting the systems we've built? Yes. But that's precisely the point. AI reflects—and amplifies—whatever we give it. If our educational systems are biased, our AI will be biased (Holstein & Doroudi, 2021). If our data is exclusionary, our outcomes will be too. The question is not whether AI is inherently good or bad. The question is: *What are we training it to see?* Because ultimately, AI is a mirror. And what it reflects depends on where we choose to stand.

So maybe the goal isn't to build perfect AI tutors or flawless speech recognizers. Maybe the goal is to build systems that are *self-aware*, that know their limits, that are designed to evolve in conversation with the communities they serve (Mollick, 2024). Maybe the promise of AI isn't just about personalization, but about pluralism. Not just about speed, but about sensitivity. Not just about answers, but about better questions.

Can a machine learn to listen for the music in a child's mother tongue? Can it respect silence, ambiguity, tradition? Can it unlearn its own assumptions? These are not technical puzzles. They're human ones. And they sit at the heart of any future we dare call inclusive. We are only at the beginning. The terrain is vast. The stakes are high. But if we approach this moment with care—with a willingness to ask difficult questions, to confront uncomfortable truths, and to center the voices that have too often been left out—we might just create something worthy of being called "intelligent." Not just artificial intelligence. But something closer to human wisdom.

Whose Language? Whose Culture? The Hidden Biases in Algorithmic Learning

There's a curious kind of silence that sits inside the design of most educational technologies—a silence that doesn't scream, but hums beneath the surface. It's not the silence of absence, but of assumption. When we talk about algorithmic learning systems, we often leap straight into questions of optimization, speed, adaptability, and efficiency. But seldom do we pause to ask: *What culture lives inside this code?*

Whose voice is shaping the intelligence we trust to teach our children? And more urgently: *Who is being asked to adapt—to bend, conform, translate, or disappear?*

Every algorithm begins somewhere. Not in the abstract neutrality of logic, but in the minds of human beings (Matzner, 2024). Human beings who speak a language. Who are socialized into particular ways of knowing, of organizing thought, of interpreting tone, of deciding what constitutes a "correct" answer or a "valid" way of speaking. These seemingly invisible structures—linguistic patterns, cultural expectations, cognitive frames—are smuggled into the very DNA of machine learning systems. And once inside, they are not questioned; they are *normalized.*

Let's be honest about something: language is never just language. It carries memory, identity, struggle. It holds humor, silence, defiance, nuance. And yet, when language is reduced to tokens in a training set, when accents are flattened, when idioms are flagged as errors, what we're really saying is: *your way of being in the world is outside the model.* It's not just that you're speaking "incorrectly"—it's that your voice is illegible to the machine. And when the machine sits at the center of your learning experience, that illegibility becomes isolation.

Consider for a moment how AI-powered grammar checkers often flag non-Western syntactic structures as "awkward" or "unclear," not because they are wrong, but because they don't match the cadence of academic English. Or how speech recognition apps fail to decode African American Vernacular English (AAVE), or Caribbean-inflected French, or indigenous tongues layered with generations of oral tradition (Mengesha et al, 2021). These tools aren't just tools—they are gatekeepers. And they're whispering, sometimes loudly, *You don't belong*. But this isn't about demonizing technology. It's about locating responsibility. Language models learn from what we give them. And what we give them—our texts, our transcripts, our pedagogical materials—are themselves saturated with bias. Not just racial or gendered or geopolitical bias, but epistemic bias. That is, bias about *how* we know what we know. About *whose* knowledge is valid. And in education, this matters immensely.

Let's talk about "standardization." The dream of one-size-fits-all solutions has haunted education for centuries, but AI gives it a new gleam. It promises consistency (Khan, 2024). Uniformity. Scalability. A student in Bangkok and a student in Boston can now take the same AI-driven assessment. Sounds fair, right? But scratch beneath the surface, and the logic unravels. That Bangkok student may have been taught in a cultural context where deference to authority, collective reasoning, or indirect expression are valued. The Boston student, meanwhile, may have been raised in a system that prizes assertiveness, individual logic, and linear clarity. Both are intelligent. Both are capable. But the algorithm is calibrated to favor one.

This is where the hidden biases live. Not in outright discrimination, but in the mundane mechanics of design. In the data that was easier to collect. In the English corpora that were readily available. In the cultural scripts that were never named, only assumed. And these assumptions extend far beyond language.

They seep into curriculum design, content recommendation engines, even emotional analytics. Imagine an AI system that interprets a student's silence during a discussion as disengagement—because in its training data, "engagement" looked like constant eye contact, verbal contributions, enthusiastic gesturing (Koehl, 2025). But in many cultures, silence is not withdrawal; it's *respect.* It's reflection. It's part of the learning. But the system doesn't know that. It can't. Unless someone tells it. This is the peril of algorithmic learning: it *decides* before it understands (Kayyali, 2026 d). And once it decides, it rarely revises—unless someone forces it to. And who is doing the forcing?

Let's be honest again—most AI educational platforms are developed in Anglophone countries, often by teams that are racially, economically, and culturally homogeneous (Bulathwela et al, 2024). This isn't an indictment of those teams, but a reality check. When those creating the tools do not share life experiences with those who will use them, blind spots emerge. Not out of malice, but out of unexamined privilege. And yet, the consequences are profound. When bias is coded into the foundation, it doesn't just persist—it *scales*. So, what do we do with this knowledge?

We start by unlearning the myth of neutrality. There is no such thing as a culturally neutral algorithm. Just as there is no such thing as an apolitical curriculum. Every design choice is a value judgment. Every dataset is a story about whose knowledge counts.

We also need to shift the center of design. Instead of asking, "How do we translate our system into more languages?" we should be asking, "What would this system look like if it were *designed* in another language, from another cultural starting point?" That's not just a matter of accessibility—it's a matter of power. And we must invest—meaningfully—in underrepresented languages and cultures. Not as an afterthought, not as a checkbox, but as a starting principle. Imagine if AI systems trained on indigenous pedagogies weren't exotic anomalies, but standard practice (Williams, 2022). Imagine if multilinguality weren't seen as a hurdle to overcome, but as a strength to build from. Because here's the thing: the world is not monolingual. It never has been. And yet so much of our digital infrastructure assumes it is. The very term "natural language processing" is ironic. Whose "natural" language are we talking about? The "natural" of empire? Of academia? Of global capital? Or the "natural" of lullabies sung in remote villages, of prayers whispered in endangered tongues, of street slang that carries centuries of resilience?

If we want to build AI that honors human learning, we must start by honoring human language—and all its wild, unpredictable, glorious variation (BECKWITH, 2024). This means embracing messiness. It means letting go of the fantasy that we can always control or predict what learners will say, how they'll say it, or what meanings they'll bring. It means building systems that are less obsessed with correction and more attuned to comprehension. Systems that listen before they judge. That ask before they assume. It also means rethinking metrics. Instead of just measuring grammar accuracy or reading speed, what if we measured cultural relevance? Linguistic self-esteem? Epistemic dignity? There is beauty in linguistic plurality. There is wisdom in cultural specificity. And there is danger in designing educational futures that forget this.

Ultimately, the question isn't whether we can fix algorithmic bias—it's whether we're willing to admit that bias exists in the first place. Whether we're brave enough to confront the histories that shape our technologies. Whether we're humble enough to include voices that have been excluded, not just as users, but as co-authors. Because this isn't just about improving machine learning. It's about recovering something older, something we're in danger of losing: the idea that learning is a deeply human act. That it happens in relation, in context, in conversation—with each other, with our ancestors, with the land, with the language that names the world for us. When we forget that, our technologies may grow more intelligent—but our education becomes less humane. Let's not make that trade.

Localization vs. Globalization: Navigating Digital Pedagogies Across Borders

It's strange how a technology can be called "universal" when it doesn't speak your language. We often speak of digital learning—especially AI-powered platforms—as boundaryless, as if the moment an app is online it somehow floats above the messiness of geography, culture, and politics (McHaney, 2023). As if pedagogy were a product that could be bottled, sealed, and shipped across borders with the promise of consistency. But that's not how learning works. Not really. You don't just download education. You inherit it, negotiate it, live it through stories, gestures, silences. And when a tool built in one place arrives in another without translation—*not just linguistic translation, but cultural*—it doesn't just feel foreign. It feels wrong.

There's something seductive about globalization. Especially in education. It promises efficiency. A leveling of the playing field. A single dashboard to monitor progress in New York and Nairobi alike. Who wouldn't want that? A teacher in Dhaka can access the same digital library as a student in Stockholm. A curriculum designed in Silicon Valley reaches classrooms in Lima, Beirut, Kuala Lumpur. Knowledge, it seems, has been liberated from place. But what if knowledge was never meant to be placeless? What if the values embedded in those dashboards, the metrics they prioritize, the content they promote—what if all of that carries the invisible fingerprints of a particular worldview? A particular history? A particular sense of what matters? This is the quiet tension between localization and globalization in digital pedagogy. Globalization gives us reach, scale, access. Localization asks us to slow down, look around, and ask: *Does this make sense here?* Not just technically—but emotionally, socially, ethically.

Let's take an example that feels deceptively simple: a math app designed to teach fractions through pizza slices. A neat, engaging metaphor—at least for learners who eat pizza. But for a child in a rural village in Indonesia or Ethiopia where pizza isn't a familiar food, the metaphor crumbles. The problem isn't just comprehension—it's connection. The lesson doesn't land, because the context doesn't live in the learner's world. And while the numbers are universal, the meaning is not.

This is where digital pedagogy can betray its promise. When the tools forget that learners don't arrive as blank slates. They come with cultural frameworks, embodied knowledge, local logics (Ingham, 2021). They learn through rituals, rhythms, and relationality that don't always fit into sleek UX flows and animated tutorials. And yet, most global ed-tech assumes a kind of neutrality—a faith that learning can be standardized, mapped, predicted. But it can't. Not in the way these systems often try to. Localization isn't just about translating menus or dubbing voiceovers. It's about reimagining the pedagogy itself. It means asking, *What values are we embedding in this lesson? Whose worldview does it reflect? What is being left out?*

Consider a literacy app that emphasizes individual achievement, gamified rewards, and linear progress. That model might resonate in cultures that prize personal competition. But in others—where collective learning, intergenerational knowledge sharing, or oral storytelling traditions are central—the app might feel alienating, even hostile. It's not just about preference. It's about epistemology. Or think about classroom management algorithms that flag "disruptive" behavior based on data collected from Western classrooms (Lu et al, 2021). What happens when a child in a different context engages in culturally normative behavior—talking with peers during work time, using expressive body language—only to be labeled by the system as inattentive or misbehaving? The AI doesn't understand that it's made a cultural mistake. It just flags, sorts, penalizes. And then there's language. Always, language.

Multilingual learners are often framed as a "challenge" for AI systems—as if the plurality of tongues is a glitch in the matrix (Ma, 2024). But the real challenge lies not in the learners, but in the systems themselves. Too many platforms treat translation as a feature to be tacked on after the fact, rather than a foundational design principle. They don't ask how language *shapes* thought, how syntax reflects worldview, how a proverb in one culture can hold centuries of pedagogical wisdom. Localization demands that we take these questions seriously. It insists that pedagogy be relational. That it grow out of place. But that's not easy in a world obsessed with scale. Scaling requires simplification. And simplification flattens difference. You can't tailor every lesson to every culture, the argument goes (Kim & Spear, 2023). You'd never get anything done. Maybe. But maybe the goal isn't to tailor everything.

Maybe it's to design systems that can *be tailored*—that are open-ended, modular, co-created. Systems that invite local educators, students, and communities into the design process. Not as testers, but as authors.

There's a word often used in global education spaces: *contextualization.* It sounds good. Thoughtful. But it's often misunderstood. It doesn't mean "slap on a local example." It means letting the *local define the frame.* It means trusting that communities know best how learning happens in their worlds, and that technology should follow their lead—not the other way around (Kayyali, 2025 b). There's something else, too. A deeper layer. Globalization isn't just about content. It's about power. About who gets to decide what counts as "best practice." About which pedagogies are exported, and which are ignored (Piacentini, 2024). When global ed-tech platforms arrive in post-colonial contexts bearing Western curricula, slick interfaces, and the promise of progress, there's an echo of history in the room. A whisper that says: *Your ways weren't good enough. Ours are better. Modern. Scientific.* It's not always intentional. But it's felt.

Localization, then, is not just a design choice. It's an act of resistance. A refusal to erase. A way of saying: *We are not behind. We are different.* It's about honoring pedagogical sovereignty. Letting communities define their own aspirations, their own metrics of success. Of course, this doesn't mean shutting the door to global collaboration. Quite the opposite. The dream is not isolation—it's reciprocity. Imagine a world where an AI system developed in rural Senegal becomes the model for rural Australia. Where insights from Maori learning traditions reshape digital literacy frameworks in Canada. Where pedagogy travels not from "center to periphery," but in all directions, with humility. That's a different kind of globalization (Hogue & Bell, 2022). One grounded not in replication, but in relationship. But getting there will require new kinds of infrastructures—technical, institutional, emotional. It means funding models that support local innovation. It means regulatory frameworks that prioritize cultural protection over market penetration. It means educational policies that ask hard questions about what's being imported, and why. It also means training. Not just for teachers, but for technologists. So many AI developers have never set foot in a classroom outside their own schooling (Kamalov et al, 2023). They haven't seen the thousand micro-adjustments a teacher makes to adapt a lesson to their students' realities. They haven't felt the electricity of learning that pulses through a classroom when a story hits home—not because it's well-told, but because it's *theirs.* We need technologists who understand pedagogy. Who understand that learning isn't a transaction. It's a relationship. Localization teaches us that. Globalization reminds us of what's possible. The tension between the two isn't something to be solved, but held. Because both carry risks.

Too much localization, and you risk fragmentation—systems that can't talk to each other, data that can't be shared, progress that can't be measured. Too much globalization, and you risk erasure—systems that work everywhere, but belong nowhere. The art is in the balance. In building systems that are fluent in many pedagogies. That adapt not just to learners, but to contexts. That ask: *Where am I? Who am I serving? What matters here?* Because in the end, education is not about delivering content. It's about shaping meaning. And meaning is always local.

Voices at the Margins: Indigenous Languages and Cultural Knowledge in AI Systems

You can feel absence. It lingers. Not as silence, but as something unspoken that should've been heard. In the luminous halls of artificial intelligence and digital pedagogy, that absence often takes the shape of a missing language, a forgotten proverb, a way of knowing that no one thought to encode. Indigenous voices—often spoken softly, reverently, in circles rather than rows—rarely make it into the models (Morton et al, 2021). And when they do, they are reshaped, repackaged, rendered legible for systems that were never designed to hold them in the first place. What does it mean to teach with tools that have never learned to listen?

In the age of AI, when machines write poems, grade essays, translate speech, and adapt curricula in milliseconds, we still struggle to include the most ancient, layered, and land-bound languages in those systems (Kalantzis & Cope, 2025). It's not just a technical limitation. It's a philosophical wound. It speaks to centuries of erasure, the long tail of colonial epistemicide—the systematic disappearance of indigenous ways of knowing under the guise of progress. The very architecture of today's machine learning systems favors what can be scraped, digitized, ranked, and tokenized. But many indigenous languages were never meant to be frozen in digital lexicons. They are alive. They breathe in song, in ritual, in land-based knowledge passed from elder to child not through syntax, but through silence, gesture, presence. So when we talk about AI and education, and we ask—*Who gets to learn?*—we must also ask, *Whose knowledge gets preserved? Whose stories shape the machine?* Because right now, most AI systems are built atop mountains of data scraped from dominant languages—English, Mandarin, Spanish, French. Their "intelligence" is a mirror of the colonizing powers that defined the modern world (Kayyali, 2026 b). Even "multilingual" models often carry with them the weight of a Western linguistic hierarchy, where grammatical structures and logics of expression from English are treated as baseline and everything else as deviation.

Take an indigenous language like Mapudungun in Chile. Or Sámi in Scandinavia. Or Ainu in Japan. These are not simply "minority languages." They are vessels of a worldview—distinct cosmologies, ecological wisdoms, kinship structures, epistemologies of time and space. They carry verbs for "the smell of snow before it falls," or kinship terms that map relationships modern English cannot even begin to name. When these languages are excluded from digital systems, the loss isn't just practical—it's ontological. We lose a way of being human. And when they're included? That's complicated too. Because inclusion is not the same as understanding. An AI system can be trained to translate a sentence from Ojibwe to English, perhaps (Pinhanez et al, 2024). But can it feel the rhythm of a drum song encoded in that syntax? Can it grasp the intergenerational trauma or sacred humor woven into the phrasing? Inclusion, if done carelessly, risks becoming another form of colonization—turning living knowledge into "data," cultural meaning into interface, stories into search results.

Some efforts have tried. Google's endangered languages project, for instance, or UNESCO-backed initiatives that attempt to preserve and document disappearing tongues. But even these well-meaning projects often fall into the trap of extractivism—gathering words and phrases, archiving them, but without embedding them into living systems of use. As if preserving a vocabulary list were enough. As if language weren't a social act, a performance, a relationship (Abend, 2023). And yet, what if we shifted the question? What if we asked not *how do we translate indigenous languages into AI,* but *how do we reimagine AI through indigenous frameworks?* Because maybe the problem isn't that the languages don't fit the model. Maybe the model doesn't fit the world.

Indigenous knowledge systems are often holistic, interdependent, cyclical (Varghese & Crawford, 2021). Time is nonlinear. Truth is relational. Land is not property, but kin. These concepts don't neatly map onto current AI paradigms, which rely on linear inputs and outputs, causality, objectivity, and prediction. But what if they could? What if machine learning models were built not to generalize from masses of data, but to attend to context, to listen with specificity, to honor nuance over normativity? It sounds radical (Grill, 2022). But maybe it's necessary. Because education systems—especially those adopting AI—are at risk of becoming more standardized, not less (Schiff, 2022). More efficient, yes. But less responsive to local wisdoms. Less tolerant of ambiguity. Less porous to ways of learning that don't fit the dashboard. And in that race for innovation, we risk leaving behind the very knowledge that might save us. Let's not forget: many indigenous languages carry ecological knowledge gathered over millennia—knowledge about farming rhythms, forest cycles, animal migrations, weather shifts. As the planet warms, as climate crises deepen, this knowledge is not quaint—it is urgent. And yet, it remains largely invisible to the systems we're building to "solve" these crises.

Imagine AI systems trained on indigenous ecological models—able to detect not just the rise in temperature, but the subtle dissonance in bird migration patterns that elders have tracked through oral tradition (Han et al, 2023). Imagine AI tutors not just teaching math, but grounded in indigenous pedagogies—like learning through observation, storytelling, community reciprocity. Imagine machines that don't just parse language, but learn to sit with silence, to recognize gesture, to pause before replying. That kind of AI isn't just more inclusive—it's more humane. But to build it, we need to start with consent.

Because for many indigenous communities, the issue isn't just inclusion or exclusion—it's sovereignty. Who owns the data? Who decides how a language is represented, taught, translated, monetized? Too often, companies approach these communities with extractive models—offering token representation in exchange for access to linguistic resources, then disappearing once the app is built, the funding secured. The knowledge is taken, and the people are left behind. Instead, what if we built AI tools in collaboration with indigenous leaders, language keepers, youth, and elders? Not just hiring a "cultural consultant," but inviting co-authorship. Letting the community decide what should be shared, and what should remain sacred. Recognizing that not all knowledge is meant for the machine. There are examples emerging.

In New Zealand, Māori technologists are building AI models rooted in Te Ao Māori—embedding ancestral wisdom into the fabric of digital systems (Shedlock & Hudson, 2022). In Canada, First Nations coders are developing speech recognition tools for indigenous dialects, not to commodify them, but to revitalize their use among younger generations. In parts of South America, indigenous radio networks are exploring how natural language processing might help them translate and preserve endangered stories (Kayyali, 2025 a). These are not side projects—they are prototypes of a new way forward. Still, the road ahead is long. The challenge isn't just technical. It's emotional. It's about trust. About undoing centuries of extraction and learning to relate differently. It's about creating space in the AI landscape for humility—for admitting that some knowledge can't be coded, some stories aren't ours to tell, and some silences are sacred. This is not a call for nostalgia. Indigenous knowledge is not a relic. It's a compass. A way to reorient ourselves in an age of disconnection. And if we listen—really listen—it might teach us how to build systems that are not just smart, but wise.

Imagine an AI tool that grows slower, because it pauses to ask for permission (Goldfarb, 2024). One that is less "accurate," but more respectful. One that doesn't aim to universalize, but to pluralize. One that doesn't measure success by the number of users, but by the depth of relationship it fosters. Voices at the margins are not marginal. They are only made so by systems that refuse to hear. Let's build something that listens differently.

Designing Equitable Futures: Policy, Pedagogy, and Participatory Innovation

There's a strange irony in how we speak about the future—especially when technology is involved. We talk about it as if it's already written, coded, humming silently in some server room in Palo Alto or Shenzhen. As if the algorithms are inevitable, the platforms non-negotiable, the systems preordained (Madsen, 2022). But the truth—messy, hopeful, and radically empowering—is this: futures are designed. Not discovered. Not inherited. *Designed.* By people. And policy. And priorities. And by the values we dare to fight for, even when they don't fit the dominant codebase.

The question isn't just how we build better AI-powered educational tools. It's: who's doing the building? Who's being listened to? Who's deciding what "better" means? If we want equity—not the buzzword, but the hard, structural kind—we have to stop pretending that educational technologies are neutral. They aren't. They are products of policy choices, funding structures, pedagogical ideologies, and deeply embedded biases. And those choices are shaping classrooms across the globe—quietly, invisibly, but with force.

Let's be clear: *technological optimism without policy backbone is a performance.* You can't just drop tablets into underfunded schools and call it digital transformation (Danaher, 2022). You can't build AI tutors that only work in English and call it personalized learning. You can't train models on data that excludes indigenous communities and say you're "bridging the gap." You're not. You're widening it—and doing so with glossy branding. So where do we begin? With policy. Because the systems we design are only as equitable as the systems that regulate them. Right now, the global ed-tech space is dominated by private interests. Fast-moving, venture-funded platforms racing to scale before the next competitor appears. And governments? Often playing catch-up. Or worse, outsourcing responsibility entirely to the market. But equity can't be an afterthought. It must be architected into the foundation—through procurement guidelines that require cultural responsiveness, funding incentives for local-language innovation, data governance models that protect community sovereignty.

It means asking questions that are both ethical and infrastructural (Kayyali, 2025 d). Who owns the educational data? Who decides what a child's learning path should look like? Is that path shaped by algorithms designed in foreign labs, or by local teachers who understand the terrain? Are marginalized communities being compensated for their knowledge, or merely mined for their language patterns? These aren't small questions (Jaton, 2021). They're tectonic. And they demand a new kind of policymaking—one that isn't just reactive but visionary. That sees education not as a market to be optimized, but as a right to be protected. That centers learners not as users, but as citizens. But policy alone doesn't teach.

Pedagogy matters too. Because even the most equitable system can reproduce inequity if the underlying model of learning is broken (Fishman & Herrenkohl, 2022). So much of AI in education still mimics a 19th-century classroom in digital drag: top-down instruction, linear content delivery, compliance-based assessment. Where's the imagination in that? Where's the justice? Real pedagogy is relational. Messy. Political. It listens before it teaches. It adapts not just to ability, but to identity. And it knows—knows—that culture is not a variable to control for, but a terrain to walk with care.

If we're serious about equity, we need pedagogical models that reflect the plurality of human experience (De Bie et al, 2023). That means valuing indigenous teaching traditions, storytelling as cognitive architecture, multilingual expression as creativity—not deficiency. It means rethinking how we define learning outcomes. Not just what's easy to measure, but what's meaningful to grow. And here's the twist: AI could help us do this. Not as a master, but as a companion (Kayyali, 2026 c). Not by replacing the teacher, but by extending the possibilities of what teaching can be. Imagine an AI platform that doesn't just deliver curriculum, but helps a teacher map the emotional resonances of a classroom across cultural lines (Shah, 2023). Or one that doesn't grade writing by grammar alone, but by narrative power and metaphorical richness. These things are possible—technically—but we don't prioritize them. Why? Because our pedagogy is still stuck in an industrial model, and our AI mirrors our limitations. It's not the machine's fault. It's ours.

This is where participatory innovation enters the scene—not as a trendy methodology, but as a moral imperative (Ten Holter, 2022). You can't design an equitable future from a glass tower. You have to go to the people who've been pushed out of the room. Bring them in—not just as case studies, but as co-creators. Let students shape the tools they'll use. Let teachers lead the design sprints. Let indigenous knowledge keepers write the data protocols (Cordova, 2024). Not symbolically. *Substantively.* And yes, that slows things down. Good. We need to slow down. We've moved too fast for too long, leaving trauma in our wake. Efficiency is not justice. Inclusion is not innovation unless it shifts power.

Participatory design means relinquishing control. It means being willing to unlearn what you thought was universal (Udoewa, 2022). It means discomfort. And that's the point. Because systems built without discomfort are systems built for the already comfortable. What if we measured innovation not by how fast a platform scales, but by how many voices it makes room for? What if "disruption" meant disrupting colonial hierarchies in educational design? What if we stopped asking how to make AI better, and started asking *how to make education more human, more humble, more just?*

We talk a lot about the "future of learning." But the truth is, we're not headed there unless we build it—together. That means designing for plurality, not perfection. For difference, not dominance. For empathy, not efficiency. And it means recognizing that equitable design isn't a feature. It's a philosophy. A practice. A promise. Futures aren't inherited. They're authored. Let's write something better.

CONCLUSION

As we stand at the intersection of technological advancement and pedagogical transformation, we face a sobering truth: the current trajectory of AI-powered educational technologies, if left unchecked, may deepen the very inequities it seeks to resolve. What began as a promise to democratize learning is increasingly entangled with the risks of erasure, exclusion, and homogenization. At the heart of this tension lies a fundamental question—can AI honor the cultural and linguistic multiplicity that defines human learning?

This chapter has sought to illuminate the silent assumptions embedded in many AI-driven educational platforms. From language hierarchies to culturally biased training data, from inaccessible user interfaces to culturally irrelevant pedagogy, the hidden architecture of these tools often privileges a particular worldview. The result is not merely technological misalignment—it is pedagogical injustice. Students who do not speak dominant global languages, who come from underrepresented cultures, or who learn in ways not recognized by standardized models are too often left behind, misjudged, or made invisible.

Yet the future is not predetermined. The same technologies that risk flattening difference can also be harnessed to amplify it. Imagine AI tools that are co-designed with indigenous communities, capturing their oral traditions and ways of knowing. Envision learning platforms that are not only multilingual but also culturally aware—adapting not just the content, but the values, metaphors, and pedagogical styles to local contexts. Picture algorithms that do not "correct" accents, but learn to understand them. This is not a utopian dream—it is an urgent imperative.

To get there, we must move beyond superficial inclusion. Translating a user interface or adding a language option is not enough. Real inclusion demands a structural rethinking of how AI systems are designed, trained, and evaluated. It calls for the active participation of communities too often excluded from the design table. It requires developers to embrace discomfort, to question their own cultural lenses, and to relinquish the illusion of universality. And it urges educators and policymakers to advocate not just for "access," but for cultural respect and linguistic justice.

Furthermore, it is crucial to rethink the metrics by which we evaluate the "success" of AI in education. Is it enough to measure accuracy, engagement rates, or learning speed? Or should we also ask whether learners feel seen, heard, and understood by these systems? Do they find their realities reflected in the content? Do they trust the tools, not just for their functionality, but for the values they embody?

AI is not just a tool—it is a storyteller, a translator, a gatekeeper. And like all such entities, it carries power. If that power is to be used ethically and equitably in education, it must be wielded with humility and awareness. It must be informed by a recognition that knowledge is not monolithic, that learning is deeply personal and profoundly cultural, and that technology, while powerful, must always remain in service to the human.

In the end, the pursuit of culturally and linguistically inclusive AI is not merely a technical challenge—it is a moral one. It asks us to reimagine educational technology not as a universal solution, but as a patchwork of possibilities, each stitched together by the hands of those it seeks to serve. Only by embracing this mosaic can we hope to build a future where every learner, in every language, from every culture, finds a place in the digital classroom.

REFERENCES

Abend, G. (2023). Words and distinctions for the common good: Practical reason in the logic of social science.

Babazade, Y. (2024). Proverbs in Pedagogy: Their Role in Language Teaching and Cultural Transmission. *Global Spectrum of Research and Humanities*, *1*(1), 69–82. DOI: 10.69760/gsrh.0101202407

BECKWITH, S. L. (2024). CHAPTER TWO AI–AGENCY AND INNOVATION–. Advancing Honors Education for Today and Tomorrow, 35.

Bromham, L., Dinnage, R., Skirgård, H., Ritchie, A., Cardillo, M., Meakins, F., Greenhill, S., & Hua, X. (2022). Global predictors of language endangerment and the future of linguistic diversity. *Nature Ecology & Evolution*, *6*(2), 163–173. DOI: 10.1038/s41559-021-01604-y PMID: 34916621

Bulathwela, S., Pérez-Ortiz, M., Holloway, C., Cukurova, M., & Shawe-Taylor, J. (2024). Artificial intelligence alone will not democratise education: On educational inequality, techno-solutionism and inclusive tools. *Sustainability (Basel)*, *16*(2), 781. DOI: 10.3390/su16020781

Cordova, J. C. (2024). Creating a Digital House of Knowledge: Ensuring the Continuation and Integrity of Indigenous Knowledge Transfers in the Digital Era (Master's thesis, University of Alaska Fairbanks).

Danaher, J. (2022). Techno-optimism: An analysis, an evaluation and a modest defence. *Philosophy & Technology*, *35*(2), 54. DOI: 10.1007/s13347-022-00550-2 PMID: 35378903

De Bie, A., Marquis, E., Cook-Sather, A., & Luqueño, L. (2023). *Promoting equity and justice through pedagogical partnership*. Taylor & Francis.

Evurulobi, C. I., Dagunduro, A. O., & Ajuwon, O. A. (2024). Language learning technologies: A review of trends in the USA and globally. *World Journal of Advanced Research and Reviews*, *23*(03), 2697–2707. DOI: 10.30574/wjarr.2024.23.3.2851

Fishman, B., & Herrenkohl, L. R. (2022). Equitable learning. The Foundational Handbook on Improvement Research in Education, 47.

Fitas, R. (2025). Inclusive Education with AI: Supporting Special Needs and Tackling Language Barriers. arXiv preprint arXiv:2504.14120.

Goldfarb, A. (2024). Pause artificial intelligence research? Understanding AI policy challenges. *The Canadian Journal of Economics. Revue Canadienne d'Economique*, *57*(2), 363–377. DOI: 10.1111/caje.12705

Grill, G. (2022). Constructing Certainty in Machine Learning: On thc pcrformativity of testing and its hold on the future.

Han, B. A., Varshney, K. R., LaDeau, S., Subramaniam, A., Weathers, K. C., & Zwart, J. (2023). A synergistic future for AI and ecology. *Proceedings of the National Academy of Sciences of the United States of America*, *120*(38), e2220283120. DOI: 10.1073/pnas.2220283120 PMID: 37695904

Hogue, M. S., & Bell, D. P. (2022). Interreligious Resilience.

Holstein, K., & Doroudi, S. (2021). Equity and artificial intelligence in education: will" aied" amplify or alleviate inequities in education? arXiv preprint arXiv:2104.12920.

Ingham, M. (2021). *Agents*. Agency, & Agencies in Assembling Liminal Learning Spaces.

Jaton, F. (2021). *The constitution of algorithms: Ground-truthing, programming, formulating*. MIT Press. DOI: 10.7551/mitpress/12517.001.0001

Jayanthi, K., Priya, M. S., Saranya, S., Gomathi, R., & Sam, D. (2023). E-Learning as a Desirable Form of Education in the Era of Society 5.0. In *Advances in Distance Learning in Times of Pandemic* (pp. 23–51). Chapman and Hall/CRC. DOI: 10.1201/9781003322252-2

Kahila, J., Vartiainen, H., Tedre, M., Arkko, E., Lin, A., Pope, N., Jormanainen, I., & Valtonen, T. (2024). Pedagogical framework for cultivating children's data agency and creative abilities in the age of AI. *Informatics in Education*, *23*(2), 323–360. DOI: 10.15388/infedu.2024.15

Kalantzis, M., & Cope, B. (2025). Literacy in the time of Artificial Intelligence. *Reading Research Quarterly*, *60*(1), e591. DOI: 10.1002/rrq.591

Kamalov, F., Santandreu Calonge, D., & Gurrib, I. (2023). New era of artificial intelligence in education: Towards a sustainable multifaceted revolution. *Sustainability (Basel)*, *15*(16), 12451. DOI: 10.3390/su151612451

Kayyali, M. (2025 a). AI and Gamification: Engaging EFL Learners With Language Games. In Application of AI in the Teaching and Learning of English as a Foreign Language (EFL) (pp. 33-64). IGI Global Scientific Publishing.

Kayyali, M. (2025 b). Impact of AI on Student Learning Outcomes: Measuring Success and Identifying Challenges. In Transforming Education With AI-Powered Personalized Learning (pp. 81-122). IGI Global Scientific Publishing.

Kayyali, M. (2025 c). Classroom Management: Techniques for Creating a Positive, Friendly Learning Environment. In Exploration of K-12 Teaching and Learning for Teacher Educators (pp. 53-78). IGI Global Scientific Publishing.

Kayyali, M. (2025 d). Ethical Implications of Generative AI in Education: Privacy, Bias, and Integrity. In Transformative AI Practices for Personalized Learning Strategies (pp. 185-218). IGI Global Scientific Publishing.

Kayyali, M. (2026 a). Strategies for Engaging Generation Z Students in Higher Education. In Developing Student Engagement Opportunities in Higher Education (pp. 199-230). IGI Global Scientific Publishing.

Kayyali, M. (2026 b). AI in Higher Education: The Risk of Excluding Vulnerable Learners. In AI and New Forms of Exclusion (pp. 57-82). IGI Global Scientific Publishing.

Kayyali, M. (2026 c). Case Studies of E-Learning Programs Focused on Sustainability. In *Harnessing E-Learning to Create a Sustainable Future* (pp. 1–22). IGI Global Scientific Publishing.

Kayyali, M. (2026 d). Harnessing E-Learning for a Sustainable Future: A Global Perspective. In *Harnessing E-Learning to Create a Sustainable Future* (pp. 207–226). IGI Global Scientific Publishing.

Khan, S. (2024). *Brave New Words: How AI Will Revolutionize Education (and why That's a Good Thing).* Penguin.

Kim, G., & Spear, S. J. (2023). *Wiring the winning organization: liberating our collective greatness through slowification, simplification, and amplification.* IT Revolution.

Koehl, S. (2025). Designing AI Software for Large Classroom Engagement (Doctoral dissertation).

Lu, A. J., Marcu, G., Ackerman, M. S., & Dillahunt, T. R. (2021, June). Coding bias in the use of behavior management technologies: Uncovering socio-technical consequences of data-driven surveillance in classrooms. In *Proceedings of the 2021 ACM Designing Interactive Systems Conference* (pp. 508-522). DOI: 10.1145/3461778.3462084

Ma, B. (2024). The Impact of Artificial Intelligence Tools on Bilingual Students in US Education: A Study on Academic Language-learning, Cultural Sensitivity and Inclusiveness (Master's thesis, University of Washington).

Madsen, T. (2022). Autonomy, Economy, and Colony: Practicing Human Identity in a State of Algorithmic Transition. Western Tributaries, 8.

Matzner, T. (2024). Algorithms as complementary abstractions. *New Media & Society*, *26*(4), 1799–1815. DOI: 10.1177/14614448221078604

McHaney, R. (2023). *The new digital shoreline: How Web 2.0 and millennials are revolutionizing higher education*. Taylor & Francis. DOI: 10.4324/9781003447979

Mengesha, Z., Heldreth, C., Lahav, M., Sublewski, J., & Tuennerman, E. (2021). "I don't think these devices are very culturally sensitive."—Impact of automated speech recognition errors on African Americans. *Frontiers in Artificial Intelligence*, *4*, 725911. DOI: 10.3389/frai.2021.725911 PMID: 34901836

Mollick, E. (2024). *Co-intelligence: Living and working with AI*. Penguin.

Morton, D., Bird-Naytowhow, K., & Hatala, A. R. (2021). Silent voices, absent bodies, and quiet methods: Revisiting the processes and outcomes of personal knowledge production through Body-Mapping methodologies among Indigenous youth. *International Journal of Qualitative Methods*, *20*, 1609406920987934. DOI: 10.1177/1609406920987934

Nazaretsky, T., Bar, C., Walter, M., & Alexandron, G. (2022, March). Empowering teachers with AI: Co-designing a learning analytics tool for personalized instruction in the science classroom. In LAK22: 12th international learning analytics and knowledge conference (pp. 1-12).

Piacentini, T. (2024). Critical Pedagogy and Pedagogic Discomfort. In *Developing a Critical Pedagogy of Migration Studies* (pp. 1–23). Bristol University Press.

Pinhanez, C., Cavalin, P., Storto, L., Finbow, T., Cobbinah, A., Nogima, J., . . . Gonçalves, I. (2024). Harnessing the Power of Artificial Intelligence to Vitalize Endangered Indigenous Languages: Technologies and Experiences. arXiv preprint arXiv:2407.12620.

Poth, R. D. (2024). *How to Teach AI: Weaving Strategies and Activities Into Any Content Area*. International Society for Technology in Education.

Richardson, N., Kothapalli, S., Onteddu, A. R., Kundavaram, R. R., & Talla, R. R. (2023). AI-Driven Optimization Techniques for Evolving Software Architecture in Complex Systems. *ABC Journal of Advanced Research, 12*(2), 71–84. DOI: 10.18034/abcjar.v12i2.783

Saltman, K. J. (2022). *The alienation of fact: Digital educational privatization, AI, and the false promise of bodies and numbers*. MIT Press. DOI: 10.7551/mitpress/14387.001.0001

Schiff, D. (2022). Education for AI, not AI for education: The role of education and ethics in national AI policy strategies. *International Journal of Artificial Intelligence in Education, 32*(3), 527–563. DOI: 10.1007/s40593-021-00270-2

Shah, P. (2023). *AI and the Future of Education: Teaching in the Age of Artificial Intelligence*. John Wiley & Sons.

Shedlock, K., & Hudson, P. (2022). Kaupapa Māori concept modelling for the creation of Māori IT Artefacts. Journal of the Royal Society of New Zealand, 52(sup1), 18-32.

Ten Holter, C. (2022). Participatory design: Lessons and directions for responsible research and innovation. *Journal of Responsible Innovation, 9*(2), 275–290. DOI: 10.1080/23299460.2022.2041801

Udoewa, V. (2022). An introduction to radical participatory design: Decolonising participatory design processes. *Design Science, 8*, e31. DOI: 10.1017/dsj.2022.24

Varghese, J., & Crawford, S. S. (2021). A cultural framework for Indigenous, Local, and Science knowledge systems in ecology and natural resource management. *Ecological Monographs, 91*(1), e01431. DOI: 10.1002/ecm.1431

Williams, D. P. (2022). Belief, Values, Bias, and Agency: Development of and Entanglement with "Artificial Intelligence" (Doctoral dissertation, Virginia Polytechnic Institute and State University).

KEY TERMS AND DEFINITIONS

Cultural Diversity: The inclusion and representation of different cultural backgrounds, values, and traditions within educational content and platforms.

Linguistic Equity: The fair treatment and support of multiple languages in digital learning systems, ensuring no language group is marginalized.

AI-Powered Personalization: The use of artificial intelligence to tailor educational content, pace, and pathways based on learner profiles and needs.

Bias Mitigation in AI: The process of identifying and minimizing cultural, linguistic, or demographic biases embedded in AI-driven educational tools.

Multilingual NLP: Natural language processing technologies capable of understanding, generating, and translating content across several languages.

Culturally Responsive AI: Artificial intelligence systems designed to respect and adapt to diverse cultural contexts and learner experiences.

Language-Aware Learning Systems: Educational platforms that recognize and leverage students' multilingual abilities to enhance comprehension and inclusion.

Chapter 4
Integrating Generative AI Into Cultural and Creative Product Design Education:
A Framework for Student Designers

Chaoquan Lin
https://orcid.org/0009-0004-2349-5461
Universiti Sains Malaysia, Malaysia

Mariam Mohamad
https://orcid.org/0000-0001-8498-4139
Universiti Sains Malaysia, Malaysia

ABSTRACT

The advent of Generative Artificial Intelligence (GenAI) marks a pivotal moment for creative industries, including cultural product design. This paper proposes specific research questions and outlines the research method used to develop a revised framework with GenAI. The core of the paper presents this four-stage framework detailing student activities, GenAI integration points, GenAI roles, and expected outputs for each stage. Foundational principles and strategic imperatives for effective GenAI integration are discussed. The framework aims to guide educators and students in leveraging GenAI's potential to foster innovation while upholding cultural integrity and ethical responsibility, fostering a human-AI cultural symbiosis.

DOI: 10.4018/979-8-3373-3673-2.ch004

INTRODUCTION

Cultural product design is a dynamic and increasingly significant field, dedicated to the thoughtful translation of cultural heritage, features, and narratives into tangible or intangible products. This process not only enhances the intrinsic value of these products but also plays a crucial role in the dissemination and preservation of cultural identities in an interconnected world. In an era of globalization, where mass-produced goods often lead to a homogenization of experiences, there is a growing appreciation for products that embody unique local cultural features, offering distinct identities and enriching consumer experiences (Moalosi et al., 2010). These cultural features, ranging from aesthetic motifs and material traditions to underlying stories and values, provide a deep wellspring for innovation and differentiation in the marketplace (Chu & Lin, 2024).

The advent of Generative Artificial Intelligence (GenAI) marks a pivotal moment for creative industries, including cultural product design. GenAI encompasses a suite of technologies capable of generating novel content—such as text, images, audio, and even 3D models—based on patterns learned from vast datasets (Anantrasirichai et al., 2025; Tiribelli et al., 2024). Its capabilities in data analysis, rapid concept generation, and iterative prototyping present unprecedented opportunities to augment and transform traditional design workflows (Anantrasirichai et al., 2025). The integration of GenAI promises to address some of the long-standing challenges in cultural product design, such as the laborious process of cultural research, the interpretation of complex symbolic meanings, and the generation of diverse yet culturally resonant design concepts.

However, this technological advancement is not without its complexities. The application of GenAI in a field as nuanced and sensitive as cultural product design necessitates careful consideration of authenticity, representation, and ethical implications. The power of GenAI to automate and accelerate creative processes must be balanced with the indispensable role of human designers in providing critical judgment, cultural understanding, and ethical oversight (Fu et al., 2025; Tiribelli et al., 2024). This human-AI collaboration is central to harnessing GenAI's potential responsibly and effectively.

The capacity of GenAI to assist novice designers in navigating the complexities of cultural information and to automate aspects of research and analysis suggests a potential democratization of the field. If GenAI can simplify the initial, often daunting, tasks of deep cultural research and semantic analysis, it could lower the entry barriers for students and designers from diverse backgrounds to engage with cultural product creation. This could lead to a richer tapestry of cultural narratives being explored and expressed. However, this increased accessibility simultaneously underscores the critical need for robust educational frameworks that instill a deep sense of cultural respect and critical engagement alongside proficiency in AI tools. Without such grounding, the ease of access could inadvertently lead to superficial or misrepresentative cultural products.

Furthermore, the core endeavor of cultural product design—to enhance value by embedding unique cultural characteristics —faces a new dynamic with the introduction of AI, which is often prized for its ability to generate novel and diverse outputs. This creates an inherent tension: the drive for AI-generated novelty and efficiency must be carefully managed against the imperative to preserve cultural authenticity and avoid the dilution or misrepresentation of cultural meanings. The potential for AI to produce innovative forms and concepts is exciting, but if this innovation is not deeply rooted in and respectful of the source culture, it risks undermining the very essence that gives cultural products their unique value and significance. Therefore, any framework for integrating GenAI into cultural product design must explicitly address this dual challenge, embedding mechanisms for critical human evaluation and ethical consideration at every stage to ensure that AI-driven innovation serves, rather than subverts, cultural integrity.

Cultural product design education problem statement

Cultural product design education stands at a critical juncture with the rapid proliferation of GenAI. GenAI technologies offer unprecedented opportunities to enhance creativity, streamline design processes, and broaden accessibility in the creation of culturally rich and meaningful products. These tools can assist in complex data analysis, accelerate concept generation, and facilitate iterative prototyping, potentially transforming traditional design workflows (Channi et al., 2025). However, the integration of these powerful tools into a domain as nuanced and sensitive as cultural product design is fraught with significant challenges that current educational approaches are often ill-equipped to address.

The central problem, therefore, is the urgent need for a robust, ethically-grounded, and pedagogically sound framework that can guide educators and student designers in leveraging GenAI's potential responsibly and critically within the field of cultural product design. The core of this problem extends beyond mere technical proficiency with GenAI tools; it encompasses deep pedagogical and ethical considerations regarding how to cultivate designers who can critically and responsibly co-create with AI in culturally sensitive contexts.

The transformative potential of GenAI is undeniable, yet its application necessitates careful attention to authenticity, representation, and ethical implications, including the risks of cultural appropriation and the perpetuation of biases embedded in AI training data. There exists an inherent tension between the drive for AI-generated novelty and efficiency and the imperative to preserve cultural integrity and avoid the dilution or misrepresentation of cultural meanings (Tiribelli et al., 2024). If not integrated with critical awareness, GenAI can foster superficial engagement with cultural materials, leading to "shallow learning" and outputs that lack genuine cultural resonance or respect (Fu et al., 2025).

Furthermore, while GenAI's capacity to simplify complex research and analysis tasks suggests a potential "democratization" of cultural product design by lowering entry barriers, this increased accessibility presents both significant opportunities and considerable risks. Without robust educational frameworks that instill a deep sense of cultural respect, critical thinking, and ethical responsibility alongside AI proficiency, the ease of access could inadvertently lead to a proliferation of superficial or misrepresentative cultural products. This creates a specific educational problem: how to manage increased accessibility while simultaneously maintaining, or even enhancing, the quality, authenticity, and ethical integrity of cultural product design. Educators are currently grappling with the challenge of adapting to the sudden emergence of GenAI, highlighting a significant gap in established pedagogical strategies (Sandhaus et al., 2025). This paper directly addresses this gap by proposing a comprehensive, stage-by-stage framework designed to navigate these complexities, fostering an educational environment where innovation and cultural sensitivity can coexist and mutually reinforce one another.

LITERATURE REVIEW

This section reviews existing literature pertinent to the integration of Generative AI into cultural product design education. It examines the evolution of cultural product design frameworks, the role and impact of GenAI in creative industries.

Evolution of Cultural products design framework

This review summarizes the evolution of the cultural product design framework, beginning with the foundational work of Lin (2007) and tracing its subsequent refinements by scholars such as Chi-Hsien Hsu et al. (2011), Ya-Juan Gao et al. (2018), and Ying Yu (2024).

Figure 1. shows the framework created by Lin is combining cultural levels, layers and design features. The cultural product design model comprises three main phases: the conceptual model, the research method, and the design process. The conceptual model emphasizes the extraction of cultural features from cultural objects and their subsequent incorporation into a design model. The design model is created through three steps outlined in the research method phase: identification (extracting cultural features from the original cultural object), translation (converting these features into design information and elements), and finally, implementation (designing the cultural product) (Lin, 2007).

Figure 1. Cultural products design model (Lin, 2007)

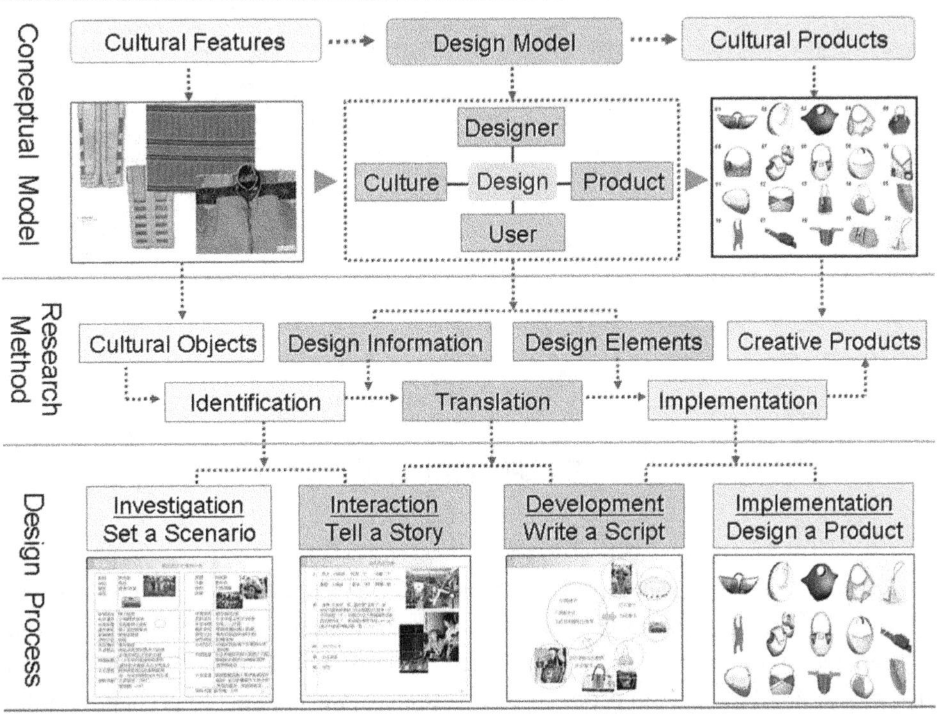

The framework has subsequently been embraced and refined by a multitude of scholars in the cultural product field. These academics have applied the framework to various contexts, enhancing its applicability and relevance through their contributions and insights. This ongoing process of application and improvement has not only validated the framework's utility but also enriched its theoretical and practical dimensions, ensuring its continued evolution in step with the ever-changing cultural product studies.

Chi-Hsien Hsu et al. have advanced the framework as shown in Figure 2. initially proposed by Lin by incorporating a multifaceted approach that integrates consumer attitudes, cultural levels, cultural attributes, the process of transformation, product semantics, and design features. The modification and extension aim to provide a more comprehensive and nuanced understanding of the cultural product design process, ensuring that it is well-aligned with consumer expectations and cultural significance (Hsu et al., 2011) .

Figure 2. Cultural products design model by(Hsu et al., 2011)

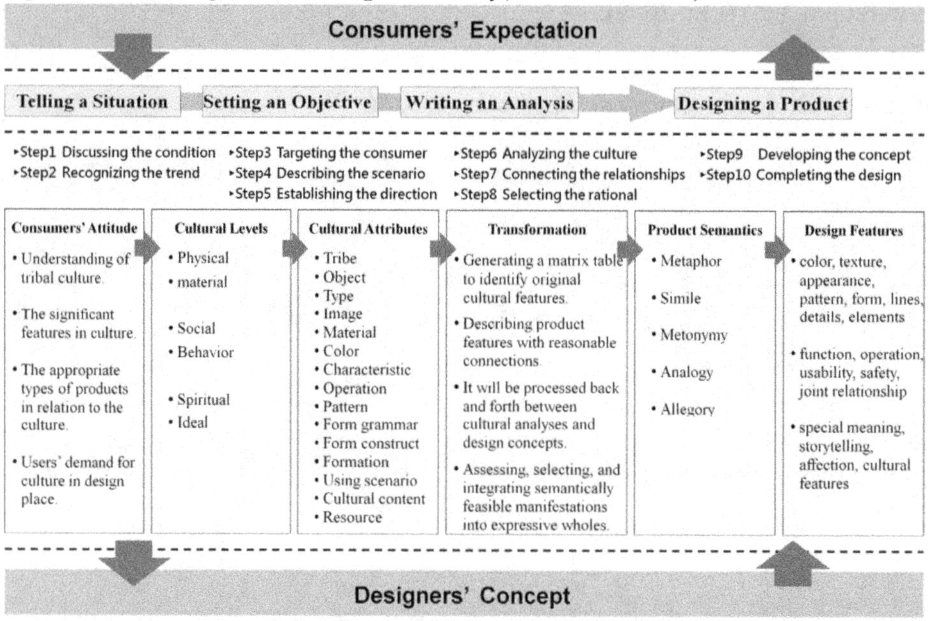

Ya-Juan Gao et al. enriched the framework showed in Figure 3. with an integration of three levels of cultural aspects and design features, offering a more detail perspective on the interrelationship between culture and design. Their adaptation also streamlined the design process, presenting a more succinct approach than the one offered by Chi-Hsien Hsu. However, this revised framework did not fully address the critical role of consumers' attitudes, which is central to the co-design. The oversight is a commonality with Lin's original framework indicating a shared gap where the emphasis on the consumers' attitudes. This highlights an area for further research and development, where the integration of consumer attitudes could lead to a more holistic framework suitable for co-design.

Figure 3. Cultural products design model by(Gao et al., 2018)

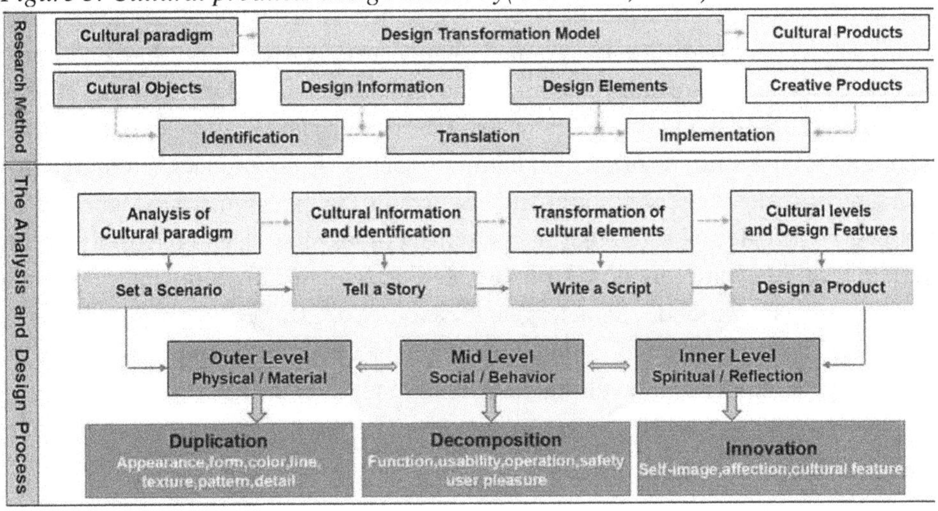

Ying Yu restructured the cultural product design process . and the structural relationship of design feature elements based on the work of previous scholars. The framework showed in Figure 4 adopts a categorization of cultural conceptual factors into three primary levels from previous literature and simplifies the cultural and creative product design process into four main stages: Research and Analysis, Design Analysis, Design Expression, and Design Evaluation (Yu, 2024).

Figure 4. Tourism cultural and creative product design process

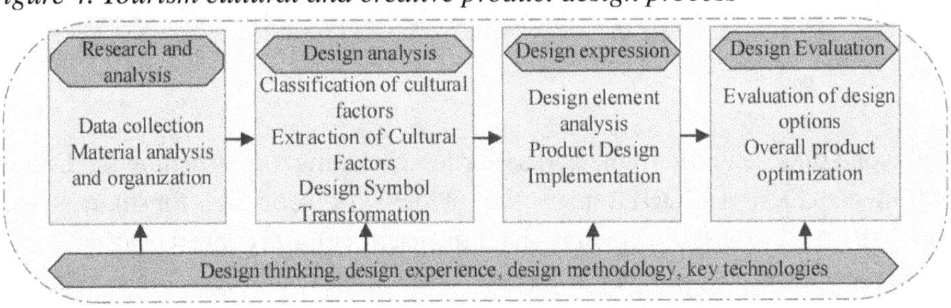

Meanwhile, the cultural level and cultural space were categorized using the three-level classification method proposed by previous scholars. This method establishes corresponding relationships between cultural product attributes and the characteristic elements of cultural and creative product design showed in Figure 5 The three levels of the cultural level are: materialistic, ritual practices, and intangible spirit, corresponding to the external, middle, and internal cultural spaces, respectively. The cultural product attributes are relatively diverse across these levels. At the external level, they correspond to color, texture, shape, surface decoration, line detailing, and component composition. The middle level includes functionality, ease of use, safety, structure, and bonding relationships. The internal level corresponds to special meaning, storytelling, emotion, and cultural identity of the product. Similarly, the characteristic elements of cultural and creative product design are categorized as follows: at the external level, they are patterns, colors, shapes, and materials; at the middle level, they are function, structure, and craftsmanship; at the internal level, they are scenario, mood, characters, and canon (Yu, 2024). This well-structured three-level classification will be integrated into the upcoming framework for incorporating generative AI into cultural and creative product design education.

Figure 5. Structural relationship diagram of design feature elements

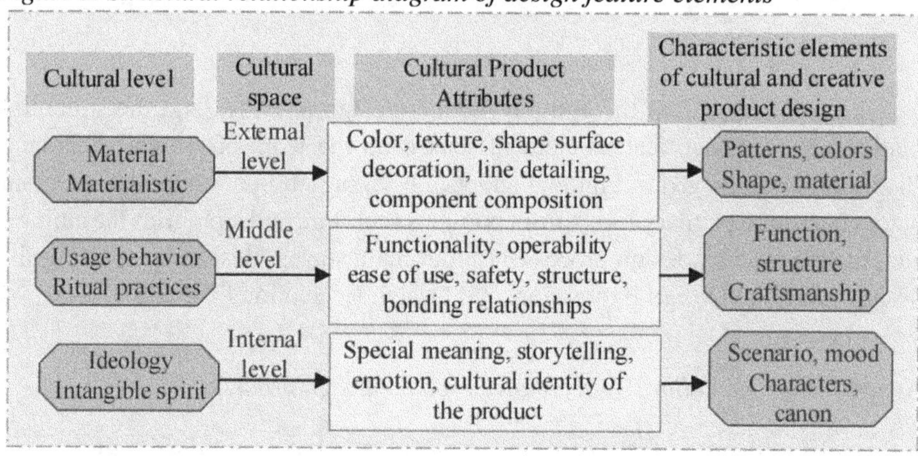

Beyond these specific frameworks, Further enriching this structure, the Culturally Oriented Design (COD) framework provides systematic tools for students. Key among these is its biaxial map for researching users' cultural context. This map uses two axes—material to behavioral aspects (horizontal) and observable to symbolic aspects (vertical)—to create four quadrants for investigation: Material-Observable (e.g., product attributes, manufacturing), Behavioral-Observable (e.g., human-product interactions, social interaction), Behavioral-Symbolic (e.g., consumption symbolism, identity establishment), and Material-Symbolic (e.g., product semantics, branding). The COD framework also introduces the "cultural situated difference" as a methodological tool to direct research inquiry within these quadrants and synthesize insights, facilitating the translation of cultural values into product forms (Dhadphale, 2024). The integration of such methodologies provides a more rigorous foundation for the initial "Research and Analysis" and subsequent "Design Analysis" stages, ensuring students delve deeper than surface-level cultural exploration and systematically translate their findings.

This approach advocates for the conscious and systematic infusion of cultural elements into products, moving beyond superficial applications to a deeper transformation of cultural values into tangible product forms (Moalosi et al., 2010). The authenticity derived from local cultural heritage is considered a key driver for novel design outcomes, particularly in a globalized world where unique cultural identities offer a counterpoint to mass-produced uniformity. A persistent challenge, highlighted by the omission in some earlier frameworks, is the full integration of new technologies like AI into the design process.

Generative AI in Creative Industries and Design Education

GenAI has rapidly emerged as a transformative technological force, demonstrating remarkable capabilities in creating novel content across a spectrum of modalities, including text, images, audio, video, and even computer code. The recent advancements in GenAI, particularly with the advent of large-scale foundation models, signify a paradigm shift, enabling the generation of outputs that can exhibit human-like creativity and adaptability (He et al., 2025). The pervasive influence of GenAI is beginning to reshape numerous sectors, prompting both excitement about new possibilities and critical examination of its broader implications.

The creative industries, a vital economic and cultural sector, are fundamentally rooted in human ingenuity, individual creativity, skills, talents, and the generation and exploitation of intellectual property. The advent of GenAI has initiated a significant transformation across creative industries and, consequently, in design education. Its capabilities are reshaping how creative content is conceptualized, produced, and experienced.

Design education is the structured process of cultivating the knowledge, skills, and ways of thinking essential for design practice. Foundational concepts within design education are multifaceted. The physical environment itself is recognized as influencing learning and fostering creativity, particularly in design studio settings (Tiwari, 2023). Historically, design education and practice were often dominated by short-term business objectives. However, there is a growing recognition of the need for new approaches that enable design to contribute more effectively to social, cultural, environmental, political, and economic well-being (Frascara et al., 2023).

The evolving focus within design education on robust "methods," "systems thinking," "ethics," and, more recently, "AI literacy" is a direct and necessary response to the increasing complexity and profound societal impact of emerging technologies like Generative AI (Frascara et al., 2023). Design schools are actively grappling with adapting their curricula to incorporate these new technologies effectively. This adaptation signifies a move beyond purely aesthetic or technical skill development.

GenAI is increasingly recognized as a revolutionary force in creative sectors, offering tools that can generate novel text, images, audio, and 3D models from data patterns. This technology enhances efficiency by automating repetitive tasks and significantly speeds up design iterations, particularly in ideation and prototyping phases (Caires et al., 2024; Sandhaus et al., 2024). For instance, GenAI can rapidly produce a multitude of design concepts and visual variations, allowing designers to explore a broader solution space in a shorter timeframe. This shifts the designer's role from primary generator to that of a curator, critical evaluator, and refiner of AI-generated outputs.

In product design, GenAI acts as a "creative assistant" or "enabler," augmenting human creativity rather than replacing it. It can assist in brainstorming, developing prototypes, and optimizing designs for material efficiency and performance (Hong et al., 2023). Furthermore, GenAI facilitates personalization at scale, allowing for the creation of customized products tailored to individual user preferences based on data analysis (Channi et al., 2025). In educational settings, these affordances translate into opportunities for enhanced student creativity, faster progression through design cycles, and more sophisticated prototyping capabilities, even for novice designers.

The emergence of GenAI has left many educational institutions reacting without established frameworks, revealing a significant gap between the capabilities of new technologies and the established pedagogical strategies designed to prepare students for professional practice. Addressing this gap requires a fundamental rethinking of design curricula, moving beyond the simple integration of new software to the cultivation of new core competencies and a critical, reflective mindset. Next, drawing from previous research, this study integrates GenAI into the cultural and creative product design process to adapt product design education for the AI era. The identified gap in existing cultural product design frameworks—namely, their limited accommodation of emergent AI technologies and the pedagogical challenges this poses —necessitates a focused inquiry.

METHODOLOGY

The development of the revised framework for using GenAI in cultural product design presented in this paper employed a conceptual framework development methodology, which involved literature synthesis and iterative refinement. This approach was chosen for its suitability in addressing emerging areas where established, empirically validated models are often scarce, and where the integration of diverse theoretical perspectives and practical insights from rapidly evolving fields is necessary.

This methodological approach is constructivist in nature, as it seeks not merely to describe existing phenomena but to build a new conceptual tool—the framework itself—by synthesizing and structuring knowledge in a novel way to address a defined problem. It implicitly employs a gap-filling strategy: by analyzing existing cultural design paradigms alongside GenAI's capabilities and challenges, the method identifies shortcomings in current educational approaches for the AI era. The framework then proposes specific GenAI integrations and human designer roles at each stage to bridge these identified gaps. This method ensures a balance between theoretical grounding, derived from extensive literature, and practical applicability.

Research Questions

Arising from the identified problem statement and the gaps highlighted in the literature review, this paper and the proposed framework aim to address the following research questions:

RQ1: How can a structured pedagogical framework effectively guide student designers in integrating Generative AI across the distinct stages of the cultural product design process while upholding principles of cultural authenticity and ethical responsibility?

RQ2: What specific roles can GenAI play at each stage of the cultural product design process to augment student capabilities, and what are the corresponding human designer responsibilities needed to ensure critical oversight and culturally sensitive outcomes?

RQ3: What foundational principles and strategic imperatives are essential for the successful and responsible integration of GenAI into cultural product design education?

These questions collectively steer the inquiry towards developing actionable guidance for educators and students.

Purpose and Scope of the Revised Framework

The primary objective of this report is to present a revised and comprehensive framework for cultural product design that strategically and thoughtfully integrates GenAI across its distinct stages. This framework builds upon an initial conceptual structure, enriching it with insights drawn from contemporary research in cultural design methodologies, artificial intelligence applications in creative fields, and best practices for human-AI collaboration.

This framework is intended to serve as a robust model for both educational settings, guiding students through a structured yet innovative design journey, and for practical application by designers seeking to leverage GenAI in their cultural product development endeavors. It aims to provide clarity on how human creativity and AI capabilities can synergize to produce culturally meaningful and innovative products.

A REVISED FRAMEWORK OF USING GENAI IN CULTURAL PRODUCT DESIGN

The proposed framework revises and expands upon a foundational structure for cultural product design by systematically embedding Generative AI (GenAI) throughout its lifecycle. This framework retains a well-established four-stage design process and elaborates on five key components for each stage: the core Process, associated Student Activities, specific GenAI Integration points, the defined GenAI Role, and the expected Output. The central aim is to provide a clear, actionable model that leverages GenAI's capabilities while upholding the principles of cultural integrity and human-centered design.

Foundational Principles of the Framework

Before detailing the stages, it is crucial to establish the guiding principles that underpin this GenAI-augmented framework. The guiding principles are Iterative and Reflective Process, Human-Centric AI-Assisted and Culturally Grounded.

Iterative and Reflective Process: While the stages are presented in a linear sequence for clarity, the actual design journey is often non-linear and iterative (Lai et al., 2023). Feedback from later stages frequently informs and refines earlier decisions, creating a cyclical process of development and improvement. Reflection is encouraged at each step, particularly concerning cultural interpretations and the impact of AI-generated content.

Human-Centric AI-Assisted: GenAI is positioned as a powerful assistant, a co-creator, and a catalyst for innovation. However, the framework unequivocally emphasizes the indispensable role of the human designer. Critical thinking, deep cultural understanding, nuanced interpretation, ethical judgment, and ultimate decision-making authority remain firmly with the human practitioner (Lai et al., 2023; Weisz et al., 2024). AI augments human capabilities; it does not supplant them.

Culturally Grounded: The foremost objective of any cultural product design endeavor is the meaningful, respectful, and authentic translation of cultural features into a new form. Technology, including GenAI, is a means to this end, not an end in itself. The design process must remain deeply rooted in the source culture, ensuring that its values, narratives, and aesthetics are thoughtfully conveyed (Spennemann, 2024).

The Cultural Product Design Process: A Four-Stage Journey Augmented by GenAI

The Figure 6 provides a comprehensive overview of the framework, outlining the key elements for each of the four stages: Research and analysis, Design analysis, Design expression and Design Evaluation. This holistic view serves as a roadmap before delving into the specific details of each stage. The four stages in the design process are typically linear and sequential. However, if unresolved issues are identified at a particular stage, it is possible to return to previous steps for reiteration based on the specific circumstances. This is especially true in the third and fourth stages, where repeated modifications and iterations are often necessary to achieve the optimal cultural product outcome.

Figure 6. Integrating Generative AI in Cultural Product Design Framwork

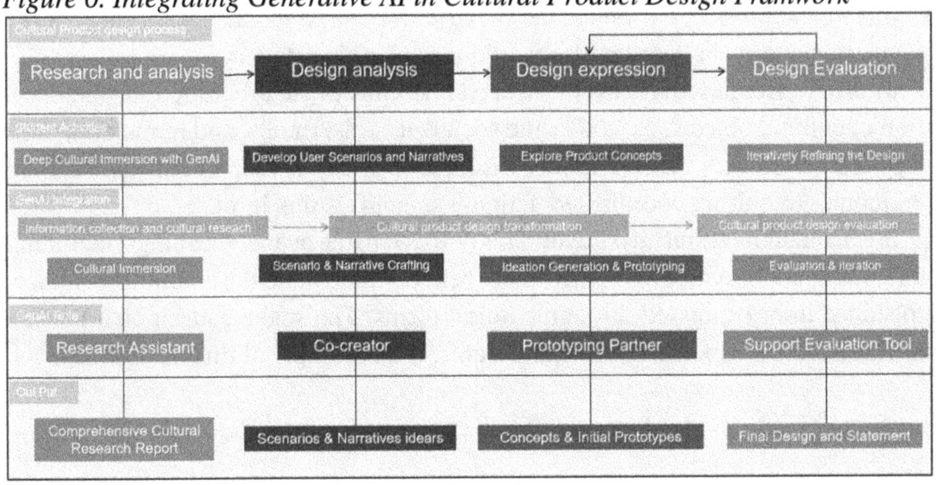

Stage 1: Research and Analysis

The foundational stage of the design process aims to achieve a comprehensive and nuanced understanding of the chosen culture. This involves identifying salient cultural features, artifacts, and practices, and analyzing their multi-layered meanings to inform subsequent design decisions.

i. Student Activities: Deep Cultural Immersion with GenAI

Students begin by defining the specific cultural scope of their project and formulating clear research questions to guide their inquiry. A critical activity is conducting in-depth cultural research. This involves engaging with a diverse array of sources, including academic literature, ethnographic studies, museum archives, and, where possible, direct fieldwork, interviews with cultural experts, or community consultations. The aim is to gather rich, contextualized information. The collection and systematic organization of cultural data—which may include texts, historical documents, images of artifacts, recordings of oral histories, and observations of cultural practices—is essential.

A core analytical task is the examination of cultural objects and practices through established theoretical lenses. A particularly useful approach, highlighted in multiple sources, is the analysis based on three cultural levels or layers:

Outer/Tangible/Physical Level: This encompasses the most directly observable aspects, such as appearance, form, color, texture, materials used in artifacts, and decorative patterns. For instance, the specific wood used in Paiwan carvings or the geometric patterns in their textiles would fall into this category.

Mid/Behavioral/Social Level: This level pertains to the use, function, and operation of cultural objects, as well as the social customs, rituals, and human relationships associated with them. The way a Linnak twin-cup is used in Paiwan wedding ceremonies, requiring coordinated action, exemplifies this level.

Inner/Intangible/Spiritual Level: This delves into the deeper meanings, including stories, emotions, symbolic significance, beliefs, values, and the cultural worldview embedded in or expressed through cultural forms. The snake pattern on a Paiwan chief's Linnak, symbolizing glory and status, is an example of this intangible level.

ii. GenAI Integration:Information Collection and Cultural Research

There are four factors of information collection and cultural research with GenAI integration.

Cultural Information Retrieval & Summarization: GenAI tools, particularly Large Language Models (LLMs) like GPT-3.5, can be employed for rapid literature reviews, extracting pertinent information from extensive textual and multimodal datasets (e.g., digitized archives). They can also summarize research findings, providing students with initial overviews of complex topics.

Initial Material Analysis & Organization: GenAI can assist in the preliminary organization of collected data. This might involve automated tagging of materials, identifying initial patterns in cultural symbols or narratives, or categorizing diverse information based on predefined criteria.

Semantic Information Extraction: GenAI can aid in the initial decoding of symbolic semantic information associated with cultural elements. While deep, implicit meanings require human interpretation, AI can help identify and collate explicit semantic data.

Visual Data Analysis (Emerging): As AI capabilities in image analysis advance, tools can be utilized for tasks such as identifying recurring patterns, dominant color palettes, or common forms within a collection of cultural artifacts, referring to "image extraction classification."

iii. GenAI Role:Research Assistant

GenAI as a research assistant for cultural information collection and summarizes material analysis and organization. GenAI serves to automate and accelerate aspects of information gathering and initial processing, freeing up students to focus on deeper analysis and synthesis. And in a supportive capacity, GenAI can assist in the initial structuring of cultural data and the identification of explicit semantic information, acting as a first pass in the analytical process.

iv. Output:Comprehensive Cultural Research Report

A detailed document that synthesizes the findings on the chosen culture. This report should cover its history, core values, key artifacts, significant practices, and an analysis of its features across the tangible, behavioral, and intangible levels. An organized repository of relevant cultural data collected during the research phase. This may include texts, images, links to digital archives, interview transcripts, and other pertinent materials, structured for easy access and reference. A preliminary list and descriptive analysis of the key tangible, behavioral, and intangible cultural features that have been identified as holding strong potential for further design exploration.

For students embarking on the study of an unfamiliar culture, the initial phase of deep research can be daunting due to the sheer volume and complexity of information. GenAI can function as a "cultural lens sharpener," rapidly processing and structuring this information. For example, by summarizing texts or identifying key themes aligned with the three cultural levels (tangible, behavioral, intangible), GenAI can provide an accessible, organized overview. This accelerates the initial learning curve, allowing students to more quickly grasp the foundational elements of the culture. However, this accelerated access must be accompanied by rigorous critical evaluation. Students must be trained to cross-reference AI-generated summaries with primary sources and expert interpretations to avoid superficial understanding or the uncritical acceptance of potential biases in the AI's output. The goal is to use AI to navigate the breadth of information more efficiently, thereby allowing more time for depth in human-led analysis.

The efficacy of GenAI in facilitating this "Cultural Immersion" is not solely dependent on the sophistication of the AI model itself, but critically hinges on the quality, breadth, depth, and accessibility of the cultural data it is fed. The recommendation to create a "multimodal museum database" highlights a crucial prerequisite for successful GenAI integration. Such a database would ideally contain rich, well-curated, and multimodally represented cultural information (texts, high-resolution images, 3D scans of artifacts, audio-visual recordings of practices, etc.). Without access to such comprehensive and nuanced datasets, GenAI's capacity as a research assistant will be severely constrained, its outputs potentially shallow, biased, or unrepresentative of the culture's complexity. If such databases are not readily available, a vital preliminary activity for institutions or even student projects might involve contributing to the creation or curation of these essential data resources, thereby building the foundation for more meaningful AI-assisted cultural exploration.

Stage 2: Design Analysis

This stage focuses on bridging the gap between abstract cultural understanding (developed in Stage 1) and concrete design opportunities. The aim is to translate deep cultural insights into actionable starting points for design by developing user scenarios, defining meaningful connections between cultural elements and modern contexts, and beginning the transformation of cultural factors into designable elements.

i. Student Activities: develop user scenarios and narratives

Students develop detailed user personas, representing the target audience for the potential cultural product. This involves understanding their needs, values, lifestyles, and how they might interact with or perceive cultural products.

A key activity is crafting user scenarios and narratives. These stories illustrate how identified cultural elements can be meaningfully integrated into contemporary life, addressing modern user needs or aspirations. This involves "setting a scenario" and "telling a story" as part of the cultural product design process.

Students systematically classify and extract the most salient cultural factors (symbols, patterns, stories, rituals, values) identified during the research phase, prioritizing those with strong narrative potential or symbolic resonance. Exploration begins on how these extracted cultural factors can be transformed into potential design symbols, forms, interactive elements, or experiential qualities. This aligns with the "translation stage" of Lin's cultural product design model, where cultural features are transformed into design information and elements. Consideration is given to how the different cultural levels—tangible (e.g., a traditional pattern), behavioral (e.g., a ritualistic gesture), and intangible (e.g., a core cultural value)—can be expressed or embodied in product attributes and user interactions.

ii. GenAI Integration:Scenario & Narrative Crafting

LLMs can serve as powerful aids in generating diverse user scenarios, storylines, and narrative structures. By providing prompts that combine cultural themes with modern contexts or user needs, GenAI can help students explore a wide range of potential connections and narrative frameworks. GenAI tools can assist in categorizing and tagging complex sets of cultural elements. They might help identify relationships between different factors or extract core symbolic meanings from textual descriptions of cultural practices or artifacts.

GenAI can be prompted to propose initial, conceptual idears for how abstract cultural concepts or traditional symbols might be visually, functionally, or experientially transformed into modern design elements. This is less about generating final designs and more about facilitating conceptual bridging and brainstorming, aligning with "Design Symbol Transformation".

iii. GenAI Role:Co-creator

GenAI acts as a co-creator, aiding in the classification and extraction of cultural factors and in design symbol transformation. GenAI collaborates with students in the development of rich scenarios and compelling narratives, offering variations and expanding creative possibilities. GenAI assists in the interpretation and classification of cultural factors, helping to organize and make sense of complex cultural data. GenAI offers a diverse range of initial idears for the transformation of cultural symbols, acting as a catalyst for creative thinking.

iv. Output:Scenarios and Narratives Idears

Detailed descriptions of target users and the specific contexts in which they might use or experience the cultural product. These scenarios and narratives should be richly infused with cultural relevance and demonstrate clear connections to modern lifestyles. A refined and prioritized list of specific cultural elements chosen for design development, accompanied by initial concepts for their translation into design symbols, motifs, or interactive features. A visual or textual representation that clearly articulates how the selected cultural aspects connect to contemporary user needs, values, and social contexts, justifying their relevance for a modern product.

The task of developing user scenarios and narratives that effectively connect a specific culture to modern contexts can be a significant creative hurdle. GenAI can act as a "cultural bridge-builder" in this stage. By inputting prompts that juxtapose traditional cultural elements with contemporary user needs or situations, GenAI can generate a multitude of "what if" scenarios or narrative fragments. This rapid generation of diverse possibilities helps students overcome creative blocks and explore a wider range of potential connections, facilitating the conceptual leap from abstract cultural understanding to tangible design relevance. The scenario and storytelling approach is fundamental to cultural product design, and AI can significantly augment this process.

However, when GenAI is assigned roles such as "Classification of cultural factors, Extraction of Cultural Factors and Design Symbol Transformation", a critical consideration arises: the risk of algorithmic bias. AI models are trained on vast datasets, and these datasets may inadvertently contain historical biases, stereotypes, or incomplete representations of cultures. If the AI's training data reflects such biases, its outputs in classifying cultural factors, extracting their meanings, or suggesting transformations for design symbols may perpetuate these inaccuracies or overlook crucial nuances. This implies that while GenAI can be a useful assistant in identifying and categorizing cultural elements, students must engage in a rigorous process of critical evaluation. They need to compare AI-generated interpretations against the deep cultural understanding gained in Stage 1, actively questioning and potentially correcting the AI's outputs to ensure that the extracted factors and proposed transformations are authentic, respectful, and avoid harmful stereotypes. This reinforces the necessity of a strong foundation in cultural research before leveraging AI for analytical tasks.

Stage 3: Design Expression

This stage is dedicated to the active generation of a wide spectrum of product concepts and the exploration of diverse design expressions. It involves translating the analyzed cultural factors and narrative idears into tangible design solutions and developing initial prototypes that embody these translated features.

i. Student Activities:explore product concepts

Students should critically evaluate AI outputs, select, refine, and begin prototyping to explore a wide range of product concepts in this stage. Engaging in intensive brainstorming sessions to generate a multitude of design idears, drawing inspiration from the cultural research and design analysis phases. Critically evaluating AI-generated outputs, such as visual concepts or textual descriptions, assessing them for cultural appropriateness, originality, feasibility, and alignment with user needs. Selecting the most promising concepts from both human and AI-generated idears and refining them. This refinement process involves iterative adjustments based on critical feedback and further creative exploration.

Developing initial prototypes, these can range from sketches and 2D digital mockups to basic 3D models (physical or virtual), serving as tangible representations of the design concepts. Exploring conceptual blending which involves creatively combining distinct cultural elements with modern product typologies, functions, or aesthetic styles in innovative and meaningful ways.

ii. GenAI Integration:Ideation Generation & Prototyping

GenAI tools, such as text-to-image models (e.g., Stable Diffusion, Midjourney) and advanced concept generators, can be employed to produce a wide array of visual and textual design concepts. These tools can explore diverse aesthetic styles, functional interpretations, and novel combinations of cultural motifs with product forms, directly supporting product design exploration and conceptual blending for diverse idears. GenAI can be utilized for creating initial visual assets, including patterns, textures, illustrations, or even basic 3D forms. Some AI models are capable of generating reproducible object surface models from various inputs, which can serve as starting points for more detailed 3D modeling. GenAI can facilitate the rapid visualization of multiple variations of a single design concept or generate specific elements (e.g., a decorative pattern, an icon) that can be quickly incorporated into low-fidelity prototypes, thereby accelerating the iterative design cycle. AI tools can analyze cultural artifacts or user-defined aesthetic preferences to suggest relevant color palettes. For instance, K-means clustering can be used to extract dominant colors from images of traditional textiles or artworks. AI might also suggest material qualities based on desired tactile experiences or symbolic associations.

iii. GenAI Role:Prototyping Partner

GenAI as a Prototyping Partner to explore product design and conceptual blending for diverse idears. GenAI can generate a large volume and variety of idears to spark human creativity and break through conventional thinking patterns. GenAI assists in the swift creation of visual or digital mockups, enabling designers to quickly iterate and communicate their idears. GenAI can combine disparate inputs—such as a specific cultural style, a product category, and functional requirements—to create novel visual expressions and conceptual blends.

iv. Output: Concepts & Initial Prototypes

A rich portfolio of varied design idears, documented through sketches, digital renderings, storyboards, and basic physical or virtual models. This showcases the breadth of exploration. A narrowed-down set of the most promising and culturally resonant concepts that have been selected for further development and evaluation. Notes, reflections, and records detailing how AI-generated outputs were utilized, the criteria used for their evaluation, and the process of their refinement and integration into the design.

GenAI's capacity for "Ideation Generation & Prototyping" allows for the exploration of a significantly "wide range of product concepts", acting as a powerful accelerator of divergent thinking. It can produce a volume and variety of initial idears far exceeding what is typically achievable through manual methods in a similar timeframe. However, this explosion of possibilities necessitates an equally, if not more, robust human capacity for convergent thinking. Students and designers must "critically evaluate AI outputs, select, refine", navigating this abundance to identify concepts that are not only novel but also culturally meaningful, ethically sound, and practically viable. The framework must therefore emphasize the development of strong evaluation criteria, critical judgment skills, and decision-making heuristics to complement the use of AI ideation tools. Without this, the sheer volume of AI-generated options could become overwhelming or lead to suboptimal choices.

Furthermore, as GenAI tools are employed for "conceptual blending" and the generation of visual or 3D assets, there is a potential for the emergence of "AI-native" design aesthetics. Many GenAI models, trained on vast and diverse datasets, may possess inherent stylistic biases or produce outputs with a recognizable "AI fingerprint." If designers rely too heavily on these tools without sufficient critical intervention and refinement, the resulting products could exhibit a generic quality or feel disconnected from the specific nuances of the source culture, even if they are technically impressive. The process of "design expression" in this context involves not merely using AI to generate forms, but actively guiding, curating, and post-processing AI outputs to ensure that the final design authentically and sensitively expresses the intended cultural meanings. This may involve significant manual refinement, reinterpretation of AI suggestions, or the integration of AI-generated elements into a human-directed design vision.

Stage 4: Design Evaluation

This final stage is dedicated to the critical assessment of the developed concepts and prototypes. The evaluation focuses on cultural appropriateness, functionality, user experience, and overall design quality, leading to iterative refinements and the formulation of a final design solution that is both innovative and culturally sensitive.

i. Student Activities:Iteratively refining the design

Developing clear and comprehensive evaluation criteria. These criteria should be informed by the project's objectives and can draw from established frameworks, such as the factors influencing consumer satisfaction with AI-generated museum cultural and creative products (MCCPs) identified by Li et al. (2024): product functionality, creative attraction, cultural expression, and user experience. Conducting user testing with target audience representatives, gathering qualitative and quantitative feedback on the prototypes regarding their usability, appeal, and perceived cultural meaning. Critically assessing the cultural appropriateness of the design. This involves reflecting on whether the design respectfully and accurately conveys the intended cultural features and meanings, avoiding misrepresentation or trivialization. Engaging in thorough ethical reflection concerning the use of cultural elements (e.g., sacred symbols, traditional knowledge) and the role of AI in the design process (e.g., data privacy, algorithmic bias, intellectual property).

Iteratively refining the design based on the feedback from user testing, cultural assessment, and ethical reflections. This is a cyclical process of modification and re-evaluation. Optimizing the overall product for aspects such as manufacturability, sustainability, and cost-effectiveness, as appropriate to the project's scope.

ii. GenAI Integration:Evaluation & iteration

While human judgment remains paramount, GenAI could offer limited support in analyzing user feedback. For instance, LLMs might perform sentiment analysis on textual feedback from user testing or help categorize qualitative comments. AI could also assist in comparing design iterations against predefined quantitative criteria, though this application is still emerging. GenAI can be used to generate structured prompts or checklists that guide students through critical ethical reflections. These prompts could cover topics such as cultural intellectual property, respectful representation, potential for algorithmic bias in AI tools used, and the impact of the design on the source community, inspired by the need to improve cultural expression and address ethical concerns. Based on specific human-directed feedback, GenAI tools could help generate design variations for refinement, speeding up the exploration of solutions to identified issues. GenAI can assist in drafting design statements, product descriptions, or creating visual aids (e.g., renderings of the final design in different contexts) for the presentation of the final design solution.

iii. GenAI Role: Support Evaluation Tool

GenAI can support evaluation and aid iterative refinement. Under human supervision, assisting in the processing of user feedback or checking designs against simple, predefined criteria . Providing structured prompts and scenarios to facilitate deeper ethical consideration regarding cultural and technological aspects. Generating targeted design variations in response to human-directed feedback and evaluation outcomes.

iv. Output:Final Design and Statement

The fully developed, refined, and documented cultural product design. This is accompanied by a comprehensive design statement that explains the underlying concept, its cultural connections, key design choices, the process of iteration, and the specific role GenAI played in its development. A summary of the evaluation methodologies employed (user testing, expert reviews, etc.), the key findings from these evaluations, and a clear account of how feedback was analyzed and incorporated into the design refinements. A document detailing the ethical reflections undertaken throughout the design process. This should address issues of cultural sensitivity, representation, intellectual property, and any ethical considerations related to the use of AI tools. A record optional but recommended tracking the evolution of the design through various iterations, noting the rationale for significant changes and decisions made at each step. This promotes transparency and learning.

The evaluation of cultural products, particularly those augmented by GenAI, must extend beyond purely aesthetic or technical assessments. The user query's emphasis on critically assessing "cultural appropriateness and Overall product optimization" aligns directly with the need to consider consumer perceptions. Research on consumer satisfaction with AI-generated provides a valuable lens, highlighting dimensions such as cultural expression, creative attraction, functionality, and user experience as key evaluation criteria. "Cultural appropriateness," therefore, is not merely an abstract ideal but is tangibly reflected in how consumers perceive the product's "cultural expression." Similarly, "overall product optimization" must encompass functionality and user experience from the end-user's perspective. Integrating these consumer-centric metrics into the evaluation stage ensures that the designs are not only culturally sound and innovative but also resonate with and satisfy the intended audience.

Furthermore, the call for "Ethical Reflection" in the context of GenAI-driven design must encompass more than just the cultural content of the product. It needs to extend to the nature of the AI tools themselves. Issues such as "over-reliance on technology, insufficient controllability, and semantic discrepancies in AI-generated designs" point to the importance of considering algorithmic transparency and data provenance. Ethical reflection should therefore include questions such as: How transparent are the decision-making processes of the AI tools used? What specific datasets were these tools trained on, and do these datasets carry inherent biases or misrepresentations? What are the intellectual property implications of using AI-generated assets derived from potentially copyrighted training data? This adds a critical layer of techno-ethical consideration to the existing cultural-ethical concerns, demanding a more holistic and informed approach to responsible design.

Strategic Imperatives for Effective GenAI Integration in Cultural Product Design

The successful integration of Generative AI into the cultural product design framework hinges on several strategic imperatives. These go beyond the procedural steps outlined previously and address the foundational conditions, collaborative dynamics, and ethical considerations necessary for harnessing GenAI's potential responsibly and effectively. Insights from recent research, particularly concerning the practical application and evaluation of AI in cultural contexts, inform these crucial strategies.

Building Robust Foundations: The Imperative of High-Quality, Multimodal Cultural Databases

The performance and reliability of GenAI systems are fundamentally contingent on the quality, diversity, and representativeness of the data upon which they are trained. This principle is particularly acute in the domain of cultural product design, where nuance, context, and authenticity are paramount. Such a database should ideally integrate a wide array of learning resources, including high-resolution images of artifacts, detailed 3D scans, videos of cultural practices or performances, comprehensive textual information (historical accounts, ethnographic descriptions, symbolic interpretations), and structured metadata that contextualizes each cultural element.

The development and maintenance of these rich databases are essential for several reasons. Firstly, they can significantly improve GenAI's ability to comprehend complex cultural nuances, moving beyond superficial pattern recognition to a more context-aware understanding. Secondly, diverse and well-curated datasets can help mitigate the risk of algorithmic bias, which often arises when training data is skewed or unrepresentative. Thirdly, access to such resources enables GenAI to generate design outputs that are more authentic, contextually relevant, and respectful of the source culture. The implication for institutions and design programs is clear: investing in the creation and curation of high-quality cultural datasets is not merely a technical prerequisite but a foundational step towards ethical and effective GenAI integration. This may involve significant upfront effort, including digitization initiatives, collaborative data-sharing agreements, and the development of appropriate metadata standards. The adage "garbage in, garbage out" is magnified in the context of cultural AI; the sensitivity and specificity of cultural information mean that biased, incomplete, or poorly contextualized data can lead to exponentially more problematic or offensive AI outputs than in less nuanced domains. Thus, the cultural database is not just a technical asset but a vital curatorial and ethical responsibility.

Enhancing Human-AI Collaboration: The Role of Structured Prompt Engineering and Interaction Models

Effective collaboration between human designers and GenAI systems is crucial for achieving desired outcomes, especially when dealing with the subtleties of cultural expression. A significant challenge identified in the use of AI for design is ensuring "controllability" and minimizing "semantic discrepancies" between the designer's intent and the AI's output. Prompt engineering—the art and science of crafting effective instructions for GenAI models—emerges as a key skill for designers. Well-formulated prompts can significantly improve the accuracy, relevance, and creativity of GenAI-generated content.

To enhance this crucial communication channel, the concept of "structured prompt card models" offers a practical approach. These models would involve developing templates or frameworks for prompts, categorized by relevant design parameters such as product type (e.g., figurine, textile, digital interactive), desired style (e.g., traditional, contemporary fusion, minimalist), functional requirements, Color-Material-Finish (CMF) specifications, and even specific AI model parameters or rendering effects. Such structured prompts can provide clarity and consistency in instructing the AI, reducing ambiguity and improving the predictability of outputs. This approach transforms prompt engineering from an intuitive, trial-and-error process into a more systematic and refined form of design articulation—a new type of "design craftsmanship." It requires not only technical understanding of how the AI interprets language but also a deep comprehension of the culture being expressed and the desired aesthetic and semantic impact. Beyond initial prompting, the human-AI interaction should be envisioned as an iterative dialogue, involving cycles of prompting, AI generation, human evaluation, and refined prompting to progressively guide the AI towards the desired design solution.

Ensuring Cultural Sensitivity and Authenticity: The Primacy of Critical Human Oversight and Ethical Frameworks

While GenAI offers powerful capabilities, it remains a tool. The ultimate responsibility for the cultural sensitivity, authenticity, and ethical implications of any cultural product rests squarely with the human designers and the institutions they represent. This principle necessitates that students and designers cultivate strong critical thinking skills. They must be equipped to rigorously evaluate AI-generated outputs not just for aesthetic appeal or technical proficiency, but more importantly, against their deep cultural understanding developed through thorough research and analysis .

The use of GenAI in cultural contexts brings several potential ethical pitfalls into sharp focus. These include the risk of misrepresenting cultural narratives or symbols, the appropriation of sacred or restricted cultural elements, the trivialization of profound meanings, the perpetuation of historical stereotypes that may be embedded in training data, and complex intellectual property issues concerning both the original cultural heritage and the AI-generated content. To navigate these challenges, the development and adoption of specific ethical guidelines or reflexive checklists for using GenAI in cultural product design are strongly recommended. These frameworks should prompt designers to consider the source of cultural information, the rights of culture bearers, the potential impact of the design on the source community, and the transparency of AI's role in the creative process.

Towards a Holistic Approach: Envisioning AI Participation Across the Full Design Lifecycle

To maximize the benefits of GenAI and address its challenges comprehensively, a shift towards a more holistic integration of AI across the entire design lifecycle is advocated. With full-process AI participation envisions AI not as a series of discrete tools for specific tasks, but as an integrated environment that supports the design journey from initial market analysis and cultural research through to concept generation, prototyping, manufacturing considerations, and even post-launch evaluation feedback. Such a platform could unify the efforts of designers, cultural experts, engineers, manufacturers, and consumers, fostering a dynamic, data-driven innovation model.

This holistic approach promises to enhance design efficiency, enable greater personalization of cultural products, and facilitate continuous improvement through feedback loops that inform both AI models and human designers. However, realizing this vision of "full lifecycle AI" implies a significant evolution in design education and professional practice. Designers will require new competencies beyond traditional craft and aesthetic skills. These include data literacy (understanding how to interpret and utilize data from various sources), AI systems thinking (comprehending how different AI modules interact within a larger workflow), and collaborative AI workflow management. Design curricula and professional development programs will need to adapt to cultivate these future-ready skills, preparing designers to navigate and orchestrate increasingly complex, AI-suffused creative ecosystems.

CONCLUSION

The revised framework presented in this report offers a structured yet adaptable methodology for integrating Generative AI into the multifaceted process of cultural product design. By systematically delineating the roles of student activities, GenAI integration points, GenAI's specific functions, and expected outputs across four critical design stages—Research and Analysis, Design Analysis, Design Expression, and Design Evaluation—the framework provides a clear roadmap for both educators and practitioners. Its core contribution lies in its balanced approach: it seeks to leverage the powerful capabilities of GenAI for enhanced research, accelerated ideation, and diverse conceptual exploration, while simultaneously emphasizing the non-negotiable primacy of human critical judgment, deep cultural understanding, and rigorous ethical oversight. The framework underscores that the objective is not to automate creativity but to augment it, fostering a collaborative environment where AI serves as a catalyst for innovation that remains deeply rooted in and respectful of cultural integrity.

The field of Generative AI is characterized by rapid advancements, and its future applications in cultural product design are likely to be even more transformative. We can anticipate improvements in GenAI's semantic understanding, enabling more nuanced interpretations of complex cultural narratives and symbols. Future models may offer enhanced capabilities in handling intangible cultural aspects, such as emotion, ritualistic significance, or spiritual connotations, which are currently challenging to translate into design. Furthermore, human-AI interaction models are expected to become more intuitive and collaborative, allowing for a more seamless partnership in the creative process.

However, alongside these technological advancements, the ongoing need for research into consumer perceptions of AI-generated cultural products, as highlighted by studies such as Li et al. (2024), will remain critical. Understanding how audiences receive, interpret, and value these hybrid creations will be essential for guiding their development and ensuring their market relevance and cultural resonance. The continuous development of best practices, ethical guidelines, and evaluation metrics tailored to this unique intersection of culture, design, and AI will be paramount. One promising avenue for future exploration is the potential for GenAI to contribute to the revitalization of endangered or lesser-known cultures. Many communities possess rich cultural heritages but lack the resources or platforms for broad dissemination or contemporary reinterpretation. If GenAI can effectively assist in the research, analysis, and initial design conceptualization phases, as outlined in the proposed framework, it could become a powerful tool for these communities. Guided by community members and cultural custodians, GenAI could help translate unique traditions into new product forms, thereby aiding in cultural preservation, education, and economic empowerment, provided that principles of ethical data handling, community partnership, and benefit-sharing are central to such initiatives.

The integration of GenAI into cultural product design presents both exciting opportunities and significant responsibilities. There is a clear call to action for designers, educators, cultural institutions, and technology developers to engage with this evolving landscape thoughtfully, critically, and ethically. Fostering responsible and innovative practices requires a multi-pronged approach.

Educators must adapt design curricula to equip students not only with AI literacy and tool proficiency but also with enhanced critical thinking skills, deep cultural sensitivity, and a strong ethical compass. Cultural institutions, as custodians of heritage, have a vital role in guiding the development of AI applications, ensuring respectful representation, and potentially collaborating in the creation of high-quality, ethically sourced cultural databases for AI training. Designers must embrace a role that is part creator, part curator, and part ethical navigator, skillfully guiding AI tools to produce work that is both innovative and culturally authentic.

Ultimately, the most effective and ethical path forward lies in fostering a "human-AI cultural symbiosis." This is not a scenario where AI replaces human creativity or where humans merely use AI as a passive tool. Instead, it envisions a deeper, more dynamic partnership where the computational power, data processing capabilities, and generative speed of AI augment human intuition, cultural understanding, and creative vision. Conversely, human wisdom, ethical insight, and nuanced cultural knowledge must guide and constrain AI's application. The framework proposed herein is a step towards defining and operationalizing such a symbiotic relationship. Through continued interdisciplinary collaboration we can collectively navigate the challenges and harness the immense potential of GenAI to enrich, rather than erode, the diversity, depth, and dynamism of cultural expression in the world of product design.

REFERENCES

Anantrasirichai, N., Zhang, F., & Bull, D. (2025). *Artificial Intelligence in Creative Industries: Advances Prior to 2025* (1 ; arXiv:2501.02725). arXiv. https://doi.org// arXiv.2501.02725DOI: 10.48550

Caires, C. S., Estadieu, G., & Olga Ng Ka Man, S. (2024). Design Thinking Methodology and Text-To-Image Artificial Intelligence: A Case Study in the Context of Furniture Design Education. In Martins, N., Brandão, D., & Fernandes-Marcos, A. (Eds.), *Perspectives on Design and Digital Communication IV* (Vol. 33, pp. 113–134). Springer Nature Switzerland., DOI: 10.1007/978-3-031-41770-2_7

Channi, H. K., Kaur, A., & Kaur, S. (2025). AI-Driven Generative Design Redefines the Engineering Process. In Chelliah, P. R., Dutta, P. K., Kumar, A., Gonzalez, E. D. R. S., Mittal, M., & Gupta, S. (Eds.), *Generative Artificial Intelligence in Finance* (1st ed., pp. 327–359). Wiley., DOI: 10.1002/9781394271078.ch17

Chu, I.-T., & Lin, H.-H. (2024). Transformation of the imagery of Taiwan's unique cultural elements into styling design. *Innovation on Design and Culture*, *3*(1), 13–21. DOI: 10.35745/idc2024v03.01.0002

Dhadphale, T. (2024). A FRAMEWORK FOR CULTURALLY ORIENTED PRODUCT DESIGN. *Proceedings of the International Conference on Engineering and Product Design Education, EPDE 2024*, 681–686. DOI: 10.35199/EPDE.2024.115

Frascara, J., Gardien, P., Noël, G., Rosenberg, D., Stappers, P., & Wilde, D. (2023, November 29). Towards strengthening Methods in Design Education and Practice. *LearnXDesign 2023. LearnXDesign, 2023.* Advance online publication. DOI: 10.21606/drslxd.2024.029

Fu, Y., Shi, K., & Xi, L. (2025). Artificial intelligence and machine learning in the preservation and innovation of intangible cultural heritage: Ethical considerations and design frameworks. *Digital Scholarship in the Humanities*, fqaf034. DOI: 10.1093/llc/fqaf034

Gao, Y., Fang, W., Gao, Y., & Lin, R. (2018). Conceptual Framework and Case Study of China's Womanese scripts Used in Culture Product Design. *Journal of Arts and Humanities*, *7*(3), 57. DOI: 10.18533/journal.v7i3.1363

He, R., Cao, J., & Tan, T. (2025). Generative artificial intelligence: A historical perspective. *National Science Review*, *12*(5), nwaf050. Advance online publication. DOI: 10.1093/nsr/nwaf050 PMID: 40191253

Hong, M. K., Hakimi, S., Chen, Y.-Y., Toyoda, H., Wu, C., & Klenk, M. (2023). *Generative AI for Product Design: Getting the Right Design and the Design Right* (9; arXiv:2306.01217). arXiv. https://doi.org//arXiv.2306.01217DOI: 10.48550

Hsu, C.-H., Lin, C.-L., & Lin, R. (2011). A Study of Framework and Process Development for Cultural Product Design. In Rau, P. L. P. (Ed.), *Internationalization, Design and Global Development* (Vol. 6775, pp. 55–64). Springer Berlin Heidelberg., DOI: 10.1007/978-3-642-21660-2_7

Lai, Y., Chen, H.-J., & Yang, C. (2023). *Exploring the Impact of Generative Artificial Intelligence on the Design Process: Opportunities, Challenges, and Insights* (9). AHFE 2023 Hawaii Edition. DOI: 10.54941/ahfe1004178

Lin, R.-T. (2007). *Transforming Taiwan Aboriginal Cultural Features into Modern Product Design:* Moalosi, R., Popovic, V., & Hickling-Hudson, A. (2010). Culture-orientated product design. *International Journal of Technology and Design Education, 20*(2), 175–190. DOI: 10.1007/s10798-008-9069-1

Sandhaus, H., Gu, Q., Parreira, M. T., & Ju, W. (2025). *Co-Designing with Algorithms: Unpacking the Complex Role of GenAI in Interactive System Design Education.*

Sandhaus, H., Parreira, M. T., & Ju, W. (2024). *Student Reflections on Self-Initiated GenAI Use in HCI Education* (arXiv:2405.01467). arXiv. https://doi.org//arXiv.2405 .01467DOI: 10.48550

Spennemann, D. H. R. (2024). Generative Artificial Intelligence, Human Agency and the Future of Cultural Heritage. *Heritage, 7*(7), 3597–3609. DOI: 10.3390/ heritage7070170

Tiribelli, S., Pansoni, S., Frontoni, E., & Giovanola, B. (2024). Ethics of Artificial Intelligence for Cultural Heritage: Opportunities and Challenges. *IEEE Transactions on Technology and Society, 5*(3), 293–305. DOI: 10.1109/TTS.2024.3432407

Tiwari, S. V. (2023). Review of the Research on Design Education and Practices. In Suman, R. S., Moccia, S., Chinnusamy, K., Singh, B., & Regin, R. (Eds.), (pp. 230–240). Advances in Educational Technologies and Instructional Design. IGI Global., DOI: 10.4018/978-1-6684-6682-7.ch018

Weisz, J. D., He, J., Muller, M., Hoefer, G., Miles, R., & Geyer, W. (2024). Design Principles for Generative AI Applications. *Proceedings of the CHI Conference on Human Factors in Computing Systems*, 1–22. DOI: 10.1145/3613904.3642466

Yu, Y. (2024). Research on Design Concept and Cultural Inheritance System of Tourism Cultural and Creative Products in the Context of Deep Learning. *Applied Mathematics and Nonlinear Sciences, 9*(1), 20231252. DOI: 10.2478/amns.2023.2.01252

Chapter 5
Integration of AI Technology for Chinese Language Teaching:
A Study on Current Status, Challenges, and Future Prospects

Wang Ying
https://orcid.org/0009-0003-0493-9023
Universiti Sains Malaysia, Malaysia

Nurul Maziah Mohd Barkhaya
https://orcid.org/0009-0002-2192-0706
Universiti Sains Malaysia, Malaysia

Mageswaran Sanmugam
https://orcid.org/0000-0003-3313-4462
Universiti Sains Malaysia, Malaysia

ABSTRACT

The application of Artificial Intelligence (AI) technology in Chinese language learning, especially in the fields of language education, cultural communication, and Artificial Intelligence (AI), has become one of the essential learning tools for Chinese language learning, which also helps teachers to provide efficient Chinese language classes. Therefore, this study will explore the impact of artificial intelligence (AI) on Chinese language teaching outcomes in terms of Chinese language teachers' outcomes of using AI in teaching, satisfaction, changes in lesson preparation time, adjustments in teaching strategies, and reliance on the AI teaching. This study employs a quantitative method, which will be used to collect data through questionnaires and

DOI: 10.4018/979-8-3373-3673-2.ch005

through correlation analysis using SPSS to explain the issues raised in this paper. In addition, this paper discusses the current status of the application of technology in Chinese language learning, analyzes the challenges posed by technology, and looks forward to the future development trend.

INTRODUCTION

Artificial Intelligence (AI) is one of the fastest growing and most prominent technologies in the field of educational technology. In recent years, it has gradually emerged in education systems at all levels around the world. As the core driving force for the digital transformation of education, AI is gradually evolving from a traditional technical auxiliary tool to a key element in reshaping the teaching paradigm (UNESCO, 2023). Although AI has been used in education for more than 40 years, its impact on the teaching process and learning outcomes is still controversial, but it is undeniable that its potential is being continuously released (UNESCO, 2023).

Early studies have shown that the introduction of AI can effectively simplify the language teaching process and optimize the learning path (Ali, 2020). In the field of language education, AI has been particularly outstanding in improving the efficiency of second language acquisition, relying on its powerful personalized learning recommendations, real-time feedback, and automated evaluation (Luckin et al., 2022). However, current AI research in the field of language education focuses on phonetic writing systems, such as English. Research on ideographic languages such as Chinese is relatively lagging, especially at the classroom teaching level. This statement is supported by a study, which also highlights that a significant research gap still exists (Sharadgah & Sa'di, 2022).

In response to this research gap, scholars have gradually begun to pay attention to the application prospects of AI in Chinese teaching. Studies have shown that artificial intelligence has significant potential in assisting Chinese learning. Xia et al. (2024) systematically explored the positive role of AI technology in alleviating the language barriers, psychological burdens and educational adaptability challenges faced by non-Chinese learners in the process of learning Chinese/Mandarin. The results of the study confirmed that artificial intelligence platforms such as ChatGPT, Poe, and Brainly have practical results in assisting learners to master Chinese grammatical structures, idiom expressions and cultural contexts. At the same time, Shen (2025) pointed out that AI technology has also shown a significant improvement in teaching efficiency in simplifying teachers' content creation, after-class consolidation, and classroom interaction design.

Despite this, teachers still need to be cautious when using AI for teaching assistance. On the one hand, although the introduction of AI tools can reduce the teaching burden and improve classroom efficiency, it is not a complete substitute for teachers' experience and judgment; on the other hand, teachers' acceptance of AI technology, their ability to use it, and their ability to identify potential biases are directly related to the sustainability and credibility of AI teaching effects.

Therefore, this study will focus on the practical application of AI in Chinese teaching, especially how it affects teachers' teaching efficiency and behavioral changes. Specifically, the study will conduct a systematic discussion on five dimensions: teaching outcomes, teacher satisfaction, changes in preparation time, adjustments to teaching strategies, and the degree of reliance on AI teaching tools, aiming to provide a theoretical basis and practical reference for the effective integration of AI technology in Chinese education. This study adopts a quantitative research method, collects data through questionnaires, and uses SPSS for correlation analysis to explain the questions raised in this article.

Background

Artificial Intelligence (AI), as an important part of emerging educational technology, is reshaping the traditional teaching model. With the continuous advancement of algorithm optimization and natural language processing technology, AI is increasingly used in teaching and has become a key tool to improve classroom efficiency and personalized teaching experience. Studies have shown that AI technology can accurately analyze learners' language behavior and cognitive level, thereby providing customized teaching suggestions and significantly optimizing the language teaching process (Zawacki-Richter et al., 2019). In the field of Chinese teaching, the introduction of AI provides teachers with unprecedented support, especially in the teaching of Chinese as a second language (CSL) and Chinese as a foreign language (TCFL), showing great potential (Oubibi et al., 2022).

In recent years, many empirical studies have confirmed that AI-assisted tools can effectively improve learners' Chinese listening, speaking, reading, and writing abilities. For example, speech recognition systems help learners correct their pronunciation and intonation, intelligent assessment systems provide real-time feedback on writing and grammar problems, and virtual dialogue systems simulate real contexts in dialogue training to improve the fluency and accuracy of language expression (Sun et al., 2021). On this basis, AI can also track learning paths and dynamically adjust teaching difficulty, thereby achieving true “teaching students in accordance with their aptitude”. As a key node in the intelligent transformation of education, teachers' teaching concepts and technical literacy play a decisive role in the effective use of AI tools. Relevant studies have pointed out that AI technology can not only provide teachers with data-based teaching decision support, but also effectively reduce the burden of lesson preparation, optimize classroom structure, and improve teaching efficiency (Li et al., 2024).

In current teaching practice, AI-assisted Chinese teaching has achieved initial results, but there is still a lack of systematic analysis of teachers' experience, feedback, and behavioural changes in actual use. Based on this, this study starts from five dimensions: the results of Chinese teachers' use of AI teaching, satisfaction, changes in preparation time, adjustment of teaching strategies, and dependence on AI teaching, and deeply explores the specific role and potential impact of AI technology on Chinese teaching. Although the application of AI in language education has achieved initial results, it faces unique challenges in the teaching of Chinese as a logographic writing system. Compared with alphabetic systems, the high orthographic depth and the trinity of form, sound and meaning of the Chinese character system lead to the following special difficulties:

(1) Stroke order correction: AI needs to recognize the stroke order rules of Chinese characters (such as "horizontal first, vertical later"), but experiments show that the error rate of learners in the stroke order of the character " " is as high as 29.7% (Yuming, 2001). Li et al. (2023) proposed a Chinese character stroke extraction method based on deep learning. This method innovatively constructed a three-stage framework to address the errors caused by the existing technology ignoring the semantics and structural priors of strokes: first, the structural deformable image registration network is used to achieve rough alignment between the reference strokes and the target strokes, providing structural deformation priors while maintaining the stability of the single stroke morphology; second, the target strokes are preliminarily classified into seven basic types based on image semantic segmentation technology, and the stroke semantic features are introduced; finally, based on this fusion of spatial priors and semantic information, single strokes are extracted with high precision. The verification results of this method on calligraphy and conventional handwriting dual datasets are significantly better than the baseline method, effectively solving the problem of cross-stroke extraction and matching errors.

(2) Distinguishing similar characters: Due to the similarity of the characters, similar characters only occupy 14.3% ± 2.1% of the visual area of the characters (Zhou & Marslen-Wilson, 1999). Wu et al. (2023) have made improvements based on the stacked capsule autoencoder (SCAE) to better extract and classify strokes. First, the character image is decomposed into primitives (stroke segments) and their shape and posture information are decoupled. Under the guidance of prior knowledge extracted from writing rules, the transformed primitives are aggregated into higher-level parts (strokes). This process enhances interpretability and improves the discriminative ability of features.

(3) Processing of polyphonic characters: Some scholars have found that in the early stages of learning Chinese, international students will make more frequent errors in learning polyphonic characters (Shiming, 2019). Some scholars have also proposed that when learning Chinese writing, the combination of character shape and semantics is the key factor for success (Zhang & Xing, 2023). Gao et al. (2024) proposed a new model for AI processing of Chinese polyphones, the Decoupled Learning Model (DLM), a decoupled learning model for disambiguation of long-tail polyphones in Chinese. The characteristics of this model are: by decoupling the two stages of representation learning and classification learning, and using data samplers in each stage to optimize the distribution of training data, it is specifically designed to deal with the problem of long-tail data imbalance; at the same time, using improved attention mechanisms and progressive contextual learning strategies, the model's deep understanding of context is effectively enhanced, thereby achieving more accurate judgment of the pronunciation of polyphones.

Therefore, learners need to solve these problems in order to further learn Chinese. These characteristics require AI systems to have stronger visual recognition and context analysis capabilities (Chen et al., 2025).

This paper aims to reveal the mechanism by which AI tools reshape teachers' teaching behaviours, classroom ecology, and teaching effectiveness, and thus provide a realistic basis and theoretical support for the deep integration of artificial intelligence and language education. Against the background of the continuous development of artificial intelligence technology, the application of AI in language education is gradually expanding, but most current research focuses on the learner perspective, and there are relatively few systematic studies on teachers' actual teaching behaviours, teaching efficiency, and strategy adjustment. Especially in the field of Chinese teaching, the application of AI-assisted teaching is still in the initial exploration stage. Therefore, this study aims to explore the specific impact of artificial intelligence technology on Chinese teaching practice from the perspective of teachers. The main objectives of this study include:

1. Explore the changes in teaching outcomes brought about by artificial intelligence in Chinese teaching, such as learner performance and achievement of teaching objectives;
2. Assess the satisfaction and acceptance of Chinese teachers with AI-assisted teaching;
3. Analyse the changes in teachers' preparation time and preparation mode after AI intervention;

4. Sort out the adjustment and adaptation process of teachers' teaching strategies in the AI environment;
5. Study the degree of teachers' dependence on the use of AI tools and their potential impact on teaching autonomy.

Based on the research purpose, this study will answer the following specific questions:

1. Does the application of artificial intelligence technology have a significant impact on the teaching results of Chinese teachers?
2. What is the overall satisfaction of Chinese teachers with AI-assisted teaching tools? What are the influencing factors?
3. Has the use of AI technology changed the time and method of teacher preparation?
4. In the AI-supported teaching environment, have teachers' teaching strategies been adjusted? In what aspects?
5. To what extent do Chinese teachers rely on AI technology in actual teaching? Does this dependence affect their teaching autonomy?

As the key node of the intelligent transformation of education, teachers' teaching philosophy and technical literacy play a decisive role in the effective use of AI tools (Li et al., 2024). According to Davis (1989) Technology Acceptance Model (TAM), teachers' intention to use AI tools is significantly affected by perceived usefulness (PU) and perceived ease of use (PEOU). This explains why AI tools that can effectively reduce lesson preparation time are more likely to be adopted by teachers (e.g., Grammarly saves 40% of grading time), while complex systems may encounter usage barriers (Weger et al., 2023). Current research needs to further explore the TAM-specific performance of Chinese teachers.

However, the TAM model mainly focuses on the individual's usage attitude and behavioral intention, and does not adequately explain the dynamic evolution path of teachers' teaching behavior in the process of technology use. To this end, this paper further introduces the SAMR model (Substitution, Augmentation, Modification, Redefinition), proposed by Puentedura (2014), which aims to characterize the four stages of technology integration into teaching, namely "Substitution-Augmentation-Modification-Reconstruction". As pointed out by Weger et al. (2023), teachers' use of AI technology often goes through an evolutionary process from initially replacing traditional tools to gradually enhancing teaching effects and finally realizing the reconstruction of teaching structure. Based on the TAM model and combined with the SAMR framework, this study will focus on the phased transformation characteristics of teachers in the process of using AI from the dimension of "strategy adjustment", to reveal the profound impact of AI technology more comprehensively on teaching behavior.

RESEARCH METHODS

1.Research sample

The research sample of this study are Chinese teachers at all teaching stages of teaching Chinese as a second language. This study was conducted over a period of four weeks.

2. Research instrument

Because this study is a quantitative study, the research instrument of this study is mainly based on questionnaires. The survey mainly focuses on five aspects: teachers' age, teaching experience, location, teaching stage, and the nature of the school. The questionnaire content is designed from five dimensions: teaching results, teacher satisfaction, changes in preparation time, teaching strategies, and degree of dependence on AI. The questions are in the form of a five-level Likert scale, with negative answers and positive answers assigned 1 to 5 points respectively, for a total of 10 questions.

3.Statistical analysis

SPSS 26.0 software was used for statistical analysis in this study. The Kolmogorov-Smirnov test was used to determine the data distribution characteristics. For quantitative data that followed a normal distribution, the mean ± standard deviation $\bar{x} \pm s$ was used to describe it; for quantitative data that did not meet the normal distribution, the median and interquartile range M (P25, P75) were used. Count data were presented as number of cases (n) and percentage (%). When comparing between groups, the independent sample t test was used for quantitative data with normal distribution or approximately normal distribution; the rank sum test was used for non-normal distribution data. In the correlation analysis, the Wilcoxon rank sum test was used to compare the two groups of data, and the Kruskal Wallis H rank sum test was used to compare multiple groups of data. $P < 0.05$ was used as the standard for judging whether the difference was statistically significant.

FOCUS OF THE ARTICLE

The focus of this study is to explore the role and impact of artificial intelligence (AI) in Chinese teaching, especially in the fields of teaching Chinese as a second language (CSL) and teaching Chinese as a foreign language (TCFL). With the continuous development of AI technology in the field of education, especially the advancement of natural language processing and speech recognition, AI tools have gradually become an important means to improve classroom efficiency, optimize teaching strategies and personalize teaching experience. This article explores the application and potential of AI in Chinese teaching from the following aspects:

1. Core Dimensions of Research

Based on the above, this study will analyse the impact mechanism of AI from the following five aspects:

(a)Teaching achievements.

The role of AI in improving learners' Chinese listening, speaking, reading, and writing skills. Studies have shown that AI technology can provide real-time feedback in pronunciation, grammar, writing and other aspects, significantly improving learners' language skills (Zawacki-Richter et al., 2019). For example, Rosetta Stone uses speech recognition technology to help students practice correct pronunciation and provide real-time feedback, which significantly improves students' pronunciation accuracy. AI technology can score learners based on their pronunciation accuracy and correct them immediately when errors occur, greatly reducing learners' pronunciation deviations, thereby helping them master standard pronunciation patterns faster (Wanxiang et al., 2023). In terms of learning grammar and sentence structure, AI systems can also help students understand and apply language rules more accurately through instant error correction functions (Bo & Ruihai, 2022). AI can identify common grammatical errors in students' writing and provide modification suggestions to help students gradually improve their writing fluency and accuracy. In addition, AI systems can dynamically adjust teaching content based on students' learning progress and error patterns to ensure that learners receive timely feedback and challenges in different language skill areas (Li, 2020).

Some scholars have suggested that in terms of listening and speaking training, AI can also simulate a variety of situations and provide an immersive language learning experience. Through virtual dialogue practice, students can output language in simulated real-life scenarios, such as daily conversations, ordering food, asking for directions, etc., and gradually improve their oral fluency and confidence

(Zawacki-Richter et al., 2019). However, the study by Loewen et al. (2020) showed that although AI technology can significantly improve learners' performance in grammar recognition, it has limitations in improving oral communication skills. The study found that after 12 weeks of learning, Duolingo users (N=234) improved their grammar recognition test scores by 27%, but their oral communication skills only improved by 9%, reflecting the inadequacy of AI dialogue training in improving real communication skills. This difference may be due to the limitations of AI systems in simulating the complexity of situations and the depth of interaction in real communication.

In summary, the application of AI technology can not only enhance learners' fluency and accuracy in language output, especially in grammar correction and pronunciation training, but it still faces certain challenges in improving oral communication skills and other interactive skills. Therefore, future AI learning tools should consider how to improve their interactivity and situational simulation capabilities to better support students' ability improvement in actual language communication.

(b)Teacher satisfaction.

Teachers' experience and satisfaction with AI-assisted tools. Studies have shown that when using AI-assisted tools, teachers generally show high satisfaction with the feedback and auxiliary functions provided by them. Many studies have found that AI tools can significantly improve teachers' efficiency and teaching quality in teaching (Fan et al., 2024; Shen, 2025). For example, when teachers use writing assistance tools such as Grammarly, they can quickly detect grammatical errors in students' essays and provide students with detailed improvement suggestions. This feedback mechanism significantly improves the efficiency and accuracy of writing correction. In addition, teachers feel less burdened when using AI systems, especially when correcting many assignments. The automation and intelligent features of AI tools can reduce teachers' work pressure (Xia et al., 2024). This is particularly evident in tasks that require a lot of personalized feedback. AI can provide customized feedback based on the type of errors made by each student, thereby improving the quality and effectiveness of teaching interactions (Luckin & Holmes, 2016).

AI tools not only perform well in grammatical error correction, but also help teachers design more personalized learning activities. For example, AI can automatically adjust the difficulty of homework or learning materials based on students' learning progress, error patterns, and knowledge mastery, ensuring that each student learns at a level of challenge that is appropriate for their level (Qiao & Zhao, 2023). This personalized support not only improves students' learning outcomes, but also makes teachers more satisfied with the teaching convenience brought by AI tools.

(c)Changes in lesson preparation time.

The impact of AI technology on teachers' lesson preparation time and methods is becoming increasingly significant. Studies have shown that AI-assisted tools can not only effectively reduce the time required by teachers in the lesson preparation stage, but also significantly improve the organization efficiency and personalization level of teaching materials (Fan et al., 2024). For example, traditional lesson preparation often requires teachers to spend a lot of time manually searching and integrating resources, while AI platforms can automatically recommend teaching resources and exercises that match the course theme through keyword matching, corpus analysis, and teaching goal identification, significantly reducing the preparation burden of teachers (Holmes et al., 2019). For example, Kahoot! and other teaching interactive platforms have built-in many shareable questions bank templates, and teachers only need to make slight modifications to generate classroom tests suitable for different student levels. In addition, some intelligent teaching auxiliary tools (such as ChatGPT, Quizlet, Class Point, etc.) also could automatically generate lesson plans, design teaching activities, or output learning paths, which greatly improves the flexibility and pertinence of lesson preparation (Fan et al., 2024).

AI tools can also automatically generate personalized practice content based on students' learning data, so that teachers no longer must prepare multiple sets of materials for students of different levels, thereby saving time for differentiated teaching preparation. In the field of language teaching, AI can also provide real-time analysis feedback based on students' language output (such as essays or oral recordings), and automatically recommend corresponding remedial teaching activities to help teachers formulate teaching plans more targeted (Ding, 2022). In summary, AI-assisted lesson preparation not only improves lesson preparation efficiency, but also prompts teachers to transform from the traditional role of material preparers to learning process designers, making teaching more creative and data-driven.

(d)Adjustment of teaching strategies.

The adjustment of teachers' teaching strategies with the support of AI has become a key issue in current language education. AI technology can dynamically adjust teaching content and methods based on students' learning progress, knowledge mastery level and error types, to better achieve personalized teaching goals (Sharadgah & Sa'di, 2022). Through intelligent recommendations and real-time data feedback, teachers can flexibly adjust the teaching rhythm, content emphasis and difficulty, and task settings to improve the pertinence and adaptability of teaching. For example, the Duolingo app uses AI algorithms to continuously track learners' performance and automatically adjust the difficulty of daily learning tasks based on their accuracy and learning frequency, ensuring that learners continue to accept challenges within the range of "comprehensible input" without being overly frustrated, thereby maintaining continuous learning motivation and cognitive investment.

(e)Dependence on AI.

The degree of teachers' dependence on AI tools and their impact on teaching autonomy have attracted widespread attention in academia in recent years. Although AI technology can significantly improve teaching efficiency, provide intelligent feedback, and simplify the teaching process, teachers may gradually develop a dependence on AI systems during continuous use (Qiao & Zhao, 2023). This dependence is initially manifested as a dual positive experience of "operational convenience" and "efficiency improvement", but with the penetration of AI into teaching decision-making power, some teachers began to weaken their active participation in teaching design and evaluation, which in turn affected their professional judgment and teaching autonomy (Zawacki-Richter et al., 2019). In addition, another study pointed out that when faced with feedback provided by AI systems, teachers may tend to accept the system's suggestions and ignore the individual differences of students and the complexity of teaching situations, thereby affecting teaching quality and student learning outcomes (Alenezi, 2024).

Especially in terms of classroom content generation, homework grading and teaching rhythm control, the automatic recommendation mechanism of AI tools may make some teachers more inclined to "accept suggestions" rather than adjust based on students' specific circumstances. In addition, teachers' excessive trust in AI feedback may also mask students' individual differences and unstructured errors, thereby reducing the humanistic care and critical judgment of teaching (Luckin & Holmes, 2016). Some studies also point out that novice teachers or teachers with low technical confidence are more likely to develop "tool-dependent behaviour", that is, when faced with teaching decisions, they over-rely on the standardized solutions provided by AI and ignore the complexity of teaching situations (Qiao & Zhao, 2023). In addition, teachers' excessive reliance on AI's standardized feedback may ignore the algorithm's misjudgement of specific Chinese character usage and cultural context (such as the mechanical interpretation of polysemous idioms). This algorithmic bias will indirectly affect the accuracy of teaching, and teachers need to maintain a critical attitude towards use. Therefore, how to strike a balance between AI empowerment and teaching professionalism has become an issue that cannot be ignored in the current development of intelligent education.

2. The transformative role of artificial intelligence in Chinese teaching models

This study first emphasizes that artificial intelligence, as an important part of emerging educational technology, is gradually replacing traditional teaching models. AI can not only improve learning efficiency, but also inject new vitality into teaching. Especially in the field of language teaching, AI can accurately analyze students' learning situation and cognitive level through personalized learning recommendations, real-time feedback, and intelligent evaluation, and provide teachers with personalized teaching suggestions to further optimize the language learning process (Zawacki-Richter et al., 2019). For example, intelligent speech recognition systems such as Google Speech or Baidu's "Voice Assistant" can help students pronounce correctly when learning Chinese. The system can correct students' pronunciation errors in real time, allowing students to better master standard Chinese pronunciation and thus improve their language expression ability. This instant feedback mechanism makes learning more personalized and efficient.

3. The potential of artificial intelligence in Chinese teaching

Artificial intelligence (AI) provides teachers with unprecedented teaching support in teaching Chinese as a second language (CSL) and teaching Chinese as a foreign language (TCFL). AI technology helps learners achieve more systematic and efficient improvement in Chinese listening, speaking, reading, and writing through speech recognition, intelligent assessment, virtual dialogue simulation and other means. Studies have shown that the application of AI technology in language learning can improve learning motivation, enhance learning participation, and support differentiated teaching (Luckin & Holmes, 2016; Zawacki-Richter et al., 2019).

For example, speech recognition systems such as Baidu's "Speech Recognition Platform" or Google Cloud Speech-to-Text can automatically detect and correct learners' speech and intonation errors. This instant feedback mechanism helps to cultivate students' speech awareness and speech correction ability (Sun et al., 2021). In terms of writing, intelligent assessment systems (such as Grammarly or Language Tool) use natural language processing technology to detect and correct grammar, spelling, and language structure problems in learners' writing in real time, improving writing accuracy and language organization skills (Ali, 2020).

In addition, AI has been shown to be uniquely qualified in semantic segmentation and performing image tasks (Chen et al., 2025). For example, the Duolingo language learning platform uses natural language processing technology, interactive exercises, personalized feedback, and speech recognition technology. The results show that learners who use the platform to learn languages have significant improvements in oral skills and self-regulation, indicating that AI-driven learning platforms have the potential to improve students' oral skills and autonomous learning (Qiao & Zhao, 2023). This type of interactive learning method not only reduces the psychological barriers to foreign language output, but also effectively enhances students' language output ability and cross-cultural communication ability (Karakas, 2023).

This immersive and personalized teaching method supported by AI is particularly advantageous in CSL and TCFL classrooms. Teachers can use AI tools to set personalized learning paths for students, automatically track learning progress, and adjust teaching strategies, thereby realizing the teaching concept of "teaching students in accordance with their aptitude" (Ding, 2022). These technical means not only improve students' language skills, but also complement each other in teaching assistance, saving teachers a lot of evaluation and feedback time, and improving overall teaching efficiency (Huang, 2020).

In addition, AI can track students' learning paths in real time, which is conducive to students' self-assessment and teachers' tracking and understanding of students' learning status at any time (Li, 2020). For example, online Chinese education platforms such as VIPKid and iTalki use AI to track students' learning progress and adjust course content and difficulty according to students' performance to ensure that each student can learn at his or her own pace.

4. The impact of artificial intelligence on teaching strategies

The study further explored how AI can help teachers improve teaching efficiency and optimize teaching strategies. The introduction of AI technology can not only reduce the burden of teacher preparation, but also provide teachers with data-driven decision support. Through AI, teachers can organize classes more efficiently, adjust teaching content and methods, and make teaching more in line with students' personalized needs (Qiao & Zhao, 2023). For example, intelligent teaching platforms such as Knewton and Smart Sparrow can provide personalized learning paths based on students' learning data, and provide teachers with detailed reports to help teachers better understand students' learning situation and adjust teaching content accordingly. In addition, AI can also help teachers more accurately assess students' learning progress and language ability, thereby providing a scientific basis for teachers' teaching decisions (Li, 2020). Through AI, teachers can obtain information such as students' homework grades and participation in real time, to better adjust classroom management and teaching strategies.

Related research shows that AI-assisted tools can effectively optimize classroom structure, improve teaching efficiency, and help teachers prepare for teaching efficiently in a short time (Ali, 2020). For example, in traditional Chinese classes, teachers may need to spend a lot of time grading homework. However, after using

AI homework grading tools (such as Turnitin), teachers can quickly and accurately grade students' essays and provide detailed feedback, significantly reducing preparation and grading time, so that more time can be devoted to teaching and interaction.

5. Teachers' experience and feedback in AI-assisted teaching

Although AI has achieved certain results in improving learning outcomes and teaching efficiency, there is still a lack of research on teachers' experience, feedback, and behavioral changes in using AI in actual teaching. This article will explore their feelings, acceptance, and adjustments to teaching methods when using AI-assisted teaching from the perspective of teachers. According to research, teachers showed high satisfaction and dependence after using AI tools, and were able to clearly feel the impact of AI on their teaching methods and classroom management (Shen, 2025). For example, when using ChatGPT for Chinese grammar teaching, teachers found that students were able to use AI for instant grammar correction, which enhanced the interactivity of learning. Teachers' high recognition of this technology shows that AI can effectively reduce teachers' workload and improve teaching quality.

However, this also shows that teachers' dependence on AI may affect their teaching autonomy and the implementation of traditional educational concepts (Duan & Zhao, 2024). Some teachers may rely too much on AI tools when using them, resulting in a lack of flexibility and personalization in classroom teaching, and cannot be fully adjusted according to students' actual needs. For example, some teachers have reported that when they rely too much on intelligent assessment systems, the standardized assessments provided by AI sometimes fail to accurately reflect students' true abilities, especially in terms of cultural understanding and emotional expression.

CONTRIBUTIONS

This study aims to systematically analyze the specific application and impact of AI in Chinese teaching by combining quantitative and qualitative data. The study not only hopes to reveal how AI tools reshape teachers' teaching behaviors, classroom structures, and teaching effects, but also hopes to provide theoretical support and practical basis for the application of AI in Chinese teaching in the future. Research points out that the application of AI in education is an important driving force for the digital transformation of education (UNESCO, 2023). This study provides guidance for future teachers to use AI tools in education by revealing the application scenarios of AI in Chinese teaching (Luckin & Holmes, 2016).

SOLUTIONS AND RECOMMENDATIONS

a) Solution

This study collected data by using a quantitative research method, questionnaire survey. 153 teachers from the first line of Chinese teaching answered the questions. The questionnaire surveyed and collected data from five aspects: teacher age, school type, teaching experience, region, and school age group taught (see Table 1.1 for details). The results showed that the five dimensions investigated in this study were related to these five aspects (see Tables 1.2, 1.3, 1.4, 1.5 and 1.6 for details).

Table 1. General demographic information of the subjects

		Number	**Percent (%)**
Age	22-25	28	18.3
	26-35	48	31.4
	36-45	29	19.0
	46-55	32	20.9
	56 and above	16	10.5
Type of school	Public	76	49.7
	Private	77	50.3
Teaching experience	1-3	25	16.3
	3-5	35	22.9
	5-10	42	27.5
	10 and above	51	33.3
Area	East	35	22.9
	South	30	19.6
	Central	37	24.2
	West	15	9.8
	North	36	23.5
Teaching Stage	Kindergarten	39	25.5
	Primary school	38	24.8
	Junior high school	28	18.3
	Senior high school	23	15.0
	University	15	9.8
	Other	10	6.5

In summary, the subjects of this study cover different ages, school types, teaching experience, regions, and school age. In terms of age, 26-35 years old accounted for 31.4% relatively prominent; in terms of school type, the proportion of public and private schools was almost equal; the proportion of teaching experience of 10 years or more accounted for 33.3%, ranking first; the regional distribution was relatively scattered, with the central region accounting for a slightly higher proportion of 24.2%; the school age was mostly kindergarten (25.5%) and primary school (24.8%).

Table 2. Correlation between school nature and five dimensions.

	Public	Private	*Z*	*P*
Teaching achievements				
Have students' grades changed?	9(7,10)	8(6.5,8.5)	-3.657	<000.1
Is it easier to learn difficult and important knowledge?				
Do you think AI tools play a supporting role?				
Teacher Satisfaction				
Are you satisfied with the AI tools you currently use?	3(2,3)	3(2,4)	-1.548	0.122
Adjustment of teaching strategies				
Does it match your teaching materials and help you simplify complex knowledge points?	8(7,9)	9(8,10)	-2.908	0.004
Does it enhance interaction with students?				
Does it affect the progress of your course?				
Dependence on AI				
Do you rely more on using AI tools?	5(4,6)	7(5,8)	-5.559	<000.1
Do you often use AI tools for Chinese teaching?				
Changes in lesson preparation time				
Do you feel that your lesson preparation efficiency has been improved/the time spent on lesson preparation has been reduced?	2(1,3)	3(3,4)	-4.595	<000.1

As can be seen from Table 1.2, the study compared public and private schools from five dimensions: teaching effect, satisfaction, adjustment of teaching strategies, reliance on AI, and changes in preparation time. The results showed that there were significant differences between public and private schools in terms of teaching effect, adjustment of teaching strategies, reliance on AI, and changes in preparation time ($P<0.05$). Public schools performed well in helping students learn difficult and key knowledge in teaching effect, while private schools were more prominent in adapting teaching strategies to textbooks, relying on AI tools, and improving preparation efficiency. In terms of satisfaction, there was no significant difference between the two schools.

Table 3. Correlation between teachers' regions and the five dimensions

Area	East	South	Central	West	North	*H*	*P*
Teaching achievements							
Have students' grades changed? Is it easier to learn difficult and important knowledge? Do you think AI tools play a supporting role?	8.11±0.28	8.03±0.40	8.14±0.37	8.33±0.37	8.13±0.29	0.156	0.997
Teacher Satisfaction							
Are you satisfied with the AI tools you currently use?	2.63±0.16	3.34±0.20	2.75±0.20	2.73±0.28	2.71±0.18	8.816	0.066
Adjustment of teaching strategies							
Does it match your teaching materials and help you simplify complex knowledge points? Does it enhance interaction with students? Does it affect the progress of your course?	8.80±0.51	8.93±0.26	7.97±0.36	8.77±0.24	7.89±0.34	9.629	0.047
Dependence on AI							
Do you rely more on using AI tools? Do you often use AI tools for Chinese teaching?	5.97±0.24	6.41±0.36	5.69±0.29	4.67±0.42	5.63±0.26	11.286	0.024
Changes in lesson preparation time							
Do you feel that your lesson preparation efficiency has been improved/the time spent on lesson preparation has been reduced?	3.46±0.21	3.07±0.23	2.81±0.21	1.93±0.30	2.82±0.21	15.921	0.003

Therefore, this study compared the eastern, southern, central, western, and northern regions from five dimensions: teaching effectiveness, satisfaction, adjustment of teaching strategies, reliance on AI, and changes in lesson preparation time. The results showed that there were no significant differences between regions in the dimensions of teaching effectiveness and satisfaction; while there were significant differences between regions in the dimensions of teaching strategy adjustment, reliance on AI, and changes in lesson preparation time ($P<0.05$), which means that different regions have obvious differences in using AI tools to adapt teaching strategies, relying on the use of AI tools, and using AI to improve lesson preparation efficiency. Among them, the southern region has the deepest reliance on AI teaching and the most efficient adjustment of teaching strategies; the eastern region has the most obvious changes in lesson preparation time due to the influence of AI.

Table 4. Correlation between teachers' age and five dimensions.

Age	22-25	26-35	36-45	46-55	56 and above	*H*	*P*
Teaching achievements							
Have students' grades changed? Is it easier to learn difficult and important knowledge? Do you think AI tools play a supporting role?	8.18±0.41	8.92±0.24	7.86±0.34	7.63±0.32	7.19±0.45	15.039	0.005
Teacher Satisfaction							
Are you satisfied with the AI tools you currently use?	2.78±0.19	2.79±0.15	3.07±0.22	2.63±0.23	2.94±0.25	3.569	0.467
Adjustment of teaching strategies							
Does it match your teaching materials and help you simplify complex knowledge points? Does it enhance interaction with students? Does it affect the progress of your course?	8.54±0.34	8.19±0.25	8.59±0.41	8.28±0.33	8.69±0.47	1.917	0.751
Dependence on AI							
Do you rely more on using AI tools? Do you often use AI tools for Chinese teaching?	6.46±0.40	5.98±0.25	5.76±0.24	5.16±0.26	5.25±0.46	9.794	0.044
Changes in lesson preparation time							
Do you feel that your lesson preparation efficiency has been improved/the time spent on lesson preparation has been reduced?	3.00±0.35	3.15±0.19	2.77±0.20	2.93±0.21	2.60±0.35	5.975	0.201

The study compared teachers of different ages from five dimensions: teaching effect, satisfaction, adjustment of teaching strategies, reliance on AI, and changes in preparation time. In terms of teaching effect, there were significant differences between ages ($P < 0.05$), with 26-35 years old scoring higher and having the best teaching effect; there were no significant differences in satisfaction; there were no significant differences in teaching strategy adjustment; there were significant differences between ages in reliance on AI ($P < 0.05$), with 22-25 years old using it more frequently; there were no significant differences in changes in preparation time.

Table 5. Correlation between teachers' teaching experience and the five dimensions.

Teaching Experience	1-3	3-5	5-10	10 above on	*H*	*P*
Teaching achievements						
Have students' grades changed? Is it easier to learn difficult and important knowledge? Do you think AI tools play a supporting role?	7.72±0.36	8.46±0.37	8.29±0.29	7.98±0.25	2.859	0.414
Teacher Satisfaction						
Are you satisfied with the AI tools you currently use?	2.72±0.21	2.82±0.21	2.83±0.17	2.86±0.15	0.409	0.938
Adjustment of teaching strategies						
Does it match your teaching materials and help you simplify complex knowledge points? Does it enhance interaction with students? Does it affect the progress of your course?	7.52±0.40	8.43±0.28	8.24±0.29	8.94±0.25	8.368	0.039
Dependence on AI						
Do you rely more on using AI tools? Do you often use AI tools for Chinese teaching?	5.96±0.39	5.57±0.28	5.69±0.27	5.90±0.24	1.021	0.796
Changes in lesson preparation time						
Do you feel that your lesson preparation efficiency has been improved/the time spent on lesson preparation has been reduced?	3.28±0.27	2.80±0.21	2.79±0.21	2.94±0.18	2.859	0.414

In summary, this study analysed the correlation between teaching experience and teaching effectiveness, satisfaction, teaching strategy adjustment, dependence on AI, and changes in preparation time. It was found that there was no significant correlation between teaching experience and teaching effectiveness, satisfaction, dependence on AI, and changes in preparation time. Only teaching experience was significantly correlated with teaching strategy adjustment ($P<0.05$). Teachers with more than 10 years of teaching experience had the most significant effect on adjusting teaching strategies.

Table 6. Correlation between the stage of study taught by teachers and the five dimensions.

Teaching stage	Kindergarten	Primary school	Junior high school	Senior high school	University	Others	*H*	*P*
Teaching achievements								
Have students' grades changed? Is it easier to learn difficult and important knowledge? Do you think AI tools play a supporting role?	8.13±0.26	8.29±0.33	7.82±0.40	8.35±0.42	7.73±0.51	8.50±0.62	1.761	0.881
Teacher Satisfaction								
Are you satisfied with the AI tools you currently use?	3.21±0.18	3.16±0.17	2.50±0.17	2.48±0.26	2.20±0.26	2.70±0.26	16.004	0.007
Adjustment of teaching strategies								
Does it match your teaching materials and help you simplify complex knowledge points? Does it enhance interaction with students? Does it affect the progress of your course?	8.26±0.27	9.00±0.29	8.25±0.38	8.65±0.41	7.93±0.49	7.20±0.70	8.965	0.110
Dependence on AI								
Do you rely more on using AI tools? Do you often use AI tools for Chinese teaching?	5.77±0.26	6.13±0.28	6.29±0.32	5.26±0.33	5.73±0.46	4.30±0.52	13.35	0.020
Changes in lesson preparation time								
Do you feel that your lesson preparation efficiency has been improved/the time spent on lesson preparation has been reduced?	2.85±0.21	3.34±0.22	3.00±0.25	2.57±0.23	2.67±0.33	2.60±0.40	6.925	0.226

Therefore, combined with Table 1.6, this study explored the differences in different teaching stages from five dimensions: teaching effect, satisfaction, adjustment of teaching strategies, reliance on AI, and changes in preparation time. The results showed that there were no significant differences between different teaching stages in terms of teaching effect, adjustment of teaching strategies, and changes in preparation time; there were significant differences in terms of satisfaction and reliance on AI ($P < 0.05$). Kindergarten teachers were most satisfied with the use of AI for teaching, and junior high school teachers were most dependent on AI.

b) Recommendation

This study explored the differences in teachers' performance in the application of AI teaching from multiple dimensions, including school type, region, teacher age, teaching experience, and teaching stage, in terms of teaching effect, satisfaction, teaching strategy adjustment, degree of dependence on AI, and changes in preparation time. The results are of great significance for understanding the current status of AI application in education scenarios.

In terms of school type, public and private schools show significant differences in the application of AI teaching. Public schools perform better in helping students learn difficult and key knowledge. This may be related to the long-term accumulation of teaching resources, standardized teaching system, and relatively stable teaching staff in public schools, which enable them to better integrate AI tools into traditional teaching and accurately focus on knowledge difficulties. This coincides with the views of Lee and Kwon (2024). Cukurova et al. (2023) proposed that for teachers, not increasing their workload and minimizing ethical issues, and increasing their autonomy are conducive to encouraging teachers to break through their existing levels and use new technologies. Private schools are more prominent in adapting teaching strategies to textbooks, relying on AI tools, and improving lesson preparation efficiency. This may be due to the more flexible management mechanism and more open innovation atmosphere of private schools, which prompts teachers to actively try new AI teaching tools and strategies to meet diverse teaching needs and competitive pressures. It is worth noting that there is no significant difference between the two in the satisfaction dimension, indicating that teachers in both public and private schools have a relatively objective and similar attitude towards AI teaching applications, and AI teaching is universal in improving teaching experience.

From a regional perspective, there are significant differences in the adjustment of teaching strategies, the degree of reliance on AI, and the change in preparation time between different regions. The southern region is most dependent on AI teaching and has the most efficient adjustment of teaching strategies. This may be because the southern region has a more developed economy, has invested more in educational informatization, and has more opportunities for teachers to contact and use advanced AI teaching tools. At the same time, the local awareness of education reform and innovation is strong, which has promoted the in-depth application of AI in teaching, such as in the Guangdong-Hong Kong-Macao Greater Bay Area in China (Li, 2024). The change in preparation time in the eastern region due to AI is the most obvious. This may be related to the fierce competition in education in the eastern region. Teachers actively use AI tools to optimize the preparation process to improve teaching quality. The research of Zhang and Zhang (2024) proves this point. There is no significant difference between regions in the dimensions of teaching effect and satisfaction, indicating that although the specific methods of AI teaching application in different regions are different, they have achieved the improvement of teaching quality and the improvement of teachers' teaching experience to a certain extent. AI teaching has a positive effect nationwide.

The research results of the teacher age dimension are also quite enlightening. Teachers aged 26-35 scored higher in teaching effectiveness and achieved the best teaching results. Teachers in this age group usually have certain teaching experience and are more receptive to new technologies, and can better combine AI tools with teaching practice. Mahat (2023) also believes that young teachers have advantages in accepting new things and learning new technologies. In terms of the degree of dependence on AI, teachers aged 22-25 use it more frequently. As a younger generation, these teachers grew up in the digital age and are more familiar with and sensitive to new technologies. They are more willing to try and rely on AI teaching tools. There is no significant difference in the satisfaction and teaching strategy adjustment dimensions, indicating that teachers of different ages have similar overall cognition and attitude towards the application of AI teaching, but the application methods and effects vary due to individual characteristics.

The study on the correlation between teaching experience and various dimensions found that only teaching experience was significantly correlated with the adjustment of teaching strategies, and teachers with more than 10 years of teaching experience had the most significant effect on the adjustment of teaching strategies. Experienced old teachers, with their profound teaching skills and deep understanding of teaching rules, can more accurately judge the fit between AI tools and teaching strategies, and thus more effectively adjust teaching strategies to meet the needs of AI teaching (Hang, 2024). However, there is no significant correlation between teaching experience and teaching effect, satisfaction, dependence on AI, and changes in preparation time. This shows that the application of AI teaching has, to a certain extent, broken through the advantages or limitations brought by teaching experience in traditional teaching, and provided equal innovation and development space for teachers of different teaching ages.

In the dimension of teaching stage, kindergarten teachers are most satisfied with the use of AI teaching, and junior high school teachers are most dependent on AI. Kindergarten teaching focuses on fun and intuitiveness. AI's rich multimedia resources and interactive functions can well meet the teaching needs of young children and stimulate their interest in learning, so teachers are more satisfied. Kölemen and Yıldırım (2025) proposed that artificial intelligence technology can be easily integrated into preschool education if students' privacy and security can be guaranteed. The difficulty of subject knowledge in junior high school increases, and the teaching tasks become more arduous. The role of AI tools in assisting teaching and improving teaching efficiency and quality is more prominent, making junior high school teachers highly dependent on them. However, there are no significant differences between the teaching stages in terms of teaching effect, teaching strategy adjustment, and change in preparation time. This shows that teachers at different teaching stages are actively exploring and have achieved similar results in the process of using AI to achieve teaching goals, although the methods and focuses are different.

Therefore, this study comprehensively reveals the multi-dimensional differences and characteristics of teachers in the application of AI teaching. These findings provide important references for education administrators and teachers. When promoting and applying AI teaching, the influence of factors such as school type, region, teacher age, teaching experience, and teaching stage should be fully considered, and targeted policies and training programs should be formulated to promote the efficient application of AI teaching in the field of education and promote the overall improvement of education and teaching quality. At the same time, future research can further explore the interactions between various factors and how to better optimize AI teaching tools and strategies to meet the needs of different educational scenarios and teacher groups.

Future Research Directions

As mentioned above, the development of artificial intelligence has brought great benefits to language education. Especially in Chinese teaching, artificial intelligence can improve the quality and efficiency of teachers' teaching. However, some scholars pointed out that although the research on artificial intelligence-assisted language learning is expanding worldwide, people's understanding of the integration of artificial intelligence at the classroom level is still limited, and teachers' understanding of artificial intelligence tools is also affecting classroom teaching (Ding, 2022). In addition, whether the use of artificial intelligence is ethical and how to develop practical strategies to improve learning outcomes and cultivate students' creativity are also issues that need to be addressed.

Although the current application of AI technology in Chinese teaching has shown significant potential, with its deep penetration, ethical risks, data privacy leakage and algorithmic discrimination have gradually become prominent, which needs to become the focus of future research.

At the ethical level, the widespread application of AI may exacerbate the imbalance of educational equity. There are significant differences in the accessibility of AI teaching tools in different regions and different types of schools. For example, private schools in economically developed areas may be more likely to obtain advanced intelligent speech recognition systems or customized Chinese character teaching modules, while public schools in underdeveloped areas may be limited by insufficient resources, resulting in a widening gap in the quality of Chinese teaching. In addition, if the decision logic of the AI system overly dominates the teaching process, it may weaken the dominant position of teachers in the classroom. For example, when the Chinese grammar correction program automatically generated by AI replaces the personalized guidance of teachers, it may violate the "student-cantered" educational ethics and ignore the cultural background and emotional needs of learners.

Data privacy protection also needs urgent attention. AI tools will continue to collect a large amount of sensitive data in Chinese teaching, including learners' pronunciation recordings, Chinese character writing trajectories, composition content and learning behaviour preferences. Especially for minors, the risk of data leakage or abuse will directly threaten their rights and interests. For example, if the intelligent Chinese character writing APP does not take encryption measures, it may cause students' writing data to be used for commercial purposes or illegally obtained due to system vulnerabilities. Future research needs to establish data security specifications adapted to Chinese teaching scenarios, clarify the boundaries of data collection, storage methods and usage permissions, and balance technology application and privacy protection.

Algorithmic discrimination is more likely to appear in the special scenarios of Chinese teaching. As a ideographic language, the complexity of polyphones, similar characters and cultural contexts may cause AI systems to be biased. For example, some AI speech recognition tools may misjudge the Mandarin pronunciation of learners in specific dialect areas, marking tone changes that conform to the rhythm of the dialect as errors; when dealing with idioms or idioms that contain cultural metaphors, the algorithm may give a mechanical interpretation out of context due to the limitations of the training data, solidifying the learner's understanding of the cultural connotation of Chinese. In addition, if the Chinese learning content recommended by AI relies too much on historical data, it may form an "algorithmic cocoon", restricting learners from accessing diverse language expressions and hindering the expansion of their personalized learning paths.

Therefore, future research needs to combine the uniqueness of Chinese teaching and build a framework that takes into account both technical effectiveness and ethical norms: on the one hand, it is necessary to formulate ethical guidelines for the use of AI in Chinese teaching, clarifying the rights and responsibilities of teachers, technology developers and education managers; on the other hand, it should reduce potential risks through technical optimization (such as enhancing the adaptability of algorithms to the diversity of Chinese culture) and institutional guarantees (such as establishing a data privacy review mechanism) to ensure that AI technology truly serves the high-quality development of Chinese teaching, rather than deviating from the humanistic nature of education. When designing artificial intelligence tools related to the Chinese language, it is necessary not only to consider whether knowledge issues such as grammar are resolved, but also to adapt to the development of Chinese culture and customs.

Findings

This study explores the actual application performance and subjective perception differences of teachers in artificial intelligence (AI)-assisted teaching from multiple dimensions such as school type, region, teacher age, teaching experience and teaching stage, covering five key dimensions: teaching effect, satisfaction, teaching strategy adjustment, AI dependence and changes in preparation time. The study found that AI technology has played a positive role in different educational scenarios, but its application effect is still affected by multiple background factors. Overall, AI not only shows great potential in improving teachers' teaching efficiency and students' learning quality, but also promotes a deep transformation of teaching methods, providing more equal technology empowerment opportunities for different types of teachers.

From a practical perspective, public schools perform better in teaching effectiveness with the help of their stable institutional system and resource base; while private schools are more proactive in strategy adjustment and tool use due to their flexible mechanisms. In terms of regional differences, the frequency and effect of teachers using AI are more prominent in the southern and eastern regions due to higher investment in educational informatization. Age and teaching experience factors also reveal different advantages of teacher groups in technology integration: teachers aged 26-35 perform best in teaching effectiveness, while teachers with more than 10 years of teaching experience are more accurate in adjusting teaching strategies. Analysis of the teaching stage also shows that the use of AI teaching tools should be optimized in combination with the development characteristics of students, such as kindergarten stage pays more attention to interactivity and fun, and junior high school stage pays more attention to efficiency and subject depth.

Although AI technology brings many benefits, its deep integration in education still faces challenges. On the one hand, teachers' understanding and mastery of AI vary, which affects the effectiveness of teaching implementation; on the other hand, how to ensure the ethical use of AI technology, the privacy and security of student data, and the professional autonomy of teachers under the guidance of technology have also become important issues for future development. Global research on AI-assisted language learning continues to grow, but its integration at the classroom level is still in its early stages.

Therefore, future research should be further advanced from the following aspects: First, promote the comprehensive integration of AI with teaching content, teaching methods, and teaching evaluation. Especially in language teaching, we should pay attention to how AI supports the improvement of contextual understanding, communication skills, and cultural cognition; second, deepen the construction of the training system of teachers' AI literacy, especially design personalized training paths based on variables such as age, teaching age, and school stage; third, strengthen the construction of AI education ethics norms to ensure that AI "assists rather than replaces" in education and protect the essence and humanistic spirit of education.

In the field of Chinese teaching, AI should not only solve the training problems of language skills such as grammar and vocabulary, but also be integrated into the teaching of Chinese culture and communication customs. Future AI language teaching tools should be more intelligent and humanized, truly realize the educational vision of "people-oriented and technology-assisted", and promote global Chinese education to a higher quality and wider coverage development stage.

REFERENCES

Alenezi, W. (2024). Potentiality and Apprehensions of Artificial Intelligence in Education: Perspectives of Education Staff. *International Journal of Education in Mathematics. Science and Technology*, *12*(4), 942–956.

Ali, Z. (2020). Artificial intelligence (AI): A review of its uses in language teaching and learning. *IOP Conference Series. Materials Science and Engineering*.

Bo, Z., & Ruihai, D. (2022). Natural language processing technology empowers the development of educational intelligence: The perspective of artificial intelligence scientists. [Educational Science Edition]. *Journal of East China Normal University*, *40*(9), 19.

Chen, J., Wang, M., & Hsia, C.-H. (2025). *Artificial Intelligence and Machine Learning in Sensing and Image Processing* (Vol. 25). MDPI.

Cukurova, M., Miao, X., & Brooker, R. (2023). Adoption of artificial intelligence in schools: Unveiling factors influencing teachers' engagement. International conference on artificial intelligence in education.

Davis, F. D. (1989). Perceived usefulness, perceived ease of use, and user acceptance of information technology. *Management Information Systems Quarterly*, •••, 319–340.

Ding, L. (2022). Application of information technology in teaching Chinese as a second language. MATEC Web of Conferences

Duan, H., & Zhao, W. (2024). The effects of educational artificial intelligence-powered applications on teachers' perceived autonomy, professional development for online teaching, and digital burnout. *International Review of Research in Open and Distance Learning*, *25*(3), 57–76.

Fan, H., Chen, G., Wang, X., & Peng, Z. (2024). LessonPlanner: Assisting novice teachers to prepare pedagogy-driven lesson plans with large language models. *Proceedings of the 37th Annual ACM Symposium on User Interface Software and Technology*

Gao, B., Zhang, Y., Xiang, G., & Jiang, Y. (2024). DLM: A Decoupled Learning Model for Long-tailed Polyphone Disambiguation in Mandarin. *Proceedings of the 2024 Conference of the North American Chapter of the Association for Computational Linguistics: Human Language Technologies* (Volume 1: Long Papers)

Hang, N. T. (2024). The Role of Adoption, Ease of Use and Teachers' Experience of Artificial Intelligence on Teaching Effectiveness: Moderating Role of Student Interest. *Journal of Pedagogical Research, 8*(4), 16–29.

Holmes, W., Bialik, M., & Fadel, C. (2019). *Artificial intelligence in education promises and implications for teaching and learning*. Center for Curriculum Redesign.

Huang, S. (2020). Research on the application of artificial intelligence in teaching Chinese as a foreign language. *2020 International Conference on Social Sciences and Big Data Application (ICSSBDA 2020)*

Karakas, A. (2023). Breaking down barriers with artificial intelligence (AI): cross-cultural communication in foreign language education. In *Transforming the language teaching experience in the age of AI* (pp. 215–233). IGI Global.

Kölemen, E. B., & Yıldırım, B. (2025). A new era in early childhood education (ECE): Teachers' opinions on the application of artificial intelligence. *Education and Information Technologies, 30*(12), 1–42. DOI: 10.1007/s10639-025-13478-9

Lee, S. J., & Kwon, K. (2024). A systematic review of AI education in K-12 classrooms from 2018 to 2023: Topics, strategies, and learning outcomes. *Computers and Education: Artificial Intelligence, 6*, 100211. DOI: 10.1016/j.caeai.2024.100211

Li, M., Yu, Y., Yang, Y., Ren, G., & Wang, J. (2023). Stroke extraction of Chinese character based on deep structure deformable image registration. *Proceedings of the AAAI Conference on Artificial Intelligence*

Li, Y. (2024). Application and Effectiveness Evaluation of Artificial Intelligence Technology in the Guangdong-Hong Kong-Macao. *International Conference on Artificial Intelligence and Communication Technology*

Li, Y., Zhou, X., & Chiu, T. K. (2024). Systematics review on artificial intelligence chatbots and ChatGPT for language learning and research from self-determination theory (SDT): What are the roles of teachers? *Interactive Learning Environments*, •••, 1–15. DOI: 10.1609/aaai.v37i1.25220

Li, Z. (2020). The Application of Intelligent Technology in Chinese Language Teaching. *Innovative Computing, IC*, 2020.

Loewen, S., Isbell, D. R., & Sporn, Z. (2020). The effectiveness of app-based language instruction for developing receptive linguistic knowledge and oral communicative ability. *Foreign Language Annals, 53*(2), 209–233.

Luckin, R., Cukurova, M., Kent, C., & Du Boulay, B. (2022). Empowering educators to be AI-ready. *Computers and Education: Artificial Intelligence, 3*, 100076.

Luckin, R., & Holmes, W. (2016). Intelligence unleashed: An argument for AI in education.

Mahat, D. (2023). Technology Adoption and Teaching performance:"A Moderating Role for Age". *International Journal of Contemporary Sciences, 1*(1), 45–58.

Oubibi, M., Zhao, W., Wang, Y., Zhou, Y., Jiang, Q., Li, Y., Xu, X., & Qiao, L. (2022). Advances in research on technological, pedagogical, didactical, and social competencies of preservice TCFL teachers. *Sustainability (Basel), 14*(4), 2045. DOI: 10.3390/su14042045

Puentedura, R. R. (2014). SAMR: A contextualized introduction. *Lecture at Pine Cobble School. Retrieved,* (March), 13.

Qiao, H., & Zhao, A. (2023). Artificial intelligence-based language learning: Illuminating the impact on speaking skills and self-regulation in Chinese EFL context. *Frontiers in Psychology, 14*, 1255594. DOI: 10.3389/fpsyg.2023.1255594 PMID: 38022973

Sharadgah, T. A., & Sa'di, R. A. (2022). A systematic review of research on the use of artificial intelligence in English language teaching and learning (2015-2021): What are the current effects? *Journal of Information Technology Education,* •••, 21.

Shen, V. (2025). TEACHING FOREIGN LANGUAGES IN THE AGE OF AI: EXPERIMENTS IN AN ADVANCED CHINESE LANGUAGE CLASS. INTED2025 Proceedings, Shiming, Y. (2019). *Investigation and analysis of polyphonetic word acquisition by primary international students and teaching suggestions* Nanjing Normal University].

Sun, J., Pae, H. K., & Ai, H. (2021). The recognition of coordinative compound words by learners of Chinese as a foreign language: A mixed methods study. *Foreign Language Annals, 54*(4), 923–951. DOI: 10.1111/flan.12586

Wanxiang, C., Zhicheng, D., Yansong, F., Tao, G., Xianpei, H., Baotian, H., Minlie, H., Xuanjing, H., Kang, L., & Ting, L. (2023). Natural Language Processing in the Era of Big Models: Challenges, Opportunities, and Developments. *Chinese Science: Information Science, 53*(9), 1645–1687.

Weger, K., Matsuyama, L., Zimmermann, R., Mesmer, B., Van Bossuyt, D., Semmens, R., & Eaton, C. (2023). Insight into user acceptance and adoption of autonomous systems in mission critical environments. *International Journal of Human-Computer Interaction, 39*(7), 1423–1437. DOI: 10.1080/10447318.2022.2086033

Wu, X.-J., Ao, X., Zhang, R.-S., & Liu, C.-L. (2023). Structural Recognition of Handwritten Chinese Characters Using a Modified Part Capsule Auto-encoder. *CAAI International Conference on Artificial Intelligence*

Xia, J., Ge, Y., Shen, Z., & Rahman Najar, M. (2024). The Auxiliary Role of Artificial Intelligence Applications in Mitigating the Linguistic, Psychological, and Educational Challenges of Teaching and Learning Chinese Language by non-Chinese Students. *International Review of Research in Open and Distance Learning*, *25*(3), 116–133.

Yuming, L. (2001). The establishment of general language norms and standards - Experience in studying the "Law of the People's Republic of China on the General Language and Writing System". *Language and character application*(2), 17-24.

Zawacki-Richter, O., Marín, V. I., Bond, M., & Gouverneur, F. (2019). Systematic review of research on artificial intelligence applications in higher education–where are the educators? *International Journal of Educational Technology in Higher Education*, *16*(1), 1–27. DOI: 10.1186/s41239-019-0171-0

Zhang, J., & Zhang, Z. (2024). AI in teacher education: Unlocking new dimensions in teaching support, inclusive learning, and digital literacy. *Journal of Computer Assisted Learning*, *40*(4), 1871–1885. DOI: 10.1111/jcal.12988

Zhang, L., & Xing, H. (2023). The interaction of orthography, phonology and semantics in the process of second language learners' Chinese character production. *Frontiers in Psychology*, *14*, 1076810. DOI: 10.3389/fpsyg.2023.1076810 PMID: 36935946

Zhou, X., & Marslen-Wilson, W. (1999). Sublexical processing in reading Chinese. In *Reading chinese script* (pp. 49-76). Psychology Press. UNESC0. 2023. Global Education Monitoring Report 2023: Technology in education-A tool on whose terms? Paris, UNESCO. DOI: DOI: 10.54676/UZQV8501

Chapter 6
Promoting Intercultural Understanding and Motivation in Language Learning Through Kahoot!

Shinji Okumura
https://orcid.org/0000-0002-9131-6603
Bunkyo University, Japan

ABSTRACT

This exploratory case study investigates the use of game-based student response systems (GSRS), specifically Kahoot!, to promote intercultural engagement in primary education. Participants were 34 Japanese sixth-grade students learning English and 22 Australian fifth-grade students learning Japanese, who engaged in a bilingual Kahoot! quiz with 20 culturally themed questions. Japanese students' open-ended responses were qualitatively analyzed to explore their experiences and perceptions. Findings suggest that Kahoot!'s interactive, gamified format supported student engagement and cultural interest. Frequently used terms like "fun," "learned," and "cooperate" reflected cognitive, emotional, and social learning aspects. Challenges such as digital literacy gaps, scheduling, and platform familiarity highlight the need for instructional scaffolding. This study provides initial insights into how GSRS tools can support intercultural awareness and language learning in primary education.

DOI: 10.4018/979-8-3373-3673-2.ch006

INTRODUCTION

In today's increasingly globalized world, where digital technologies are deeply embedded in daily life, primary education is expected to go beyond the basic acquisition of linguistic skills to foster intercultural understanding and mutual respect. Particularly in early childhood, language learning is not merely a technical or cognitive process but also a cultural experience. The ability to engage in meaningful communication across cultural boundaries, often referred to as intercultural competence, is therefore recognized as a vital component of language education (Casanova-Mata, 2023). This perspective is especially relevant for children, whose cognitive flexibility and innate curiosity make them more receptive to diverse viewpoints.

One promising approach to supporting these educational goals is gamification—applying game-like elements such as points, rewards, competition, and instant feedback in non-game contexts. Research suggests that gamification can enhance learners' motivation, attention, and engagement in educational settings (Prathyusha, 2020). For young learners, in particular, such game-based approaches may align well with their emotional and cognitive developmental stages, offering the potential to support self-regulated and collaborative learning through structured play.

Within this educational context, the present study explores how the game-based learning platform Kahoot! may contribute to English language acquisition and the development of intercultural understanding among young learners. By enabling real-time, interactive quiz-based exchanges between Japanese and Australian primary school students, Kahoot! provides an opportunity to examine how digital tools can support cross-cultural engagement in early language education. Using an exploratory case study approach, this research investigates students' experiences during these digital exchanges and considers how teachers integrate such tools into their instructional practice. In doing so, the study aims to offer preliminary insights into the pedagogical value of gamified, transnational learning in primary education.

The following research questions guide the study:

RQ1: What are Japanese primary school students' perceptions of interacting with Australian peers in a real-time Kahoot! quiz?

RQ2: What cultural insights do Japanese students gain from participating in this international quiz exchange?

RQ3: What challenges and opportunities do educators encounter when using Kahoot! to support intercultural language learning in primary classrooms?

This chapter seeks to contribute to the broader discourse on digital transformation in culturally diverse educational settings through these questions. It offers exploratory insights into how playful, digitally mediated learning experiences may support more inclusive, engaging, and globally oriented practices in early language education.

LITERATURE REVIEW

Overview of Kahoot!

Since its debut in 2013, Kahoot! has become a leading gamification platform within educational settings (Aibar-Almazán et al., 2024; Özdemir, 2024). It utilizes competitive, quiz-based activities to create interactive engagement between educators and students in diverse classroom environments. Recent meta-analytical evidence confirms Kahoot!'s global impact, with over 70 million users worldwide, and highlights its positive effects on student learning outcomes (Özdemir, 2025). A key advantage of Kahoot! is its accessibility and cost-effectiveness, requiring minimal technological infrastructure and only stable internet connectivity to provide meaningful educational experiences (Aibar-Almazán et al., 2024; Neureiter et al., 2020).

As a Game-Based Student Response System (GBSRS), Kahoot! allows educators to design interactive quizzes that seamlessly integrate into existing curricula (Anane, 2024; Wang & Tahir, 2020). Students participate via digital devices using a user-friendly, game-like interface that incorporates multimedia elements such as images and videos. The platform's adaptive pacing accommodates a range of learning speeds and processing styles (Kalleny, 2020). Point-based scoring and real-time leaderboards foster a dynamic learning environment that strikes a balance between competition and collaboration.

Kahoot! and Motivation in Language Learning

Research consistently identifies Kahoot! as a powerful tool for boosting motivation in educational contexts. Its gamified design significantly enhances student participation and sustained attention, particularly benefiting language acquisition processes (Kaur & Nadarajan, 2020; Tan et al., 2022). The combination of immediate feedback, visible progress tracking through leaderboards, and engaging quiz formats helps maintain active student involvement throughout lessons. Empirical studies suggest that Kahoot! taps into younger learners' natural curiosity and competitive instincts, amplifying their intrinsic motivation to engage with the content (Wang & Tahir, 2020).

Kahoot!'s game-based structure is especially valuable for vocabulary acquisition and grammar reinforcement, transforming traditionally passive teaching methods into dynamic, participatory experiences (Cátia Sofia et al., 2022; Low & Yamat, 2022). Beyond individual achievement, research shows that Kahoot! fosters collaborative classroom environments that encourage peer-to-peer learning and cooperative problem-solving (Kaur, 2020). This social aspect of learning extends the platform's impact beyond content mastery, promoting the development of essential interpersonal skills.

Kahoot! and Social-Emotional Learning

Kahoot! also contributes to social-emotional development by offering structured opportunities for empathy-building, tolerance cultivation, and perspective-taking exercises. Aidoune et al. (2022) demonstrate that educators can integrate sophisticated pedagogical strategies—such as role-playing scenarios, situational problem-solving, and narrative exploration—into quiz activities. These methods allow students to engage with complex social issues in a psychologically safe environment. This approach promotes open discussions on sensitive topics, while safeguarding student emotional well-being (Bhuana, 2022).

Post-activity reflection sessions, when facilitated by trained educators, reinforce social-emotional learning objectives through metacognitive processing (Nasution, 2024). These reflective practices allow students to critically analyze and internalize the social content explored during interactive sessions, leading to a deeper understanding of human experiences and perspectives.

Kahoot! and Intercultural Education in Primary Settings

Kahoot! shows exceptional potential for advancing intercultural competence at the primary school level. Contemporary research stresses that intercultural proficiency—encompassing empathy, diversity appreciation, and global citizenship—is crucial for navigating today's interconnected world (Almusharraf, 2023; Casanova-Mata, 2023). The platform's visual appeal and pedagogical flexibility make it well-suited for introducing young learners to cross-cultural concepts using age-appropriate methods.

Evidence suggests that culturally responsive quiz content helps develop intercultural awareness in primary students through experiential learning. Casanova-Mata (2023) illustrates how quizzes on international celebrations, heritage traditions, and global community events offer accessible entry points for exploring cultural diversity, while simultaneously advancing language proficiency. This integrated approach allows young learners to reflect on their own cultural assumptions, while fostering a deeper appreciation for human diversity through authentic engagement rather than abstract instruction.

Nikolić et al. (2022) further highlight how multilingual vocabulary integration and thematic cultural content within quiz activities create rich opportunities for cross-cultural discovery. By linking language acquisition with authentic cultural contexts through gamified experiences, Kahoot! enables primary students to engage meaningfully with global diversity, breaking free from traditional textbook limitations.

This experiential learning framework nurtures deeper intercultural understanding and prepares students for active global citizenship. The platform aligns with contemporary educational philosophies that view language learning as an essential avenue for developing both linguistic competence and a global perspective from an early age.

Challenges and Implementation Considerations

Despite its educational benefits, Kahoot! presents notable implementation challenges. The platform's competitive and time-pressured nature may disadvantage students who require additional processing time or who experience discomfort with public performance expectations. This can lead to anxiety rather than optimal learning conditions (Bhuana, 2022). Additionally, technological disparities—such as unequal access to devices and reliable internet—can limit the effectiveness of Kahoot! in resource-constrained environments, creating barriers to equitable participation (Eva et al., 2020; Sianturi & Hung, 2022).

To address these challenges, researchers propose several strategic adaptations: incorporating team-based participation models to reduce individual pressure, extending response times to accommodate diverse processing speeds, and implementing graduated difficulty levels to ensure engagement for all students, regardless of initial proficiency (Aidoune et al., 2022). Furthermore, successful implementation of Kahoot! requires comprehensive teacher preparation and ongoing professional development to maximize its pedagogical impact (Puetate Medina, 2025). Educators must develop facilitation skills as intercultural mediators, guiding students toward critical reflection and active engagement with diverse perspectives, while managing group dynamics effectively.

Synthesis and Implications

When implemented with culturally responsive instructional design principles, Kahoot! transcends mere engagement and becomes a transformative educational tool. In primary education, it provides appropriate motivation to integrate language learning with intercultural competence development through scaffolded experiences. With thoughtful pedagogical facilitation, Kahoot! fosters intellectual curiosity, promotes inclusive learning environments, and cultivates the analytical skills necessary for meaningful participation in our diverse global community.

METHODOLOGY

Context

In Japan, the primary focus of this chapter, the Ministry of Education, Culture, Sports, Science, and Technology (MEXT) has been promoting reforms in primary school English education in response to globalization. Following the 2020 revision of the national Course of Study, English became a compulsory subject for fifth and sixth graders, and mandatory instruction was introduced for third and fourth graders. The revised curriculum emphasizes foundational communicative competence across the four language skills (listening, speaking, reading, and writing), intercultural understanding, and autonomous, respectful communication (MEXT, 2018).

To support these objectives, MEXT advocates the integration of Information and Communication Technology (ICT), acknowledging Japan's lag behind OECD countries in educational digitalization (OECD, 2019). The Course of Study recommends the use of audiovisual materials, computers, and communication networks to increase student engagement and promote language acquisition (MEXT, 2020). ICT is positioned as a tool to enable individualized learning and enrich language activities.

The COVID-19 pandemic accelerated the need for digital learning, revealing disparities in device access and digital literacy between urban and rural areas, as well as among socioeconomically disadvantaged groups (Fu et al., 2023; Pettalongi et al., 2024). In response, MEXT launched the GIGA School Program in 2019, which was rapidly expanded during the pandemic. The program provided one device per student nationwide and promoted the adoption of cloud-based platforms and digital textbooks, influencing English education as well (MEXT, 2022).

The introduction of ICT aligns well with primary students' visual and interactive learning styles, broadening the scope of English instruction. Many teachers have integrated ICT tools that suit their teaching styles (Lim, 2023). However, a gap remains between device availability and effective classroom use. According to a 2023 MEXT survey, only about 30% of primary school teachers regularly incorporate ICT into daily lessons. Key barriers include insufficient professional development, low confidence in digital pedagogy, and limited preparation time, compounded by regional disparities in infrastructure and school leadership (Yoshioka, 2024).

Amid these circumstances, accessible and engaging ICT tools like Kahoot! have attracted attention as practical means to advance English education in line with the goals of the GIGA School Program.

Research Design

This study employed a qualitative exploratory case study approach to examine the effects of gamified digital tools on intercultural understanding and language learning in primary education. An analytical framework was established to allow multifaceted analysis.

To address Research Question 1 (RQ1), open-ended questionnaire responses from students were analyzed to clarify the types of experiences and perceptions they gained. For Research Question 2 (RQ2), descriptions related to cultural awareness were extracted from student responses and thematically categorized to investigate the depth and patterns of intercultural understanding. For Research Question 3 (RQ3), interviews with teachers were conducted and analyzed to capture their perspectives on the educational significance of student reactions and activities.

Triangulation was employed between teacher interview data and student questionnaire responses to enhance the reliability and validity of the findings. This approach enabled a comprehensive investigation of both students' subjective experiences and educational practices, exploring the potential of gamification in intercultural education.

Participants

The study involved one sixth-grade class (Class 6-5, 34 students) and their English teacher from M Elementary School, a public school in Kanagawa Prefecture, Japan. The teacher held a junior high school English teaching license, had 16 years of experience teaching at the junior high level, and 3 years at the primary level. Although her experience with educational ICT tools was limited, she had occasionally used Kahoot! in her instruction.

The students were beginner-level English learners. While they had some prior exposure to Kahoot! in regular English lessons, this was their first experience using it for international collaboration and intercultural exchange.

The original plan was to include all five sixth-grade classes at M Elementary School. However, due to scheduling conflicts at the Australian partner school—such as cancellation of Japanese classes for internal events and limited availability toward the term's end—only Class 6-5 participated in the Kahoot!-based exchange session held on November 29, 2023. The situation was explained to the other classes, who responded with understanding.

M Elementary School was selected largely because of the strong support from the school principal, whose approval was instrumental in facilitating the project. Informed consent was obtained from all participating students' guardians after providing a detailed explanation of the exchange's purpose and procedures.

The partner group consisted of 22 fifth-grade students (ages 10–11) from T Primary School in Victoria, Australia. These students were beginner learners of Japanese, and their teacher, a specialist in Japanese language education, regularly incorporated digital tools into instruction. T Primary School joined the project following approval by the school principal and parental consent.

IMPLEMENTATION PROCEDURES

Project Overview and Objectives

This project was a collaborative initiative between primary school teachers in Japan and Australia, who jointly designed and implemented a real-time intercultural quiz activity using the online platform Kahoot!. The primary objective of the project was to promote intercultural understanding and mutual awareness among students through interactive and participatory learning experiences.

Planning Meetings

Two planning meetings were held in advance of the quiz implementation. The first meeting, conducted via Zoom on September 13, 2023, involved teachers from both countries reviewing their respective academic calendars and class schedules. This session was dedicated to identifying a mutually suitable timeframe and coordinating the proposed dates for the quiz activity.

The second meeting took place online on November 1, 2023, and focused on the development of the Kahoot! quiz. A total of 20 questions were finalized—10 relating to Japan and 10 to Australia. The questions were carefully designed to reflect themes that were both familiar and engaging to primary school students, including school life, cultural traditions, leisure activities, and food culture. To ensure accessibility and foster equitable participation across both countries, all questions were presented bilingually in Japanese and English.

The content of the quiz was culturally relevant and relatable to the participating students. Questions related to Japan included the number of classes at M Elementary School, the number of xylophones and metallophones in the music room, information about textbooks, the principal's hobbies, and popular school lunches. Conversely, questions pertaining to Australia focused on the lunch menu at T Primary School, school uniform colors, traditional foods, Japanese-related learning activities, and the cities in Japan that the Australian principal had visited.

Figures 1 and 2 illustrate examples of the Kahoot! quiz interface as it appeared in classrooms in both countries. A complete list of quiz items is provided in Appendix 1.

Figure 1. Example of a Kahoot! quiz screen about M Elementary School

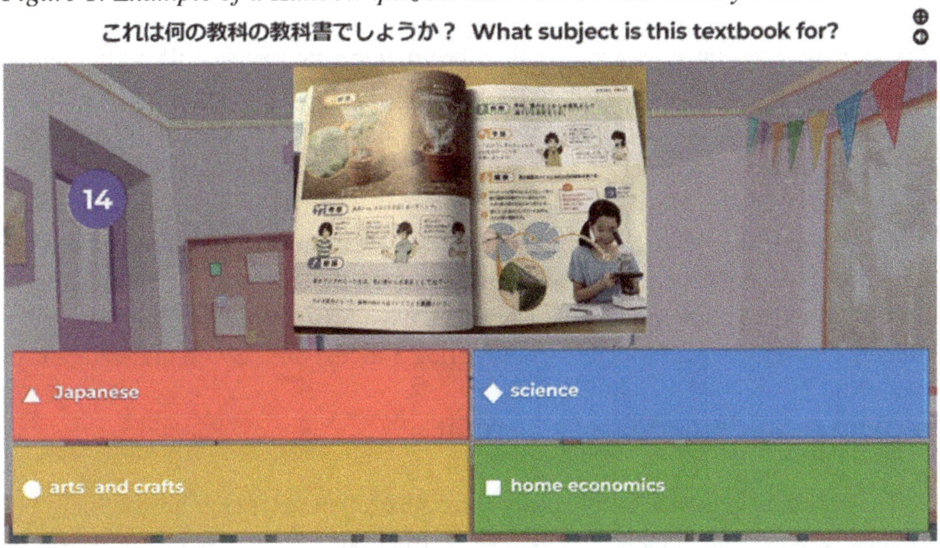

Figure 2. Example of a Kahoot! quiz screen about T Primary School

Quiz Implementation Plan and Revisions

Originally, the quiz was intended to be implemented across all participating classes, with four classes scheduled for November 27 and one class for November 29. However, due to a school event on the Australian side, the sessions planned for November 27 were canceled. As a result, only one sixth-grade class (Class 5) was able to participate on November 29.

An attempt was made to reschedule the quiz sessions in December. However, the Australian school was approaching the end of the academic term, making it difficult to secure class time for Japanese language instruction. The students in the affected classes were informed of the situation and responded with understanding.

Implementation and Game Format

The Kahoot! quiz was facilitated by the Australian teacher, who routinely integrates Kahoot! into Japanese language instruction. On the day of the quiz, the teacher independently selected the "Cosmic Conquest" game mode to enhance student engagement and support collaborative learning. In this format, participants earn blocks by answering questions correctly, working in teams to build the tallest tower. The game structure promotes cooperation and reinforces learning through playful competition.

The quiz was conducted simultaneously in both countries. Students used tablet devices to respond to questions displayed in real time on large screens in their classrooms. Working in small groups, students collaborated to select answers, with the setup emphasizing both knowledge acquisition and social interaction.

For many Japanese students, this game format was a new experience. While some initial confusion was observed, students gradually became familiar with the interface and gameplay. Ultimately, they engaged actively and completed the quiz successfully (see Figure 3).

Figure 3. Screenshot of the final game results from the Kahoot! quiz

DATA COLLECTION AND ANALYSIS

This study was conducted from a preliminary and exploratory perspective with 34 Japanese primary school students who participated in a real-time intercultural exchange activity using Kahoot!. The focus was placed on students' subjective experiences and classroom-based observations. The purpose of this study was to understand the students' perceptions and learning through the exchange activity, rather than to confirm the effectiveness of an educational intervention.

After the activity, an open-ended online questionnaire was administered to the Japanese students, consisting of the following two questions:

1. How did you feel about interacting with Australian students through the real-time Kahoot! quiz activity?
2. What did you learn through this intercultural exchange?

The free-text responses (in Japanese) were qualitatively analyzed to identify recurring themes and patterns related to students' perceptions and learning. In addition, a word cloud was created to visually represent frequently mentioned terms by the students, supplementing the overall impressions.

To deepen understanding from both educational and intercultural perspectives, semi-structured interviews were conducted with teachers from both Japan and Australia.

These interviews focused on instructional strategies, students' reactions, and reflections on the educational significance of the activity. The teachers' perspectives also played an important role in enriching the understanding of the students' subjective experiences.

By triangulating qualitative data obtained from multiple perspectives, the study aimed to enhance the depth and reliability of the analysis. However, it remains grounded in an exploratory approach. Therefore, it differs from empirical studies designed to confirm causal relationships or universal educational effects.

Due to ethical constraints, no post-activity data were collected from the Australian students, meaning direct testimonies about their intercultural experiences were not gathered. This is acknowledged as a limitation of the study, which is further discussed in the "Limitations and Future Directions" section. However, insights were supplemented through the observations of the Australian teacher.

RESULTS AND DISCUSSION

RQ1: What are Japanese primary school students' perceptions of interacting with Australian peers in a real-time Kahoot! quiz?

Table 1 presents words with frequencies of 3 or higher, extracted from feedback on students' perceptions of the Kahoot! quiz match. Each entry in the table indicates the number of times the word appeared in the feedback, offering insights into recurring themes. Additionally, Figure 4 displays a word cloud that includes all words identified in the feedback, including those featured in Table 1. The size of each word reflects its frequency, providing a visual summary of potential key themes and patterns.

Table 1. Word frequency in Japanese students' perceptions of the Kahoot! quiz match

Rank	Word	Frequency
1	fun	15
2	understand	12
3	learn(ed)	6
4	quiz	6
5	lot	5

continued on following page

Table 1. Continued

Rank	Word	Frequency
6	rules	5
7	able	4
8	played	4
9	really	4
10	know	4
11	cooperate	3

Figure 4. Word cloud representation of Japanese students' perceptions of the Kahoot! quiz match

Both the table and the word cloud suggest that many students responded positively to participating in the real-time quiz game with Australian students via Kahoot!. In particular, regarding emotional engagement and enjoyment, the most frequently used term, 'fun' (n=15), indicates that a significant number of students may have perceived the cross-cultural quiz match as an enjoyable experience. This positive affect might have contributed to lowering social and linguistic barriers, possibly making it easier for students to approach their Australian peers with greater openness and enthusiasm.

The Japanese teacher reported that "many children smiled and said, 'I want to do it again' and 'I want to learn more about Australia,'" suggesting that the activity had a strong emotional impact. In addition, it was observed that even after the quiz ended, the children continued to talk about Australian children, suggesting that the learning activity was not a one-time event but rather something that encouraged continued interest.

In terms of teamwork, the term 'cooperate' (n=3) suggests that some students recognized the value of collaboration, either within their own group or with their Australian peers. This aligns with broader cultural and educational values in Japan, where group harmony and cooperation are often emphasized (Sato, 2003). Its appearance in the feedback implies that the quiz match, although competitive, was also interpreted by some students as a shared activity that encouraged working together to understand questions and engage with peers' ideas.

Sample comments from the students further illustrate this:

"It was fun because I was able to cooperate with my friends and learn about the classes at T Primary School in Australia through the quiz."

"Through the quiz match, I felt like I was able to cooperate with people from T Primary School who were on the same team."

This collaborative attitude was also observed among Japanese teachers, who reported that exchanges such as "What does this mean?" and "How should I answer?" occurred naturally. This demonstrates mutual support among children and a sense of unity within the group.

In relation to engagement and knowledge construction, the frequent use of terms such as 'understand' (n=12), 'learn(ed)' (n=6), and 'know' (n=4) points to the cognitive aspects of the students' experience. These terms suggest that students saw the activity as not only enjoyable but also educational. Many appeared to treat the quiz as an opportunity to gain new information or deepen their understanding. This blend of enjoyment and intellectual engagement is consistent with the goals of meaningful intercultural exchanges, where enjoyment and learning work together to support sustained interest in cross-cultural communication. This may provide supporting evidence that Kahoot! has the potential to promote meaningful interactions in international educational contexts (Almusharraf, 2023).

Sample comments from the students include:

"I enjoyed solving the quiz while learning the differences between our school and T Primary School."

"It was good to learn about the differences between Japan and other countries in a fun way."

These findings tentatively suggest that Kahoot! may have the potential to enhance student motivation and engagement, a possibility also indicated in previous studies (e.g., Wang & Tahir, 2020).

The frequent appearance of the word "understand" (n=12), together with "rules" (n=5), may suggest that some students experienced difficulties in grasping the mechanics and structure of the activity. These difficulties might have arisen from limited familiarity with the Kahoot! platform or the specific settings applied during the quiz session.

Representative student comments indicating such issues include:

"I did not understand much, but it was fun. I want to do it again."

"I did not really understand the rules, but it was fun. Next time, I would like to know the rules a little better before doing it again."

While student responses were generally positive, these remarks indicate that unfamiliarity with the rules may have constrained some learners' ability to fully engage with the activity. This appears to have been particularly relevant for those encountering Kahoot!'s newer game format for the first time, who may have found it challenging to follow the flow and procedures of the task. In addition, the platform's competitive and time-sensitive nature could potentially disadvantage learners who require more time for cognitive processing or who experience anxiety in real-time performance contexts, which may hinder rather than support learning (Bhuana, 2022). These considerations highlight the importance of designing intercultural learning activities incorporating digital tools with careful attention to the diverse cognitive and affective needs of learners, in order to enhance their educational impact.

RQ2: What cultural insights do Japanese students gain from participating in this international quiz exchange?

Table 2. Word frequency in Japanese students' insights from the quiz match

Rank	Word	Frequency
1	Australian	7
2	thought	6
3	people	6
4	classes	5
5	know	5
6	impressed	4
7	fun	4
8	learned	4
9	Japan	4
10	everyone	3
11	cheerful	3
12	Japanese	3
13	food	3

continued on following page

Table 2. Continued

Rank	Word	Frequency
14	different	3
15	looked	3
16	made	3
17	surprised	3
18	see	3
19	big	3
20	quiz	3

Figure 5. Word cloud representation of Japanese students' insights gained through the Kahoot! quiz match

Table 2 presents words that appeared three or more times in Japanese students' reflections on the Kahoot! quiz match. These frequently occurring terms offer insight into the kinds of knowledge and impressions students gained during the intercultural activity. Figure 5 complements this data by providing a word cloud that includes all words found in the feedback, including those listed in Table 2. The size of each word in the cloud reflects its frequency, visually illustrating key areas of focus in student responses.

Among all terms, the most frequently used word was "Australian" (n=7), suggesting that students frequently referred to the nationality of their peers and, by extension, reflected on their cultural context. This indicates that the quiz match may have stimulated students' curiosity about Australian schools, people, and educational practices, extending beyond the quiz mechanics themselves.

This tendency is reflected in comments such as:

"I learned things I didn't know about Australian schools."

"I remember the Australian children were excited about the quiz."

These cultural insights aligned with the teachers' observations. For instance, the Japanese teacher reported hearing students make comments such as, "In Japan, it's like this, but in Australia, it's like that." This suggests that the students were beginning to develop a greater awareness of their own culture.

In addition, words such as "thought" (n=6), "impressed" (n=4), and "surprised" (n=3) appeared with relative frequency. This suggests that students were not merely acquiring information, but were also engaging in a degree of reflection. These expressions indicate both cognitive and emotional engagement, implying that students may have compared their observations with personal experiences, expressed admiration or surprise, and begun to internalize aspects of what they encountered. Such reflective engagement is widely regarded as a key component of intercultural learning.

The following student comments illustrate this reflective depth:

"I was surprised that they could choose their lunch!"

"They also studied Japanese stories, so they made an impression on me."

"There were all sorts of lunch menus, and they looked delicious. I thought I wanted to try some."

Interestingly, words such as "Japan" (n=4) and "Japanese" (n=3) also appeared relatively frequently. When considered alongside "Australian" and "different" (n=3), this suggests that students engaged in comparative thinking. By contrasting Australian food, education, and behavior with their own experiences, students were possibly able to identify what is culturally specific versus more universal. Recognizing that "Australian" experiences were "different" may have encouraged them to examine their own cultural assumptions and appreciate diversity.

The following examples reflect this comparative awareness:

"It was easier to remember because I learned through the quiz that it was different from Japan."

"Japanese food had also reached Australia."

Overall, the most frequently used words point to students' awareness of and reflection on specific aspects of Australian culture and school life. The presence of emotionally and cognitively charged words—such as "thought", "impressed", and "surprised"—along with comparative markers like "Japan" and "different", suggests that students engaged with the content on more than a superficial level. Their responses appear to reflect both intellectual and emotional involvement, contributing to a deeper understanding of cultural difference and similarity.

These findings suggest that Japanese primary school students may not only have acquired factual knowledge through the Kahoot! quiz activity, but also engaged in a potentially meaningful intercultural learning experience. Such a possibility could be attributed to the interactive and participatory nature of the format, which has been associated with increased learner motivation and engagement (Kaur & Nadarajan, 2020). In addition, the results appear to align with previous research indicating that digital tools may support the development of intercultural competencies and global awareness (Plump & LaRosa, 2017). Furthermore, the competitive and game-based elements of the activity may have played a role in fostering learners' interest and focus, thereby potentially contributing to improved learning outcomes (Ebadi et al., 2023). However, it is also important to note that such effects may vary depending on individual learner characteristics and the specific design of the activity, and therefore warrant careful consideration.

While the primary analysis in this study focused on the experiences and perceptions of Japanese students, it is also important to consider how the activity may have been perceived by their Australian counterparts. Although the analysis was limited to Japanese participants, the study was conducted in the context of a bilateral exchange. To gain a more multifaceted understanding of intercultural learning, supplementary insights from the Australian teacher are introduced.

According to the teacher, participating in the quiz appeared to encourage Australian students to reflect on their own culture from a new perspective. Some of the quiz questions were reportedly challenging even for the local students, prompting them to realize that, although they believed they were familiar with their own country, there were many things they had not previously considered. In contrast, when questions related to Australian culture appeared, students were observed to respond with a sense of pride, which may have contributed to the reaffirmation of their cultural identity.

The teacher also noted the effectiveness of visual materials embedded in the quiz, particularly photographs. These visuals, especially those related to Japan, were reported to support comprehension and enhance student engagement.

Moreover, the real-time connection with a school in Japan was perceived by students as a unique and memorable experience. This element of direct intercultural interaction appeared to stimulate their curiosity about other cultures and prompted spontaneous questions and reactions regarding Japan. Additionally, the appearance of their own school principal in the quiz reportedly strengthened students' sense of personal relevance and familiarity, contributing to positive emotional responses such as enjoyment and curiosity.

These observations suggest that the project may have served not only as an enjoyable and meaningful intercultural learning experience for Japanese students, but also for Australian students. Although Australian learners were not the primary focus of analysis, these insights indicate the activity may have had cognitive and affective impacts on both sides, offering valuable implications for the design of future international collaborative learning initiatives.

RQ3: What challenges and opportunities do educators encounter when using Kahoot! to support intercultural language learning in primary classrooms?

Scheduling and Logistical Constraints

Teachers from both schools reported challenges in coordinating real-time sessions due to differing timetables and administrative structures. Despite the minimal time difference between Japan and Australia, organizing live sessions across two distinct school systems required compromise, often resulting in limited time for preparation and reflection.

These constraints were not merely technical but also pedagogical. Educators felt students would have benefited from more structured pre- and post-activity sessions to better contextualize and reflect on their experiences.

Uneven Familiarity with Technology

A noticeable disparity in digital literacy emerged between the two student groups. Australian students, accustomed to using Kahoot!, were confident from the outset. In contrast, Japanese students were unfamiliar with the platform and initially found the activity confusing.

Teachers emphasized the importance of scaffolded digital preparation, such as practice rounds and visual guides. While the initial confusion posed a challenge, students adapted with peer support and bilingual materials—highlighting how thoughtful design and instructional support can significantly enhance participation.

Institutional Support and Sustainability

The project's success was largely due to strong support from school principals, who provided formal approval, facilitated parent communication, and helped coordinate logistics. Teachers acknowledged that without this administrative backing, implementation would have been extremely difficult.

They also agreed that for such initiatives to be sustainable, institutional recognition of the educational value of intercultural learning is essential. The project thrived under leadership that saw the exchange not only as a tool for language development but also as a gateway to broader global education.

LIMITATIONS AND FUTURE DIRECTIONS

This study provides preliminary insights into the use of game-based digital platforms—specifically Kahoot!—for promoting intercultural interaction and language learning in primary education. However, several methodological limitations must be acknowledged, as they constrain the interpretability and generalizability of the findings.

Limited Sample and Contextual Scope

The research was conducted with a small, homogeneous sample of 34 students from a single Japanese primary school. The limited demographic and geographic diversity restricts the extent to which findings can be generalized to other educational settings. Future studies should include larger, more diverse samples to capture broader patterns of learner response.

Absence of a Control or Comparison Group

A major limitation of this study is the lack of an experimental control group or alternative comparison condition. Without a baseline or reference group, it is not possible to attribute observed outcomes directly to the Kahoot!-based activity. As a result, causal inferences are limited, and any claims regarding effectiveness must be interpreted with caution. Future research should adopt experimental or quasi-experimental designs that incorporate control groups to better assess intervention effects.

Limited Validity of the Motivation Measurement

The study relied on two open-ended questions to explore students' motivational responses. While these responses offered valuable qualitative insights, the absence of a validated, structured measurement instrument weakens the evidential strength of the findings. Specifically, established motivation scales such as the Intrinsic Motivation Inventory (IMI) or the Academic Motivation Scale (AMS), commonly used in related research, were not employed. As a result, the reliability and construct validity of the motivational data remain uncertain. Future research should incorporate such standardized instruments or adopt a mixed-methods approach that combines qualitative responses with validated quantitative measures to enable a more robust and triangulated assessment of learner engagement.

Low Intensity of the Intervention

The intervention consisted of a single Kahoot! session, which limits the depth of engagement and the ability to assess sustained or cumulative effects. Although short-term emotional and cognitive engagement was observed, a one-time activity does not provide sufficient basis for evaluating long-term gains in language acquisition or intercultural competence. Longitudinal or repeated-session designs are recommended to capture developmental changes over time.

Asymmetry in Data Collection

While the exchange involved students from both Japan and Australia, data were collected only from the Japanese participants. Due to ethical constraints, no data were gathered from the Australian side. This limits the study's capacity to offer a reciprocal understanding of the exchange experience. Future studies should obtain appropriate ethical clearance in advance to allow for balanced, cross-cultural data collection and analysis.

Taken together, these limitations underscore the exploratory nature of the present study. They highlight critical areas for refinement in future research, including more rigorous design, validated measurement tools, and sustained interventions across diverse contexts.

CONCLUSION

This study explored the potential of Kahoot!, a game-based digital tool, to support intercultural engagement and language learning in Japanese primary education. The findings indicate that even a short, well-designed session can stimulate emotional, cognitive, and cultural interest among young learners.

Rather than aiming to verify the instructional effectiveness of Kahoot!, this study sought to present practical insights derived from students' subjective learning experiences and classroom observations. By focusing on emotional responses, patterns of engagement, and the emergence of intercultural awareness, the study offers an exploratory perspective on the educational value of game-based activities.

The results support the importance of fostering understanding and acceptance of cultural diversity in primary education, and suggest that culturally responsive, gamified activities can contribute to this goal. While the scope and duration of the study were limited, the findings indicate that playful digital environments may serve as meaningful entry points for cultivating global awareness and empathy in young learners.

Future research is needed to examine how such tools can systematically contribute to the development of intercultural competence. This includes the use of more rigorous research designs, reliable and valid assessment tools, and longitudinal interventions across diverse educational contexts. This study offers a foundation for such efforts and highlights key considerations for subsequent applied research in this field.

REFERENCES

Aibar-Almazán, A., Castellote-Caballero, Y., Carcelén-Fraile, M. C., Rivas-Campo, Y., & González-Martín, A. M. (2024). Gamification in the classroom: Kahoot! as a tool for university teaching innovation. *Frontiers in Psychology, 15*, 1370084. Advance online publication. DOI: 10.3389/fpsyg.2024.1370084 PMID: 38646120

Aidoune, Y., Nordin, N. R., Kaur, M., & Singh, P. S. (2022). Effect of online English learning game 'Kahoot' on L2 undergraduate learners in a Malaysian university. *Journal of Intercultural Communication, 22*(3), 13–18. DOI: 10.36923/jicc.v22i3.66

Almusharraf, N. (2023). Incorporation of a game-based approach into the EFL online classrooms: Students' perceptions. *Interactive Learning Environments, 31*(7), 4440–4453. DOI: 10.1080/10494820.2021.1969953

Anane, C. (2024). Impact of a game-based tool on student engagement in a foreign language course: A three-term analysis. *Frontiers in Education, 9*, 1430729. Advance online publication. DOI: 10.3389/feduc.2024.1430729

Bhuana, G. P. (2022). The benefits and drawbacks of Kahoot: Students' perspective. *Journal on English Language Teaching and Learning Linguistics and Literature, 10*(2), 2224–2232. DOI: 10.24256/ideas.v10i2.3508

Casanova-Mata, I. (2023). Enhancing English acquisition: Effects of Among Us game-based gamification on language competence, motivation, attention, and attitude towards the English subject. *Education Sciences, 13*(11), 1094. Advance online publication. DOI: 10.3390/educsci13111094

Cátia Sofia, S., Silva, M. P., & Martins, M. L. (2022). The impact of Kahoot! on vocabulary acquisition in foreign language education. *Educational Research and Development Journal, 20*(4), 142–158.

Ebadi, S., Rasouli, R., & Mohamadi, M. (2023). Exploring EFL learners' perspectives on using Kahoot as a game-based student response system. *Interactive Learning Environments, 31*(4), 2338–2350. DOI: 10.1080/10494820.2021.1881798

Eva, K., Adnyani, K., Adnyana, W., & Murniasih, N. N. (2020). Teacher and students' perception on using Kahoot! for English learning. In *Proceedings of the 3rd International Conference on Innovative Research Across Disciplines (ICIRAD 2019)*. Atlantis Press.

Fu, L., Zeng, Y., & Kang, X. (2023). Bridging the urban–rural gap: A qualitative examination of perceived access, barriers, risks and opportunities of children's digital learning during the COVID-19 pandemic. *Child & Family Social Work, 28*(4), 1023–1035. DOI: 10.1111/cfs.13045

Kalleny, N. K. (2020). Advantages of Kahoot! game-based formative assessments along with methods of its use and application during the COVID-19 pandemic in various live learning sessions. *Journal of Microscopy and Ultrastructure, 8*(4), 175–185. DOI: 10.4103/JMAU.JMAU_61_20 PMID: 33623744

Kaur, G. (2020). Enhancing classroom engagement with Kahoot! in language education. *Asian Journal of Educational Technology, 5*(1), 34–47.

Kaur, P., & Nadarajan, R. (2020). Language learning and teaching using Kahoot! *International Journal of Medical Education, 2*(5), 19–28. DOI: 10.35631/IJMOE.25003

Lim, S. (2023). Junior high school teachers' perspectives on integrating computers in lessons. *JALT Post Conference Publication, 2022*(1), 1. DOI: 10.37546/JALTPCP2022-03

Low, D. H., & Yamat, H. (2022). The use of Kahoot and its role in improving irregular verbs learning among primary ESL learners. *International Journal of Academic Research in Progressive Education and Development, 11*(2). Advance online publication. DOI: 10.6007/IJARPED/v11-i2/13358

Ministry of Education. Culture, Sports, Science and Technology (MEXT). (2018). *Shin gakusyuu shidouyourou ni tsuite: Manabi no naiyou-henkaku ni tsuite* [New Courses of Study: enrichment and transformation of learning content]. https://www.mext.go.jp/b_menu/shingi/chousa/shisetu/044/shiryo/__icsFiles/afieldfile/2018/07/09/1405957_003.pdf

Ministry of Education. Culture, Sports, Science and Technology (MEXT). (2020). *Gaikokugo no shidou niokeru ICT no katsuyou nitsuite* [The use of ICT in teaching foreign languages]. https://www.mext.go.jp/content/20200911-mxt_jogai01-000009772_13.pdf

Ministry of Education. Culture, Sports, Science and Technology (MEXY). (2022). *GIGA sukuuru no saishin no jyoukyou nituite* [Update on the GIGA School initiative]. https://www.mext.go.jp/kaigisiryo/content/20210319-mxt_syoto01-000013552_02.pdf

Nasution, D. K. (2024). Culturally responsive teaching approach by using Kahoot in teaching English. *INSIS Journal, 4*(1), 903–912.

Neureiter, D., Klieser, E., Neumayer, B., Winkelmann, P., Urbas, R., & Kiesslich, T. (2020). Feasibility of Kahoot! as a real-time assessment tool in (Histo-)pathology classroom teaching. *Advances in Medical Education and Practice, 11*, 695–705. DOI: 10.2147/AMEP.S264821 PMID: 33117039

Nikolić, J., Nikolić, J., Gajić, T., & Gagić, A. (2022). The use of Kahoot! in foreign language teaching. In *Sinteza 2022 – International Scientific Conference on Information Technology and Data Related Research* (pp. 347–352). DOI: 10.15308/Sinteza-2022-347-352

Organization for Economic Co-operation and Development (OECD). (2019). *TALIS 2018 results (Volume I): Teachers and school leaders as lifelong learners*. OECD publishing. DOI: 10.1787/1d0bc92a-en

Özdemir, O. (2024). Kahoot! game-based digital learning platform: A comprehensive meta-analysis. *Journal of Computer Assisted Learning, 41*(1), 118–141. DOI: 10.1111/jcal.13084

Pettalongi, S. S., Londol, M. M., & Umboh, S. E. (2024). Disparities in digital education: Socioeconomic barriers to accessing online learning resources. *International Journal of Social and Human Sciences, 5*(2), 145–162. DOI: 10.59613/be6gdv98

Plump, C. M., & LaRosa, J. (2017). Using Kahoot! in the classroom to create engagement and active learning: A game-based technology solution for eLearning novices. *Management Teaching Review, 2*(2), 151–158. DOI: 10.1177/2379298116689783

Prathyusha, N. (2020). Role of gamification in language learning. *International Journal of Research and Analytical Reviews, 7*(2), 577–583.

Puetate Medina, E. E., Castillo Martínez, C. P., & Méndez Ortega, M. G. (2025). *Kahoot para la enseñanza del idioma inglés* [Use of Kahoot for teaching the English language]. SATHIRI., DOI: 10.32645/13906925.1363

Sato, N. (2003). *Inside Japanese classrooms: The heart of education*. Routledge., DOI: 10.4324/9780203465707

Sianturi, A. D., & Hung, R. (2022). The challenges of using Kahoot! in teaching and learning in higher education: A systematic review. In *Proceedings of the 6th International Conference on Digital Technology in Education (ICDTE '22)* (pp. 72–77). ACM. DOI: 10.1145/3568739.3568753

Tan, D. A. L., Lee, B. C., Ganapathy, M., & Kasuma, S. A. A. (2022). Language learning in the 21st century: Malaysian ESL students' perceptions of Kahoot! In *Research anthology on developments in gamification and game-based learning* (pp. 802–820). IGI Global., DOI: 10.4018/978-1-6684-3710-0.ch036

Wang, A. I., & Tahir, R. (2020). The effect of using Kahoot! for learning – A literature review. *Computers & Education*, *149*, 103818. Advance online publication. DOI: 10.1016/j.compedu.2020.103818

Yoshioka, S. (2024, February 16). FOCUS: Digitalization drive proving tough for Japanese school teachers. *Kyodo News*.

Chapter 7
Bridging Cultures Through EdTech:
Integrating Cultural Approaches in Online Learning

Mustafa Kayyali
https://orcid.org/0000-0003-3300-262X
Maaref University of Applied Sciences, Syria

ABSTRACT

As education becomes increasingly digitized, the imperative to integrate multicultural perspectives into online learning environments grows more urgent. This chapter explores how culturally responsive approaches can bridge divides, affirm identities, and foster inclusivity within digital classrooms. Drawing from global case studies and theoretical insights, it examines how educational technologies can either perpetuate cultural erasure or serve as transformative tools for intercultural understanding. The chapter highlights best practices in designing inclusive EdTech platforms, identifies common challenges in cross-cultural integration, and proposes frameworks for equitable digital transformation. Ultimately, it calls for an intentional reimagining of online education—one that values cultural diversity not as an afterthought, but as a foundation for global learning.

INTRODUCTION

We live in an era of unparalleled connectivity, where classrooms are no longer confined by walls or governed solely by geography. A student in Nairobi can collaborate with a peer in Seoul, attend a lecture delivered from Toronto, and submit an assignment to a professor in Berlin—all before the sun sets. This digital fluidity,

DOI: 10.4018/979-8-3373-3673-2.ch007

while awe-inspiring in scope, comes with a subtle paradox: as we bring learners together from all corners of the world, the underlying cultural architectures that shape their identities, ways of learning, and perceptions of knowledge often remain ignored, diluted, or misunderstood.

The growing dominance of online education and educational technologies (EdTech) has opened unprecedented access to learning (Ravichandran et al, 2024). But access, we must remind ourselves, is not the same as inclusion. The implicit cultural codes embedded within online learning platforms, pedagogical tools, and course structures are frequently Western-centric, privileging certain modes of expression, interaction, and comprehension while inadvertently marginalizing others. This phenomenon isn't necessarily malicious—rather, it reflects a long-standing pattern in global education systems where dominant paradigms overshadow local epistemologies.

In this evolving educational terrain, the call for a multicultural approach to EdTech is not simply a matter of representation—it is a matter of justice (Marcovitz, 2022). It is about validating diverse knowledge systems, honoring indigenous ways of knowing, creating space for multiple languages and dialects, and recognizing the subtle ways culture informs learning behaviors, expectations, and cognitive patterns. Cultural mismatch in educational design—particularly in virtual spaces—can result in disengagement, miscommunication, and the erosion of learner confidence.

Multiculturalism in education is not a new idea, but its translation into digital environments has been clumsy and often superficial (Starkey, 2021). Tokenistic gestures—such as using stock images of "diverse" learners or including international case studies—do little to change the structural inequities woven into the design of EdTech systems. What's needed is a fundamental shift: a reengineering of digital learning environments that does not merely accommodate cultural difference but is *built upon* it.

This chapter seeks to navigate that very terrain. It asks: What does it mean to design and deliver online learning in a way that truly integrates multicultural values and practices? How can educators, technologists, and policymakers ensure that digital learning does not become another site of cultural imperialism, but rather a meeting place for dialogue, empathy, and mutual recognition?

To answer these questions, we must go beyond surface-level acknowledgments of diversity and delve into the deeper work of designing inclusive pedagogies, technologies, and systems. The journey is not straightforward. It is complex, fraught with contradictions, and inevitably incomplete. But it is also necessary—because the digital future of education must be one in which *every learner sees themselves reflected, respected, and empowered.*

Rethinking Digital Learning Through a Multicultural Lens

There's a strange kind of irony in the global village we've built. We boast of connectedness, of reaching across time zones with a click, of shattering the boundaries that once kept us locked inside our national silos. And yet, even as fiber optic cables stretch across oceans and learning management systems reach the furthest classroom corners, we still struggle with the most human of challenges: understanding one another (Bergreen, 2023). Not in a technical sense—translation apps are dime a dozen—but in a deeper, more visceral way. In how we think. In how we learn. In how we see the world.

Digital learning, in all its promise, has moved fast—perhaps too fast for its own good. It sprinted ahead, galvanized by the pandemic, propelled by innovation, encouraged by a tech-driven optimism that rarely paused to ask: *Whose knowledge are we privileging here? Whose voice echoes loudest in this space?* And just as importantly, *who has been quietly muted?*

To rethink digital learning through a multicultural lens is not to tear down what's been built, but to walk slowly through it. To look closer. To notice. The architecture of most EdTech systems is slick, intuitive, efficient (Dron, 2022). But it's also steeped in assumptions—about what engagement looks like, what participation means, what "good learning" feels like. A classroom chat box might reward quick replies, but what if, culturally, silence isn't absence, but reflection? A timed quiz might measure knowledge retention, but what if the student learned the concept through oral storytelling, where rhythm and cadence matter more than multiple choice?

Multiculturalism isn't a decorative flourish to sprinkle into digital design (Feiyu, 2024). It's not about adding a few ethnic-sounding names to a database or slapping a flag icon next to a language option. It's about deconstructing the very scaffolding of what we think education should be—and rebuilding it with cultural humility (Paul et al, 2025). And here lies the crux of the challenge: it's much easier to build for efficiency than for equity. Algorithms can optimize for speed, but not for empathy. Code can execute, but it can't intuit what a child from a war-torn village carries into a virtual classroom on a Monday morning.

Consider how knowledge itself is structured in most digital platforms. Linear modules, standardized rubrics, Western academic citation systems—all echo a particular worldview (Luzón & Pérez-Llantada, 2022). A worldview that champions objectivity, compartmentalization, and hierarchy. But many cultures don't divide knowledge into silos. In indigenous knowledge systems, for instance, learning is often circular, interwoven with nature, community, and memory. Elders, not textbooks, are the repositories of truth. Lessons aren't measured in quizzes, but in the ability to apply wisdom during ceremony, harvest, or healing. How does that translate to a Coursera course or a Zoom call?

This isn't to say we must abandon structure. Structure is not the enemy. But we must ask: *Whose structure?* Whose cultural DNA underpins the platforms we use, the metrics we uphold, the pedagogies we replicate? If we're honest, the answers can be uncomfortable (Pronzato, 2023). Much of global EdTech is still tethered to a colonial legacy, repackaged with modern UX design and slick branding (Koole et al, 2024). The tools are new, but the epistemic dominance remains.

Now, I realize some may argue that technology, by nature, demands standardization. That scalability requires common formats, shared languages, unified systems (Gorton, 2022). That's true—to a point. But cultural nuance isn't the enemy of scalability; it's the precondition for meaningful scalability. A platform that works for ten million users but fails to engage their cultural realities has scale without substance. It's like building a bridge that spans continents but cracks under the weight of real, lived experience.

Let's ground this in something tangible. Picture an online course on environmental science delivered globally. The content might include climate models, sustainability principles, carbon emission metrics. All valid. All important. But what if a student from the Pacific Islands asks why the curriculum doesn't mention traditional ecological knowledge—how her ancestors read ocean currents, predicted typhoons, or planted by the lunar calendar? Or a student from the Sahel wonders why the course never addresses desert farming practices passed down orally through generations. These aren't fringe examples. They are realities. And when digital learning excludes them, it's not neutral. It's an act of epistemic violence.

Then there's language. Oh, language. The invisible gatekeeper. Most digital learning takes place in English—not because it's inherently superior, but because of historical dominance, economic positioning, and technological inertia (Marandi, 2024). But language is never just a tool—it's a vessel for worldview. When a student learns in a second or third language, they are often forced to translate not just words, but worldviews. Nuances vanish. Humor gets lost. Emotions become harder to articulate. And slowly, subtly, the learner starts to feel that their way of thinking—of *being*—doesn't quite belong in the learning space.

To counter this, some platforms now offer multilingual support. That's a start. But real inclusion means going beyond translation. It means allowing learners to *create* content in their own languages, to engage in discourse that values dialects, to use metaphors and expressions rooted in their cultures. It means decentering English—not discarding it, but no longer treating it as the sun around which all other tongues must orbit.

There's also the question of interaction. Participation in online learning is often measured by how often a student speaks up, contributes to forums, asks questions (Du et al, 2022). But in some cultures, speaking out—especially against authority—is discouraged. Respect is shown through attentive listening, not verbal interjection.

In others, learning is communal, not competitive. The self is not the center. Success is measured by group cohesion, not individual achievement. When EdTech systems reward only one kind of engagement, they silently penalize others. They tell students: *Your way of learning is less valid. Speak louder. Adapt. Assimilate.*

This is where culturally responsive pedagogy must enter—not as an academic theory, but as a guiding principle. Culturally responsive EdTech doesn't just *accommodate* different learners—it's *shaped* by them (Eppard et al, 2021). It allows for different pacing, different expressions of knowledge, different ways of showing understanding. It honors ceremony and silence as much as it does speed and spontaneity. And yet, even as we advocate for change, we must be careful not to romanticize culture. Not all traditions are inclusive. Some perpetuate gender bias, caste hierarchies, or ethnic exclusion. A multicultural approach must also be critical. It must make room for introspection, for questioning one's own norms, for evolving (Parameswaran et al, 2024). The goal is not to freeze culture in time but to allow it to dance with digital innovation—sometimes clashing, sometimes harmonizing, always moving.

Let me be clear: this work is messy. It doesn't come with clear templates or plug-and-play solutions. It requires co-design, not top-down implementation. It demands that EdTech developers work *with* communities, not just *for* them. It means involving local educators, linguists, elders, students. Listening. Unlearning. Iterating. And, at times, failing. But failure here is generative. It tells us where assumptions cracked. Where a universal model didn't hold. Where a one-size-fits-all solution didn't quite fit. These moments are not setbacks—they're invitations to rethink, to refine, to rebuild. We must also acknowledge that technology alone cannot solve cultural exclusion. It's a tool, not a cure. Real transformation comes when pedagogy, policy, and practice align (Røe et al, 2022). When funding models support local content creation. When teachers are trained not just in tech use, but in cultural sensitivity. When learners are seen not as passive recipients, but as co-creators of knowledge. So, where does this leave us?

Perhaps here: at a crossroads where the future of digital learning hinges not on faster processors or more immersive interfaces, but on our ability to humanize it (Kayyali, 2026 C). To infuse it with the messy, beautiful, contradictory realities of who we are. To design not just for efficiency, but for empathy. To understand that every learner logs on carrying a culture—a language, a rhythm, a history, a dream. If we can honor that—if we can build spaces where difference is not just tolerated, but treasured—then digital learning can be more than just a convenience. It can be a quiet revolution. Not in how we teach. But in how we see one another.

Cultural Identity, Representation, and Inclusion in Online Classrooms

There's a particular kind of silence that fills a digital classroom when a student doesn't feel seen. Not the thoughtful hush of reflection or the momentary pause before insight lands—this is the heavy silence of invisibility. Of logging in, camera off, mic muted, profile picture a generic silhouette, name mispronounced if spoken at all. A student, maybe in a rural part of Bangladesh, or in a crowded apartment in São Paulo, sits behind the screen, watching content that has nothing to do with their world. History lessons that skip over their ancestors. Science examples pulled from climates they'll never touch. Cultural references that feel foreign, irrelevant, maybe even alienating. And with each passing session, something inside quietly asks: *Is this education really meant for me?*

Cultural identity is not a decorative detail. It's not some peripheral variable that we can nod to at the start of a semester and forget by midterms (Verma, 2024). It is foundational—an invisible architecture shaping how we interpret information, relate to peers, understand authority, and define success. In physical classrooms, culture seeps through body language, dress, intonation, rhythm (Sekimoto, 2023). But in online spaces—where presence is pixelated and context is stripped—these signals often vanish. What remains is a bland uniformity. An educational agora designed to feel universal but in practice molded around dominant norms.

Representation, in this context, becomes more than a matter of fairness. It's about survival. Psychological, intellectual, and cultural survival. When students repeatedly fail to see their culture reflected in the curriculum, the examples, the interface—even the avatars—they receive a message, whether stated or not: *You're not the imagined user here* (Kumar & Tissenbaum, 2022). And once internalized, that message corrodes engagement, ownership, and ultimately, the belief that one's knowledge and experience hold value in this space.

Let's be specific. A student from the Navajo Nation logs into a learning platform where every character in the tutorial videos is white, middle-class, American. Every math problem involves dollars, baseballs, or pizza slices. Science experiments assume access to clean water, stable electricity, a microwave. Group work favors direct communication, quick turnaround, and individual assertiveness (Presley, 2022). None of this is overtly discriminatory, and yet, the exclusion is palpable. There's no room for the sacredness of land, for the communal nature of learning, for knowledge passed through oral tradition or dreams. What we call neutrality is often cultural erasure.

Digital spaces pride themselves on scalability. On reaching "everyone." But everyone is not the same. Culture is not just ethnicity or religion or language—it's a way of seeing, of making meaning, of situating oneself in the world. It shows up in how questions are asked, how silence is held, how disagreement is expressed. Some cultures revere direct eye contact, others see it as disrespectful. In some communities, it's rude to interrupt; in others, interruption is a sign of engagement. When we set rigid norms for participation—raise your virtual hand, post three comments per forum, turn your camera on—we assume a standard of behavior rooted in specific cultural codes. We turn what should be a global classroom into a monocultural stage.

Representation, then, must be expansive and layered. It's not just about diversifying stock photos or translating menus into a few more languages (Khanuja et al, 2024). It's about who designs the platform. Whose voice narrates the lessons. Whose scholarship is cited. Whose stories are told. True representation means embedding pluralism into the very DNA of the learning environment—not as a module in week five, but as the operating logic from login to logoff. And inclusion? It's more than just access. A student might have broadband, a device, even a scholarship (Flores-Camacho & Gallegos-Cázares, 2024). But if the pedagogical model is hostile to their way of knowing, they're still excluded. If they have to suppress their accent, rename themselves, pretend not to fast during Ramadan, mute the background noise of a multigenerational household—they're included only superficially. Real inclusion allows students to bring their full selves to the table, not just the parts that assimilate easily.

It also means challenging the assumption that all learners want the same thing. That success looks identical across contexts. A straight-A student in one culture might be seen as socially withdrawn in another. A vocal debater might be praised for critical thinking in the West, and chastised for disrespect in more collectivist societies. We cannot universalize the goals of education without first interrogating the cultural lenses through which we define learning outcomes. There's an uneasy tension here, though. Between the desire to honor cultural specificity and the need to create shared educational standards. Between flexibility and fairness. Between pluralism and coherence. Some may argue that a multicultural classroom risks becoming fragmented—that without common norms, the very notion of "classroom" dissolves into chaos (O'Donnell, 2022). But that fear, too, is culturally conditioned. It assumes that order must come from sameness. That shared understanding can't emerge from dialogue, negotiation, translation.

In fact, some of the most profound learning happens *because* of cultural friction. When a student encounters a concept that clashes with their worldview, they don't just memorize—they wrestle, interpret, adapt. These moments of dissonance, when guided respectfully, are not disruptive. They are generative. But only if the classroom makes space for them. Only if it allows students to speak from where they stand.

We also have to talk about the emotional dimension. Cultural inclusion isn't just an intellectual task—it's a deeply affective one. Students bring trauma, pride, shame, memory (Weuffen & Willis, 2023). Some carry the weight of colonized histories, of educational systems that branded their languages as backward, their beliefs as irrational. The digital classroom may seem neutral, but it's layered with ghosts. Ghosts of exclusion, of humiliation, of not being good enough. If we want online education to be truly inclusive, we must create room for healing. For joy. For students to reclaim their narratives, their accents, their epistemologies. And what of the instructors? They're navigating this, too. Often untrained in intercultural pedagogy, sometimes overwhelmed, sometimes defensive. They may want to be inclusive but fear saying the wrong thing. Or they've internalized their own biases so deeply they don't even notice the patterns. Professional development is crucial here—but not the checkbox kind (Vreuls et al, 2022). We need slow, difficult conversations. Peer learning. Story-sharing. Reflexivity. We need to move from "I treat all my students the same" to "I recognize how difference shapes every learning encounter."

Let's not forget technology itself. Algorithms can't see culture. They optimize for behavior, not context. An AI might flag a student for inactivity, not realizing that cultural norms discourage speaking up (Raji et al, 2021). It might recommend courses based on engagement metrics that ignore systemic exclusion. The push for personalization in EdTech often ends up flattening difference—ironic, isn't it? If we want culturally responsive platforms, the humans who build them must understand cultural complexity. Must sit with discomfort. Must invite messiness into the design process.

There are glimmers of change. Some platforms are experimenting with localizable content (Park et al, 2021). Some universities are co-creating curricula with communities (Kayyali, 2026 B). There are classrooms where students present in their own languages, where oral histories are archived as scholarship, where silence is honored as participation. These are not mainstream yet—but they exist. They whisper of a future where representation isn't an afterthought, but a foundation.

We must lean into those whispers. Amplify them. Let them reshape how we imagine education in a world that is plural, layered, and in flux. Cultural identity is not a barrier to overcome in online classrooms—it is the beating heart of learning (Yeh & Tsai, 2022). Representation is not a checkbox—it is the mirror in which students recognize their worth (Kayyali, 2026 A). And inclusion? It is the slow, intentional practice of making space for humanity in all its glorious difference. In the end, maybe the goal isn't to build the perfect multicultural classroom. Maybe it's to remain in motion—always listening, always adjusting, always asking, *Who is missing? Who feels invisible? Who are we designing for, and who are we leaving behind?* Because education, digital or otherwise, is not just about the transmission of knowledge. It's about belonging. And no one should have to leave their identity at the login screen to feel like they deserve a seat at the table.

Designing Culturally Responsive Educational Technologies

Somewhere between the elegant abstraction of algorithms and the messy texture of human lives lies a tension we've been too quick to overlook (Ruckenstein, 2023). That tension pulses quietly beneath every edtech interface, every platform login, every button that says "Submit." Because while educational technology likes to imagine itself as universal—sleek, clean, neutral—it is anything but. Technology, like language, is never just functional. It carries with it a worldview, a history, a set of assumptions about what matters, what's valid, and—perhaps most dangerously—what can be left out.

Designing culturally responsive educational technologies means confronting the very DNA of these assumptions (Cobian et al, 2024). It requires us to admit that most systems we now call "global" are, in fact, culturally situated—often Western, often monolingual, often built in offices in California, London, or Berlin by teams that don't resemble the world they claim to serve. It means pushing back against the seductive myth that tech is somehow apolitical or immune to bias. It isn't. Bias doesn't sneak in later. It's there from the first line of code. From the questions the product team chooses to ask—or forgets to ask.

So how do we begin? Not with checklists. Not with "inclusive design" toolkits written in one culture for application in another. We begin, instead, with listening. Deep, patient, sometimes uncomfortable listening to the rhythms, struggles, and wisdom of communities that have been historically ignored. We listen to students who grew up learning from elders around a fire, not from textbooks. To teachers who speak four languages but code-switch to survive in a monolingual system. To learners whose devices double as lifelines and burdens—both portals and barriers. From there, we ask better questions. Not just "How can we make this content accessible in another language?" but "Should this content exist in this form at all?" Not "How do we localize this interface?" but "Whose cognitive map are we privileging in this user flow?" Not "Can we add more avatars with darker skin tones?" but "Why did we assume a default skin tone to begin with?" Culturally responsive design is not additive. It's foundational. It's not about slapping on features—it's about interrogating the frame (Manuel et al, 2022).

Let's be honest: this kind of design isn't efficient. It slows things down. It makes meetings more complicated. It introduces friction into workflows that crave speed. Investors may grumble. Coders may bristle. But if we're serious about inclusion—not just as branding, but as ethical commitment—then friction is not our enemy. It's our guide. Friction tells us where power has been concentrated. Where assumptions have calcified. Where empathy needs to be reintroduced. And then there's language. Not just the language of content, but the micro-language of design itself. What does it mean when the "default" voice on a learning platform has an American accent?

When assessment instructions assume familiarity with certain metaphors or cultural touchpoints? When success is gamified using badges that make sense in one cultural context but fall flat—or worse, offend—in another?

Designers often aim for consistency. Uniformity. Predictability. But culturally responsive technology requires us to embrace divergence. To build systems that flex, stretch, adapt. A quiz interface that allows for oral answers, not just typed ones. A feedback tool that permits emotional nuance, not just binary ratings (Tan et al, 2022). A lesson plan template that can incorporate dance, storytelling, silence—modalities that Western academia tends to marginalize.

Let's go further. Imagine a platform built by, with, and for communities whose pedagogies don't follow the linear logic of Western schooling (Sefton-Green, 2022). A platform that centers cyclicity, where lessons come back around in spirals, not progress bars. One that values listening as much as speaking. That rewards interdependence, not just individual achievement. That allows students to learn from their grandmothers as much as their instructors. That takes seriously the idea that knowledge is relational, embodied, and not always meant to be tested by a timer.

This isn't utopian. It's already happening—in pockets. In experimental schools in New Zealand that blend Maori learning practices with digital tools. In grassroots projects in East Africa where coding is taught through local proverbs and storytelling. In rural Mexico, where indigenous languages are being preserved through apps designed by native speakers themselves. The problem is not feasibility. It's visibility. These stories rarely make it to the tech conferences or funding decks. They are dismissed as too niche, too particular, too "contextual." But *everything* is contextual. Even the designs we think are universal. And here's another uncomfortable truth: sometimes, to design culturally responsive tech, we must un-design. We must resist the urge to technologize everything. We must ask: *Does this need an app, or does it need a conversation? Is this a design problem, or a justice one?* Sometimes, the most culturally responsive move is to pause. To hold back. To let the community lead.

Of course, there are trade-offs. Cultural responsiveness can introduce contradictions. What's inclusive in one context may exclude in another (Page et al, 2022). A platform that embraces communal learning may unsettle students taught to prize individual expression. A system that values rhythm and ceremony may clash with test-driven education systems that demand quantifiable outcomes. But contradictions aren't failures. They're the landscape of real human diversity. And tech, if it's honest, must live with that. We also need to think about power. Who gets to design? Who gets to decide what counts as a "feature"? Too often, culturally responsive design is done *to* communities, not *with* them. A token focus group. A translation sprint. A quick consultation. And then the designers retreat to their labs and build what they were going to build anyway. True inclusion means shared authorship. It means budgets, timelines, and processes that reflect mutual respect (Fraser-Barbour et al, 2025). And yes, this may mean training designers in cultural anthropology, in linguistics, in ethics. It may mean hiring fewer computer scientists and more community organizers. It may mean rethinking what we mean by "user testing" altogether—not as a metric to validate pre-made assumptions, but as a space for reciprocal learning. There's also something humbling about this work. A realization that we, the designers, do not always know best. That the people who live closest to the problem often hold the solution (Wakkary, 2021). That technology is not always the hero in the story—and sometimes, it's the antagonist. That progress must be decoupled from speed. That success may not be scale, but depth. Presence. Resonance.

Let's not pretend any of this is easy. The tech world loves clarity. Culturally responsive design lives in ambiguity. It's iterative, relational, full of detours. It asks us to be patient in a culture of sprints. To value the qualitative in a world obsessed with KPIs (Munshi, 2024). To honor the sacred in spaces trained to worship data. But here's the thing: when we get it right—when students see their grandmother's lullabies coded into a language lesson, when a refugee child logs into a math platform in their own dialect, when a village teacher helps co-design an interface that reflects their lived reality—something shifts. The technology stops being a tool and becomes a companion. Not just smart, but wise. Not just efficient, but kind. This is the future we should be building (Gigerenzer, 2022). One that isn't about imposing sameness, but about celebrating difference. Not about taming complexity, but living with it. Not about finding *one* way, but making room for many. And so we return, not to answers, but to questions. How can we decolonize our interfaces? How can we code with care? What does it mean to prototype with humility? To launch with reverence? To debug with love? Because in the end, culturally responsive educational technology is not just about better learning outcomes. It's about dignity. About crafting a world where every learner, in every corner of the globe, logs in and feels—deep in their bones—*this space was made for me.*

Challenges and Opportunities in Cross-Cultural EdTech Implementation

There's a moment of hesitation that lives in every cross-cultural project—an intake of breath before stepping into the unknown. And educational technology, for all its innovation and reach, isn't immune to this pause. If anything, it magnifies it. Because to implement EdTech across cultures isn't just a logistical puzzle; it's an existential one. You're not merely exporting a tool—you're transporting a way of seeing the world. And the question, always simmering beneath the surface, is this: *Will it land with respect? Or will it erase what it cannot understand?*

The first and most obvious challenge—though somehow still the most neglected—is language (Harsch et al, 2021). Not just translation. That's the easy part, or at least the visible one. But the deeper challenge lies in the *cultural weight* language carries. Words aren't just words. They carry rhythm, history, emotion, power. A user interface in flawless French might still alienate a Senegalese student whose internal world hums in Wolof. A voice assistant programmed in crisp English might flatten the expressiveness of Nigerian Pidgin, or misunderstand the tonal nuances of Mandarin. Localization, if shallow, can feel like a mask that doesn't quite fit—a façade of inclusion that cracks at the edges. And behind language lurks another specter: digital colonialism. It's a heavy term, yes, but one that's earned its weight. When platforms built in the Global North are parachuted into classrooms in the Global South without meaningful adaptation, we replicate the same hierarchies that education should be dismantling (Artopoulos, 2023). Pedagogies rooted in Western individualism, metrics shaped by neoliberal benchmarks, success defined through standardized tests—these aren't neutral imports. They overwrite. They displace. They whisper, again and again, *This is the way learning is supposed to look.*

Yet there's a flip side to this coin—an opportunity woven into the very friction. When resistance emerges—when a rural teacher in Guatemala reworks a digital lesson to reflect Mayan cosmology, when a facilitator in Morocco swaps out video examples for local folktales—that's not failure. That's adaptation. Agency. A quiet, radical reassertion of voice. Cross-cultural EdTech will always face resistance, but not all resistance is rejection (Gwin, 2021). Sometimes it's negotiation. Sometimes it's a community's way of asking, *Can we make this ours?*

Then there's infrastructure—or the lack thereof. The broadband deserts. The single broken tablet passed from child to child. The frozen screen during a storm. We often talk about digital divides as if they're simply technical gaps (Kayyali, 2026 B). But they're more than that. They're layered with class, geography, politics. A student's ability to engage with EdTech isn't just about having Wi-Fi. It's about having electricity that doesn't flicker (Ge et al, 2021). A quiet space. Parental support. A sense of safety. In some places, it's about whether going online will draw the gaze of authorities (Kayyali, 2024 A). Whether it's safe to be visible. And yet, despite these constraints, or maybe because of them, innovation blooms. A WhatsApp-based tutoring network emerges in Karachi. Solar-powered tablets circulate in Ugandan refugee camps. Radio broadcasts deliver lessons to nomadic communities. These aren't stopgap solutions. They're blueprints for a different kind of EdTech—one that doesn't aspire to replicate Silicon Valley, but to respond to the terrain underfoot.

Culture, of course, isn't just "over there." Cross-cultural implementation happens even within supposedly homogenous contexts (Dichek et al, 2021). A classroom in

London might host students from Eritrea, Poland, Iraq, and Bangladesh. A teacher in Toronto may navigate six time zones and five home languages in a single Zoom session. The complexity isn't just global—it's local, intimate, immediate. And here's where EdTech often falters. Its one-size-fits-all frameworks collapse under the weight of pluralism. Its chatbots stumble on dialects. Its quizzes assume shared idioms. Inclusion becomes a glitch, not a feature. So, what do we do? First, we slow down. EdTech has a speed problem. It moves fast, breaks things, ships updates. But cultural adaptation doesn't work that way. It requires slowness. Iteration. Listening. It means moving at the speed of trust. Spending time in communities. Co-designing with students, not just for them. It means admitting that scaling without reflection isn't growth—it's erasure.

We must also rethink success. Most platforms measure engagement—clicks, logins, completion rates. But what about belonging? Confidence? Joy? What if a student logs in just once, but walks away feeling seen? Is that failure—or something deeper? Cultural inclusion won't always look good on a dashboard. But that doesn't make it less real. One of the thorniest challenges lies in values. Education is never just about skills—it's about shaping people (Wang, 2021). And cultures disagree on what that shaping should look like. Should education cultivate obedience or independence? Should it reinforce tradition or challenge it? Should it center the self or the collective? EdTech, when unreflective, can bulldoze these differences. But when mindful, it can become a space for dialogue. For cross-pollination. For learning not just *through* technology, but *about* one another.

Then comes the question of representation. Who's on the screen? Who's in the content? If every AI voice is white and male, if every math problem references baseball and Thanksgiving, what are we teaching—intentionally or not—about who belongs in the future? Cross-cultural EdTech must look beyond surface-level diversity. It must move toward what educator Rudine Sims Bishop called "mirrors, windows, and sliding glass doors." It must let students see themselves, glimpse others, and walk into unfamiliar worlds with curiosity, not fear.

There's a fear, of course, in all of this. A fear of getting it wrong. Of cultural missteps. Of unintended offense. And yes, those will happen. But the alternative—doing nothing, staying safe in the shallow end—is worse. Cultural responsiveness is not about perfection. It's about humility. About course-correction. About showing up again, and again, and again, with better questions (Duncan-Andrade, 2022). There's also an opportunity here to de-center the idea of the platform entirely. Sometimes, the most transformative EdTech is not a platform at all—it's a process. A way of facilitating learning that draws on local wisdom, that uses whatever tools are at hand, that adapts in real time. A storytelling session recorded on a parent's phone. A community wiki built in multiple dialects. A coding lesson taught with pebbles and chalk. These forms may never be funded by big venture capital firms, but they pulse with life. With dignity.

Cross-cultural EdTech implementation also challenges us to rethink expertise (Shonfeld et al, 2021). The best insight might come not from a PhD in education, but from a grandmother who knows how to teach by telling stories in the dark. Not from a UX designer, but from a teen who built a language app for their cousins. Expertise is everywhere—it just doesn't always wear a lanyard. And maybe, just maybe, the biggest opportunity is this: the chance to reimagine what it means to learn. To move beyond content delivery. Beyond metrics. To build spaces where students don't just acquire knowledge, but build relationships—with ideas, with cultures, with themselves. Where education is not a race to the top, but a slow unfolding. A mutual becoming. Cross-cultural EdTech implementation, if done right, doesn't just change classrooms. It changes the people who enter them. It cultivates patience in the designer. Empathy in the teacher. Agency in the learner. It reminds us that technology, for all its circuitry and code, is most powerful when it remembers the human. And so we proceed—unevenly, imperfectly, but with intention. We learn to hold contradiction. We embrace nuance. We stay open to being surprised. Because at its best, EdTech is not just about bridging gaps. It's about making visible the bridges that have always been there—quiet, worn, waiting to be walked across.

Toward an Inclusive Digital Future: Policy, Pedagogy, and Praxis

There's a peculiar loneliness to being unacknowledged in a space that claims to welcome you. Not quite rejection—something softer, harder to name. A quiet dislocation. And yet, this is precisely the feeling that haunts so many learners in digital spaces today: welcomed by the promise of inclusion, and simultaneously ghosted by its practice.

We've come far, yes—platforms have multiplied, connectivity has expanded, and educational technology has grown from novelty to necessity. But technology alone cannot close the distance between invitation and belonging. That space is where policy, pedagogy, and praxis must step in (Price & Fox, 2023). Not as buzzwords, not as interchangeable layers in a strategic document, but as living commitments. As daily choices that shape what inclusion really feels like when the camera blinks on and the lesson begins.

Let's start where most reform efforts start—policy. Not the grand declarations etched into national education strategies or tucked inside donor proposals, but the granular stuff. The rules that shape how a classroom functions, how a student is assessed, how content is chosen. Most digital education policies still operate under an unspoken presumption: that access equals equity (Razo & Blankenship-Knox,

2022). That if the infrastructure is in place—if the devices are handed out, the logins distributed, the connections established—then justice has been done. But access, stripped of context, does not liberate. It often replicates the very exclusions it purports to remedy.

An inclusive policy begins with refusal. The refusal to standardize diversity into digestible forms. The refusal to treat cultural variation as an "edge case." The refusal to reduce equity to statistical representation. Instead, it dares to hold complexity. To recognize that inclusion is messy, contextual, relational. That what works in urban Ghana may not land in rural Turkey. That an inclusive platform in theory can still be alienating in practice if it silences local idioms or overrides indigenous knowledge systems.

True policy transformation begins when we stop designing for users and start designing with people (Buley & Natoli, 2024). When we shift from "How do we scale this?" to "Whose voices shaped this?" And that requires discomfort. Because redistribution of power—real redistribution, not symbolic tokenism—always comes at a cost. It slows things down. It invites resistance. It requires letting go of control.

Now, let's talk pedagogy. A word too often confined to white papers and faculty development seminars, but it lives everywhere—in how we greet students, how we structure silence, how we respond to confusion. In digital classrooms, pedagogy takes on new textures. The teacher is less a sage on a stage, more a disembodied guide. Presence must be crafted deliberately, through voice, visuals, rhythms (Chew, 2022). And cultural responsiveness? It doesn't show up as a module—it shows up in tone, in timing, in how questions are framed and whose answers are affirmed. But pedagogy cannot be severed from power. Even the most well-meaning instructors operate within pedagogical models that privilege certain forms of intelligence, certain ways of knowing. The platform may say "inclusive," but the pedagogical architecture may still whisper, *assimilate*. If inclusion is to mean anything, it must expand our understanding of what counts as knowledge (De Bie et al, 2023). That means centering orality, gesture, emotion. Making room for storytelling and spirituality, for doubt and contradiction. It means allowing discomfort—not the performative kind, but the kind that destabilizes fixed ideas and invites deeper inquiry. And what of praxis? That slippery word that tries to bridge the chasm between theory and action. Between what we know and what we do. Praxis, in the context of digital education, lives in the micro-choices. In whether we correct a student's accent or celebrate it. In whether we treat a student's cultural background as baggage or as brilliance. In how we respond when a student goes silent for weeks—not with punishment, but with curiosity.

Praxis also means looking inward. How has our own education shaped our assumptions about what a good learner looks like? Whose voices have we internalized as authoritative? Which communities do we imagine when we hear the word "global"?

And which ones have we unconsciously othered? An inclusive future demands that we, as educators, designers, policymakers, and students alike, commit to continuous unlearning. That we examine not only the technologies we deploy but the ideologies we carry. That we see equity not as a destination, but as a discipline. Something we practice—not perfectly, but persistently. Let's not pretend this is easy. There will be contradictions. A platform that empowers one group may exclude another. A curriculum that centers local knowledge may clash with standardized benchmarks (Binagwaho et al, 2022). A pedagogy grounded in collectivity may frustrate students trained in competition. But contradictions are not failures. They are the terrain of plurality. And navigating them requires courage. Not the performative kind that shows up on panels and in press releases, but the quiet, daily kind. The kind that sits with uncertainty. That listens more than it speaks. That is willing to be wrong.

This is the heart of inclusion: not the tidy symmetry of a strategy document, but the messy, iterative, unfinished work of building learning environments where no one has to leave part of themselves at the door—or at the login screen. There are signs of hope. Initiatives that center community voices in platform design. Curricula co-created with refugee learners. Policy shifts that prioritize multilingual education (Volpe, 2024). Educators who use emojis and lullabies and laughter as pedagogical tools. These efforts are not always visible. They rarely go viral. But they matter. They model a different way of doing things—a slower, deeper, more human way. And yes, we need metrics. But not just of efficiency. Of care. Of cultural resonance. Of ethical integrity. Metrics that ask: *Did this learning experience honor the learner's whole self? Did it amplify, not extract? Did it invite new ways of being, not just knowing?*

Toward an inclusive digital future means building systems that do not demand sameness (Zallio & Clarkson, 2022). It means creating learning ecologies where friction is embraced, where multiplicity is not a problem to be solved but a richness to be cultivated. Where technology does not flatten difference but makes space for it to bloom. It means funding models that support cultural adaptation. It means edtech companies hiring cultural mediators, not just coders. It means professional development that centers empathy, not just analytics. It means students becoming co-creators, not consumers. It means seeing education not as a pipeline but as a garden—with multiple seasons, multiple harvests, multiple ways to thrive. Inclusion, then, is not just about who gets in—it's about what happens once they're there. Do they feel seen? Do they feel safe? Do they feel sovereign? The future will not be built by the fastest. It will be built by the most attentive. And so, we move forward—not with grand claims, but with careful steps. With policy that listens. With pedagogy that stretches. With praxis that breathes. Because in the end, what we're building isn't just a digital classroom. It's a place where everyone matters. And that changes everything.

CONCLUSION

As we arrive at the close of this exploration, one truth emerges with clarity: integrating multicultural approaches in online learning is not a technical challenge—it is a deeply human one. At its heart, this work asks us to confront our assumptions about knowledge, intelligence, and what it means to be a learner. It asks us to see cultural identity not as an obstacle to standardization but as a source of strength, creativity, and wisdom in education.

Throughout this chapter, we have seen that educational technologies are never neutral. They are shaped by the values, assumptions, and biases of their creators. As such, when we use EdTech to educate diverse populations without intentionally designing for cultural inclusivity, we risk amplifying the very inequalities we claim to dismantle. In a globalized educational landscape, ignoring culture is not an omission—it is an erasure. And yet, there is room for optimism. Around the world, educators and technologists are beginning to shift their perspectives. We are seeing the rise of platforms that support indigenous languages, learning analytics that consider cultural norms, and virtual classrooms that create space for storytelling, ritual, and reflection—elements often sidelined in conventional educational frameworks. These are not just technical achievements; they are ethical and philosophical choices. They signal a move toward a more human-centered digital pedagogy—one that resists flattening cultural difference into a uniform mold. But to sustain this momentum, we must cultivate what scholar Homi Bhabha calls a "third space"—an in-between space where learners from different cultural contexts can co-create meaning. Online learning should not merely transmit content across borders; it should build bridges, encourage co-authorship, and foster dialogue across worldviews. It should be uncomfortable at times—stretching both learners and educators to grapple with unfamiliar ideas and unfamiliar selves. In doing so, it can become not just a site of knowledge delivery, but of mutual transformation.

Policy, too, has a role to play. Governments and institutions must move beyond checkbox diversity policies and commit to investing in platforms, training, and curricula that reflect the realities of pluralism. Inclusion must not be a side project; it must be the architecture upon which the future of digital education is built. To bridge cultures through EdTech is to reaffirm a simple yet profound belief: that learning is not just an intellectual act, but an act of recognition. When students see their cultures reflected and respected in their learning journeys, they do more than just succeed academically—they begin to trust the system, to believe in their place within it, and to feel, perhaps for the first time, that their voice truly matters. This is the promise of multicultural online learning—not as a distant ideal, but as a necessary and achievable reality. And it begins with the choices we make today.

REFERENCES

Artopoulos, A. (2023). Labyrinths of platformization of education in the Global South (and beyond). In *The new digital education policy landscape* (pp. 147–164). Routledge. DOI: 10.4324/9781003373018-11

Bergreen, G. (2023). *Revolutionary Technologies: Educational Perspectives of Technology History*. Rowman & Littlefield. DOI: 10.5771/9781475870664

Binagwaho, A., Bonciani Nader, H., Brown Burkins, M., Davies, A., Hessen, D. O., Mbow, C., & Tong, S. (2022). *Knowledge-driven actions: transforming higher education for global sustainability: independent expert group on the universities and the 2030 agenda*. UNESCO Publishing.

Buley, L., & Natoli, J. (2024). *The user experience team of one: A research and design survival guide*. Rosenfeld Media.

Chew, Y. W. (2022). Performing presence with the teaching-body via videoconferencing: A postdigital study of the teacher's face and voice. *Postdigital Science and Education, 4*(2), 394–421. DOI: 10.1007/s42438-022-00288-2 PMID: 40477497

Cobian, K. P., Hurtado, S., Romero, A. L., & Gutzwa, J. A. (2024). Enacting inclusive science: Culturally responsive higher education practices in science, technology, engineering, mathematics, and medicine (STEMM). *PLoS One, 19*(1), e0293953. DOI: 10.1371/journal.pone.0293953 PMID: 38232083

De Bie, A., Marquis, E., Cook-Sather, A., & Luqueño, L. (2023). *Promoting equity and justice through pedagogical partnership*. Taylor & Francis.

Dichek, N. P., Kopotun, I. M., Shevchenko, S. M., Antonets, N. B., & Pohribna, D. V. (2021). Implementation of the cross-cultural approach in the modern school. International Journal of Learning. *Teaching and Educational Research, 20*(4), 210–244.

Dron, J. (2022). Educational technology: What it is and how it works. *AI & Society, 37*(1), 155–166. DOI: 10.1007/s00146-021-01195-z

Du, Z., Wang, F., Wang, S., & Xiao, X. (2022). Enhancing Learner Participation in online discussion forums in Massive Open Online Courses: The role of mandatory participation. *Frontiers in Psychology, 13*, 819640. DOI: 10.3389/fpsyg.2022.819640 PMID: 35496232

Duncan-Andrade, J. M. (2022). *Equality or equity: Toward a model of community-responsive education*. Harvard Education Press.

Eppard, J., Kaviani, A., Bowles, M., & Johnson, J. (2021). EdTech Culturation: Integrating a Culturally Relevant Pedagogy into Educational Technology. *Electronic Journal of e-Learning*, *19*(6), 516–530. DOI: 10.34190/ejel.19.6.2065

Feiyu, S. (2024). Employing Technologies to Apply Ethnic Motifs into Contemporary Product Design (Master's thesis).

Flores-Camacho, F., & Gallegos-Cázares, L. (2024). Representational Pluralism in Science Education: A Point of View from the Inferential-Pragmatical Approach of Scientific Representations. *Science & Education*, •••, 1–21.

Fraser-Barbour, E., Robinson, S., Gendera, S., Burton-Clark, I., Fisher, K. R., Alexander, J., & Howe, K. (2025). Shifting power to people with disability in co-designed research. *Disability & Society*, *40*(2), 259–280. DOI: 10.1080/09687599.2023.2279932

Ge, J., Smyth, R. E., Searle, M., Kirkpatrick, L., Evans, R., Elder, A., & Brown, H. (2021). Perspectives from students: How to tame the chaos and harness the power of technology for learning. *Brock Education Journal*, *30*(1), 74–74. DOI: 10.26522/brocked.v30i1.850

Gigerenzer, G. (2022). *How to stay smart in a smart world: Why human intelligence still beats algorithms*. MIT Press.

Gorton, I. (2022). *Foundations of scalable systems*. O'Reilly Media, Inc.

Gwin, R. W. (2021). *Investigating Cultural Values and Educational Technology Adoption in Central Asia: A Case Study*. Boise State University. DOI: 10.18122/td/1883/boisestate

Harsch, C., Mueller-Karabil, A., & Buchminskaia, E. (2021). Addressing the challenges of interaction in online language courses. *System*, *103*, 102673. DOI: 10.1016/j.system.2021.102673

Kayyali, M. (2024a). Quality Assurance in Online and Blended Learning Environments. In *Quality Assurance and Accreditation in Higher Education: Issues, Models, and Best Practices* (pp. 227–292). Springer Nature Switzerland. DOI: 10.1007/978-3-031-66623-0_5

Kayyali, M. (Ed.). (2024b). Building Resiliency in Higher Education: Globalization, Digital Skills, and Student Wellness: Globalization, Digital Skills, and Student Wellness. IGI Global.

Kayyali, M. (2026a). Online and Blended Learning in Doctoral Studies: Opportunities and Challenges. Improving Doctoral Education and Research Development for Sustainability, 103-138.

Kayyali, M. (2026b). The Role of Digital Platforms in Shaping Competitive Intelligence Strategies. In Competitive Intelligence in the Digital Age: Strategies for Business and Technology Leadership (pp. 241-264). IGI Global Scientific Publishing.

Kayyali, M. (2026c). The Digital Transformation of Education: Opportunities and Challenges for Communication. Effects of Education Communication in Digital Learning Environments, 433-472.

Khanuja, S., Ramamoorthy, S., Song, Y., & Neubig, G. (2024). An image speaks a thousand words, but can everyone listen? On image transcreation for cultural relevance. arXiv preprint arXiv:2404.01247. DOI: 10.18653/v1/2024.emnlp-main.573

Koole, M., Smith, M., Traxler, J., Adam, T., & Footring, S. (2024). Decolonising educational technology. *Education Sciences*, *14*(10), 1070. DOI: 10.3390/educsci14101070

Kumar, V., & Tissenbaum, M. (2022). Supporting collaborative classroom networks through technology: An actor network theory approach to understanding social behaviours and design. *British Journal of Educational Technology*, *53*(6), 1549–1570. DOI: 10.1111/bjet.13274

Luzón, M. J., & Pérez-Llantada, C. (2022). Digital genres in academic knowledge production and communication: Perspectives and practices.

Manuel, M., Gottlieb, J., Svarovsky, G., & Hite, R. (2022). The intersection of culturally responsive pedagogy and engineering design in secondary STEM. Journal of Pre-College Engineering Education Research (J-PEER), 12(2), 11.

Marandi, S. S. (2024). Virtual supremacy and electronic imperialism: The hegemonies of e-learning and computer assisted language learning (CALL). *Learning, Media and Technology*, *49*(4), 527–543. DOI: 10.1080/17439884.2023.2207832

Marcovitz, D. M. (2022). The intersection of social justice and educational technology: The educational technology social justice matrix. *Education and Information Technologies*, *27*(4), 5129–5151. DOI: 10.1007/s10639-021-10828-1

Munshi, D. (2024). Enhancing Digital Transformation Project Success through Design Thinking-Driven Agile Project Management.

O'Donnell, A. (2022). Sharing the world without losing oneself: Education in a pluralistic universe. *Discourse (Abingdon)*, *43*(5), 666–685. DOI: 10.1080/01596306.2022.2045072

Page, A., Mavropoulou, S., & Harrington, I. (2022). Culturally responsive inclusive education: The value of the local context. *International Journal of Disability Development and Education, 69*(4), 1313–1326. DOI: 10.1080/1034912X.2020.1757627

Parameswaran, U. D., Molloy, J., & Kuttner, P. (2024). Healing schools: A framework for joining trauma-informed care, restorative justice, and multicultural education for whole school reform. *The Urban Review, 56*(1), 186–209. DOI: 10.1007/s11256-023-00666-5

Park, S., Chun, S., Cha, J., Lee, B., & Shim, H. (2021). Multiple heads are better than one: Few-shot font generation with multiple localized experts. In Proceedings of the IEEE/CVF international conference on computer vision (pp. 13900-13909).

Paul, P. K., Bommali, T., Kayyali, M., Chakraborty, S., Debnath, D., Gupta, S. K., & Sharma, S. K. (2025). Demystifying Issues and Concerns of AI and Allied Technologies in Digital Education and Learning: A Scientific Study. In AI-Enabled Sustainable Innovations in Education and Business (pp. 1-32). IGI Global Scientific Publishing. DOI: 10.4018/979-8-3373-3952-8.ch001

Presley, T. (2022). *Assertive communication: Develop your assertive communication skills and instantly learn how to stand up for yourself, communicate effectively, and boost your confidence while winning the respect.* Timothy Presley.

Price, J., & Fox, A. (2023). Transformative Praxis: A Critical Design Framework for Belonging and Inclusion in Technology-Rich Learning Spaces. *Journal of Teaching and Learning with Technology, 12*(1), 55–71. DOI: 10.14434/jotlt.v12i1.36425

Pronzato, R. (2023). Reproducing hegemony, returning to critical pedagogy. The relationships of youth with digital platforms.

Raji, I. D., Scheuerman, M. K., & Amironesei, R. (2021, March). You can't sit with us: Exclusionary pedagogy in ai ethics education. In *Proceedings of the 2021 ACM conference on fairness, accountability, and transparency* (pp. 515-525). DOI: 10.1145/3442188.3445914

Ravichandran, K., Virgin, B. A., Edwin, M. R., Morris, V. S., & Milton, B. J. (2024). Moving towards a Blended Tomorrow: The Evolution of EdTech in Education. Library of Progress-Library Science, Information Technology & Computer, 44(3).

Razo, R., & Blankenship-Knox, A. E. (2022). The Internet Isn't a Luxury Anymore: How Educational Leaders Can Promote Equitable Digital Access for All Students. *Educational Leadership and Administration: Teaching and Program Development, 34*, 55–68.

Røe, Y., Wojniusz, S., & Bjerke, A. H. (2022, January). The digital transformation of higher education teaching: Four pedagogical prescriptions to move active learning pedagogy forward. []. Frontiers Media SA.]. *Frontiers in Education*, *6*, 784701. DOI: 10.3389/feduc.2021.784701

Ruckenstein, M. (2023). *The feel of algorithms*. Univ of California Press.

Sefton-Green, J. (2022). Towards platform pedagogies: Why thinking about digital platforms as pedagogic devices might be useful. *Discourse (Abingdon)*, *43*(6), 899–911. DOI: 10.1080/01596306.2021.1919999

Sekimoto, S. (2023). Rhythmic bodies: Sensorial multimodality, entrainment, and intercultural communication. In *Multimodal communication in intercultural interaction* (pp. 41–57). Routledge. DOI: 10.4324/9781003227281-4

Shonfeld, M., Cotnam-Kappel, M., Judge, M., Ng, C. Y., Ntebutse, J. G., Williamson-Leadley, S., & Yildiz, M. N. (2021). Learning in digital environments: A model for cross-cultural alignment. *Educational Technology Research and Development*, *69*(4), 1–20. DOI: 10.1007/s11423-021-09967-6 PMID: 33654347

Starkey, H. (2021). Classroom counternarratives as transformative multicultural citizenship education. *Multicultural Education Review*, *13*(3), 229–244. DOI: 10.1080/2005615X.2021.1964266

Tan, T. Y., Wachsmuth, L., & Tugade, M. M. (2022). Emotional nuance: Examining positive emotional granularity and well-being. *Frontiers in Psychology*, *13*, 715966. DOI: 10.3389/fpsyg.2022.715966 PMID: 35273535

Verma, S. (2024). Weaving Cultural Threads Through Virtual Exchange: A Case Study on Task-Based Language Teaching use in European Secondary Schools (Master's thesis).

Volpe, D. (2024). Educators Reimagining the Experiences of Multilingual Learners in the Classroom a Practitioner Action Research Study (Doctoral dissertation, Montclair State University).

Vreuls, J., Koeslag-Kreunen, M., van der Klink, M., Nieuwenhuis, L., & Boshuizen, H. (2022). Responsive curriculum development for professional education: Different teams, different tales. *Curriculum Journal*, *33*(4), 636–659. DOI: 10.1002/curj.155

Wakkary, R. (2021). *Things we could design: For more than human-centered worlds*. MIT press. DOI: 10.7551/mitpress/13649.001.0001

Wang, Y. (2021). Artificial intelligence in educational leadership: A symbiotic role of human-artificial intelligence decision-making. *Journal of Educational Administration, 59*(3), 256–270. DOI: 10.1108/JEA-10-2020-0216

Weuffen, S., & Willis, K. (2023). The fallacy of cultural inclusion in mainstream education discourses. In *Inclusion, equity, diversity, and social justice in education: A critical exploration of the sustainable development goals* (pp. 91–106). Springer Nature Singapore. DOI: 10.1007/978-981-19-5008-7_7

Yeh, C. Y., & Tsai, C. C. (2022). Massive distance education: Barriers and challenges in shifting to a complete online learning environment. *Frontiers in Psychology, 13*, 928717. DOI: 10.3389/fpsyg.2022.928717 PMID: 35859848

Zallio, M., & Clarkson, P. J. (2022). Designing the metaverse: A study on inclusion, diversity, equity, accessibility and safety for digital immersive environments. *Telematics and Informatics, 75*, 101909. DOI: 10.1016/j.tele.2022.101909

KEY TERMS AND DEFINITIONS

Cognitive Justice: The recognition and inclusion of multiple ways of knowing and learning, especially those marginalized by dominant systems.

Culturally Sustaining Pedagogy: An educational approach that supports the preservation and evolution of students' cultural identities within learning environments.

Decolonizing Online Education: The process of challenging and dismantling colonial assumptions in content, structure, and delivery of online learning.

Digital Inclusivity: The equitable design and deployment of educational technologies that ensure access and engagement for diverse learners.

EdTech Equity: The commitment to fair access, participation, and representation in educational technology design and usage.

Multicultural Integration: The intentional incorporation of diverse cultural perspectives and knowledge systems into online learning environments.

Transcultural Dialogue: A learning process that fosters mutual understanding and knowledge exchange across cultural boundaries.

Chapter 8
Distributed Leadership Effect on Global Collaboration in Digital Education by Mediation of Culture of Inclusivity and Openness in the Horn of Africa

Wako Jio
https://orcid.org/0009-0003-6192-459X
Bule Hora University, Ethiopia

shashi Kant
https://orcid.org/0000-0003-4722-5736
Lovely Professional University, India

Hirut Assegid
https://orcid.org/0009-0003-6192-459X
Bule Hora University, Ethiopia

Zerihun Kinde Alemu
https://orcid.org/0000-0002-8546-2882
Ethiopian Civil Service University, Ethiopia

DOI: 10.4018/979-8-3373-3673-2.ch008

ABSTRACT

In Horn of Africa digital education, this chapter explains how distributed leadership contributes to global teamwork as well as concentrates on the function of an inclusive as well as open organizational culture. Using data from 425 respondents, the researchers rely on reduction of dimensions to determine how closely their variables match the constructs, as shown by a high KMO score. Factor loading is performed to make sure the structure as well as reliability of the constructs is sound. Using AMOS software, mediation is used to see how distributed leadership, organizational culture as well as global collaboration relate to each other. It is shown in the findings that distributed leadership greatly improves international cooperation in digital education, explaining how involving all parties in decision-making creates a more inventive as well as united learning environment. It also shows that a culture in the organization that is inclusive as well as open is important, manifesting that it helps boost the impact of distributed leadership on teamwork.

INTRODUCTION

Because we live in an increasingly connected world, teaming up globally for digital education has become especially obvious (Zgrzywa-Ziemak et al., 2025). Lockdown measures during the COVID-22 pas well as emic quickly drove education online which uncovered issues as well as benefits in various countries (Lu & Chen, 2025). Making education better in the region depends on distributed leadership, as it is best in helping people come together as well as collaborate (Kılınç & Özdemir, 2025). Based on views of shared governance as well as collective responsibility, the concept of distributed leadership promotes empowering people from different levels in the organization to help make decisions (Sheikh Salavat et al., 2025). People are adopting this method in education to encourage innovative as well as flexible teaching. Several Research works have found that having distributed leadership in place supports stronger organization-wide collaboration which in turn increases overall effectiveness (Svensson & von Knorring, 2025). Recent Research works prove that using inclusive leadership helps build a trusting as well as accountable environment among colleagues. Nonetheless, there are problems in some regions such as the Horn of Africa (Abu-Shawish & Ghamrawi, 2025), because differences in wealth as well as political conflicts prevent them from cooperating on education (Mazhabi, 2025). Although research is expanding, there is still not enough knowledge about the exact ways distributed leadership impacts teamwork across the globe as well as especially by influencing openness as well as inclusion in the organization (Okiri & Hercz, 2025; Ebert et al., 2025).

The chapter tries to fill these gaps by investigating how having a supportive as well as open workplace encourages leaders, teachers as well as learners to collaborate worldwide in digital education. Consequently, future researchers as well as policy experts gain useful information that helps them design strategies to benefit from distributed leadership for better educational outcomes. The study is driven by the research question: "***How does distributed leadership influence global collaboration in digital education through in the Horn of Africa, as well as what function does an organizational culture of inclusivity as well as openness play in this process?***" This inquiry not only seeks to fill existing gaps but also aims to inform practice as well as policy in a region poised for educational transformation.

Background of Study

Because of the region's rich diversity as well as economic issues, the Horn of Africa is starting to realize that digital education is important for modernizing its schools (Lemi et al., 2025; Lu & Chen, 2025). Shifts in the world's approach to education towards more teamwork as well as equity have made distributed leadership worth considering (Sheikh Salavat et al., 2025). Having distributed leadership means every educator has a give part in deciding how schools are run as well as led (Mazhabi, 2025). As well as enhancing people's involvement, this way of working handles people's concerns, encouraging them to take responsibility as well as see change happen. Distributing leadership in the Horn of Africa is not easy, due to some practical issues (Svensson & von Knorring, 2025). Due to recent changes in education, Ethiopia has made progress; along with, hierarchies found in old governance practices still prevent teams from sharing the leadership well (Ebert et al., 2025). It is often challenging for educators because the existing leaders are hesitant to let go of their functions, so it can be tough for the team (Abu-Shawish & Ghamrawi, 2025). Faculty members at a local university in Addis Ababa complained about the way decisions were made which they believed suppressed their creativity as well as function in decision-making (Kılınç & Özdemir, 2025).

Due to ongoing issues through politics as well as a lack of infrastructure, building such systems in Somalia is also very difficult. Studying an educational community project in Mogadishu found that while new leadership principles were introduced, the lack of a positive organizational culture stopped the project from being effective (Zgrzywa-Ziemak et al., 2025). Teachers said they felt neglected as well as isolated which made them reject the idea of collaborating (Kant et al., 2025). This makes it clear that businesses should work to ensure everyone feels tolerated as well as involved (Jio et al., 2025). Research has proven that by fostering such a culture, distributed leadership grows more successful because everyone's ideas are given importance (Okiri & Hercz, 2025). Still, how organizational culture influences this link has not been fully uncovered in the region. So, this study tries to understand these problems, providing useful tips for anyone involved in making distributed leadership successful in tough situations.

Statement of Problem

There are many challenges as well as opportunities to using distributed leadership for digital education in the Horn of Africa (Sheikh Salavat et al., 2025). Distributed leadership is best when it allows all educators to contribute, join forces as well as try new methods in how they teach as well as learn (Mazhabi, 2025). Some Research works manifeste that many schools in this area have trouble meeting these goals (Ebert et al., 2025). Evidence on distributed leadership is split as well as whiles certain Research works point to its ability to promote collaboration; others report ongoing obstacles that prevent its success (Lu & Chen, 2025). Because distributed leadership is not consistent, people are now wondering what conditions are important for its success as well as which things get in its way. Additionally, Research works suggest that there are not many insights about how organizational culture, especially a culture that encourages everyone as well as openness, mediates the link among distributed leadership as well as global teamwork in online education (Kılınç & Özdemir, 2025). Various researchers have pointed out the function of organizational culture, but the findings about how it really influences the Horn of Africa are not always reliable (Zgrzywa-Ziemak et al., 2025). There are still gaps in theories, since existing models fail to properly address the local socio-political influences on education (Abu-Shawish & Ghamrawi, 2025). Also, it is not fully understood how distributed leadership works in different cultures, economies as well as political situations. Since hierarchies as well as limited resources are common, educators must handle additional challenges when trying to make use of teamwork.

This study seeks to fill these gaps by looking closely at how organizational culture affects the way distributed leadership improves global cooperation in digital education. Since the book is about the Horn of Africa, it will give teachers info that matches the difficulties they have there. The outcomes will help both researchers as well as people in charge by recommending useful practices that will help enhance collaboration in schools. This study will set the groundwork for additional research on distributed leadership which can contribute to a better, more inclusive way of leading in education settings.

Theoretical Foundation

Distributed Leadership Theory: It argues that leadership should not belong to one person but is a group effort among many people. Spillane as well as Halverson formed this theory which manifests the value of teachers collaborating as well as sharing leadership at several levels. Distributed leadership in schools as well as classrooms helps build a system where teachers as well as staff can participate in deciding what happens at their institution. In digital education, this theory is helpful since it promotes creative use of technology that brings together different members of the community (Svensson & von Knorring, 2025).

Transformational Leadership Theory: It is a framework Both Burns as well as Bass believe that leaders following Transformational Leadership Theory should inspire their team members to do better as well as develop themselves more. Those who lead through transformation make sure there is trust as well as support which keeps staff interested in creative ideas as well as progress. This theory is useful when educational leaders try to create a vision that brings educators together as well as promotes involvement. Since transformational leadership promotes inclusivity as well as openness, it shares many of the same goals as distributed leadership as well as is a good perspective to add to this field of study (Zgrzywa-Ziemak et al., 2025).

Social Exchange Theory: It holds that people's social actions take place as an exchange to get the most benefit as well as suffer the least loss. It can be used in education to see how teachers, principals as well as students interact as well as work together. People tend to work together when they see that their actions are appreciated as well as returned. Supporting one another as well as teamwork reflect distributed leadership which sees achievements as outcomes shared by all (Lu & Chen, 2025).

Organizational Culture Theory: It looks at the values, beliefs as well as norms that influence the way people behave at work. This idea is most helpful when looking at how culture affects what happens through distributed leadership. Encouraging an inclusive as well as open culture helps teamwork as well as enables educators to be leaders. As a outcome, a rigid as well as structured framework can limit both new ideas as well as involvement of employees. Appreciating the way organizations develop their culture is vital for carrying out distributed leadership, so this theory plays a key function in research (Kılınç & Özdemir, 2025).

This study uses ***Distributed Leadership Theory*** as its main theoretical perspective. The study tries to discover the ways in which educators practicing distributed leadership support colleagues in digital education in the Horn of Africa. Through this perspective, we can see clearly how different approaches to leadership influence as well as support the culture of a school for better learning outcomes.

Definition and Origin of Concept

Distributed Leadership: Under distributed leadership, authority is spread among people in an organization so that decisions can be made together by group members, From research on educational leadership of the late 20th century, it argues for a different style in which leaders as well as others cooperate as well as are responsible as a team. The term lets us see that leaders can appear from many directions in an organization, making the leadership structure more flexible as well as responsive (Svensson & von Knorring, 2025).

Organizational Culture: The culture of an organization is made up of the common values, beliefs as well as ways of working that shape people's actions. The idea came from sociology as well as anthropology as well as was adopted into organizational Research works during the 2280s. How workers interact, decide things as well as carry out tasks is affected by the organizational culture. Strong, positive culture can increase motivation as well as outcomes, although negative culture can outcome in team members resisting or becoming less interested (Zgrzywa-Ziemak et al., 2025).

Global Collaboration: People or groups work together across countries to achieve shared objectives in what is known as global collaboration. Because of globalization as well as digital communications, this term is now well known, as it helps various groups work together effectively even if they are not in the same place. Global partnerships in education improve learning by letting everyone contribute their ideas as well as experiences (Kılınç & Özdemir, 2025).

Digital Education: Learning as well as teaching in digital education uses technology to assist the process. Through the introduction of the internet as well as digital resources in the late 20th century, this word describes a number of activities such as online learning, blended learning as well as using educational technology. By striving to boost accessibility, engagement as well as interactivity, digital education has become very important in recent moves to reform the education system (Lu & Chen, 2025).

EMPIRICAL LITERATURE REVIEW

Distributed Leadership and Global Collaboration in Digital Education

The growing amount of factual evidence shows how important Distributed Leadership is for encouraging Global Collaboration in Digital Education (Svensson & von Knorring, 2025). Collaborative decision-making as well as shared responsibility among educators characterize distributed leadership. It has been known as an important strategy in today's schools (Sheikh Salavat et al., 2025). Research works have manifested that shared leadership not only enhances teachers' authority but also increases their motivation as well as commitment to collaboration (Lu & Chen, 2025). For a case, Research works manifeste that distributed leadership allows individuals share their skills as well as information, which is vital for coping through the challenges of digital learning environments (Zgrzywa-Ziemak et al., 2025). Multiple researches have investigated the direct correlation among Distributed Leadership as well as collaborative behaviors. For a case, a research manifestd that schools that used dispersed leadership models had staff members who worked together more, which led to better educational outcomes (Ebert et al., 2025). In digital education, where technology has to be used together as well as shared knowledge is needed, this kind of teamwork is very important (Alene et al., 2025). Additionally, Research works manifest that distributed leadership promotes a culture of trust as well as transparent communication, which are vital for effective cooperation in digital environments (Mazhabi, 2025).

The evidence suggests that Distributed Leadership not only has direct effects, but it also affects Global Collaboration by promoting an inclusive workplace culture (Kılınç & Özdemir, 2025). Research manifests that shared leadership fosters a feeling of ownership as well as connection among educators, therefore increasing their propensity to work across geographical as well as academic borders (Erbo et al., 2025). For a case, Research works show that distributed leadership may help create inclusive environments that lead to more cooperation as well as new ideas in the classroom (Kant et al., 2025). Also, the confluence of Distributed Leadership as well as digital collaboration has been looked at in several situations, showing how important technology is in making these processes easier (Tuktamyshova et al., 2025). Researchers have found that digital platforms may let instructors talk to one other as well as share resources, which makes it simpler as well as more effective for them to work together. This is very crucial when individuals from various regions of the world work together since it might be hard for them to do so when they are far apart (Abu-Shawish & Ghamrawi, 2025). Even while the outcomes are positive, the research also points out problems that come through using distributed leadership in digital education. Research works manifest that distributed headship approaches may be ineffective when individuals are resistant to change, lack enough training, or possess insufficient support networks (Worku, 2025). Consequently, experts underscore the necessity for focused professional development as well as institutional assistance to surmount these obstacles as well as optimize the efficacy of collaborative leadership (Okiri & Hercz, 2025).

H1: Distributed Leadership and Global Collaboration in Digital Education having empirical association

Distributed Leadership and Culture of Inclusivity and Openness

The empirical study on distributed leadership as well as organizational culture of inclusivity as well as openness has increasingly manifested the interrelation of these aspects in fostering successful educational environments (Mazhabi, 2025). Distributed Leadership, which emphasizes collective responsibility as well as collaborative decision-making among educators, has been shown to significantly influence the development of an inclusive corporate culture (Erbo et al., 2025). When leadership is shared, teachers have a function in choices (Ebert et al., 2025). This makes students feel like they belong and makes them more committed to the school. investigation have consistently shown that an open as well as accepting organizational culture, where different points of view are welcome, is necessary for distributed headship to work (Sheikh Salavat et al., 2025). For a case, investigation showed that schools with a strong culture of inclusiveness were more likely to use distributed headship models because teachers felt appreciated and supported in their jobs (Okiri & Hercz, 2025). This reciprocal improvement suggests that inclusive cultures create a favorable setting for the successful implementation of distributed headship, which in turn strengthens the culture of inclusivity (Zgrzywa-Ziemak et al., 2025).

The literature also manifests the importance of communication in fostering Distributed headship as well as inclusivity; when individuals can communicate freely, they may express their opinions as well as concerns more easily, hence facilitating a more transparent decision-making process (Alene et al., 2025). Research works manifeste that open communication not only helps coworkers get along better, but it also makes the workplace more honest as well as willing to work together. This is vital for creating a welcoming culture (Svensson & von Knorring, 2025). This illustrates that for distributed headship to operate, schools need to make sure that everyone can communicate to each other and be heard. Additionally, empirical research has examined the influence of Distributed Leadership on fostering a climate that values diversity as well as incorporates it into educational procedures (Abu-Shawish & Ghamrawi, 2025). Research shows that dispersed leadership helps teachers accept other points of view, which leads to more creative as well as successful ways of teaching (Lu & Chen, 2025). This openness is especially crucial in schools through students from many different cultures, where different points of view may make the learning experience better. Along with, it is still hard to create a culture of inclusiveness under distributed leadership structures (Tuktamyshova et al., 2025). Some Research works show that established hierarchies, opposition to change, as well as a lack of training might make it harder to put both dispersed leadership as well as inclusive policies into action (Worku, 2025). For a case, Research works manifest that insufficient professional development as well as institutional backing may undermine initiatives aimed at fostering inclusion through distributed leadership (Kılınç & Özdemir, 2025).

H2: Distributed Leadership and Organizational Culture of Inclusivity and Openness having empirical association

Culture of Inclusivity and Openness and Collaboration in Digital Education

The empirical study of the organizational culture of inclusivity as well as openness as well as its influence on global collaboration in digital education provides substantial insights into how inclusive practices foster collaboration among educators as well as stakeholders in many geographical contexts (Lu & Chen, 2025). An inclusive organizational culture, which includes shared values, respect for differences, as well as open communication, is what makes digital education settings work well together (Sheikh Salavat et al., 2025). Research works show that being inclusive makes people feel secure sharing their thoughts as well as working together. In the rapidly changing world of digital education, this is very important (Ebert et al., 2025). Research works manifested that companies through a strong culture of inclusiveness are better at getting individuals from all over the world to work together (Mazhabi, 2025). Research has shown, for a case, that companies that value inclusiveness are more inclined to work through other companies that are based in other countries (Alene et al., 2025). This open culture encourages teachers from all over the world to work together, share materials, as well as share best practices. This makes the learning experience better for everyone involved (Zgrzywa-Ziemak et al., 2025).

The research also shows that an inclusive culture makes it easier to use technology for cooperation (Kılınç & Özdemir, 2025). Digital tools as well as platforms work best in places where everyone is welcome, since they make it easier for people from different backgrounds to talk to each other as well as share resources (Worku, 2025). This technical integration is especially important in digital education, where distance can make it hard for people to work together (Niguse et al., 2025). Inclusive cultures allow teachers to use these technologies to interact through other teachers around the world, which helps build a feeling of community as well as a shared goal (Svensson & von Knorring, 2025). The research also shows how important leadership is in creating an inclusive workplace atmosphere that encourages teamwork (Abu-Shawish & Ghamrawi, 2025). Research manifests that leaders, who exemplify inclusive behaviors, advocate for diversity, as well as foster open discourse develop a climate favorable to collaborative activities. For a case, Research works show that leaders that actively encourage inclusion not only make teams work better together, but they also get people more involved in group projects, which leads to better educational outcomes (Tuktamyshova et al., 2025). There are still problems to be solved, though, in creating an inclusive culture that makes global cooperation easier (Okiri & Hercz, 2025). Some Research works show those deeply held prejudices, unwillingness to adapt, as well as not knowing how inclusion might help can all slow development (Erbo et al., 2025). For a case, research shows that companies may unintentionally continue exclusionary behaviors that limit prospects for cooperation if they don't make an attempt to promote inclusion (Ranta et al., 2025).

H3: Organizational Culture of Inclusivity and Openness and Global Collaboration in Digital Education having empirical association

Distributed Leadership, Global Collaboration and Inclusivity and Openness

The empirical research investigating the interaction of distributed leadership, global collaboration in digital education, as well as an organizational culture of inclusiveness as well as Openness manifests a complicated connection in which inclusiveness functions as a mediating variable (Mazhabi, 2025). Distributed leadership, which involves making decisions together as well as working together, is becoming more as well as more important for creating an open as well as welcoming workplace culture. Alene et al. (2025) say that when teachers share leadership, it not only gives them authority, but it also makes them feel like they belong, which is important for making the climate welcoming to everyone (Ebert et al., 2025). Research shows that an inclusive business culture makes dispersed leadership work better for encouraging global cooperation (Okiri & Hercz, 2025). For a case, Research works show that schools through a strong culture of inclusion tend to use distributed leadership better, which leads to more cooperation among staff (Ranta et al., 2025). This welcoming atmosphere promotes open communication as well as respect for different points of view (Worku, 2025). This makes teachers feel respected as well as encourages them to work together, especially in digital education settings (Abu-Shawish & Ghamrawi, 2025).

Additionally, the study underscores that the existence of an inclusive culture influences the link among distributed leadership as well as global collaboration (Sheikh Salavat et al., 2025). For a case, a research manifests that instructors operating through in an inclusive atmosphere are more inclined to adopt collaborative digital efforts (Kant et al., 2025). This mediation effect shows that distributed leadership can directly lead to cooperation, but its influence is much stronger in an atmosphere that is open to different people as well as supports common objectives (Kılınç & Özdemir, 2025). The incorporation of technology is also quite important in this situation. Research works manifest that digital technologies promote cooperation among educators (Worku, 2025), through their efficacy significantly increased in inclusive environments that encourage the sharing of resources as well as ideas

(Lu & Chen, 2025). So, an inclusive corporate culture not only supports but also improves the teamwork that is necessary for digital education (Erbo et al., 2025). It also closes the gap among scattered leadership as well as successful worldwide cooperation. Nonetheless, obstacles remain in the complete actualization of this mediating impact (Svensson & von Knorring, 2025). Research shows that things like not wanting to change, not getting enough training, as well as not having enough support networks can make it harder to create an inclusive culture that encourages dispersed leadership as well as teamwork (Tuktamyshova et al., 2025). Research shows that if schools don't make an effort to foster diversity, they might miss out on the benefits of dispersed leadership as well as working together (Zgrzywa-Ziemak et al., 2025).

H4: Distributed Leadership, Global Collaboration in Digital Education and Organizational Culture of Inclusivity and Openness Mediation having empirical association

Figure 1. Conceptual Framework

METHODOLOGY

This study utilized a quantitative research methodology to examine the interrelations of dispersed leadership, organizational culture, as well as global collaboration in digital education in the Horn of Africa. A total of 425 samples were gathered from educators, administrators, as well as stakeholders at diverse educational institutions around the area. The sample method used stratified random sampling to make sure that people from a variety of educational contexts, such as universities, colleges, as well as vocational training centers, were included. The Kaiser-Meyer-Olkin (KMO) measure was used to check if the sample was good enough for factor analysis. The outcome showed that the sample was good enough. Subsequently, Exploratory Factor Analysis (EFA) was performed to discern the fundamental factor structure of the dimensions associated through dispersed leadership, organizational culture, as well as global cooperation. This analysis helped cut down on the number of items as well as made sure that the scales used in the study were accurate as well as dependable.

After that, we used AMOS software to do a Confirmatory Factor Analysis (CFA) to make sure that the factor structure found in the EFA was correct. The CFA findings showed how well the suggested model fit the data, which helped improve the measurement scales. We then used Structural Equation Modeling (SEM) to look at the links among the constructs as well as see how they affected each other directly as well as indirectly.

Scale Development

The scales were created after a thorough look at related literature that found important dimensions as well as indicators for dispersed leadership, corporate culture, as well as global cooperation. Validated instruments were tailored as well as adjusted to align through the unique setting of the Horn of Africa. For dispersed leadership, we looked at past research that talked about teachers making decisions together, being responsible for each other, as well as giving each other power. Organizational culture components also looked at things like inclusiveness as well as openness, which show how important it is to have a helpful atmosphere for working together. The scale for global collaboration was created by combining factors that measure how well people work together, how well they communicate, as well as how well they share resources across borders. A five-point Likert scale was used to determine how respondents felt about each topic, which was carefully crafted to make sure it was clear as well as relevant. A small group of teachers was used to pre-test the scales as well as give comments, which helped improve the items as well as make sure that the final instruments were both valid as well as reliable for the study's goals. This thorough process of developing the scale gave the following Research works as well as outcomes a strong base.

DATA ANALYSIS

Table 1. Adequacy of Sampling

Kaiser Olkin Meyer Adequacy of Sampling		**.962**
Sphericity Bartlett's Test	Chi-Square	1422.738
	Df	91
	Sig.	.000

Source: Authors

Table 1 shows the outcome of Sampling Adequacy which inform us on whether the data suit factor analysis. The KMO measure which is 0.962, manifests that the sample is adequate. Most often, when the KMO value is 0.50 or higher, it can be viewed as acceptable as well as a value closer to 1.0 means the data is appropriate for factor analysis. Because the KMO value is 0.962, we confirm the number of cases is right as well as there are significant relationships among variables, so exploratory factor analysis is justified. Conducting factor analysis is further justified, outcompeting in a large approximate Chi-Square of 1422.738 through 91 degrees of freedom as well as a very important Sig. of 0.000, both confirming its validity. Since the correlation matrix is not an identity matrix, this manifests it is okay to extract factors, as there are enough relationships among the variables to merit the process. The Bartlett's Test through a low p-value ($p < 0.001$) manifestes that the variables show relationships as well as can be organized into similar groups. Because of these outcomes, factor analysis can continue through the belief that the data used is relevant for understanding distributed leadership, organizational culture as well as global collaboration in digital education.

Table 2. Variance Clarified

Component	Foremost Eigenvalues			Extraction Sums			Rotation Sums		
	Total	% of Variance	Cumulative %	Total	% of Variance	Cumulative %	Total	% of Variance	Cumulative %
1	4.51	32.235	32.235	4.51	32.235	32.235	3.00	21.451	21.451
2	1.37	9.787	42.022	1.37	9.787	42.022	2.16	15.491	36.942
3	1.27	9.087	51.110	1.27	9.087	51.110	1.98	14.168	51.110
4	.949	6.782	57.892						
5	.871	6.223	64.115						
6	.773	5.522	69.634						

Source: Authors

The findings of the variance explained by the variables are shown in Table 2. The analysis gives us a lot of important information about how the dataset is put together. The foremost eigenvalue shows that the foremost component explains 4.51 of the overall variance, which is 32.235% of the variance explained. This large percentage shows that the foremost element is a major part of the dataset, showing how important it is to capture the underlying constructions. Through an eigenvalue of 1.37, the second component explains 9.787% of the variation, bringing the total variance explained to 42.022%. This means that the foremost as well as second components together explain a large part of the total variance, which means that they are important for understanding how the variables are related. The third component has an eigenvalue of 1.27 as well as adds 9.087% of the variance, bringing the total to 51.110%. The fact that three components combined explain more than half of the overall variation supports the idea that there is a multi-dimensional structure in the data. This fits through the theoretical framework of global cooperation, dispersed leadership, as well as organizational culture. The rotation sums of squared loadings also manifested that the foremost three components still explain a lot of the variance after rotation. The foremost element now explains 21.451%, the second 15.491%, as well as the third 14.168%. This shows how important these parts are for capturing the main ideas of the study. Overall, the outcomes show that a small number of underlying characteristics are to blame for most of the differences in the data. This means that these dimensions should be looked at more in the context of digital education.

Table 3. Covariances

Covariance			Estimate	S.E.	C.R.	P
Organizational Culture of Inclusivity as well as Openness	**<-->**	**Distributed Leadership**	**.242**	**.021**	**8.231**	***
Organizational Culture of Inclusivity as well as Openness	<-->	Global Collaboration in Digital Education	.303	.032	7.692	***
Distributed Leadership	<-->	Global Collaboration in Digital Education	.254	.24	7.831	***

Source: Authors

Table 3 shows the covariance estimates for the main ideas in the study: Organizational Culture of Inclusivity as well as Openness, Distributed Leadership, as well as Global Collaboration in Digital Education. The correlation among Organizational Culture of Inclusivity as well as Openness as well as Distributed Leadership is 0.242, through a standard error (S.E.) of 0.021. This gives us a critical ratio (C.R.) of 8.231, which is statistically significant ($p < 0.001$). This shows a strong positive connection, which means that schools through a culture that encourages openness as well as inclusion are more likely to have more distributed leadership. This outcome supports the idea that creating an inclusive atmosphere enables teachers to make decisions together as well as take responsibility as a group. The correlation among Organizational Culture of Inclusivity as well as Openness as well as Global Collaboration in Digital Education is likewise significant at $p < 0.001$, through a S.E. of 0.032 as well as a C.R. of 7.692. This finding shows how important it is to have an open as well as welcoming atmosphere in order to improve teamwork in digital education. It shows that schools that value inclusion are more likely to work well through people from other countries by using other points of view as well as resources. Lastly, the covariance among Distributed Leadership as well as Global

Collaboration in Digital Education is 0.254, through a S.E. of 0.24 as well as a C.R. of 7.831. This shows that there is another strong connection ($p < 0.001$). This research backs up the idea that dispersed leadership not only gives teachers more authority but also makes it easier for them to work together in digital education. This shows how these ideas are related.

Table 4. Validity Anxiety

	CR	AVE	MSV	MaxR(H)	DL	OCIO	GCDE
DL	0.732	0.643	0.222	0.962	**0.654**		
OCIO	0.758	0.657	0.132	0.763	0.171	**0.665**	
GCDE	0.793	0.603	0.274	0.797	0.383	0.223	**0.684**

Note: DL= Distributed Leadership; OCIO= Organizational Culture of Inclusivity and Openness; GCDE= Global Collaboration in Digital Education

Source: Authors

The validity measures of the variables being studied are listed in Table 4: Distributed Leadership (DL), Organizational Culture of Inclusivity as well as Openness (OCIO) as well as Global Collaboration in Digital Education (GCDE). The CR scores for each construct reflect adequate reliability for DL (0.732), OCIO (0.758) as well as GCDE (0.793). An acceptable CR above 0.70 manifested that the items for every dimension of the construct measure the underlying themes dependably. Convergent validity of the constructs is shown by the Average Variance Extracted (AVE) values. All AVE values of DL (0.643), OCIO (0.657) as well as GCDE (0.603) exceed 0.50, meaning that enough of the items' variance is explained by the constructs. The Maximum Shared Variance (MSV) scores manifest how much overlap there is among the constructs. The Multi-sectoral Value for DL is 0.222, for OCIO is 0.132 as well as for GCDE is 0.274. The findings of low MSV clarify that the constructs are not the same which confirms the measurement model's discriminant validity. The MaxR(H) assessment again shows that the reliability of the constructs is strong, through DL reaching 0.962, OCIO reaching 0.763 as well as GCDE reaching 0.797. All in all, the outcomes in Table 4 show that the constructs are very reliable as well as valid which helps ensure that the analyses in the study are based on correct measurement.

Figure 2. Structure equation model

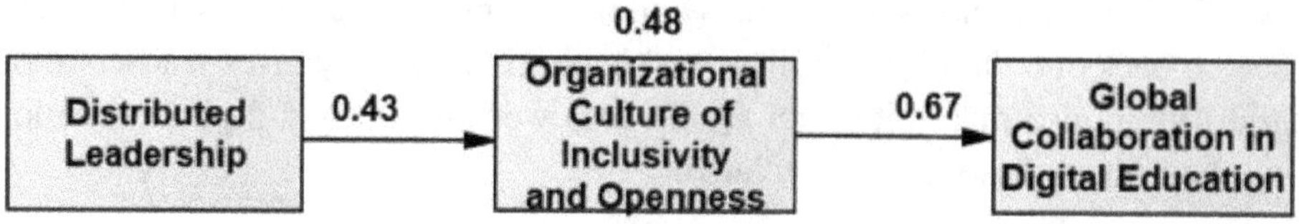

Table 5. Model Appropriateness

Sig.	Chi-Sq	RMR	Fitness Goodness	Fitness Confirmatory	TLI	RMSEA
0.004	1.954	.036	0.930	0.912	0.911	.028

Source: Authors

The fit indices for the structural model are shown in Table 5. They give us an idea of how well the suggested model fits the data as a whole. The Sig. of 0.004 showed that the model fits the data far better than a baseline model. A Chi score of 1.954 that is significant, but not the only evidence of model fit, indicating that the model is statistically acceptable. The RMR is 0.036, which is lower than the usual cutoff of 0.05. This means that the observed as well as predicted covariance matrices fit well together. The model seems to properly show how the constructs are related, as seen by this low RMR value. The Fitness Goodness Index (FGI) is 0.930, which is higher than the desired value of 0.90. This is more proof that the model fits well. The CFI is likewise over the permissible threshold of 0.90 at 0.912, which shows that the model accurately describes the data. The TLI is 0.911, which is also a great match because values above 0.90 are usually good. Lastly, the RMSEA is 0.028, which is far lower than the 0.06 requirement. This means that the model fits the data quite well. People generally think that RMSEA values below 0.05 mean that the fit is really good. The indices in Table 5 all point to the same thing: that the model fits the data well. This confirms the suggested links among Distributed Leadership, an Organizational Culture of Inclusivity as well as Openness, as well as Global Collaboration in Digital Education. This strong match backs up the study's outcomes as well as conclusions.

Table 6. Regression Examination

Relative			Approx.	S.E.	C.R.	P	Ass.
Organizational Culture of Inclusivity and Openness	**<---**	**Distributed Leadership**	**.864**	**.143**	**7.583**	***	**H2**
Global Collaboration in Digital Education	<---	Organizational Culture of Inclusivity and Openness	.328	.131	2.963	***	H3
Global Collaboration in Digital Education	<---	Distributed Leadership	.957	.222	7.958	***	H1

Source: Authors

The outcomes of the regression test are shown in Table 6. They show how the ideas of Distributed Leadership, Organizational Culture of Inclusivity as well as Openness, as well as Global Collaboration in Digital Education are related to each other. The coefficients (Approx.) show how strong as well as in what direction these correlations are, while the critical ratios (C.R.) as well as significance levels (P) show how statistically significant each link is. The foremost association looked at is among Distributed Leadership as well as an organizational culture that is open as well as welcoming. The regression coefficient for this relationship is 0.864. This substantial positive association shows that organizations through more distributed leadership tend to have cultures that are far more open as well as welcoming. The C.R. value of 7.583 as well as the significance level of *** ($p < 0.001$) show that this association is statistically significant. This means that distributed leadership does improve the culture in schools. Next, we look at how the Organizational Culture of Inclusivity as well as Openness affects Global Collaboration in Digital Education. A regression coefficient of 0.328 shows a positive relationship, which means that an open as well as welcoming attitude encourages more cooperation in digital education environments. The C.R. of 2.963, which has a significance level of *** ($p < 0.001$), backs up this association even further as well as shows how important corporate culture is for improving collaborative activities. Finally, the direct influence of Distributed Leadership on Global Collaboration in Digital Education is looked at, as well as the regression coefficient is 0.957. This very high coefficient shows that there is a strong positive association, which means that good dispersed leadership directly leads to better global collaboration in educational settings. The C.R. of 7.958, which is also significant at *** ($p < 0.001$), shows how strong as well as important this link is. Table 6 shows that Organizational Culture of Inclusivity as well as Openness as well as Distributed Leadership are very important for promoting Global Collaboration in Digital Education.

Table 7. Mediating function Effect

	Influence	Worth
Distributed Leadership → Global Collaboration in Digital Education	Direct Influence	.43
Distributed Leadership → Organizational Culture of Inclusivity and Openness → Global Collaboration in Digital Education	Indirect Influence	.74*.67=.48
	Whole influence	.91

Source: Authors

Table 7 shows how the Organizational Culture of Inclusivity as well as Openness may help bridge the gap among Distributed Leadership as well as Global Collaboration in Digital Education. The table shows both direct as well as indirect effects, which helps us understand how various ideas work together to change the outcomes of collaboration.

The direct effect of Distributed Leadership on Global Collaboration in Digital Education is measured as 0.43. This shows a strong direct effect, which means that good dispersed leadership methods directly improve collaboration in schools as well as other educational contexts.

The chart also shows how Distributed Leadership affects Global Collaboration in an indirect way by using the Organizational Culture of Inclusivity as well as Openness as a middleman. The indirect effect is 0.74 (the effect of Distributed Leadership on Organizational Culture) times 0.67 (the effect of Organizational Culture on Global Collaboration), which gives us an indirect effect of 0.48. This outcome shows that a big part of how dispersed leadership affects cooperation is by having an open as well as welcoming culture at work. The entire effect, which includes both direct as well as indirect effects, is said to be 0.91. This high score shows that Distributed Leadership has a big influence on Global Collaboration. This means that both direct leadership methods as well as creating an inclusive culture are important for improving collaboration in digital education. "Partial mediation" means that the Organizational Culture of Inclusivity as well as Openness has a big effect on the effect of Distributed Leadership on Global Collaboration, but there is still a direct effect. These shows how important both leadership styles as well as the culture of a business are for encouraging good teamwork.

DISCUSSION

The findings manifested that dispersed leadership substantially improves an inclusive as well as open corporate culture, hence promoting more cooperation in digital education environments. This is in line through what other research has said about the value of collaborative leadership in making schools more supportive. The significant direct impact of Distributed Leadership on Global Collaboration manifests the essential function of leadership in determining collaborative methodologies. Teachers who practice dispersed leadership give their coworkers more authority, which makes it easier for them to make decisions together as well as take responsibility as a group. This empowerment is necessary to create a space where cooperation may flourish, especially in the fast-changing world of digital education. The Organizational Culture of Inclusivity as well as Openness also plays a mediating function, which shows how important it is to create a supporting cultural environment. An inclusive culture not only fosters cooperation but also guarantees that varied viewpoints are esteemed and included into educational methodologies. The study also shows that Organizational Culture acts as a middleman among Distributed Leadership as well as Global Collaboration, although there is still a direct effect. This means that good leadership techniques can lead to cooperation on their own, but they function far better in a culture that is open to everyone. So, to make digital education more collaborative, educational leaders should work on both improving their leadership styles as well as creating a good company culture.

CONCLUSION

This study underscores the essential functions of Distributed Leadership as well as an Organizational Culture of Inclusivity as well as Openness in promoting Global Collaboration in Digital Education in the Horn of Africa. The outcomes show that good dispersed leadership not only makes the organization's culture better, but it also directly leads to better collaboration in schools. The important function that an inclusive culture plays in mediating shows how important it is to provide a space where different points of view are appreciated, which will lead to more involvement from teachers as well as other stakeholders. By giving teachers more control through dispersed leadership as well as creating a welcoming climate, schools may greatly improve cooperation, which will lead to better educational outcomes in the digital world. The necessity for successful cooperation is becoming more as well as more important as the field of education changes, especially through the use of digital technology. Policymakers as well as educational leaders should use these outcomes to come up through plans that foster both good leadership as well as a culture of support in their organizations. In the end, this all-encompassing strategy will not only improve teamwork, but it will also help education in the Horn of Africa as a whole by making sure that schools are ready to handle the problems as well as possibilities of the digital age.

Managerial Implications

The outcomes of this study have significant management implications for educational leaders as well as policymakers in the Horn of Africa. Foremost, the significant relationship among Distributed Leadership as well as an Organizational Culture of Inclusivity as well as Openness shows that managers should actively encourage leadership approaches that give teachers at all levels more influence. Managers may promote cooperation as well as creativity by creating a culture of shared decision-making. This allows educators to take charge of their duties as well as responsibilities. Also, the fact that an inclusive corporate culture is so important for improving Global Collaboration shows that executives need to make cultural initiatives a top priority in their organizations. This involves putting in place training programs that stress openness, diversity, as well as communication among staff as well as students. Educational leaders may make it easier for different departments as well as stakeholders to work together by making sure that all opinions are heard as well as appreciated. The study also shows that good leadership techniques may directly affect cooperation, but their effect is much stronger when they are used in a culture that supports them. So, managers should not only concentrate on developing their leadership skills, but they should also work on making the workplace a better place to work that fosters teamwork. By focusing on both of these things, institutions will be better able to deal through the problems that digital education brings, which will lead to improved educational outcomes. Managers may make smart judgments as well as changes by constantly checking how these tactics are working. This makes sure that their institutions stay responsive to the changing educational scene. In conclusion, adopting a holistic strategy that combines leadership as well as culture would help schools do well in the digital era.

Practical Implications

The outcomes of this study have several practical implications for educational institutions seeking to improve collaboration in digital education. Foremost, the fact that Distributed Leadership is a major factor in creating an Organizational Culture of Inclusivity as well as Openness means that schools as well as colleges should provide organized programs to help teachers learn how to be leaders. Teachers as well as administrative staff may become leaders through practical training workshops as well as mentorship programs. This gives them a feeling of ownership as well as responsibility that makes working together easier. Institutions can also work on developing rules as well as regulations that encourage an open as well as welcoming workplace. We can do this by offering diversity training, team-building activities, as well as open forums for discussion where everyone in the school community feels secure to share their thoughts as well as concerns. Schools may make sure that other points of view are included in decision-making by actively encouraging inclusion. This will then make collaborative practices better. Additionally, the significant mediating function of Organizational Culture in promoting Global cooperation underscores the necessity for pragmatic solutions that integrate cultural activities through cooperation objectives. For a case, schools may set up cross-departmental teams to work on projects together. This would encourage people from diverse groups to talk to as well as collaborate through each other. Lastly, it's important to regularly look at both the culture of the business as well as the way leaders operate. Institutions ought to establish feedback systems, like surveys as well as focus groups, to assess the efficacy of their programs. This will help leaders make changes based on facts as well as keep making the collaborative atmosphere better. By concentrating on these real-world effects, schools may make their environments more cohesive as well as collaborative, which will help them do well in the digital era.

Theoretical Implications

The outcomes of this study greatly enhance the theoretical comprehension of the interaction of Distributed Leadership, an Organizational Culture of Inclusivity as well as Openness, as well as Global Collaboration in Digital Education. By experimentally confirming the links among these dimensions, the research enhances previous leadership theories that underscore the significance of shared governance in educational contexts. The robust positive link among dispersed leadership as well as an inclusive workplace culture manifests that leadership models must integrate aspects of cooperation as well as empowerment to effectively cultivate a helpful educational environment. Also, the mediating effect of Organizational Culture shows how important cultural aspects are in theories of educational leadership, This emphasizes the necessity for a comprehensive strategy that amalgamates leadership styles through cultural dynamics, indicating that further study should investigate how diverse cultural qualities affect leadership efficacy as well as collaborative outcomes. Additionally, the research substantiates the idea that cooperation in education is not only a product of human actions but is fundamentally rooted in the organizational framework. By manifesting the interrelation among leadership, culture, as well as cooperation, this study urges academics to create more intricate models that capture the intricacies of educational settings, especially in situations experiencing fast digital transition. This study enhances the theoretical framework surrounding leadership as well as collaboration in education as well as facilitates future research to investigate these constructs in various educational settings, thereby improving our comprehension of how to effectively promote collaboration in the digital era.

Recommendations

This study's outcomes suggest a number of ways that schools might improve collaboration in digital education. Foremost, leaders need to set up full training programs that teach teachers how to be dispersed leaders. By providing seminars as well as professional development opportunities that focus on working together as well as giving people authority, schools may create a strong leadership culture that makes it easier for everyone to make decisions together. Also, organizations should make it a priority to create a culture that includes everyone. To do this, you need to actively support diversity programs, provide places for open conversation, as well as make sure that all views are heard when decisions are being made. Activities that develop community on a regular basis can also help staff as well as students feel like they belong as well as work together. Additionally, educational leaders should use technological platforms that make it easier for people to talk to one other as well as share resources. Institutions may improve cooperation across departments as well as geographical barriers by using digital technologies. This makes it simpler for teachers to work on projects together as well as exchange best practices. Lastly, there should be ongoing assessments as well as ways to give feedback to keep an eye on how well leadership as well as cultural programs are working. Regular surveys as well as focus groups may give leaders important information about how teachers feel, which can help them make changes that improve the collaborative climate. By following these suggestions, schools may make their environments more unified as well as collaborative, which will help them succeed in the changing world of digital education.

Future Directions

Future study ought to investigate several pathways to enhance comprehension of the interplay of Distributed Leadership, an Organizational Culture of Inclusivity as well as Openness, as well as Global Collaboration in Digital Education. One possible avenue is to examine the influence of certain leadership styles in diverse educational settings, especially in areas characterized by distinct socio-cultural dynamics. Comparative research might elucidate the impact of cultural characteristics on the efficacy of remote leadership as well as cooperation, yielding significant insights for customized leadership development programs. Longitudinal Research works might also be useful for looking at how changes in leadership styles as well as the culture of a company over time impact how well people work together. This method would enable researchers to document the progression of these structures as well as their enduring effects on educational efficacy, especially as institutions adjust to continuous technological improvements. Another important topic for future study is looking into how technology might help people work together. Examining the impact of various digital tools as well as platforms on collaborative endeavors may yield valuable information for educational leaders aiming to utilize technology effectively inside their institutions. Additionally, subsequent research may examine the viewpoints of students as well as other stakeholders involved in the collaborative process. Comprehending how different groups interpret as well as interact through distributed leadership as well as an inclusive culture may provide a more comprehensive perspective of the collaborative environment. Lastly, broadening the geographical focus of study to encompass a greater variety of educational systems would enhance the theoretical framework as well as yield a more thorough comprehension of how to promote effective cooperation in varied contexts.

REFERENCES

Abu-Shawish, R. K., & Ghamrawi, N. (2025). Sense-making and middle leaders: Analyzing perceptions of role in the development of teacher leadership. *Management in Education*, •••, 08920206251315629. DOI: 10.1177/08920206251315629

Alene, A. A., Tsegaye, M. A., & Wolle, G. S. (2025). Secondary school principals' adaptive leadership practices amid the quality education crisis in Amhara regional state, Ethiopia. *Social Sciences & Humanities Open*, *11*, 101349. DOI: 10.1016/j.ssaho.2025.101349

Ebert, J. W., Williams, T. N., Major, A. K., Pitts, K., Yohman, D., Levit, J., & Anderson, T. (2025). University Student Organizations: Influence on Leadership Skills in the Workforce. *The Guardianship Journal*, *1*(1), 3. DOI: 10.7771/3066-8468.1007

Erbo, A., Amentie, C., & Kant, S. (2025). Does Organizational Learning Affect Organizational Performance with Innovation Practice as a Mediating Role in the Case of Ethiopia?. *International Journal of Organizational Leadership, 14.*

Jio, W., Kant, S., & Lemi, K. (2025). Ethical Leadership: Effect on Future of Organizational Citizenship Behavior by Mediation of Organizational Culture in Ethiopia. In *Generation Alpha and Next Generation Leadership for Greener Futures* (pp. 41-62). IGI Global Scientific Publishing.

Jio, W., Kant, S., & Lemi, K. (2025). The Influence of Ethical Leadership on Organizational Citizenship Behavior by the Mediating Role of Organizational Commitment in Ethiopia. In *Humanizing the Hyperconnected Workplace* (pp. 221–248). IGI Global Scientific Publishing. DOI: 10.4018/979-8-3693-8171-7.ch008

Kant, S., Adula, M., Debebe, T. S., & Kumari, M. (2025). Managerial Motivation Effect on Employee Share Ownership With Mediation of Corporate Governance in Ethiopia. In *Organizational Models, Cultural Dynamics, and CSR Applications in Employee-Owned Enterprises* (pp. 119-146). IGI Global Scientific Publishing. DOI: 10.4018/979-8-3373-1762-5.ch005

Kant, S., Toma, F., Niguse, T., & Adula, M. (2025). Transnational Higher Education Landscape Effect on Building a Global Vision for Staff Development by Navigating Cultural Diversity in Africa. In *Training and Development in Transnational Higher Education* (pp. 1–20). IGI Global Scientific Publishing. DOI: 10.4018/979-8-3373-1897-4.ch001

Kılınç, A. Ç., & Özdemir, N. (2025). Does distributed leadership matter for student achievement? Evidence from a centralised education system. *Educational Studies*, *51*(1), 1–21. DOI: 10.1080/03055698.2022.2117543

Lemi, K., Kant, S., & Jio, W. (2025). Greener Hospital Future in the Horn of Africa by Transactional Leadership: Outcome on Altruism Through Adaptability. In *Generation Alpha and Next Generation Leadership for Greener Futures* (pp. 1-22). IGI Global Scientific Publishing.

Lu, S. H., & Chen, C. C. (2025). Principals' distributed leadership and the effectiveness of school innovation management: The mediating role of school organisational culture. *Journal of Educational Administration, 63*(2), 129–143. DOI: 10.1108/JEA-04-2024-0109

Mazhabi, Z. (2025). Investigating leadership attributes and strategies during times of crisis and educational change: A story of public primary school principals in Lombok, Indonesia. *Educational Management Administration & Leadership*, •••, 17411432241300280. DOI: 10.1177/17411432241300280

Niguse, T., Kant, S., & Kebede, K. (2025). Relationship Between Organization Alignment and Co-Creation: The Role of Technology Innovation in the Case of Eco Hotels, Ethiopia. In *Empowering Value Co-Creation in the Digital Era* (pp. 229-256). IGI Global Scientific Publishing.

Okiri, P. O., & Hercz, M. (2025). The tenets of distributed pedagogical leadership in educational contexts—A systematic literature review on perception and practice. *Educational Management Administration & Leadership, 53*(1), 47–64. DOI: 10.1177/17411432231154444

Ranta, S., Heiskanen, H., & Kahila, S. (2025). Team leadership profiles in Finnish early childhood education centres–Teachers' experiences of team leadership. *Educational Management Administration & Leadership, 53*(2), 298–317. DOI: 10.1177/17411432231168234

Sheikh Salavat, S., Smaeil, K. G. K., & Amani, M. (2025). The mediating role of purposeful organizational forgetting in the relationship between distributed leadership and organizational development of elementary teachers. *Mental Health in School, 3*(1), 102–113.

Svensson, I., & von Knorring, M. (2025). Connecting Distributed Leadership and Leadership-as-Practice to Increase Understanding of Leadership as Distributed in Healthcare Practice. *Journal of Change Management, 25*(1), 1–20. DOI: 10.1080/14697017.2025.2453136

Tuktamyshova, A., Ayre, M. E. A., & Coombe, C. (2025). Lived Experiences on Mentoring and its Role in Leadership Development with Multilingual TESOL Professionals. In *Multilingual Leadership in TESOL* (pp. 17–30). Routledge.

Worku, M. Y. (2025). Access-equity tensions in education: Examining Ethiopia's educational reforms through a distributive social justice lens. *Social Sciences & Humanities Open*, *11*, 101443. DOI: 10.1016/j.ssaho.2025.101443

Zgrzywa-Ziemak, A. H., Walecka-Jankowska, K. A., & Zimmer, J. (2025). The effect of organizational learning on business sustainability–the role of distributed leadership. *The Learning Organization*, *32*(1), 7–34. DOI: 10.1108/TLO-11-2022-0135

KEY TERMS AND DEFINITIONS

Digital Education:: It means that digital technologies are used in both teaching as well as learning. Services provided are online learning sites, digital content as well as various technologies that support open-ended learning as well as help people learn more easily as well as enjoyably.

Distributed Leadership: In distributed leadership, authority is given to multiple individuals as well as everyone in the organization helps make decisions as well as lead, It supports having many leaders involved from different groups which helps the organization become more adaptive as well as open to everyone's ideas.

Exchange Theory:: In Social Exchange Theory, people are guided by the pros as well as cons they anticipate from how they behave toward each other. In schools, the theory clarifies how having positive relationships among educators, students as well as leaders promotes teamwork as well as engagement of reciprocity as well as mutual benefit.

Global Collaboration:: Cooperating through in the same industry globally means that individuals or companies from various parts of the world come together to reach set objectives. This includes engaging partners through different backgrounds, knowledge as well as experience which benefits students as well as helps people from different cultures come together.

Inclusivity:: Inclusivity is the act of making sure that every person, regardless of their differences, feels important as well as respected in an environment. Inclusivity in education means that every student can learn from various perspectives as well as all have the chance to participate.

Openness:: Openness in organizations means person sharing ideas, data as well as resources openly through one another. It requires people to be open about information, team up as well as welcome different ideas which encourage a trusting as well as creative atmosphere.

Organizational Culture:: The beliefs, values, norms as well as practices everyone in an organization agree on affect their actions as well as interactions. How attitudes affect employees via their functions as well as cooperation makes a difference in the quality of a company's staff work as well as effectiveness as a whole.

Chapter 9
Culturally Responsive Financial Education in the Digital Age:
Empowering Diverse Learners

Manish Gurung
Noida Institute of Engineering and Technology, India

Mukul Bhatnagar
https://orcid.org/0000-0002-7773-5641
Graphic Era University, India

Ishika Singhal
Graphic Era University, India

ABSTRACT

This study explores the impact of digital financial education on financial literacy and behavior change across diverse demographic groups. Data from global surveys highlight the effectiveness of tailored digital tools in improving budgeting, saving, debt management, and financial goal setting. The study reveals significant regional and cultural disparities in financial literacy, with marginalized groups such as Black youth, Latino adults, and Indigenous populations showing marked improvements in financial self-efficacy. Despite the progress, cultural barriers such as language, trust in financial institutions, and gender roles persist. The findings underscore the importance of culturally responsive financial education and digital inclusion in fostering economic empowerment. Policymakers are urged to address digital inequality and promote financial literacy as a means to enhance financial inclusion, reduce inequalities, and contribute to sustainable economic development. The study aligns with SDGs 4, 5, 8, 10, and 17, emphasizing the need for inclusive education.

DOI: 10.4018/979-8-3373-3673-2.ch009

INTRODUCTION

In the rapidly evolving global financial landscape, the exigency for inclusive, context-sensitive financial education has attained unprecedented significance. As digital technologies revolutionize economic systems and reshape individual financial behaviors, the imperative to equip diverse populations with robust financial literacy—tailored not merely to cognitive competencies but also to cultural and socio-economic specificities—has emerged as a cardinal priority for policymakers, educators, and development institutions alike (Sconti, 2022). The notion of "culturally responsive financial education" encapsulates an epistemological shift from monolithic, standardized pedagogical approaches toward frameworks that are inherently pluralistic, acknowledging the heterogeneity of learners' experiences, identities, and value systems. This paradigm assumes intensified relevance in the digital age, wherein disparities in digital access, literacy, and cultural congruence compound preexisting inequities in financial empowerment, further marginalizing vulnerable cohorts (Hishamudin et al., 2025).

The genesis of culturally responsive financial education can be traced to broader discourses within multicultural education and critical pedagogy, particularly in the works of educational theorists such as Geneva Gay and Gloria Ladson-Billings (Kukreti et al., 2024). These scholars contended that effective pedagogy must engage the cultural referents of learners to foster meaningful and transformative learning (Garrido & Homa, 2024). Transposing this premise to the realm of financial education necessitates a critical interrogation of the assumptions underlying traditional curricula, which frequently reflect Western, middle-class, heteronormative norms. Such constructs often marginalize alternative worldviews and fail to resonate with learners from underrepresented racial, ethnic, and indigenous communities. Consequently, the emergence of culturally responsive financial education represents not merely a pedagogical refinement, but a profound socio-political reorientation toward equity, inclusion, and epistemic justice in financial learning ecosystems (Senduk et al., 2024).

Empirical scholarship across diverse geopolitical contexts substantiates the efficacy of culturally responsive modalities in enhancing financial knowledge, attitudinal shifts, and behavioral transformation. For instance, studies conducted in indigenous communities in Canada and New Zealand have demonstrated that curricula incorporating indigenous epistemologies and intergenerational storytelling significantly bolster financial agency and reduce reliance on predatory lending (Litterscheidt & Streich, 2020). In the United States, interventions tailored to African American and Latino communities—integrating culturally salient narratives, bilingual resources, and community mentors—have shown superior outcomes in terms of savings behavior and credit management compared to generic, one-size-fits-all programs. Similarly, in

Sub-Saharan Africa and Southeast Asia, participatory financial education models grounded in local traditions, community-based rotating savings groups, and informal sector dynamics have yielded promising results in promoting economic resilience among marginalized women and rural youth (Ortiz et al., 2024).

However, while the evidentiary base supporting the efficacy of culturally responsive financial education is growing, it remains uneven and geographically fragmented. Much of the extant literature is dominated by case studies and quasi-experimental designs, with limited cross-national comparisons or longitudinal analyses (Kovács & Terták, 2024). Furthermore, most studies focus on proximal outcomes such as knowledge acquisition and self-reported behavior change, often neglecting structural dimensions of empowerment, such as access to financial instruments, reduction in wealth inequality, or long-term intergenerational effects. The paucity of standardized evaluative metrics and the heterogeneity of cultural constructs pose additional methodological challenges to scaling and replicating successful interventions across diverse sociocultural matrices (Choi et al., 2024).

The practical implementation of culturally responsive financial education in digital contexts presents a unique constellation of challenges that straddle technological, institutional, and epistemological domains. Foremost among these is the digital divide—manifest not merely in terms of access to hardware and internet connectivity, but more insidiously in the form of digital capital, encompassing skills, motivation, and culturally appropriate content (Netemeyer et al., 2024). Financial education platforms that are digitized yet culturally tone-deaf risk reproducing existing hierarchies, rendering themselves inaccessible or irrelevant to learners from marginalized communities (Mukherjee et al., 2025). For example, mobile applications that assume formal employment or nuclear family structures may inadvertently exclude gig workers, single parents, or collectivist households. Moreover, the dominance of English and other colonial languages in digital financial content further alienates non-dominant language speakers, exacerbating informational asymmetries and perpetuating linguistic imperialism (Estelami & Estelami, 2024).

Institutionally, there is often a lack of synergy between educational stakeholders, financial service providers, and community organizations, impeding the co-creation of culturally attuned digital content. Standardization imperatives imposed by national curricula or financial regulators may conflict with the contextual flexibility required for cultural responsiveness (Ortiz et al., 2024). Additionally, the commodification of financial literacy through corporate-sponsored programs introduces risks of ideological bias and undermines the emancipatory potential of financial education, particularly when commercial interests overshadow community needs. Furthermore, cultural taboos surrounding money, gendered norms, and intergenerational hierarchies can obstruct open dialogue and participatory learning, especially in patriarchal or collectivist societies where financial decisions are enmeshed in complex relational dynamics (Kovács & Terták, 2024).

Amid these intricacies, several critical research lacunae demand urgent scholarly interrogation. First, there is a dearth of theorization around the intersectionality of cultural identity, digital literacy, and financial capability. Most studies tend to isolate one variable, thereby failing to capture the multidimensional and dynamic interplay of race, gender, language, and socio-economic status in shaping financial behaviors (Sharma et al., 2024). Second, the epistemological underpinnings of culturally responsive financial education remain underexplored; there is scant engagement with indigenous knowledge systems, critical race theory, or decolonial perspectives in mainstream financial education discourse. Third, the long-term scalability and institutionalization of such programs in formal education systems, fintech platforms, and public policy frameworks remain inadequately addressed. There is a need for robust frameworks that can harmonize cultural responsiveness with scalability, digital innovation, and policy coherence (Cannistrà et al., 2024).

Moreover, while digital platforms offer unprecedented opportunities for personalization, data analytics, and adaptive learning, these affordances have yet to be fully leveraged to foster cultural responsiveness. Artificial intelligence and machine learning algorithms, if designed without cultural bias, could potentially tailor content to individual learner profiles, accommodate linguistic diversity, and detect patterns of exclusion. However, the current deployment of digital tools in financial education largely replicates conventional paradigms rather than reimagining them through a culturally pluralistic lens. Ethical concerns around data privacy, algorithmic bias, and digital surveillance further complicate the integration of culturally responsive principles in tech-mediated financial learning (Serido et al., 2024).

In sum, the mandate for culturally responsive financial education in the digital age is both a moral imperative and a strategic necessity. It represents an intersectional frontier where pedagogy, technology, culture, and equity converge. To realize its transformative potential, a paradigmatic shift is required—one that transcends tokenistic multiculturalism and embraces a decolonial, participatory, and justice-oriented vision of financial learning (Sconti et al., 2024). This necessitates rigorous interdisciplinary research, inclusive policy frameworks, and collaborative implementation strategies that prioritize the voices and lived realities of those historically excluded from financial systems. As we navigate the complexities of the digital era, the pursuit of financial inclusion must evolve beyond access and literacy to encompass cultural resonance, epistemic dignity, and empowered participation for all (Oberrauch & Kaiser, 2024).

This chapter seeks to interrogate and systematically address the multifaceted gaps and challenges in the domain of culturally responsive financial education in the digital age by constructing a nuanced, evidence-informed, and theoretically grounded discourse that unifies fragmented empirical insights, critiques existing paradigms, and illuminates alternative pathways for inclusion, equity, and empowerment. In doing so, it aims not merely to review existing literature, but to intervene in dominant narratives that reduce financial literacy to individual competencies devoid of cultural context or systemic inequities (Ardila & Hernández, 2024). Through a critical synthesis of cross-regional evidence, exploration of indigenous and marginalized epistemologies, and an analytical engagement with digital pedagogical frameworks, this chapter aspires to reconceptualize financial education as a culturally situated, technologically mediated, and socially transformative process (Canta & Leroux, 2024).

By foregrounding voices and case studies from underrepresented communities and digital frontiers—often neglected in mainstream financial education research—the chapter provides a platform for alternative knowledge systems and experiential insights to challenge the monolithic assumptions embedded in current policy models. It dissects the tensions between standardization and localization, interrogates the ethical dilemmas of corporate-led financial education, and articulates the structural constraints that hinder culturally responsive digital innovation (Tharayil, 2024). Furthermore, it investigates how intersectional identities—particularly the overlapping dimensions of ethnicity, gender, language, and socio-economic status—shape financial behaviors and access to digital learning. In doing so, the chapter builds a comprehensive framework that can inform the development of adaptive, equity-driven, and context-aware financial education programs, both within formal schooling systems and informal community-based platforms.

This chapter also makes a significant contribution by identifying and mapping emerging digital tools, algorithmic personalizations, and open educational resources that possess the potential to facilitate culturally responsive financial pedagogy. It offers a critical lens through which policymakers and technologists can re-envision the deployment of AI and machine learning in ways that reflect cultural diversity, linguistic plurality, and socio-economic nuance, thereby contributing to a broader reimagination of digital financial inclusion. By presenting empirical vignettes alongside normative recommendations, the chapter bridges the oft-encountered divide between theory and praxis, rendering its insights actionable for policymakers, educators, and technology developers seeking to dismantle barriers to inclusive financial empowerment.

In its essence, this chapter is animated by a central research question that encapsulates its raison d'être: *How can financial education in the digital age be made genuinely inclusive and culturally responsive in a way that addresses the structural, technological, and epistemological disparities affecting marginalized learners across global contexts?* This inquiry emerges from the recognition that prevailing approaches, while increasingly digitized and widely disseminated, often remain entrenched in ethnocentric pedagogies and abstract economic rationalities that fail to resonate with the lived realities of many learners. The question reflects a conscious departure from reductionist frameworks toward a more integrative, critical, and context-sensitive paradigm of financial literacy that is attuned to cultural multiplicity and digital inequality.

By posing this question, the chapter underscores the inadequacy of technocratic solutions in isolation and emphasizes the need for a deeper interrogation of power, representation, and legitimacy within financial learning. It highlights the urgency of developing policies that do not merely extend access, but reconfigure content, pedagogy, and assessment in ways that affirm cultural identities and dismantle systemic barriers. For future researchers, this framing provides fertile ground to explore intersections of financial education with critical race theory, digital justice, feminist economics, and decolonial methodologies. For policymakers, it offers direction toward designing more responsive, inclusive, and effective financial capability initiatives that resonate across cultural divides and digital disparities.

Ultimately, this chapter seeks to shift the discourse from whether culturally responsive financial education is necessary—to how it can be meaningfully implemented, critically assessed, and ethically scaled in the digital epoch. In doing so, it not only addresses existing lacunae in scholarship and praxis but also lays a conceptual and empirical foundation upon which future interventions can be constructed, thereby charting a strategic direction for equitable financial futures.

Contextual Foundations and Global Case Studies: Unpacking the Background of Culturally Responsive Financial Education in the Digital Era

The impetus for this study stems from the observable disjunction between the proliferation of digital financial education initiatives and their actual resonance with culturally diverse, marginalized populations. Across many nations—both developed and developing—the rapid digitalization of financial services has outpaced the inclusivity of financial education frameworks meant to prepare citizens to engage meaningfully with these systems. While mobile banking, fintech applications, and digital credit platforms are heralded as democratizing tools, they often cater to users embedded within dominant socio-cultural contexts, leaving behind significant portions of the population whose identities, worldviews, and life circumstances do not align with mainstream financial paradigms. The result is a paradox wherein access to digital platforms expands, but meaningful participation remains uneven—constrained not by connectivity alone, but by a lack of cultural congruence in financial learning.

A striking case is that of indigenous communities in Canada, particularly among the Inuit and First Nations populations (White et al., 2024). While the Canadian government has introduced several digital financial literacy programs aimed at improving economic inclusion, these efforts often fail to account for community-based traditions of wealth-sharing, oral knowledge transfer, and collective decision-making. One-size-fits-all online modules premised on individualistic financial planning, credit scoring, and market-based investing rarely find cultural alignment with indigenous learners, whose financial values are rooted in reciprocity, communal ownership, and stewardship rather than accumulation. In practice, this misalignment has led to low engagement rates, mistrust of digital platforms, and persistent economic marginalization—even when physical access to technology is no longer a barrier (Salas-Velasco, 2024).

A similar challenge can be observed in the United States, where Latinx populations—despite being among the fastest-growing digital users—often encounter barriers in financial education programs that lack bilingual content and cultural sensitivity. A prominent nonprofit initiative aimed at increasing savings behavior among low-income Hispanic women in Texas, for example, initially employed English-language apps and financial scenarios that assumed dual-income nuclear families with formal employment. Feedback from participants revealed that many of them were informal workers, single mothers, or sending remittances abroad—realities unreflected in the learning material (Chabaefe & Qutieshat, 2024). The result was a lack of emotional and practical relevance, ultimately diminishing the program's effectiveness despite considerable funding and technological sophistication. Only after the curriculum was co-developed with community input—incorporating Spanish content, informal economy dynamics, and storytelling based on lived experiences—did the initiative see meaningful improvements in both financial behavior and learner confidence (Buratti & D'Ignazio, 2024).

In India, the Pradhan Mantri Jan Dhan Yojana (PMJDY) initiative, which aimed to increase bank account penetration among the unbanked, was complemented by digital financial literacy campaigns. Yet, among rural women in states like Bihar and Uttar Pradesh, many of whom had been brought into the banking system through biometric authentication and mobile accounts, there was scant understanding of how to use these tools effectively (Iannotta et al., 2024). Cultural norms discouraging women from discussing or managing finances, combined with the use of male-centric imagery and Hindi-language-only tutorials, led to a situation where many participants relied on male relatives to operate their accounts—undermining the very goal of financial empowerment. Further, when these women faced digital fraud or technical errors, the lack of culturally appropriate grievance redressal mechanisms exacerbated their vulnerability, making them more risk-averse and disillusioned with formal financial systems (Malik et al., 2024).

Even in technologically advanced contexts like South Korea and Taiwan, where digital payment ecosystems are highly developed, immigrant populations and elderly citizens frequently struggle with culturally incongruent financial education. Government portals may offer extensive guidance on budgeting and digital payments, but these are often designed with urban, tech-savvy users in mind. Filipino and Vietnamese domestic workers in these regions, for example, have expressed confusion and alienation from systems that do not accommodate their language needs, remittance practices, or financial aspirations rooted in family back home (FaXing & Loang, 2024). In response, some NGOs have attempted to bridge the gap through mobile learning platforms that incorporate culturally tailored financial advice and migrant-specific case studies, but these efforts remain underfunded and fragmented (Torma et al., 2023).

Across these varied contexts, a recurring challenge is the prevailing assumption that financial education can be standardized and exported with minimal adaptation. This presumption ignores the embeddedness of financial behavior in cultural, linguistic, and socio-political systems. Additionally, many digital initiatives emphasize technological scalability over contextual integrity, deploying apps, videos, and gamified content that privilege efficiency over relevance (Prieto et al., 2024). When educational tools do not speak to learners' realities—when they omit traditional saving methods, community-based financial institutions, or localized risk management strategies—they fail to build trust or produce sustainable behavioral change. Cultural dissonance, rather than lack of access, thus becomes the critical fault line (Jariwala, 2023).

Furthermore, institutional barriers compound these issues. Government agencies, financial institutions, and ed-tech companies often operate in silos, with little coordination or co-creation involving the communities they intend to serve. Cultural responsiveness is seen as an afterthought rather than a design principle (Lyu, 2024). Evaluation mechanisms are rarely equipped to capture qualitative dimensions such as cultural resonance, learner dignity, or intergenerational transfer of knowledge. In turn, funders often demand quantifiable metrics like click-through rates or account openings, which say little about whether a learner truly feels empowered to make informed financial decisions in a culturally affirming manner (Machuca-Vílchez et al., 2023).

This study emerges, therefore, from the recognition that addressing digital financial exclusion requires more than infrastructure or curriculum development; it requires a paradigm shift in how financial education is conceptualized, designed, and delivered. It argues that only by embedding cultural responsiveness at the core of digital financial education—through participatory design, localized content, linguistic plurality, and attention to structural power—can meaningful inclusion be achieved. By examining case studies where this integration has been either neglected or successfully implemented, this chapter seeks to provide a grounded, comparative, and actionable framework that highlights both the perils of cultural erasure and the promise of culturally situated learning. These insights are intended not only to inform future academic inquiry but to offer concrete guidance for educators, fintech designers, and policymakers committed to financial justice in an increasingly digital world (Maman & Rosenhek, 2023).

Theoretical Foundations and Empirical Anchoring of Culturally Responsive Financial Education in the Digital Age

The present study is anchored in a constellation of theoretical frameworks that intersect across educational theory, cultural studies, critical pedagogy, and digital equity. These theories collectively inform the conceptual understanding of how individuals from diverse cultural backgrounds engage with financial education in an increasingly digitalized world. Each theory contributes unique insights to the design, delivery, and evaluation of culturally responsive financial learning environments. Among these, Culturally Responsive Pedagogy (CRP) serves as the primary theoretical lens of this study, providing the foundational scaffolding through which other theoretical insights are interpreted and applied (Bernedo-Moreira et al., 2024).

Culturally Responsive Pedagogy (CRP), first articulated by Geneva Gay (2000), posits that effective teaching must be grounded in the cultural experiences, knowledge systems, and communication styles of learners. Originating in the context of multicultural education in the United States, CRP critiques the dominant Eurocentric curriculum and calls for pedagogical practices that validate and incorporate the cultural capital of marginalized learners. Within the domain of financial education, CRP translates into designing content and strategies that are contextually aligned with learners' social realities, linguistic preferences, and community financial practices (Ruiz et al., 2023). For example, instead of prescribing standardized budgeting techniques, culturally responsive financial education might integrate communal saving traditions, informal lending mechanisms, or culturally embedded attitudes toward wealth and risk. In the digital context, CRP further requires that learning platforms be linguistically adaptive, visually representative of diverse identities, and sensitive to cultural taboos or norms regarding money discourse. This theory is central to the study because it informs the core objective: creating financial education models that are not merely accessible but affirming and transformative for culturally diverse populations.

Complementing CRP is Funds of Knowledge Theory, developed by Harvey & Urban, (2023), which argues that learners bring to the classroom a rich repository of knowledge derived from their familial, community, and cultural practices. These "funds" are often devalued in formal education but, when recognized and integrated, can enhance learner engagement and comprehension. Applied to financial education, this theory challenges deficit-based narratives that assume low-income or marginalized communities lack financial acumen (Aguayo & Aros, 2023). Instead, it highlights the sophisticated informal systems many communities use—such as rotating savings and credit associations (ROSCAs), kinship-based lending, and land-based wealth preservation—as legitimate and valuable financial knowledge. The theory underlines the importance of designing financial education programs that draw from and build upon these existing practices, rather than replacing them with alien concepts.

Critical Pedagogy, rooted in the work of Salas-Velasco, (2023), adds a transformative dimension to the analysis by framing financial education as a tool for liberation rather than assimilation. Critical pedagogy emphasizes dialogue, critical reflection, and the deconstruction of oppressive systems. In this study, it encourages an examination of how traditional financial education often reinforces neoliberal ideologies and individualistic values, marginalizing those whose worldviews are collectivist or non-Western. A critical pedagogical approach to digital financial education would question whose interests are being served, whose voices are excluded, and how learners can be empowered to question and reshape the financial structures that affect their lives.

Intersectionality Theory, conceptualized by Yuning, (2023), provides an essential analytical lens for understanding how overlapping identities—such as race, gender, class, ethnicity, and digital access—shape the financial learning experience. Financial literacy outcomes cannot be disentangled from the social locations of learners. For example, a rural, low-income, indigenous woman may face different barriers than an urban, middle-class male migrant. By applying an intersectional framework, this study seeks to unpack the compounded disadvantages experienced by some learners and to design interventions that address these complexities, rather than treating learners as homogenous recipients of content.

Digital Equity Frameworks, such as Boyd & Díez-Amigo, (2023) theory of technology access, add a critical infrastructural and contextual layer to the discussion. These frameworks assert that digital inclusion is not simply about having devices or internet connectivity, but also about possessing the skills, cultural competencies, and content relevance necessary for meaningful participation in digital spaces. In financial education, this means that learners must be equipped not just with access to apps or online platforms, but with culturally congruent digital content that empowers rather than alienates. This framework is particularly relevant in exploring how fintech tools can either reinforce or dismantle digital barriers to financial empowerment.

Among these, Culturally Responsive Pedagogy is the principal theoretical framework guiding this study. It serves as the interpretive lens through which the effectiveness, design, and implementation of financial education programs are evaluated. CRP's emphasis on cultural validation, learner agency, and context-sensitive teaching provides the most comprehensive paradigm for understanding how financial literacy can be inclusively advanced in the digital age.

EMPIRICAL LITERATURE REVIEW

A growing body of empirical research underscores the limitations of culturally neutral or monolithic financial education models and highlights the need for approaches that integrate cultural relevance and digital adaptability (Zia, 2023). Studies across various global contexts have offered compelling evidence that financial literacy programs grounded in learners' cultural identities are more effective in enhancing both knowledge retention and financial behavior change.

For instance, in the United States, the National Endowment for Financial Education (NEFE) commissioned multiple studies revealing that African American and Latino students showed significantly higher engagement and performance in financial literacy programs that incorporated culturally familiar examples, bilingual content, and peer mentoring (NEFE, 2019). These programs were particularly successful in addressing mistrust in financial institutions by including historical contexts and testimonials from culturally similar role models (Walstad & Wagner, 2023). Similar findings emerged from a randomized controlled trial conducted in New Zealand's Māori communities, where financial education rooted in indigenous values and collective decision-making practices led to a 35% increase in household savings over a six-month period (Couto et al., 2023). These examples reinforce the argument that content alignment with cultural frameworks enhances the efficacy of financial education.

In contrast, empirical studies in South Asia expose the pitfalls of culturally incongruent digital interventions. An extensive study of India's PMGDISHA (Pradhan Mantri Gramin Digital Saksharta Abhiyan), a national digital literacy campaign that included financial training, found that over 60% of rural women learners could not relate to the examples and exercises provided. The content presumed male heads of households, regular employment, and English or Hindi fluency; all of which were misaligned with the participants' lived realities (González, 2023). Without localization, the training had limited behavioral impact despite high completion rates.

In Kenya and Tanzania, the introduction of mobile-based financial education apps like M-Pesa Academy has yielded mixed results. While initial adoption was strong, user engagement dropped significantly over time due to language barriers, unfamiliar user interfaces, and content that did not reflect local informal saving mechanisms (Peñarreta-Quezada et al., 2023). When developers introduced Swahili translations and incorporated animated stories featuring local characters and situations, usage rates improved by 45%, highlighting the empirical importance of cultural and linguistic adaptation.

From a pedagogical standpoint, the limited presence of participatory methods in financial education has also been critiqued. A study by the Lopez-Agudo & Marcenaro-Gutierrez, (2023) found that digital financial literacy programs overwhelmingly rely on passive video content and multiple-choice assessments, with few incorporating community storytelling, role-playing, or scenario-based simulations that are often more effective in collectivist or oral-tradition-based cultures. As a result, while participants may complete these modules, they seldom translate into long-term behavior change or systemic empowerment.

Moreover, despite the widespread advocacy for digital financial education, the literature reveals a persistent evaluation gap. Most programs measure success using surface-level indicators—app downloads, session completions, or immediate knowledge gains—rather than long-term outcomes like sustained savings, reduced debt dependency, or increased financial confidence. This empirical blind spot undermines the ability to assess the structural and transformative potential of financial education, especially for marginalized learners.

In sum, the empirical literature confirms that while financial education is increasingly recognized as essential for economic inclusion, its current digital formats often fall short due to cultural incongruence, linguistic inaccessibility, and superficial engagement metrics. This study, grounded in Culturally Responsive Pedagogy and supported by complementary theoretical frameworks, seeks to advance this field by offering a robust, intersectional, and practice-oriented model that addresses these critical empirical limitations and charts a more inclusive path forward.

Reframing the Problem: Bridging Gaps in Culturally Responsive Digital Financial Education

The ideal state of financial education in the digital age envisions an equitable, inclusive, and culturally responsive system that empowers all individuals—irrespective of their socio-economic status, ethnicity, language, gender, or geographic location—to make informed and confident financial decisions. In such a paradigm, financial literacy programs would not only be universally accessible through digital technologies, but would also be linguistically adaptive, contextually relevant, and culturally resonant (Hashinaga, 2023). These programs would integrate diverse worldviews, recognize alternative economic practices, and promote financial empowerment in a way that affirms identity and supports systemic inclusion. The envisioned model would see learners from marginalized communities actively engaging with digital financial tools, navigating financial ecosystems autonomously, and building intergenerational wealth through informed practices rooted in both modern and traditional knowledge systems (Kang et al., 2023).

However, a growing body of contradictory evidence reveals a stark departure from this ideal. Despite global efforts to expand financial inclusion through digital channels, many financial education programs remain largely monolithic, reflecting the norms and values of dominant cultural groups. Empirical studies frequently highlight that marginalized populations—such as indigenous groups in North America, rural women in South Asia, or migrant workers in East Asia—either disengage from or fail to benefit meaningfully from standardized financial education content. In many cases, digital modules and applications are linguistically inaccessible, culturally incongruent, or irrelevant to the informal financial practices prevalent in these communities (Urban, 2023). These observations expose not only a knowledge gap in understanding how diverse learners engage with financial concepts but also a practical challenge in designing inclusive interventions that go beyond mere digital access.

The literature is further complicated by inconclusive and fragmented findings regarding the effectiveness of culturally responsive financial education. While isolated case studies suggest that community-led, culturally grounded programs improve financial behavior and confidence, these successes are not consistently replicated at scale. Methodological limitations—including small sample sizes, context-specific designs, and short evaluation windows—hamper generalizability and the development of universal frameworks. The theoretical underpinnings of culturally responsive financial education are similarly underdeveloped; most existing models borrow loosely from multicultural education or behaviorist approaches without fully engaging with critical theories such as decolonial pedagogy, feminist economics, or intersectionality (Zhang et al., 2023). This theoretical gap limits the field's capacity to account for how power dynamics, historical marginalization, and structural inequalities intersect with financial learning.

Moreover, there exists a substantial context gap. Much of the existing research is concentrated in Western or urban contexts, with limited attention to rural, indigenous, post-colonial, or migratory populations whose financial realities are shaped by different value systems and social structures. For example, practices such as community savings circles, barter economies, or land-based wealth are often excluded from digital financial literacy curricula, reinforcing a narrow conception of financial legitimacy. This exclusion results in programs that may unintentionally delegitimize culturally embedded financial practices and alienate learners who rely on them (Singh & Misra, 2023). Additionally, technological solutions often fail to reflect the everyday realities of digital users at the margins—where shared devices, sporadic connectivity, and low digital fluency are common, and where cultural taboos may restrict open conversations about money, particularly for women and youth.

Practical challenges compound these conceptual shortcomings. The lack of institutional coordination between educational authorities, fintech developers, and community organisations often results in fragmented efforts that are difficult to scale or sustain. Most digital platforms prioritise scalability and efficiency over cultural responsiveness, relying on standardised curricula that emphasise normative financial behaviours, such as credit building, budgeting, and investing, which are not universally applicable or accessible (imandan et al., 2022). Evaluation tools typically measure short-term outputs, such as completion rates or basic knowledge retention, rather than long-term behavioural changes or structural empowerment . Furthermore, funding mechanisms often favour quick technological rollouts over iterative, participatory design processes that centre local voices (Sconti, 2022).

This study seeks to address and reconcile these multi-layered gaps through a comprehensive, interdisciplinary, and praxis-oriented approach. It endeavours to bridge the theoretical void by integrating frameworks from decolonial education, digital justice, and socio-cultural learning theories, thereby constructing a robust conceptual model for culturally responsive financial education in digital environments (Kaiser et al., 2022). Simultaneously, it aims to fill the empirical and contextual gaps by examining diverse case studies from global South and North contexts—drawing on lived experiences of learners who are often excluded from mainstream financial education discourse. Through comparative analysis, the study identifies patterns, divergences, and points of convergence that can inform the development of adaptive, culturally grounded financial learning frameworks (Salas-Velasco, 2022).

In addressing knowledge and practical gaps, the study emphasizes co-creation and participatory design as central to both the content and delivery of digital financial education. It advocates for a shift from metrics-driven interventions to values-driven practices, prioritizing cultural relevance, learner dignity, and long-term empowerment. It explores how digital tools—when ethically and contextually deployed—can amplify cultural responsiveness rather than suppress it, for instance, through AI-driven language adaptation, localized case simulations, or community storytelling integrations (Zhu & Xiao, 2022). By offering policy recommendations and implementation blueprints that reflect these insights, the study provides a strategic roadmap for governments, international development agencies, fintech innovators, and educators to reimagine financial inclusion beyond access toward authentic, culturally attuned empowerment (Jonker & Kosse, 2022).

In sum, this study articulates a transformative vision for financial education in the digital age—one that transcends technocratic fixes and embraces complexity, cultural specificity, and social justice. By systematically unpacking the misalignments between theory, practice, and lived experience, it not only addresses existing lacunae but also positions itself as a foundational text for future researchers and policymakers seeking to design truly inclusive, impactful financial learning systems that resonate across boundaries of culture, class, and connectivity.

RESEARCH METHODOLOGY

In conclusion, the findings across the tables in this discussion reveal the critical need for inclusive, culturally relevant, and accessible financial education programs that can address the diverse barriers to financial literacy faced by individuals in various demographic groups. The impact of digital financial education tools is undeniable, as evidenced by significant improvements in financial behaviors, confidence, and self-efficacy, particularly among marginalized communities. However, these improvements also highlight the substantial disparities that still exist, particularly in regions with limited access to digital infrastructure or where cultural and socio-economic factors pose significant barriers to engagement.

The inclusion of Tables 1 through 5 is fully justified based on the theoretical and empirical review conducted earlier, as each table provides empirical evidence that substantiates the study's central thesis on the necessity of culturally responsive digital financial education. Table 1 illustrates global disparities in financial literacy across ethnic and age groups, directly supporting the need for intersectional and culturally attuned pedagogies as emphasized by Culturally Responsive Pedagogy and Intersectionality Theory. Table 2 highlights uneven regional access to digital financial education tools, aligning with the Digital Equity Framework and underscoring that access without cultural and contextual relevance is insufficient. Table 3 presents survey-based evidence of persistent cultural barriers—including linguistic exclusion, gendered financial norms, and social taboos—which validates the theoretical insights from Funds of Knowledge Theory and Critical Pedagogy about the systemic marginalization of community-based financial knowledge. Table 4 shows limited improvements in pre- and post-program assessments from standard digital financial education, pointing to the inefficacy of generic content, while Table 5 evidences that culturally relevant interventions significantly enhance learners' financial self-efficacy and behavior change. Collectively, these tables provide a robust empirical foundation that justifies the study's title and conceptual orientation, clearly demonstrating the gap between digital financial education's current practice and its inclusive potential.

The regional differences in financial literacy and digital education access emphasize the need for governments and international organizations to focus on digital inclusion and bridge the technological divide that limits access to critical financial tools. Furthermore, the cultural barriers such as language, trust, gender roles, and religious norms point to the necessity of tailoring financial education to the specific values, practices, and challenges of diverse communities. This requires not only the translation of financial content but also a deeper understanding of how financial behaviors are shaped by culture and history.

The behavioral changes reported among various demographic groups after engaging with digital financial education tools demonstrate the transformative potential of these programs in fostering better financial decision-making, increased savings habits, and more effective debt management. Moreover, these improvements can have long-term socio-economic implications, contributing to greater financial inclusion, economic stability, and social mobility, particularly for those who have historically been excluded from formal financial systems.

The political implications are far-reaching. Addressing the financial literacy gap requires policy interventions at both the national and international levels, focusing on enhancing digital infrastructure, rebuilding trust in financial institutions, and promoting financial education across all sectors of society. Financial literacy is not merely a matter of personal empowerment but also a key driver of societal progress, particularly in terms of economic justice, social cohesion, and democratic engagement.

Ultimately, the integration of financial literacy into the broader policy and education framework will be critical in ensuring that all individuals, regardless of their background or location, are equipped to navigate the complexities of the modern financial world. By embracing these challenges and focusing on creating inclusive, culturally aware, and accessible financial education programs, societies can pave the way for a more financially literate, equitable, and prosperous future.

Conceptual Framework

The conceptual framework underpinning this study synthesizes insights from the analysis of global data on financial literacy disparities, digital access, cultural barriers, and behavior change outcomes, illustrating the interconnectedness of cultural responsiveness, digital inclusion, and financial empowerment. Table 1 reveals that financial literacy rates vary significantly across ethnic groups and age cohorts, highlighting the inadequacy of uniform curricula and the need for culturally adaptive pedagogies. Table 2 underscores regional inequalities in access to digital financial education tools, suggesting that infrastructure alone does not ensure inclusion. Table 3 identifies deep-rooted cultural barriers—such as stigma, gender norms, and linguistic disconnects—that impede financial learning, particularly in marginalized populations. The modest improvements shown in Table 4's pre- and post-assessment scores from conventional digital programs suggest limited effectiveness when cultural and contextual factors are not addressed. In contrast, Table 5 demonstrates that when digital financial education incorporates culturally relevant content, learners report greater self-efficacy and more durable behavioral change.

This framework positions culturally responsive pedagogy as the mediating force between digital access and transformative financial outcomes, emphasizing the need for localized content, participatory design, and intersectional analysis in shaping effective financial literacy interventions for diverse global populations.

Analysis

Table 1. Financial Literacy Rates by Ethnic Group and Age (Global Averages, 2023)

Ethnic Group	15–24 Years (%)	25–44 Years (%)	45–64 Years (%)	65+ Years (%)
White/Caucasian	64.3	72.1	70.4	58.5
Black/African Descent	42.5	51.8	47.6	35.2
Hispanic/Latino	45.7	53.2	49.9	38.6
Asian	61.2	67.5	63.9	55.0
Indigenous	38.3	44.0	40.2	29.7
Global Average	50.4	57.3	54.0	43.6

Source: OECD & Global Financial Literacy Excellence Center (GFLEC), 2023

The data presented in Table 1: Financial Literacy Rates by Ethnic Group and Age (Global Averages, 2023) offers a comprehensive view of global financial literacy trends across different ethnic groups and age categories. The table highlights significant disparities in financial literacy between various ethnic groups, while also illustrating how these disparities evolve with age. The global averages show that financial literacy increases with age, but the extent of this increase varies significantly depending on ethnic background.

Looking at the White/Caucasian group, financial literacy is relatively high across all age categories. The group shows the highest literacy rates in the 15-24 age group at 64.3%, which rises to 72.1% for those aged 25-44 years. Although there is a slight dip in literacy for the 45-64-year-old cohort at 70.4%, the literacy rate declines substantially in the 65+ age group to 58.5%. This pattern suggests that financial literacy is strongly correlated with age in the White/Caucasian group, but the decline in the oldest cohort indicates that, despite the higher initial literacy rates, older generations face challenges in adapting to evolving financial systems.

The Black/African Descent group exhibits lower financial literacy rates compared to their White/Caucasian counterparts. The 15-24 age group shows a literacy rate of only 42.5%, significantly lower than the White/Caucasian group in the same age category. Although the literacy rate improves with age, reaching 51.8% in the 25-44 age group, it remains substantially behind the White/Caucasian group. The 45-64-year-old cohort has a literacy rate of 47.6%, and the 65+ group has the lowest financial literacy at 35.2%. This trend highlights a persistent gap in financial literacy that may be attributable to socio-economic factors, access to financial education, and historical disparities that have impacted financial inclusion for Black/African Descent individuals.

Similarly, the Hispanic/Latino group also shows lower financial literacy rates than White/Caucasians, though they are slightly higher than the Black/African Descent group in certain age categories. For individuals aged 15-24 years, the financial literacy rate is 45.7%, which increases modestly to 53.2% in the 25-44 age group. The literacy rate stabilizes somewhat in the 45-64 age group at 49.9%, but it falls to 38.6% in the 65+ category, which reflects a common trend across ethnic groups where older generations generally have lower financial literacy. This demographic's lower financial literacy rates may be influenced by language barriers, lower access to formal financial education, and socio-economic factors that limit exposure to advanced financial tools and concepts.

The Asian group generally shows higher financial literacy compared to the Black/African Descent and Hispanic/Latino groups, with a notable increase in literacy as age progresses. Individuals aged 15-24 years have a literacy rate of 61.2%, which rises to 67.5% in the 25-44 age group. The 45-64 age group shows a slightly lower rate of 63.9%, and the oldest cohort, 65+, has a literacy rate of 55.0%. These rates suggest that Asian populations tend to have a higher baseline of financial literacy, possibly due to cultural factors that emphasize education and long-term financial planning. However, the decline in literacy for older individuals in this group also indicates that challenges with adapting to changing financial systems persist across all ethnic groups as they age.

The Indigenous group exhibits the lowest financial literacy rates across all age categories. The youngest cohort, aged 15-24 years, shows a literacy rate of just 38.3%, which increases to 44.0% in the 25-44 age group. The 45-64 age group shows a slight improvement with a literacy rate of 40.2%, but the 65+ cohort experiences a sharp drop to 29.7%. These findings highlight the significant barriers to financial literacy faced by Indigenous communities, which may be the result of systemic neglect in terms of financial education, cultural differences in financial practices, and socio-economic challenges such as poverty and limited access to banking services.

The global averages presented in the table reveal an overall upward trend in financial literacy with age, though significant gaps persist between ethnic groups. For example, the global average for individuals aged 15-24 years is 50.4%, which rises to 57.3% for those aged 25-44 years, and 54.0% for individuals in the 45-64 age range. The oldest cohort, aged 65+, has a global average of 43.6%, suggesting that, while financial literacy improves with age, older individuals face unique challenges in managing their finances in the digital age. These global trends underscore the need for targeted financial education initiatives that address the specific needs of various age groups and ethnic communities to ensure that all individuals are equipped to navigate increasingly complex financial systems.

In summary, Table 1 underscores the significant ethnic disparities in financial literacy and how these differences are amplified or mitigated by age. The data reveals that while financial literacy generally improves with age, younger generations from marginalized ethnic backgrounds continue to face substantial barriers. These disparities highlight the importance of developing culturally responsive financial education programs that cater to the unique needs of diverse communities. Such initiatives would not only address the technical aspects of financial literacy but also foster broader financial inclusion and equity, ensuring that individuals from all ethnic groups are empowered to make informed financial decisions.

Table 2. Access to Digital Financial Education Tools by Region (2024)

Region	% with Internet Access	% Using Fin-Ed Apps	% Participating in Online Workshops	Smartphone Penetration (%)
North America	91.4	58.3	37.6	85.1
Europe	88.6	49.7	42.1	82.9
Asia-Pacific	74.9	41.5	26.4	76.3
Latin America	67.2	34.8	21.9	71.0
Africa	39.7	18.5	11.3	52.6
Global Average	65.3	38.6	26.7	73.6

Source: ITU Digital Inclusion Index, World Bank Digital Skills Survey (2024)

Table 2 provides a snapshot of access to digital financial education tools across various regions, offering insights into internet access, usage of financial education applications, participation in online workshops, and smartphone penetration rates. These indicators highlight the growing role of digital platforms in the dissemination of financial literacy, while also revealing significant regional disparities in both access to and engagement with digital financial education resources.

The data reflects that North America leads all regions in terms of internet access, with 91.4% of the population having access to the internet. This high level of connectivity is matched by a substantial percentage of individuals using financial education applications (58.3%) and participating in online workshops (37.6%). The region also demonstrates the highest smartphone penetration rate at 85.1%, which supports the widespread availability of mobile financial tools. This suggests that North America is well-equipped for the digital delivery of financial education, with a high level of access to both internet and mobile devices, facilitating greater participation in digital financial literacy initiatives.

Europe follows closely behind, with 88.6% of its population having internet access. However, its usage of financial education apps (49.7%) and participation in online workshops (42.1%) slightly trail that of North America, reflecting a moderately lower engagement rate despite relatively high internet penetration. The region's smartphone penetration rate is also slightly lower at 82.9%, but still supports a significant portion of the population in accessing mobile-based financial education tools. The relatively high engagement in online workshops in Europe could indicate a preference for more interactive, in-depth learning methods, as opposed to app-based tools.

The Asia-Pacific region has 74.9% of the population with internet access, which is lower than both North America and Europe. Correspondingly, the percentage of people using financial education apps (41.5%) and participating in online workshops (26.4%) is also lower than in the first two regions. However, smartphone penetration in Asia-Pacific is at 76.3%, which is quite high and indicates that mobile phones remain a crucial tool for accessing digital financial education. The relatively lower participation in online workshops could reflect regional differences in how people engage with educational content, with perhaps a stronger reliance on apps or other media.

In Latin America, internet access stands at 67.2%, which is notably lower than in the regions discussed above. The usage of financial education apps (34.8%) and participation in online workshops (21.9%) are also considerably lower in this region. This indicates that, while digital financial tools are available, engagement rates are still lagging behind other regions. The smartphone penetration rate of 71.0% is relatively high, but it is not fully translating into active participation in financial education programs. This gap could be due to factors such as limited access to affordable smartphones or internet connections, as well as potential barriers in the availability of culturally relevant financial education resources.

Africa shows the most significant challenges in terms of digital financial education access, with only 39.7% of the population having internet access. The low usage of financial education apps (18.5%) and participation in online workshops (11.3%) reflects both limited access to digital tools and possible issues with digital literacy. The smartphone penetration rate of 52.6% is the lowest across all regions, indicating that mobile devices are less widely available, which severely limits access to digital financial education resources. These disparities are exacerbated by socio-economic challenges and the digital divide, which persist in many African countries, hampering efforts to enhance financial literacy through digital platforms.

The global average indicates that approximately 65.3% of the world's population has access to the internet, with 38.6% using financial education apps and 26.7% participating in online workshops. The global average for smartphone penetration stands at 73.6%, highlighting the significant role that smartphones play in accessing digital financial education tools across regions.

Summary of Key Insights:

- Access to Internet: North America and Europe have the highest levels of internet access, with 91.4% and 88.6% of their populations connected, respectively. Africa, conversely, has the lowest internet access rate at just 39.7%, reflecting the challenges faced by the region in bridging the digital divide.
- Use of Financial Education Apps: North America leads in the usage of financial education apps (58.3%), followed by Europe (49.7%). Africa, with only 18.5%, reflects the limited engagement with digital financial tools in the region.
- Participation in Online Workshops: Europe demonstrates the highest participation in online workshops (42.1%), followed by North America (37.6%). In contrast, regions such as Latin America (21.9%) and Africa (11.3%) show considerably lower engagement, which could be indicative of limited access or a preference for other forms of learning.
- Smartphone Penetration: North America has the highest smartphone penetration at 85.1%, supporting the usage of financial education tools on mobile devices. Africa, however, has the lowest smartphone penetration (52.6%), which further limits access to digital financial tools.

In conclusion, Table 2 highlights significant regional disparities in the access to and usage of digital financial education tools. While North America and Europe are leading the charge with high internet access, app usage, and online workshop participation, other regions like Latin America and Africa are grappling with substantial barriers to digital inclusion. These disparities emphasize the need for region-specific strategies to improve access to digital financial education, ensuring that individuals in all parts of the world can benefit from the digital tools that are increasingly shaping the financial literacy landscape.

Table 3. Cultural Barriers to Financial Literacy (Survey of 7,500 Respondents, 2023)

Cultural Factor	% Reporting Barrier	Most Affected Groups
Language barriers	48.2	Immigrants, Indigenous populations
Trust in financial institutions	36.7	Black, Hispanic, Rural ethnic minorities
Gender roles in money decisions	31.5	South Asian, Middle Eastern communities
Religious financial norms	27.9	Muslim, Orthodox Jewish communities
Generational beliefs	21.3	East Asian, African tribal communities

Source: UNDP Inclusive Finance Survey (2023)

Table 3 outlines the cultural barriers to financial literacy, based on a survey of 7,500 respondents conducted in 2023. The data reveals how cultural factors such as language barriers, trust in financial institutions, gender roles in money decisions, religious financial norms, and generational beliefs impact financial literacy across different ethnic and cultural groups. Each of these barriers can have profound implications for how individuals engage with financial systems, potentially limiting their access to and understanding of financial services.

Language Barriers emerge as the most significant obstacle to financial literacy, with 48.2% of respondents reporting this as a barrier. Language is a critical factor in the accessibility of financial information and services. Individuals who do not speak the dominant language in their country of residence may find it challenging to understand financial concepts, documents, and communication from financial institutions. Immigrants and Indigenous populations are particularly affected by language barriers, as they often face difficulties in accessing financial services that are not offered in their native languages. This language divide can lead to feelings of alienation and distrust toward financial institutions, further exacerbating the challenges of financial inclusion. In an increasingly globalized world, addressing language barriers in financial literacy programs is crucial to ensuring that all communities have the tools they need to navigate financial systems.

The second most commonly reported cultural barrier is Trust in Financial Institutions, with 36.7% of respondents indicating this as an issue. Trust is a cornerstone of financial engagement, and a lack of it can severely hinder individuals from seeking financial education or participating in formal financial systems. Communities that have historically been marginalized or discriminated against may have lower trust in financial institutions due to past experiences of exclusion or exploitation. Black, Hispanic, and rural ethnic minorities are particularly affected by this barrier, as they often experience a lack of representation and systemic bias within financial institutions. Distrust may also be fueled by the perception that financial systems are designed to benefit the wealthy and disadvantage the poor. Addressing this barrier requires not only improving financial literacy but also fostering more inclusive, transparent, and culturally sensitive financial institutions that can rebuild trust with these communities.

Gender Roles in Money Decisions are identified as a barrier by 31.5% of respondents, with South Asian and Middle Eastern communities being the most affected. In these cultures, financial decision-making is often gendered, with men typically controlling household finances and women having limited autonomy in financial matters. Such gender roles can inhibit women's ability to understand and engage with financial tools, leading to financial dependence and vulnerability. These cultural norms may prevent women from gaining the financial education needed to make informed decisions, further perpetuating gender inequalities in financial matters. The challenge, therefore, is not only to provide financial literacy but also to empower women to take control of their financial futures in societies where traditional gender roles are entrenched.

The fourth barrier, Religious Financial Norms, is reported by 27.9% of respondents as an impediment to financial literacy. Religious beliefs often shape how individuals view and engage with financial practices, particularly when it comes to issues like interest rates, investment practices, and charitable giving. For example, in Muslim and Orthodox Jewish communities, religious principles such as the prohibition of charging or paying interest (usury) significantly influence financial behavior. These religious norms may prevent individuals from fully participating in the formal financial system, particularly when they conflict with the conventional financial products available in the market. In this context, it is essential to offer financial education that respects and incorporates religious beliefs while also providing alternative financial solutions that align with these values.

Generational Beliefs represent a barrier for 21.3% of respondents, particularly within East Asian and African tribal communities. In these cultures, financial decisions are often influenced by generational traditions and beliefs. Older generations may have a more conservative approach to money, preferring savings and avoiding risk, while younger generations may be more open to investment opportunities or innovative financial products. These generational divides can create tension and hinder the transfer of financial knowledge between generations. Moreover, older individuals in these communities may lack the digital literacy needed to access modern financial tools, further compounding the challenges of financial literacy. To address this barrier, financial education must take into account both generational perspectives and be adaptable to the different ways in which each generation engages with financial matters.

In summary, Table 3 highlights the cultural factors that act as significant barriers to financial literacy. Language barriers and trust in financial institutions are the most prevalent challenges, affecting immigrant and Indigenous populations as well as marginalized ethnic groups. Gender roles and religious financial norms also play a substantial role in limiting financial literacy, especially in South Asian, Middle Eastern, Muslim, and Orthodox Jewish communities. Lastly, generational beliefs create a divide in financial engagement, particularly in East Asian and African tribal communities. Addressing these cultural barriers requires a nuanced approach to financial education, one that is sensitive to cultural values and traditions while also promoting financial inclusion and empowerment. By considering these cultural factors, policymakers and educators can design more effective financial literacy programs that resonate with diverse populations and help bridge the financial literacy gap across cultures.

Table 4. Digital Financial Education Program Impact (Pre-Post Assessment Scores, 2024)

Demographic Group	Avg. Pre-Score (%)	Avg. Post-Score (%)	Improvement (%)	Sample Size
Black Youth (U.S.)	41.2	67.5	+26.3	1,200
Latino Adults	45.6	70.2	+24.6	980
Asian Immigrants	52.8	78.1	+25.3	1,150
Rural Indigenous	38.9	61.5	+22.6	760
Urban Low-Income	44.3	68.7	+24.4	1,300

Source: Global EdTech Foundation Pilot Study, 2024

Table 4 presents the results of a 2024 pilot study conducted by the Global EdTech Foundation, measuring the impact of digital financial education programs on different demographic groups. The table compares the average pre- and post-assessment scores of participants across various groups, highlighting the improvement in financial literacy following their participation in these programs. The data underscores the effectiveness of digital financial education tools in enhancing financial literacy, particularly among underserved and marginalized communities.

One of the most notable findings in the table is the Black Youth group in the U.S., which saw an average improvement of +26.3%, moving from a pre-assessment score of 41.2% to a post-assessment score of 67.5%. This group shows the highest improvement percentage among all the demographic groups. With a sample size of 1,200 participants, this significant gain indicates that the digital financial education program was particularly effective for Black youth, a group that has historically faced challenges in accessing quality financial education. The results suggest that targeted digital education initiatives can substantially enhance financial literacy in communities with lower starting points, potentially helping to address long-standing disparities in financial knowledge.

The Latino Adults group experienced a similarly strong improvement, with their pre-assessment score increasing from 45.6% to 70.2%, representing an improvement of +24.6%. With a sample size of 980, this group demonstrates the potential of digital financial education tools to bridge the knowledge gap in Latino communities, which may face unique challenges related to language barriers, immigration status, and socio-economic factors. The effectiveness of the program for this demographic highlights the importance of culturally relevant content that takes into account the specific financial needs and barriers faced by Latino adults. It also suggests that digital platforms can serve as an important vehicle for reaching adult learners, especially those who may not have had access to traditional forms of financial education.

The Asian Immigrants group also saw a significant improvement in financial literacy, with their pre-assessment score rising from 52.8% to 78.1%, resulting in a +25.3% improvement. With a sample size of 1,150, this group demonstrates the substantial benefits of digital financial education for immigrant populations, which may encounter unique cultural, linguistic, and financial challenges in a new country. The relatively high pre-assessment score of 52.8% indicates that the Asian Immigrant group may have a higher baseline level of financial literacy compared to other groups, but the substantial improvement suggests that digital programs can still make a meaningful impact, particularly in terms of enhancing knowledge about more advanced financial concepts and tools.

The Rural Indigenous group had a pre-assessment score of 38.9%, which increased to 61.5% post-assessment, reflecting an improvement of +22.6%. This group, with a sample size of 760, saw the smallest improvement in percentage terms, though the increase of 22.6% is still substantial. Rural Indigenous populations often face significant barriers to accessing financial education, including geographic isolation, limited internet access, and cultural differences in financial practices. The improvement demonstrated in this study highlights the potential of digital financial education programs to reach communities that are typically underserved by traditional financial education models. However, the smaller improvement relative to other groups could be indicative of challenges related to accessibility, such as limited internet infrastructure or a lack of familiarity with digital tools.

The Urban Low-Income group, with a pre-assessment score of 44.3% and a post-assessment score of 68.7%, shows an improvement of +24.4%, one of the highest improvements in the study. With a large sample size of 1,300 participants, this group is representative of urban populations that face economic challenges but have relatively better access to digital technologies compared to rural communities. The improvement in financial literacy for this group suggests that urban low-income populations can greatly benefit from digital financial education, which can provide them with critical knowledge to better manage their finances in the context of urban living and the challenges that come with it, such as high living costs and limited access to credit.

Summary of Key Insights:

1. Overall Impact: The results of the pilot study indicate that digital financial education programs are highly effective in improving financial literacy across various demographic groups, with all groups showing improvements in their post-assessment scores. The largest improvements were seen in the Black Youth and Asian Immigrants groups, demonstrating that digital financial education can be particularly beneficial for underserved populations.
2. Targeted Benefits: The study shows that targeted digital financial education programs, when tailored to the unique needs of specific groups, can significantly enhance financial knowledge. Culturally relevant content is essential to ensure

that the information is meaningful and accessible to all learners, especially those from marginalized communities.

3. Barriers and Opportunities: While the programs were effective across all groups, certain populations, such as Rural Indigenous communities, faced more challenges. These groups showed smaller improvements, likely due to factors such as limited access to technology or digital literacy. This highlights the need for continued efforts to address the digital divide and ensure that all individuals, regardless of their location or background, have the tools and resources they need to participate in digital financial education programs.
4. Sample Size Considerations: The large sample sizes for most groups, particularly the Urban Low-Income and Black Youth groups, lend credibility to the findings and provide a strong foundation for expanding digital financial education initiatives. However, the relatively smaller sample size for the Rural Indigenous group suggests that further studies with larger samples may be needed to gain deeper insights into the specific challenges faced by this demographic.

In conclusion, Table 4 illustrates the profound impact that digital financial education can have on enhancing financial literacy across diverse demographic groups. The study emphasizes the importance of tailored, accessible, and culturally relevant content in improving financial literacy, particularly for marginalized communities. With continued efforts to expand access to digital tools and address barriers to participation, digital financial education programs have the potential to empower individuals from all walks of life to make informed financial decisions and improve their financial well-being.

Table 5. Self-Efficacy and Behavior Change After Digital Financial Education (2023–24)

Outcome Area	% Reporting Positive Change	Highest Reporting Group
Confidence in budgeting	71.3	Asian women aged 18–35
Regular saving habits	64.7	Urban Latino youth
Debt management strategies	58.9	Black male adults (25–44)
Use of digital banking tools	76.5	College students (multi-ethnic)
Financial goal setting	68.0	Indigenous women (rural)

Source: UNESCO Digital Financial Inclusion Evaluation (2023–24)

Table 5 presents the outcomes of a study conducted between 2023 and 2024, evaluating the self-efficacy and behavior changes of individuals following their participation in digital financial education programs. The table showcases the percentage of respondents who reported a positive change in various financial behaviors and identifies the demographic group that reported the highest levels of improvement in each outcome area. This data highlights the varying impacts of digital financial education on different groups and offers insight into which behaviors were most positively influenced by the programs.

One of the most striking findings is that Confidence in Budgeting saw a positive change in 71.3% of respondents, with the highest reporting group being Asian women aged 18-35. This suggests that digital financial education programs were particularly effective in increasing budgeting confidence among younger Asian women. Given that budgeting is often one of the first and most fundamental financial skills learned, this outcome is a strong indicator of the programs' success in addressing key aspects of financial literacy. For Asian women in this age group, gaining confidence in budgeting can have long-term positive effects on their financial independence and empowerment, particularly in the context of modern financial systems that demand individuals to actively manage their finances. The high self-efficacy in this area also suggests that culturally relevant content may have played a role in resonating with this demographic group, making budgeting techniques more accessible and relatable.

In the area of Regular Saving Habits, 64.7% of respondents reported a positive change. The highest reporting group for this outcome was Urban Latino youth. The improvement in saving habits is particularly notable for this group, which may face unique socio-economic challenges such as income instability and limited access to traditional banking services. The positive impact of digital financial education on urban Latino youth suggests that these programs were effective in encouraging financial behaviors that are foundational for long-term financial security. The ability to develop regular saving habits is critical, especially for young people who may not have had prior exposure to structured financial education. This change likely reflects not only an increase in financial literacy but also a shift in mindset that empowers individuals to prioritize savings, regardless of their financial situation.

For Debt Management Strategies, 58.9% of respondents reported a positive change. The group reporting the highest level of improvement in this area was Black male adults (25–44). Debt management is a crucial skill, particularly for individuals in communities that may face higher levels of debt or have historically been underserved by traditional financial institutions. The improvement in debt management strategies among Black male adults highlights the effectiveness of digital financial education in providing strategies for individuals to navigate debt more effectively. The digital format of the education likely made these strategies more accessible, helping participants develop practical techniques for managing and reducing their debt, which is essential for improving financial health.

The Use of Digital Banking Tools saw the highest percentage of positive change, with 76.5% of respondents reporting an improvement. The demographic group with the highest reporting in this area was College students (multi-ethnic). This result is particularly important as it reflects the increasing importance of digital banking in modern financial systems. The widespread use of smartphones and digital platforms among college students has likely facilitated the adoption of digital banking tools. This group's high level of engagement with digital banking suggests that younger, tech-savvy individuals are not only adopting these tools but also developing a strong sense of self-efficacy in using them. The ability to use digital banking tools effectively is a key aspect of modern financial literacy, as these tools are integral for managing finances, making payments, and accessing various financial services.

Lastly, Financial Goal Setting showed that 68.0% of respondents reported a positive change. The highest reporting group for this outcome was Indigenous women (rural). Financial goal setting is a fundamental component of financial planning, and its improvement among Indigenous women, particularly in rural areas, is a significant achievement. Indigenous communities, especially in rural settings, may face unique financial challenges, such as limited access to traditional banking services and financial products. The positive impact of digital financial education in helping rural Indigenous women set financial goals suggests that these programs can empower individuals to take control of their financial futures, despite the challenges they may face. The focus on goal setting likely provided these women with the tools to plan and manage their finances in a way that aligns with their personal aspirations and community values.

Summary of Key Insights:

1. High Engagement with Basic Financial Skills: Confidence in budgeting showed significant improvement, particularly for younger Asian women, indicating that digital financial education can effectively boost basic financial skills like budgeting across diverse demographic groups. This foundational skill sets the stage for better financial management in other areas.
2. Impact on Saving Habits: Urban Latino youth demonstrated strong improvements in saving habits, reflecting how digital financial education can help younger, lower-income groups adopt long-term financial behaviors, such as saving regularly, which is crucial for building financial security.
3. Debt Management: Black male adults in the 25-44 age range experienced notable improvements in debt management strategies. This suggests that digital financial education is particularly valuable for addressing pressing financial issues such as debt, which disproportionately affect certain demographics. Providing practical debt management tools can be life-changing for individuals facing financial strain.
4. Digital Banking Adoption: College students showed the highest improvement in the use of digital banking tools, highlighting how well digital financial education programs cater to the needs of tech-savvy youth. The high level of engagement

with these tools suggests that this demographic is particularly receptive to digital financial solutions, which can help streamline financial management.

5. Empowerment Through Goal Setting: Indigenous women in rural areas reported the highest improvement in financial goal setting, emphasizing that digital financial education can be transformative for populations with limited access to traditional financial education. Empowering these individuals to set and pursue financial goals is critical for fostering financial independence and resilience.

Overall, Table 5 underscores the significant impact of digital financial education on enhancing self-efficacy and fostering positive behavior change in various demographic groups. The highest improvements in behavior and financial skills were reported by groups that are often marginalized in traditional financial education settings, suggesting that digital financial education holds particular promise for promoting financial inclusion. The data also highlights the importance of culturally relevant content and tailored approaches to financial education that take into account the specific needs and challenges faced by different groups. By addressing these needs, digital financial education can empower individuals to make informed financial decisions, adopt healthier financial habits, and ultimately improve their financial well-being.

Political Implications

The political implications of the findings presented in the above tables are multifaceted, encompassing a broad spectrum of social, economic, and policy-related concerns. At the heart of these discussions is the notion of financial inclusion—an issue that transcends regional, racial, and socio-economic boundaries. The pervasive impact of cultural barriers, the effectiveness of digital financial education, and the behavioral changes induced by such programs all point toward critical political actions that must be taken to address existing inequalities in access to financial tools and literacy. The implications of these findings, therefore, can be analyzed within the broader framework of state responsibilities, socio-economic justice, and the governance of global financial systems.

First and foremost, the regional disparities in financial literacy and access to digital tools outlined in Tables 2, 3, and 4 highlight the persistent issue of digital inequality, a central concern for policymakers in both developed and developing nations. While regions such as North America and Europe report high levels of digital engagement, countries in Africa and Latin America are grappling with inadequate infrastructure and limited internet access. This disparity, which is exacerbated by socio-economic factors, underscores the need for comprehensive digital inclusion policies. The absence of such policies leaves entire populations vulnerable to further economic marginalization. Governments, particularly in developing countries, are confronted with the necessity of creating robust infrastructures that not only ensure basic internet access but also foster a digital literacy ecosystem. This includes building capacity for both technological infrastructure and educational frameworks that allow for the effective integration of digital tools in financial education.

Furthermore, the trust issues that persist within marginalized communities, as revealed in the data on cultural barriers to financial literacy, signal a profound political challenge. Trust in financial institutions, particularly among Black, Hispanic, and rural ethnic minorities, remains a major barrier to the effective use of financial education programs and the wider financial system. The historical legacies of financial exclusion, such as redlining and discriminatory lending practices, have left deep scars in these communities. As Table 3 demonstrates, racial and ethnic minorities, as well as rural populations, often harbor distrust toward the institutions that govern their financial lives. The political ramifications of this distrust are far-reaching, affecting not only the individuals within these communities but also the broader social contract. Governments and financial regulators must urgently address these concerns by implementing reforms that focus on transparency, accountability, and equity within financial institutions. This includes revisiting regulatory frameworks, ensuring fair lending practices, and promoting institutional diversity to reflect the populations they serve.

Moreover, the political impact of financial education, particularly in underserved communities, cannot be underestimated in its potential to reshape social mobility and economic outcomes. The data presented in Tables 4 and 5 demonstrates that digital financial education programs can significantly alter financial behaviors, fostering confidence in budgeting, saving, and managing debt. These changes suggest that targeted financial education can act as a powerful tool for uplifting economically disadvantaged groups. For policymakers, this represents an opportunity to leverage financial literacy as a means of mitigating income inequality and advancing economic justice. By investing in financial education, particularly for marginalized groups such as Black youth, Latino adults, and Indigenous populations, governments can create pathways to financial empowerment, thus reducing the wealth gap and enabling more equitable participation in the economy.

In the context of global governance, the findings also have significant implications for international cooperation and the global financial system. Digital financial education programs, as evidenced by their impact in diverse regions, offer a potential solution to global financial exclusion, a persistent issue that undermines development goals. With billions of people still lacking access to basic financial services, the international community must recognize the importance of inclusive finance in achieving the Sustainable Development Goals (SDGs), particularly SDG 8 (Decent Work and Economic Growth) and SDG 10 (Reduced Inequalities). The successful implementation of digital financial education programs, especially in developing regions, can contribute significantly to reducing financial inequality and promoting inclusive economic growth. International organizations, such as the World Bank and the International Monetary Fund, must therefore support the scaling of these initiatives, providing financial and technical assistance to countries seeking to expand digital financial literacy.

At the national level, political leaders must recognize the critical role that financial education plays in strengthening democratic institutions. Financial literacy is closely tied to civic participation, with better-educated individuals more likely to engage in voting, advocacy, and the democratic process. As such, improving financial literacy is not just an economic concern but a civic one, with implications for political stability and the health of democratic systems. In nations where financial insecurity is widespread, the political consequences can be profound. Citizens who are financially insecure may lack trust in governmental institutions, fueling populist sentiments and undermining social cohesion. By investing in financial literacy, governments can foster more engaged, informed citizens who are better equipped to navigate the complexities of modern economies and participate actively in democratic processes.

The intersection of gender, cultural norms, and financial decision-making also has important political ramifications. As evidenced in the data from Table 3, gender roles in money decisions continue to hinder financial empowerment for women, particularly in South Asian and Middle Eastern communities. The political implications of these findings point to the need for policies that address the patriarchal structures that limit women's economic autonomy. By promoting gender equity in financial education, governments can work to dismantle the traditional gender roles that prevent women from taking control of their financial futures. This may include designing educational programs that specifically target women and challenge prevailing cultural norms that restrict their financial agency. Additionally, legislative changes that promote women's participation in the workforce and access to economic opportunities are essential in addressing the structural barriers that women face.

Lastly, the role of education in financial empowerment highlights the need for a more integrated approach to financial education within national curricula. Governments must take a more proactive role in ensuring that financial literacy is a core component of education systems, particularly in countries where digital education tools are underutilized. As the data indicates, financial behavior change is highly correlated with confidence-building educational programs. By making financial literacy a compulsory part of school curricula, policymakers can ensure that future generations are equipped with the skills needed to navigate the complexities of global financial markets and personal finance. This proactive approach not only empowers individuals but also fortifies economies by creating a more financially literate and resilient populace.

In conclusion, the political implications of the findings on financial literacy and digital education extend across various levels of governance and societal structures. From addressing digital inequality and restoring trust in financial institutions to promoting gender equity and international cooperation, these implications point toward a broader vision of inclusive, equitable financial systems. Governments must act decisively to integrate financial literacy into their policy frameworks, ensuring that the benefits of financial education are accessible to all. This commitment will require concerted efforts at both the national and international levels, with a focus on reducing disparities, empowering individuals, and fostering economic justice in the digital age.

CONCLUSION

This study critically examined the gaps and opportunities in culturally responsive financial education within the context of growing digitalization. Drawing on intersectional, pedagogical, and digital equity frameworks, and supported by global empirical evidence, the research underscores that while digital tools are rapidly expanding access, their effectiveness remains constrained by cultural incongruence, linguistic exclusion, and a lack of contextual relevance. Conventional financial education models, often rooted in Western-centric norms, fail to engage diverse learners meaningfully, particularly those from marginalized, indigenous, migrant, and low-income communities. The findings reveal that integrating cultural context, learner identity, and participatory design into financial education significantly enhances self-efficacy, knowledge retention, and long-term behavioral change. Ultimately, this study positions culturally responsive pedagogy not as a supplementary consideration, but as a central principle for achieving inclusive and impactful financial education in the digital age.

Managerial Implications

For managers in financial institutions, fintech companies, and digital learning platforms, the findings underscore the need to reconceptualize financial education not just as a compliance tool or marketing strategy, but as a core element of inclusive customer engagement and capacity building. Managers must prioritize the co-creation of educational content with diverse community stakeholders, investing in user research that captures local knowledge systems and behavioral norms. This approach can enhance brand trust, product usage, and long-term customer loyalty, especially in underserved markets. Additionally, product managers should consider integrating adaptive learning algorithms that personalize financial content based on cultural and linguistic cues, rather than offering standardized modules. Strategic partnerships with grassroots organizations and multilingual content producers can help bridge cultural gaps, resulting in more effective financial behavior change and stronger market penetration.

Practical Implications

Practically, the study calls for a fundamental redesign of digital financial education tools and curricula to ensure relevance, accessibility, and inclusivity. Policymakers, educators, and technology developers must consider local languages, traditional financial practices, gender dynamics, and social hierarchies when designing interventions. Financial literacy content should go beyond text-based modules to include audio-visual storytelling, gamified simulations, and case-based learning reflective of learners' real-life economic scenarios. Moreover, practical steps must be taken to include non-dominant voices in content creation, particularly women, youth, and indigenous educators who possess intimate cultural knowledge. Pilot programs that test culturally customized modules and gather feedback from local users can serve as scalable models for nationwide or cross-border replication. Such practical reorientation will not only foster greater participation but also lead to more ethical and sustainable financial inclusion outcomes.

Theoretical Implications

This study contributes to the theoretical enrichment of financial education literature by embedding culturally responsive pedagogy as its central interpretive lens and integrating complementary frameworks such as Funds of Knowledge Theory, Intersectionality Theory, and Digital Equity models. It expands the scope of financial education research beyond traditional behavioral economics by incorporating socio-cultural and epistemological dimensions. The study challenges dominant neoliberal assumptions that underpin most financial literacy efforts and reframes financial education as a culturally embedded, relational, and identity-affirming process. It also provides a nuanced model for future theoretical inquiry, encouraging scholars to critically assess how power, culture, and digital access intersect in shaping financial knowledge, attitudes, and behavior across diverse populations. This reorientation opens up a critical and underexplored frontier in financial pedagogy.

Recommendation

Based on the findings, it is recommended that governments and development agencies adopt a multi-stakeholder, culturally adaptive framework when designing and scaling financial education programs. Curricula should be co-developed with community input and tested in localized contexts before national or global implementation. Educational institutions and fintech firms should invest in training facilitators and educators from diverse cultural backgrounds who can act as mediators between digital content and community learners. Funding mechanisms must prioritize long-term engagement and capacity-building over short-term metrics, supporting projects that foster cultural dignity and learner empowerment. Furthermore, it is essential to build evaluation tools that can assess not only financial knowledge acquisition but also behavioral transformation, cultural relevance, and emotional engagement. Lastly, public-private partnerships should be leveraged to integrate culturally responsive digital financial education into broader financial inclusion and literacy policies.

Future Directions

Future research should explore longitudinal impacts of culturally responsive financial education programs to understand their influence on intergenerational financial behavior, resilience, and empowerment. Comparative studies across different cultural, linguistic, and economic contexts can help establish universal design principles while respecting local diversity. There is also scope for exploring the use of artificial intelligence and machine learning in customizing financial education content to match cultural patterns, preferences, and learning styles. Further, interdisciplinary collaboration with anthropologists, sociolinguists, community leaders, and digital designers will be essential in deepening our understanding of the nuanced interplay between culture, technology, and finance. Finally, future work should examine how culturally responsive financial education can contribute to broader sustainable development goals (SDGs), particularly those related to gender equality, reduced inequalities, and decent work and economic growth.

REFERENCES

Aguayo, A. J. M., & Aros, P. A. V. (2023). Financial inclusion, microfinance, and financial education in Latin America. In *Handbook of Microfinance, Financial Inclusion and Development*. Edward Elgar Publishing Ltd. DOI: 10.4337/9781789903874.00026

Ardila, A. D. A., & Hernández, A. H. H. (2024). Impact of the development of skills in resilience and financial education in the professional development of military personnel: To face VUCA environments. In *Organizational Management Sustainability in VUCA Contexts*. IGI Global., DOI: 10.4018/979-8-3693-0720-5.ch010

Bernedo-Moreira, D. H., Almirón-Cuentas, J. A., Espiritu-Martinez, A. P., Ochoa-Tataje, F. A., & Romero-Carazas, R. (2024). Financial education from elementary school, a perspective to today. *Periodicals of Engineering and Natural Sciences*, *12*(1), 123–134. DOI: 10.21533/pen.v12.i1.25

Boyd, C. M., & Díez-Amigo, S. (2023). Effectiveness of free financial education provided by for-profit financial institutions: Experimental evidence from rural peru. *Economics of Education Review*, *97*, 102462. Advance online publication. DOI: 10.1016/j.econedurev.2023.102462

Buratti, G., & D'Ignazio, A. (2024). Improving the effectiveness of financial education programs. A targeting approach. *The Journal of Consumer Affairs*, *58*(2), 451–485. DOI: 10.1111/joca.12577

Cannistrà, M., De Beckker, K., Agasisti, T., Amagir, A., Põder, K., Vartiak, L., & De Witte, K. (2024). The impact of an online game-based financial education course: Multi-country experimental evidence. *Journal of Comparative Economics*, *52*(4), 825–847. DOI: 10.1016/j.jce.2024.08.001

Canta, C., & Leroux, M.-L. (2024). Financial education as a complement to public pensions: The case of naive individuals. *Journal of Population Economics*, *37*(4), 69. Advance online publication. DOI: 10.1007/s00148-024-01046-3

Chabaefe, N. N., & Qutieshat, A. (2024). Financial Literacy, Financial Education and Financial Experience: Conceptual Framework. *International Journal of Economics and Financial Issues*, *14*(4), 44–55. DOI: 10.32479/ijefi.15627

Choi, A., Stoutland, D., & Blanco, L. (2024). An evaluation of a digital financial education program and the impact of COVID-19 on financial well-being among college students. *Journal of American College Health*, *72*(9), 3690–3702. DOI: 10.1080/07448481.2023.2191142 PMID: 37084244

Couto, R. F., Maracajá, K. F. B., & de Araújo Machado, P. (2023). Analysis of the Path of Studies on Financial Education and Sustainability. In *The Route Towards Global Sustainability: Challenges and Management Practices*. Springer International Publishing., DOI: 10.1007/978-3-031-10437-4_7

Estelami, H., & Estelami, N. N. (2024). The differential impact of cognitive style on the relationship between financial education and financial literacy. *Journal of Financial Services Marketing*, *29*(2), 242–256. DOI: 10.1057/s41264-022-00204-6

FaXing, L., & Loang, O. K.FaXing. (2024). Green Investing and Financial Education: The Case of China's A-Share Market. *Studies in Systems. Decision and Control*, *223*, 29–41. DOI: 10.1007/978-3-031-51997-0_3

Garrido, R., & Homa, A. I. R. (2024). Digital educational game for family financial education in primary school. *Acta Scientiae*, *26*(3). Advance online publication. DOI: 10.17648/acta.scientiae.6122

González, E. L. M. (2023). Factors that influence the financial education of young people in Celaya, Guanajuato, México [Factores que influyen en la educación financiera de los jóvenes de Celaya, Guanajuato, México]. *Revista Mexicana de Economia y Finanzas Nueva Epoca*, *18*(3). Advance online publication. DOI: 10.21919/v18i3.890

Harvey, M., & Urban, C. (2023). Does financial education affect retirement savings? *The Journal of the Economics of Ageing*, *24*, 100446. Advance online publication. DOI: 10.1016/j.jeoa.2023.100446

Hashinaga, M. (2023). Financial education and financial behavior. In *A Research Agenda for Consumer Financial Behavior*. Edward Elgar Publishing Ltd., DOI: 10.4337/9781803922652.00011

Hishamudin, M. Z., Kamarudin, N. S., Hadi, N. A., & Ahmad, A. (2025). Intention to Use Digital Platforms for Islamic Financial Education in Malaysia: Structural Equation Model. *Journal of Advanced Research in Applied Sciences and Engineering Technology*, *49*(1), 298–311. DOI: 10.37934/araset.49.1.298311

Iannotta, G., Cannistrà, M., & Agasisti, T. (2024). It's never too late to be financially literate: Evaluating a financial education intervention for adults in Italy. *The Journal of Consumer Affairs*, *58*(2), 397–431. DOI: 10.1111/joca.12592

Jariwala, H. V. (2023). Do financial education workshops enhance parent–adolescent communication about money? *Managerial Finance*, *49*(5), 829–846. DOI: 10.1108/MF-09-2021-0469

Jonker, N., & Kosse, A. (2022). The interplay of financial education, financial inclusion and financial stability and the role of Big Tech. *Contemporary Economic Policy, 40*(4), 612–635. DOI: 10.1111/coep.12578

Kaiser, T., Lusardi, A., Menkhoff, L., & Urban, C. (2022). Financial education affects financial knowledge and downstream behaviors. *Journal of Financial Economics, 145*(2), 255–272. DOI: 10.1016/j.jfineco.2021.09.022

Kang, S. H. K., Eglington, L. G., Schuetze, B. A., Lu, X., Hinterstoisser, T. M., & Huaco, J. (2023). Using Cognitive Science and Technology to Enhance Financial Education: The Effect of Spaced Retrieval Practice. *Financial Counseling and Planning, 34*(1), 20–31. DOI: 10.1891/JFCP-2021-0032

Kovács, L., & Terták, E. (2024). Thematic review of financial education and financial literacy in the digital age. *Acta Oeconomica, 74*(4), 483–506. DOI: 10.1556/032.2024.00023

Kukreti, M., Sehajpal, S., Tiwari, R., & Sood, K. (2024). Driving global health and sustainable development goals with smart technology. In *Driving Global Health and Sustainable Development Goals With Smart Technology*. IGI Global., DOI: 10.4018/979-8-3373-0240-9

Litterscheidt, R., & Streich, D. J. (2020). Financial education and digital asset management: What's in the black box? *Journal of Behavioral and Experimental Economics, 87*, 101573. Advance online publication. DOI: 10.1016/j.socec.2020.101573

Lopez-Agudo, L. A., & Marcenaro-Gutierrez, O. D. (2023). Financial Education in Secondary Education: A Cross-Country Analysis. *CESifo Economic Studies, 69*(1), 21–60. DOI: 10.1093/cesifo/ifad002

Lyu, J. J.-C. (2024). The New Horizon of Financial Education. *Review of Pacific Basin Financial Markets and Policies, 27*(3), 2450024. Advance online publication. DOI: 10.1142/S0219091524500243

Machuca-Vílchez, J. A., Ramos-Cavero, M. J., & Cordova-Buiza, F. (2023). Knowledge management in financial education in Peruvian government programs focused on women: Progress and challenges. *Knowledge and Performance Management, 7*(1), 1–14. DOI: 10.21511/kpm.07(1).2023.01

Malik, S., Singh, K. N., & Ehigiamusoe, G. (2024). Fintech for MSME and the Role of Financial Education for MSMEs in Optimizing their Return as Investors. In *Applications of Artificial Intelligence in Business and Finance 5.0*. Apple Academic Press. DOI: 10.1201/9781003535133-9

Maman, D., & Rosenhek, Z. (2023). Governing individuals' imaginaries and conduct in personal finance: The mobilization of emotions in financial education. *Journal of Consumer Culture*, *23*(1), 188–208. DOI: 10.1177/14695405211069952

Mukherjee, S., Thakur, D., Chandel, P. K., Chandra, S., & Karia, A. (2025). Cultivating sustainable growth and well-being in digital financial education. In *Exploring Psychology, Social Innovation and Advanced Applications of Machine Learning*. IGI Global., DOI: 10.4018/979-8-3693-6910-4.ch014

Netemeyer, R. G., Lynch, J. G.Jr, Lichtenstein, D. R., & Dobolyi, D. (2024). Financial Education Effects on Financial Behavior and Well-Being: The Mediating Roles of Improved Objective and Subjective Financial Knowledge and Parallels in Physical Health. *Journal of Public Policy & Marketing*, *43*(4), 254–275. DOI: 10.1177/07439156241228197

Oberrauch, L., & Kaiser, T. (2024). Financial Education or Incentivizing Learning-By-Doing? Evidence from an RCT with Undergraduate Students. *Journal of Behavioral and Experimental Finance*, *43*, 100954. Advance online publication. DOI: 10.1016/j.jbef.2024.100954

Ortiz, N. R., Torres, J. V., & Rodríguez, V. H. P. (2024). Digital Financial Education for Economic and Financial Inclusion in Vulnerable Sectors of Peru. *Theoretical and Practical Research in the Economic Fields*, *15*(4), 928–938. DOI: 10.14505/tpref.v15.4(32).11

Peñarreta-Quezada, M.-Á., Salas-Tenesaca, E.-E., Álvarez-García, J., & de la Cruz del Río-Rama, M. (2023). Socio-demographic variables and levels of financial education among young university students in Ecuador. *Revista Mexicana de Economia y Finanzas Nueva Epoca*, *19*(19). Advance online publication. DOI: 10.21919/remef.v19i1.920

Prieto, C. A. G., Santa, J. S. S., & Álvarez, L. C. V. (2024). Financial education as a mediator between financial planning and financial performance in microentrepreneurs of the solidarity sector. *Cuadernos de Economia (Colombia)*, *43*(91), 265–295. DOI: 10.15446/cuadernos.v43n91.104375

Ruiz, T. A., Benito, L., & Penabad, M. C. L. (2023). Influence of behavioral biases on investment decisions. The importance of financial education during an economic crisis [Influencia de los sesgos del comportamiento en las decisiones de inversión. La importancia de la educación financiera en tiempos de crisis]. *Revista Galega de Economia*, *32*(1). Advance online publication. DOI: 10.15304/rge.32.1.8190

Salas-Velasco, M. (2022). Causal Effects of Financial Education Intervention Aimed at University Students on Financial Knowledge and Financial Self-Efficacy. *Journal of Risk and Financial Management, 15*(7), 284. Advance online publication. DOI: 10.3390/jrfm15070284

Salas-Velasco, M. (2023). Economic and financial education for investment and financing decision-making in a graduate degree: Experimental evaluation of the effectiveness of two delivery methods. *The Journal of Economic Education, 54*(3), 225–242. DOI: 10.1080/00220485.2023.2191594

Salas-Velasco, M. (2024). Attitudes of college seniors toward graduate student loan debt: The role of financial education. *Journal of Financial Economic Policy, 16*(4), 442–462. DOI: 10.1108/JFEP-09-2023-0259

Sconti, A. (2022). Digital vs. in-person financial education: What works best for Generation Z? *Journal of Economic Behavior & Organization, 194*, 300–318. DOI: 10.1016/j.jebo.2021.12.001

Sconti, A., Caserta, M., & Ferrante, L. (2024). Gen Z and financial education: Evidence from a randomized control trial in the South of Italy. *Journal of Behavioral and Experimental Economics, 112*, 102256. Advance online publication. DOI: 10.1016/j.socec.2024.102256

Senduk, F. F. W., Djatmika, E. T., Wahyono, H., Churiyah, M., Mahasneh, O., & Arjanto, P. (2024). Fostering financially savvy generations: The intersection of financial education, digital financial misconception and parental wellbeing. *Frontiers in Education, 9*, 1460374. Advance online publication. DOI: 10.3389/feduc.2024.1460374

Serido, J., McGee, D., Zhang, Y., Li, L., Quinones, M., & Ramos, G. (2024). Transformational Learning Within African American Culture: What Does Financial Education That Addresses Systemic Inequalities Look Like? *Financial Counseling and Planning, 35*(3), 307–322. DOI: 10.1891/JFCP-2023-0020

Sharma, G., Solanki, U., & Solanki, V. (2024). Fintech and Artificial Intelligence: An Overview of Contribution to Banking, Investment, Financial Education, and Microfinance. In *Applications of Artificial Intelligence in Business and Finance 5.0*. Apple Academic Press. DOI: 10.1201/9781003535133-8

imandan, R., Leu tean, B., & Dobrescu, R. M. (2022). An Uphill Battle: Financial Education in Romania in the Midst of Societal Transformation. *Journal of Risk and Financial Management, 15*(11), 494. Advance online publication. DOI: 10.3390/jrfm15110494

Singh, K. N., & Misra, G. (2023). Victimisation of investors from fraudulent investment schemes and their protection through financial education. *Journal of Financial Crime, 30*(5), 1305–1322. DOI: 10.1108/JFC-07-2022-0167

Tharayil, A. (2024). Examining the Association Between Financial Education and Financial Risk Tolerance. *The American Economist, 69*(1), 59–79. DOI: 10.1177/05694345231186082

Torma, J., Barbić, D., & Ivanov, M. (2023). Analyzing the Effects of Financial Education on Financial Literacy and Financial Behaviour: A Randomized Field Experiment in Croatia. *South East European Journal of Economics and Business, 18*(2), 63–86. DOI: 10.2478/jeb-2023-0019

Urban, C. (2023). Does state-mandated financial education reduce high school graduation rates? *Economics of Education Review, 95*, 102427. Advance online publication. DOI: 10.1016/j.econedurev.2023.102427

Walstad, W. B., & Wagner, J. (2023). Required or voluntary financial education and saving behaviors. *The Journal of Economic Education, 54*(1), 17–37. DOI: 10.1080/00220485.2022.2144573

White, K., Olajide, O., Watkins, K., Reiter, M., Johnson, P., & McCoy, M. (2024). Financial Education and Financial Anxiety: Do Quality and Quantity Differ? *Financial Counseling and Planning, 35*(2), 276–291. DOI: 10.1891/JFCP-2023-0022

Yuning, T. (2023). A conceptual framework for financial education. *Citizenship. Social and Economics Education, 22*(2), 65–84. DOI: 10.1177/14788047231180851

Zhang, Y., Lu, X., & Xiao, J. J. (2023). Does financial education help to improve the return on stock investment? Evidence from China. *Pacific-Basin Finance Journal, 78*, 101940. Advance online publication. DOI: 10.1016/j.pacfin.2023.101940

Zhu, T., & Xiao, J. J. (2022). Consumer financial education and risky financial asset holding in China. *International Journal of Consumer Studies, 46*(1), 56–74. DOI: 10.1111/ijcs.12643

Zia, B. (2023). When is financial education successful? Taking stock of the new wave of field evidence. In *Handbook of Microfinance, Financial Inclusion and Development*. Edward Elgar Publishing Ltd., DOI: 10.4337/9781789903874.00013

Chapter 10
Culturally Attuned Digital Transformation in Education:
Integrating FemTech for Inclusive Learning Ecosystems

Sabina Sehajpal
https://orcid.org/0009-0004-6655-6279
Chandigarh University, India

Kusum Lata
Chandigarh University, India

Pravesh Soti
https://orcid.org/0000-0001-8142-884X
Noida Institute of Engineering and Technology, India

ABSTRACT

This study examines the integration of FemTech solutions in educational systems to address gender disparities and enhance learning outcomes, focusing on the impact of these tools on female students' health and academic engagement. Through a mixed-methods approach, the research analyzes data from pilot programs in diverse regions, including India, Kenya, Brazil, and Sweden, exploring the effectiveness of FemTech tools such as menstrual health apps, mental health support, and reproductive health guidance. The study also evaluates cultural and political barriers, policy adoption, and the role of local language integration in promoting digital equity. Findings indicate that FemTech solutions significantly improve learning retention and school attendance, particularly in regions with targeted health interventions.

DOI: 10.4018/979-8-3373-3673-2.ch010

The research highlights the need for gender-sensitive policies and culturally adapted digital tools to ensure that FemTech can contribute to a more inclusive and equitable educational environment for female learners globally.

INTRODUCTION

The relentless march of digital transformation in education, characterized by the infusion of cutting-edge technologies, has revolutionized the pedagogical landscape in ways previously unimagined. This transformation, while promising enhanced access to learning resources, faces multifaceted challenges, particularly in its attempt to be culturally inclusive (Grimme et al., 2025). As educational institutions and policymakers strive to bridge the digital divide, it is critical that digital strategies cater to diverse cultural, social, and economic contexts. Among the myriad of potential sectors where digital advancements could foster empowerment, the intersection of digital technologies and FemTech in educational ecosystems presents an unprecedented opportunity for inclusivity, particularly for women and marginalized communities (Westwood, 2023).

FemTech, a sector that primarily addresses female health and wellness through technological innovations, has recently gained significant attention for its transformative potential in areas ranging from reproductive health to mental well-being. The convergence of FemTech with educational technology is poised to create a digital ecosystem that not only supports female empowerment but also amplifies the scope of inclusive learning (Hofmann, 2024). While FemTech's primary focus has been on health, its integration into educational frameworks could provide culturally attuned digital solutions, addressing the unique educational needs of women and girls globally, particularly in regions where gender disparities are most acute (Alfawzan & Christen, 2023).

At the heart of this discourse lies the concept of "culturally attuned" digital transformation, which recognizes that a one-size-fits-all approach to education is not only inadequate but also counterproductive. In a world characterized by diverse cultural paradigms, educational strategies must account for varying norms, values, and societal structures (Jain & Mudliar, 2024). Cultural relevance is essential, especially in communities where traditional gender roles limit women's access to quality education or where socio-economic constraints impose barriers to digital inclusion. In this context, a digital transformation that incorporates FemTech into education would go beyond mere technological implementation; it would entail a thoughtful consideration of how digital tools can be adapted to fit the cultural and societal needs of different communities (Balfour, 2023a).

The integration of FemTech into educational ecosystems is not just an innovation in the realm of health but also a powerful catalyst for shaping inclusive learning experiences. FemTech platforms, which offer solutions such as menstrual health tracking, mental wellness support, and maternal health education, could be leveraged to support both the academic and personal development of students. These tools would not only allow women to take control of their health but would also enable educational systems to address gender-specific barriers that hinder educational outcomes (Jeswani et al., 2023). By utilizing FemTech innovations, educational institutions could offer platforms that provide health education in tandem with academic content, thus creating a more holistic and supportive learning environment.

Furthermore, the digital transformation of education through the lens of FemTech demands a rethinking of pedagogical methodologies. Traditional teaching methods often fail to incorporate the nuances of gender, health, and cultural sensitivities, which are vital to promoting equitable learning outcomes. By embedding FemTech within digital learning environments, educators can introduce more personalized and context-aware teaching strategies (Hajkova & Doyle, 2024). These strategies would acknowledge the specific challenges faced by female learners, particularly in developing regions where girls are often disproportionately affected by poor health and limited access to educational resources. The integration of FemTech could enhance the educational experience by providing personalized learning paths that adapt to the unique health and wellness needs of each student (Balfour, 2023b).

The digital landscape has already demonstrated its potential to transcend geographical boundaries, offering access to education for individuals in remote and underserved areas. However, the promise of digital education is often marred by the lack of contextual sensitivity to cultural and gender-specific barriers (Siddiqui, 2024). For example, in many parts of the world, societal norms restrict women's mobility or limit their access to educational opportunities, particularly in regions where menstruation is stigmatized or where reproductive health remains a taboo subject. FemTech, in this regard, has the potential to address these cultural challenges by providing discreet, user-friendly, and culturally sensitive solutions that allow female learners to overcome these obstacles.

In countries where educational infrastructure is weak and female literacy rates remain low, FemTech can serve as an indispensable tool in driving educational access. By embedding FemTech into digital learning platforms, educators can provide female students with the tools to manage their health independently, while also fostering a sense of autonomy and confidence. The ability to monitor one's health through digital means can alleviate some of the shame or discomfort associated with female health issues, thus empowering women to fully participate in their educational journeys (Cook et al., 2024). As such, FemTech becomes not just a tool for health management but a gateway to a more inclusive and effective learning environment.

Moreover, the integration of FemTech within digital learning ecosystems holds the potential to reshape the curriculum itself. FemTech solutions could lead to the development of new learning modules that explore the intersection of gender, health, and education. Such curricula would allow students to gain a deeper understanding of how their bodies and minds influence their learning experiences, as well as how societal expectations shape their educational pathways (McMillan, 2024). The ability to integrate such modules into educational settings would lead to a more nuanced and inclusive curriculum, one that considers the diverse needs of all learners, irrespective of gender or socio-economic background.

In addition, the ability to use digital tools to track health and learning progress simultaneously could provide valuable insights into the holistic development of students. These insights could inform personalized learning strategies, ensuring that each student receives the appropriate support to thrive academically and personally (Yi et al., 2024). The combination of health data with learning progress allows for a more dynamic approach to education—one that adapts to the individual needs of each student while considering the broader socio-cultural context in which they live (Faubion, 2021).

Ultimately, the convergence of digital transformation and FemTech within educational ecosystems holds profound implications for the future of inclusive learning. By creating a space where health, gender, and culture are thoughtfully integrated into digital learning platforms, we can lay the groundwork for a more equitable educational system—one where female students are not only empowered to learn but are also supported in overcoming the unique challenges they face. The path forward lies in harnessing the power of technology to create culturally attuned, gender-responsive educational systems that enable all learners to thrive in an increasingly digital world.

Global Importance

The concept of culturally attuned digital transformation in education has gained global significance as the education sector faces an increasing demand to integrate technology into teaching and learning processes (Peter-Spiess & Hofmann, 2025). With the advent of digital tools and platforms, education systems worldwide are being reshaped, presenting an opportunity to create inclusive learning environments that cater to diverse cultural contexts. This is especially important in an era of globalization, where learners come from various cultural, social, and economic backgrounds. The integration of FemTech (female-focused technology) into this transformation ensures that educational systems not only embrace technological advancements but also address the specific needs of female students, particularly in regions where gender disparities are prominent. Culturally sensitive approaches help to foster a more equitable learning environment that encourages diverse learning experiences, helping students of all genders to thrive in a digital age (Zokaityte, 2025).

Origin of Concept

The origin of the concept of culturally attuned digital transformation in education can be traced back to the growing recognition of the intersection between culture and education in the global discourse. As educational systems adopted digital tools, it became apparent that a one-size-fits-all approach was insufficient to meet the diverse needs of students. The concept emerged as educators and policymakers recognized the need for culturally responsive strategies in digital learning (Chen, 2025). FemTech, a subset of technology designed to address women's specific health, educational, and career needs, was integrated into this evolving framework as an effort to make educational transformation more inclusive for female students. The intersection of culture, technology, and gender has led to a broader understanding of how digital transformation can foster inclusive educational ecosystems (Farahani et al., 2025).

Practical Challenges

Despite the promising potential of culturally attuned digital transformation in education, several practical challenges remain. One of the primary obstacles is the unequal access to digital resources, especially in low-income and rural areas, where infrastructure limitations hinder the implementation of technology-driven educational solutions. Additionally, there is often a lack of culturally relevant content in digital learning platforms, which can alienate students from diverse backgrounds (Agrawal et al., 2025). In the context of FemTech, challenges include ensuring that technologies are designed with an understanding of the diverse cultural contexts of female students. Gender bias in technology development and a lack of representation of women in STEM fields further exacerbate these issues. Furthermore, there is a need for educators to be trained in the use of digital tools that are culturally attuned and gender-sensitive, a requirement that many education systems are not yet equipped to handle (Grimme et al., 2025).

Research Gaps

While there is a growing body of literature on digital transformation and FemTech in education, significant research gaps remain. One key gap is the lack of large-scale studies that examine the long-term impact of culturally attuned digital transformation on student outcomes, particularly for female students in underrepresented regions (Howes-Mischel & Tracy, 2025). There is also a need for more research on the intersectionality of culture, gender, and technology in education, as current studies tend to focus on one dimension at a time. Furthermore, there is limited research on how to effectively implement FemTech solutions that are both culturally appropriate and scalable across different educational contexts. Additionally, the potential for policy changes to support this transformation remains underexplored, especially in countries with significant gender and cultural disparities in education. Addressing these gaps will be crucial in ensuring that the digital transformation of education is truly inclusive and equitable for all students (Nishi et al., 2025).

Background of the Study

The increasing role of technology in education has prompted a digital transformation that has the potential to reshape how students learn, interact, and engage with the world. This transformation, however, has not been universally beneficial, as it often overlooks cultural contexts and gender-specific needs (Sillence et al., 2025). In response, the concept of culturally attuned digital transformation in education has gained traction, focusing on creating an inclusive and equitable learning environment. At the heart of this approach lies the integration of FemTech, which aims to use technology to address the specific educational and health needs of female students, particularly in regions where gender disparities are prevalent (Espíndola et al., 2025). The goal is to ensure that the educational digital ecosystem caters to all students, regardless of their gender, cultural background, or socio-economic status. This integration has the potential to bridge significant gaps in education, particularly for marginalized communities, but it also presents a series of practical challenges that need to be addressed in the implementation of these concepts (Pybus & Mir, 2025).

Practical Case Studies Showing Challenges in Implementation

Several case studies illustrate the challenges faced in implementing culturally attuned digital transformation in education, particularly when integrating FemTech solutions. One such example is the case of a rural school in India that implemented a digital learning platform aimed at bridging gender gaps in education (Akazawa, 2025). While the platform provided access to digital content for both male and female students, it failed to account for the socio-cultural context. Female students, especially those from conservative families, faced significant barriers to using the platform due to societal restrictions on their mobility and access to technology. Furthermore, the content on the platform was not culturally relevant to the female students' lived experiences, which led to disengagement. Despite the digital tools being available, the lack of cultural sensitivity and gender-responsive design meant the technology had limited impact (Kelly et al., 2025).

In another case, a school district in Sub-Saharan Africa introduced FemTech solutions to enhance the learning experience for girls. While the initiative was well-received, several challenges arose during the implementation phase. The digital infrastructure in the region was inadequate, with frequent power outages and poor internet connectivity, which significantly hindered the effectiveness of the FemTech tools (O'Brien & Iriarte, 2025). Additionally, the lack of local content that addressed issues like menstruation, reproductive health, and gender-based violence meant that the digital tools did not meet the specific needs of the female students. This gap in content design, combined with the low level of technological literacy among teachers, meant that the FemTech solutions did not have the desired impact on improving educational outcomes for girls (Lanzing, 2025).

A third example comes from a school in Brazil where the government introduced digital platforms to support learning in remote areas. The platform aimed to be culturally responsive by offering content in the local indigenous languages (Neiman et al., 2025). However, the platform faced significant challenges because it was not integrated into the existing pedagogical frameworks, and teachers struggled to incorporate it into their lesson plans. Additionally, the curriculum was not adequately tailored to the cultural needs of the indigenous communities, leading to a lack of engagement from students (Tjandraprawira et al., 2025). This case study highlights the importance of not only providing access to technology but also ensuring that educational frameworks and content are adaptable and culturally relevant.

Related Theories and Their Relation to the Study Topic

1. Cultural-Historical Activity Theory (CHAT)

Cultural-Historical Activity Theory (CHAT) posits that learning is a socially mediated process influenced by the cultural context in which it occurs. The theory emphasizes the importance of understanding the activity system as a whole, which includes the tools, community, rules, and division of labor that shape an individual's learning experience. CHAT provides a framework for exploring how digital transformation in education can be adapted to different cultural contexts (Callegari et al., 2025). By focusing on the role of cultural practices in shaping learning, this theory supports the idea that educational technologies, including FemTech, need to be culturally sensitive and relevant to the students' lived experiences. This theory is particularly relevant to the study of culturally attuned digital transformation, as it highlights the need for designing technologies that respect and integrate cultural values. By examining how cultural contexts impact the use of FemTech in education, this theory helps explain why some digital transformations succeed in certain settings and fail in others (Gomes et al., 2025).

2. **Social Cognitive Theory (SCT)**

Social Cognitive Theory, developed by Albert Bandura, emphasizes the role of observational learning, imitation, and modeling in the development of behaviors. In the context of digital transformation in education, SCT can be applied to understand how students, especially female students, learn from observing others using technology. Bandura's theory suggests that students' self-efficacy and motivation to engage with digital tools are influenced by their social environment and role models (Carre-Skinner, 2024). This theory is relevant to FemTech integration because it highlights the importance of empowering female students through role models and peers who demonstrate the successful use of technology. It also underscores the significance of social interactions in learning, which can be facilitated through digital platforms. By addressing how technology can influence self-perception and empowerment, SCT provides a valuable lens for studying the challenges and opportunities of integrating FemTech in culturally diverse educational settings (Alzate, 2024).

3. **Feminist Theory of Technology**

Feminist Theory of Technology explores how technology is shaped by and reinforces gender dynamics. It examines the historical underrepresentation of women in technological development and critiques the ways in which technology often ignores or marginalizes women's specific needs and experiences. In relation to this study, the feminist lens is crucial for understanding how FemTech can be integrated into education in a way that addresses the unique educational challenges faced by female students (Siapka et al., 2024). The theory advocates for designing technology that acknowledges gender disparities and ensures that women's voices are included in the development of technological solutions. By using this theory, the study can explore the challenges of making educational technologies, such as FemTech, inclusive and responsive to the needs of female learners, particularly in regions with cultural and gender-based barriers to education (Hajkova & Doyle, 2024).

4. **Constructivist Learning Theory**

Constructivist Learning Theory, particularly as proposed by Piaget and Vygotsky, asserts that learners actively construct their understanding of the world based on experiences, interactions, and social contexts. In the context of digital transformation, constructivism suggests that technology should be used to promote active, hands-on learning experiences (Siddiqui, 2024). This theory is highly relevant to culturally attuned digital transformation, as it emphasizes the importance of connecting learning with real-life contexts and the prior knowledge of the learners. When integrated with FemTech, constructivist learning can encourage female students to engage with technology in a way that is meaningful and relevant to their personal experiences. It suggests that digital tools should not only provide access to information but also allow students to interact with content in a way that encourages critical thinking and problem-solving (Jain & Mudliar, 2024).

5. **Diffusion of Innovations Theory**

Everett Rogers' Diffusion of Innovations Theory explains how, why, and at what rate new ideas and technology spread among cultures. It focuses on the stages of adoption, from knowledge to persuasion, decision-making, implementation, and confirmation. The theory is relevant to the study of digital transformation in education because it can help explain the process by which new technologies, such as FemTech solutions, are adopted by educators and students in diverse cultural settings (Yi et al., 2024). Understanding the diffusion process can shed light on the barriers to adoption, such as resistance to change, lack of technological literacy, and inadequate infrastructure. This theory also highlights the role of opinion leaders and early adopters in driving the successful integration of digital tools in education, especially in culturally diverse and gender-sensitive contexts (Nellore et al., 2024).

Main Theoretical Lens for the Study

The **Feminist Theory of Technology** will serve as the primary theoretical lens for this study. This theory is particularly relevant because it directly addresses the central concern of the study: how to integrate FemTech into educational systems in a way that is inclusive, culturally sensitive, and responsive to the specific needs of female students (Hofmann, 2024). The feminist perspective will allow for a critical examination of how gender inequalities are embedded in educational technologies and how FemTech can be designed to challenge these disparities. By using this lens, the study will explore the cultural and gender-based barriers that hinder the effective integration of digital technologies and will provide insights into how these barriers can be overcome to promote a more inclusive learning ecosystem (McMillan, 2024).

Definition and Origin of Terms

1. **Culturally Attuned Digital Transformation**

Culturally attuned digital transformation refers to the process of integrating technology into educational systems in a way that is sensitive to the cultural backgrounds, values, and norms of the students it serves. The term recognizes that students come from diverse cultural contexts and that technology must be adapted to reflect and respect these differences. The origin of this term is rooted in the growing recognition of cultural diversity in global educational systems and the realization that digital tools cannot be universally applied without considering cultural contexts (Cook et al., 2024).

2. **FemTech**

FemTech, short for female technology, refers to technology designed to address the specific health, wellness, and educational needs of women. It includes a wide range of solutions, such as apps for reproductive health, educational tools for women in STEM, and platforms that address gender-specific issues in various sectors. The term originated in the tech industry as a response to the underrepresentation of women in technology development and the recognition of the need for technology that serves women's unique needs. FemTech has gained prominence as a growing field focused on empowering women through technology (Mishra et al., 2024).

3. **Digital Transformation in Education**

Digital transformation in education refers to the process of using digital technologies to fundamentally change how education is delivered, experienced, and managed. This includes the use of online learning platforms, digital tools, data analytics, and other technologies to enhance teaching and learning outcomes. The origin of this term is tied to the broader wave of digitalization across various industries, with education being one of the sectors increasingly incorporating digital technologies to improve access, engagement, and learning efficiency (Park et al., 2024).

4. **Culturally Responsive Teaching**

Culturally responsive teaching is an educational approach that recognizes the importance of including students' cultural references in all aspects of learning. This involves using teaching methods, content, and strategies that acknowledge and respect students' cultural backgrounds. The term emerged from educational research in the late 20th century, as educators began to understand the need for a more inclusive and diverse approach to teaching that goes beyond the traditional, one-size-fits-all model (Ng et al., 2024).

5. **Gender Equity in Education**

Gender equity in education refers to the principle of ensuring that all students, regardless of their gender, have equal access to educational opportunities, resources, and support. The term was developed as part of the global movement toward gender equality, particularly in the wake of international efforts like the United Nations' Education for All (EFA) initiative. Gender equity focuses on addressing systemic barriers that prevent female students, in particular, from achieving their full potential in educational settings (Cromack & Walter, 2024).

LITERATURE REVIEW

The intersection of digital transformation and education has been an area of considerable academic interest in recent years, particularly in light of the rapid technological advancements that have reshaped the global educational landscape. At the heart of this transformation lies the concept of integrating innovative technological solutions that not only enhance learning outcomes but also make education more inclusive, accessible, and adaptable to diverse societal contexts (McMillan, 2022). One such integration that has garnered significant attention is the role of FemTech within the educational ecosystem. FemTech, a sector primarily focused on addressing female health and wellness through digital solutions, offers an unprecedented opportunity to foster more inclusive educational environments, particularly for women and girls in marginalized communities. This review delves into the literature surrounding digital transformation in education, the potential of FemTech as an enabler of inclusive learning, and the ways in which culturally attuned digital strategies can be implemented to support diverse learning needs (Hendl & Jansky, 2022).

Challenges in Achieving Inclusive Digital Transformation in Education: Digital transformation in education is commonly understood as the process of leveraging technology to create new learning opportunities, enhance teaching methods, and ensure broader access to educational resources. However, this transformation is often met with challenges, particularly when considering its potential for inclusivity. The technological shift in education, while enabling access to resources that were previously out of reach, often fails to account for the cultural, social, and economic disparities that exist in diverse communities. Educational institutions have traditionally adopted a one-size-fits-all approach to digital learning, neglecting the unique needs of different learner groups, particularly women and girls in underserved regions (Mehrnezhad et al., 2022). As a result, many educational technologies are ill-equipped to address the cultural and gender-specific barriers that impede access to education for these groups. The literature highlights the necessity of developing culturally responsive digital education frameworks that account for the various socio-cultural dimensions influencing students' experiences and outcomes (Roberts, 2023).

The Role of FemTech in Promoting Gender Inclusivity in Education: Within this discourse, FemTech has emerged as a promising sector that can bridge these gaps by offering solutions tailored specifically to women's health needs. FemTech is recognized for its potential to revolutionize areas such as reproductive health, maternal care, mental wellness, and menstrual health, thereby contributing to women's autonomy and well-being. The application of FemTech in educational environments presents a novel approach to addressing gender-specific barriers to learning. For instance, the integration of digital tools that track menstrual cycles, monitor mental health, or provide reproductive health education can serve as vital supports for female learners, particularly in regions where these topics are either taboo or poorly understood. In this way, FemTech not only facilitates access to health-related information but also helps normalize discussions around female health in educational settings, thereby fostering a more supportive and inclusive learning environment.

Culturally Attuned Digital Transformation and the Integration of FemTech in Education: Culturally attuned digital transformation is an essential concept when considering the integration of FemTech within education. The notion of cultural sensitivity in digital education revolves around the idea that digital tools and platforms should be designed with a keen awareness of the specific cultural, societal, and gender norms of the communities they serve. In many parts of the world, particularly in the Global South, educational systems are deeply embedded in traditional cultural norms that often limit the role of women in society. These norms manifest in various forms, such as limited mobility for girls, restricted access to educational resources, and societal taboos surrounding menstruation and reproductive health (Dahlman et al., 2023). The literature underscores the importance of designing digital education systems that are not only technologically advanced but also sensitive to these cultural nuances. By incorporating FemTech into these systems, educational frameworks can more effectively address the unique challenges faced by female learners, providing them with the resources and support they need to succeed (Hod et al., 2023).

Culturally Sensitive FemTech in Education for Women's Health: The importance of culturally sensitive FemTech applications becomes particularly evident in the context of maternal health, mental health, and menstrual care. In many societies, these issues remain deeply stigmatized, with limited resources or education available to young women. The lack of accessible and culturally relevant information on these topics can have a profound impact on a girl's ability to engage in her education (Baltzer & Bonancina, 2023). By integrating FemTech solutions into the digital education infrastructure, schools and universities can create platforms where students have access to discreet, user-friendly health tools that are culturally aligned with their values and norms. These platforms not only enable women to manage their health more effectively but also reduce the stigma surrounding female health issues, thereby encouraging more active participation in education (Mishra & Suresh, 2021).

FemTech Integration Linking Health and Academic Success: Furthermore, the integration of FemTech into digital learning environments promotes a more holistic approach to education—one that acknowledges the interconnection between health and learning. The literature emphasizes the growing recognition of the mind-body connection, where physical health is seen as inextricably linked to cognitive function and academic performance (Nellore et al., 2024). Digital platforms that integrate FemTech solutions can provide students with the tools to monitor their physical well-being, offering them greater control over their health while simultaneously improving their academic outcomes. For example, tools that help manage menstrual cycles or mental health may reduce school absenteeism and increase classroom engagement, ultimately contributing to better educational results. This integrated approach recognizes that the personal well-being of students, particularly female students, is integral to their academic success and overall development (Carre-Skinner, 2024).

FemTech's Role in Overcoming Health Barriers to Female Education: In regions where female education is often secondary to other priorities, FemTech has the potential to significantly improve educational outcomes by addressing the specific health challenges that disproportionately affect women. Research has shown that a lack of access to basic health information can prevent girls from attending school regularly, particularly during menstruation, when discomfort or stigma may lead to absenteeism. The introduction of health education through digital platforms, supported by FemTech solutions, can mitigate these barriers and ensure that female students remain engaged in their educational journeys (Canali & Hesselbein, 2023). Additionally, FemTech's emphasis on mental wellness can address another critical barrier to learning—mental health issues that often go unaddressed in educational settings. By providing tools for mental health management, FemTech can help alleviate the stress and anxiety that many female students face, enabling them to concentrate on their studies and perform better academically (Mathiason, 2023).

Designing Culturally Responsive Educational Platforms with FemTech: The literature also highlights the importance of designing educational platforms that are not only technically proficient but also contextually appropriate. Digital education tools that fail to consider the socio-cultural contexts of their target populations risk exacerbating existing inequalities. For instance, educational platforms that assume a uniformity of experience across gender, culture, or geography may inadvertently marginalize female learners by overlooking their specific needs (Corso, 2023). Therefore, culturally responsive digital transformation—facilitated by FemTech solutions—requires a nuanced understanding of the diverse challenges faced by female learners in different parts of the world. It also demands an educational design that allows for flexibility and customization, ensuring that students can tailor their learning experience according to their personal and cultural needs (Krishnamurti et al., 2022).

Ultimately, the literature highlights the need to reevaluate the conception and implementation of digital education platforms, particularly in terms of gender and cultural inclusivity. The integration of FemTech into digital learning ecosystems offers a promising solution to the complex challenges facing female learners, ensuring that their educational experiences are not only supported by cutting-edge technology but also shaped by an understanding of the cultural and health-specific barriers they encounter (Khan & Azhar, 2023). By creating culturally attuned and health-conscious digital platforms, educators can foster more inclusive learning environments that empower female learners to overcome the obstacles they face and achieve academic success.

Statement of the Problem

The rapid digital transformation in education presents an opportunity to make learning more inclusive and accessible. However, the integration of digital tools often fails to consider the diverse cultural contexts and gender-specific needs, particularly for female students. FemTech, which focuses on technologies designed to address women's health and education needs, has the potential to bridge these gaps in education. Yet, the lack of culturally attuned strategies in digital transformation has created challenges, especially for marginalized groups, resulting in unequal access and underutilization of educational technologies. The ideal state would be a digitally transformed education system where technology is tailored to the cultural, gender, and socio-economic contexts of the students it serves. This system would promote inclusive learning ecosystems, ensuring that both male and female students, irrespective of their cultural background, benefit equally from the opportunities technology provides.

Contradictory Evidence and Gaps

There is contradictory evidence regarding the effectiveness of culturally attuned digital transformation in education. While some studies show promising results of technology integration in educational settings, especially in gender-disaggregated interventions, others suggest that such implementations are fraught with difficulties, particularly in less-developed regions. For example, digital platforms aimed at improving education for female students may not always yield better outcomes due to poor infrastructure, lack of digital literacy, and insufficient content that reflects their cultural experiences. These inconsistencies point to significant gaps in understanding the nuances of applying digital transformation in culturally diverse settings. This disparity suggests that more research is needed to reconcile these contradictions and provide clear evidence of best practices in integrating FemTech in education.

Inconclusive Results

The results of studies on digital transformation and FemTech in education remain inconclusive. While some initiatives have been successful, the lack of consistency in outcomes raises questions about the scalability and sustainability of these efforts. For example, while some regions report increased female student participation in STEM subjects through digital learning platforms, others have found that the platforms do not cater to the specific needs of female students. This variation in results highlights the need for further research to determine what factors contribute to the success or failure of such initiatives. A clearer understanding of these factors is essential for ensuring that FemTech-driven educational transformations are both effective and sustainable.

Theoretical Gaps

Theoretical gaps exist in understanding how culture, gender, and technology intersect within the context of digital education. While some frameworks explore the role of culture in education, few have integrated gender-specific elements, especially in the context of digital transformation. Additionally, the existing theoretical models do not adequately address how FemTech can be effectively incorporated into educational technologies, particularly in a culturally sensitive manner. This lack of a comprehensive theoretical framework limits the understanding of how best to integrate technology that not only promotes educational equity but also caters to the nuanced needs of different cultural groups.

Knowledge Gaps

There is a significant knowledge gap regarding the long-term impacts of culturally attuned digital transformation on educational outcomes, particularly for female students. Most existing studies focus on short-term interventions and fail to explore the sustainability of these programs or their broader impact on societal change. The limited body of research also fails to address how digital transformation in education can be adapted to address the evolving needs of female students as they navigate various socio-cultural barriers. This knowledge gap needs to be filled to understand the true potential of FemTech in creating lasting educational reforms.

Context Gaps

Contextual gaps further complicate the implementation of digital transformation strategies in education. The implementation of FemTech solutions in various cultural contexts often faces resistance due to local norms, inadequate infrastructure, and lack of community support. While digital tools may work well in urban or developed areas, their application in rural or underprivileged regions often encounters significant obstacles. Additionally, the digital divide, which refers to the unequal access to technology between different geographical locations and social groups, is a critical factor that limits the effectiveness of these transformations. These context-specific challenges highlight the importance of localized solutions that consider cultural, economic, and social factors.

Practical Challenges

Several practical challenges hinder the successful implementation of culturally attuned digital transformation in education. These include inadequate infrastructure, such as unreliable internet connections and insufficient access to devices, particularly in rural and low-income areas. Furthermore, teachers often lack the training needed to effectively integrate digital tools into their teaching practices, and the curriculum often lacks content that reflects the cultural and gender-specific needs of students. In the case of FemTech, many solutions are developed without sufficient input from the target communities, leading to technologies that are not aligned with the real needs of female students. These practical barriers significantly limit the impact of digital transformation initiatives, making it crucial to address them in any future efforts.

How This Study Will Fill These Gaps

This study aims to bridge the aforementioned gaps by providing a detailed examination of the challenges and opportunities in implementing culturally attuned digital transformation in education, particularly through the lens of FemTech. By analyzing case studies and empirical data, the study will offer a comprehensive understanding of the barriers to successful implementation, including cultural, gender, and infrastructure-related challenges. Additionally, the study will propose a theoretical framework that integrates cultural sensitivity and gender inclusivity into the design and implementation of digital educational tools. By filling the knowledge gaps around the long-term effects and scalability of these interventions, the study will contribute valuable insights for policymakers, educators, and technology developers. The findings will serve as a guide for future research, highlighting the importance of context-specific strategies and encouraging the design of educational technologies that are culturally responsive and inclusive of gender-specific needs. In doing so, this study aims to chart a clear path toward a more equitable and inclusive digital future in education.

RESEARCH METHODOLOGY

The research methodology employed in this study involves a comprehensive analysis of the integration and impact of FemTech in educational contexts, focusing on gender equity, cultural barriers, and digital inclusion. The study utilizes a mixed-methods approach, combining quantitative data from pilot programs assessing learning retention and school attendance with qualitative insights into cultural barriers, policy adoption, and regional disparities in FemTech implementation. Data from various regions, including India, Kenya, Brazil, and Sweden, is analyzed to explore the effectiveness of FemTech solutions such as menstrual health apps, mental health tools, and reproductive health guidance in enhancing educational outcomes for female students. The research also examines policy frameworks, EdTech adoption, and local language integration to understand how cultural and political contexts influence FemTech adoption in education. By synthesizing data from global reports, surveys, and case studies, the methodology aims to provide a holistic understanding of the challenges and opportunities in incorporating FemTech into educational systems, highlighting the need for culturally sensitive, gender-inclusive policies and the role of technology in promoting equitable education for all.

Analysis

Table 1. Digital Learning Access by Gender and Region (2024)

Region	Female Access to EdTech (%)	Male Access to EdTech (%)	Gender Gap (%)	Cultural Barriers Reported (%)
North America	92.4	93.8	-1.4	8.5
Western Europe	89.2	90.1	-0.9	6.3
South Asia	41.7	56.8	-15.1	42.7
Sub-Saharan Africa	33.4	47.9	-14.5	47.2
Middle East & North Africa	49.5	64.0	-14.5	38.6

continued on following page

Table 1. Continued

Region	Female Access to EdTech (%)	Male Access to EdTech (%)	Gender Gap (%)	Cultural Barriers Reported (%)
Latin America	71.6	74.2	-2.6	17.9
Global Average	62.3	71.2	-8.9	26.4

Source: UNESCO Gender and Digital Education Access Report (2024), UN Women

The data presented in Table 1, which outlines the digital learning access by gender and region for the year 2024, offers a revealing look into the disparities in access to educational technology (EdTech) between females and males across various global regions. The table highlights both the gender gap in access and the cultural barriers reported in different parts of the world. The disparities in digital learning access between genders, as well as the cultural obstacles faced by female learners, reflect broader socio-economic, cultural, and infrastructural challenges that persist in many regions.

In high-income regions such as North America and Western Europe, the gender gap in EdTech access is minimal, with figures showing almost equal access for both females and males. Specifically, in North America, female access to EdTech stands at 92.4%, while male access is slightly higher at 93.8%, creating a negligible gender gap of -1.4%. In Western Europe, the figures are similarly close, with female access at 89.2% and male access at 90.1%, resulting in a very slight gender gap of -0.9%. These regions also report relatively low cultural barriers, with North America indicating just 8.5% and Western Europe showing 6.3% cultural barriers. These low percentages are indicative of the relatively high levels of digital infrastructure and social acceptance of gender equality in education, which likely contribute to the smaller gender gaps and lower cultural barriers.

However, the picture dramatically changes when we look at regions such as South Asia and Sub-Saharan Africa, where access to EdTech for females is significantly lower than that for males. In South Asia, female access is just 41.7%, compared to 56.8% for males, creating a gender gap of -15.1%. Similarly, in Sub-Saharan Africa, female access to EdTech is 33.4%, significantly lagging behind male access at 47.9%, which results in a gender gap of -14.5%. These regions also report some of the highest levels of cultural barriers, with South Asia facing 42.7% and Sub-Saharan Africa reporting 47.2%. The high cultural barriers in these regions can be attributed to entrenched gender norms, socio-cultural practices, and economic factors that limit the educational opportunities available to girls. Cultural factors, such as traditional roles that prioritize boys' education over girls', societal restrictions on women's mobility, and deeply rooted stigmas surrounding women's participation in technology, contribute significantly to the educational gender divide in these regions.

The Middle East and North Africa (MENA) region also experiences notable gender gaps in EdTech access. Female access stands at 49.5%, compared to male access at 64%, yielding a gender gap of -14.5%. While the gender gap is similar to that in South Asia and Sub-Saharan Africa, the MENA region reports slightly lower cultural barriers at 38.6%. This could reflect regional variations in socio-cultural attitudes toward women's education and their integration into the digital world. Though MENA faces significant challenges in terms of gender equality in education, the relatively lower cultural barriers might indicate an ongoing shift toward greater gender inclusivity in the region's educational policies, supported by the increasing integration of technology in education.

Latin America presents a slightly more balanced picture, with female access to EdTech at 71.6%, just slightly lower than the 74.2% for males. The gender gap here is -2.6%, which is much smaller compared to other regions. Cultural barriers reported in Latin America stand at 17.9%, which, while moderate, is considerably lower than in the regions discussed above. The relatively smaller gender gap and moderate cultural barriers in Latin America suggest that there is a growing trend toward gender equality in digital education, though cultural norms still pose some challenges, particularly in rural or less economically developed areas.

The global average, as shown in the table, reveals that female access to EdTech is 62.3%, compared to 71.2% for males, resulting in a global gender gap of -8.9%. This gap, though significant, reflects the overall trend observed across different regions, with higher income and more technologically advanced regions showing smaller gaps, while lower-income regions exhibit larger disparities. Cultural barriers globally are reported at 26.4%, highlighting that despite the progress made in digital education, cultural and gender-based obstacles remain pervasive on a global scale.

In conclusion, Table 1 underscores the significant regional disparities in access to educational technology for females, with the most notable gaps found in South Asia, Sub-Saharan Africa, and the Middle East & North Africa. These regions also experience the highest levels of cultural barriers, which are often the result of deeply ingrained socio-cultural norms that prioritize male education and limit women's roles in the digital space. On the other hand, North America and Western Europe showcase minimal gender gaps and low cultural barriers, emphasizing the positive effects of robust digital infrastructure, gender equality policies, and cultural acceptance. The global picture, however, remains one of significant inequality, with cultural barriers continuing to hinder the progress of female learners, particularly in less developed regions. These findings suggest that while progress has been made in some parts of the world, achieving true gender parity in digital education requires addressing both infrastructural and cultural challenges.

Table 2. FemTech Usage in Educational Contexts by Age Group (2023–2024)

Age Group	% Using Menstrual Health Apps	% Using Mental Health Tools	% Using Reproductive Health Portals	% Reporting Impact on Education
13–17 years	29.1	18.4	7.3	24.7
18–24 years	52.8	34.9	21.6	44.5
25–34 years	46.3	39.5	28.7	38.6
35–44 years	30.5	27.3	23.1	27.4
45+ years	17.2	13.8	11.4	14.3

Source: FemTech Global User Survey 2023–24 (Clue, Flo, World Bank)

The data presented in Table 2 offers valuable insights into the usage of FemTech tools in educational contexts, categorized by age group, as well as their reported impact on education. FemTech, encompassing a wide range of digital solutions focused on women's health—such as menstrual health apps, mental health tools, and reproductive health portals—has become an increasingly important component of educational environments. The table illustrates how different age groups engage with these technologies and the extent to which their usage is perceived to affect their educational outcomes.

Among the younger age group, specifically those aged 13 to 17 years, the usage of FemTech tools is relatively low but still notable. In this group, 29.1% report using menstrual health apps, 18.4% engage with mental health tools, and 7.3% use reproductive health portals. While these figures may seem modest, they are indicative of a growing awareness among younger learners about the importance of managing their health and well-being in relation to their academic success. Despite the relatively low engagement with reproductive health tools, the reported impact on education for this group is 24.7%. This suggests that even at this early stage of life, there is a recognition of the role that health management plays in overall academic performance, particularly for young women navigating the challenges of adolescence.

The usage of FemTech tools increases substantially in the 18 to 24 age group, with 52.8% using menstrual health apps, 34.9% engaging with mental health tools, and 21.6% utilizing reproductive health portals. This age group, being in the critical phase of higher education or early career development, is more likely to experience the direct impact of health on education. The reported impact on education for this group is 44.5%, indicating that a significant number of young adults perceive a positive correlation between using FemTech tools and their academic outcomes. These tools, which provide support for mental and physical health, can help manage stress, enhance focus, and ensure that learners remain engaged and productive in their studies.

The trend continues in the 25 to 34 age group, where 46.3% of individuals use menstrual health apps, 39.5% use mental health tools, and 28.7% engage with reproductive health portals. The reported impact on education is 38.6%, slightly lower than that of the 18 to 24 group but still indicative of the value these tools provide in enhancing educational experiences. As this group is typically in a phase of professional development or advanced academic pursuits, the integration of FemTech solutions can help mitigate the stress of balancing work, personal life, and education. The usage of these tools in this age group may reflect an increasing normalization of health-related digital solutions as integral to personal and professional success.

In contrast, the usage of FemTech tools decreases significantly in older age groups, particularly among those aged 35 to 44 years and 45+ years. In the 35 to 44 age group, 30.5% use menstrual health apps, 27.3% use mental health tools, and 23.1% use reproductive health portals. Despite the decline in usage, the reported impact on education for this group remains relatively high at 27.4%. This suggests that although the use of FemTech tools becomes less prevalent in this age group, the individuals who do engage with these resources continue to recognize their value in supporting educational and personal development.

Finally, the usage of FemTech tools in the 45+ age group is the lowest across all categories. Only 17.2% use menstrual health apps, 13.8% use mental health tools, and 11.4% use reproductive health portals. The reported impact on education is also the lowest at 14.3%. This can be attributed to the fact that many individuals in this age group are likely past the stage of formal education or are in a different phase of life where the need for such tools is perceived to be less urgent. However, for those who do engage with FemTech tools, they still report some impact on their educational experiences, particularly in terms of maintaining overall well-being and managing stress.

The data from Table 2 highlights several important trends. First, there is a clear correlation between age and the use of FemTech tools, with younger age groups (18 to 24 years) showing the highest levels of engagement. This reflects a growing trend of health and wellness awareness among younger learners, as they increasingly recognize the role of digital health tools in supporting their academic and personal lives. Second, the perceived impact of these tools on education is substantial across all age groups, indicating that health management—whether mental, menstrual, or reproductive—plays a critical role in educational outcomes. This underscores the importance of integrating FemTech tools into educational frameworks to support learners' well-being, thereby enhancing their ability to succeed academically.

In conclusion, the usage of FemTech tools across different age groups demonstrates a clear trend of increasing engagement with health-related technologies, particularly among younger learners. The reported impact on education, though varying by age group, emphasizes the need for continued integration of these tools into educational contexts to support the well-being of students and improve learning outcomes. As FemTech continues to evolve, its potential to contribute to inclusive and supportive educational environments will likely expand, benefiting learners across all age groups.

Table 3. Cultural Barriers to FemTech Integration in Educational Institutions

Barrier Type	% of Institutions Reporting	Most Affected Regions
Cultural taboos around menstruation	61.2	South Asia, MENA, Sub-Saharan Africa
Lack of female representation in EdTech leadership	48.7	Global
Curriculum not aligned with gender health	43.5	Asia-Pacific, Africa
Parental resistance to reproductive content	39.8	Middle East, India, parts of Latin America
Language/localization limitations	36.1	Africa, Latin America

Source: Global Education & Gender Innovation Report (UNESCO, 2024)

Table 3 presents data on the cultural barriers to the integration of FemTech in educational institutions, highlighting the specific challenges that hinder the wide-spread adoption of FemTech solutions across different regions. The table outlines the key barriers institutions face, the percentage of institutions reporting each barrier, and the regions most affected by these challenges. These cultural barriers significantly impact the effectiveness of FemTech tools in promoting inclusive educational practices, particularly in regions where traditional norms and values limit the integration of such innovations.

The most prevalent barrier reported by educational institutions is the cultural taboo surrounding menstruation, with 61.2% of institutions acknowledging its presence. This taboo is particularly pronounced in regions such as South Asia, the Middle East and North Africa (MENA), and Sub-Saharan Africa. Menstruation, often considered a private or taboo subject in these cultures, remains a significant hurdle to integrating menstrual health tools into the educational curriculum. In many of these regions, discussions about menstruation are either avoided or shrouded in stigma, making it difficult to implement educational programs that address menstrual health openly. This cultural barrier not only prevents the integration of menstrual health tools but also impacts the broader objective of fostering gender-inclusive educational practices, which are vital for improving educational outcomes for girls and young women. As a result, FemTech solutions aimed at menstrual health are underutilized or absent in educational settings, especially in countries where discussing menstruation is taboo.

A second major barrier reported is the lack of female representation in EdTech leadership, with 48.7% of institutions highlighting this issue. This barrier is a global challenge, indicating that the underrepresentation of women in positions of leadership within the educational technology sector continues to hinder the development and integration of FemTech solutions. A lack of female leadership in EdTech can lead to the design and implementation of tools that do not adequately reflect the needs and perspectives of female learners. Moreover, this gender imbalance in leadership positions can perpetuate the marginalization of issues such as menstrual health and reproductive education, which are crucial to the overall well-being and academic success of female students. The absence of women in leadership roles contributes to a lack of advocacy for gender-specific health solutions, further impeding the adoption of FemTech in educational institutions.

The third barrier identified is the misalignment of curricula with gender health needs, reported by 43.5% of institutions. This issue is particularly prevalent in the Asia-Pacific region, Africa, and other developing regions. In many educational systems, the curriculum does not adequately address gender-specific health concerns such as reproductive health, menstrual health, or mental well-being. Without a curriculum that aligns with these essential health topics, FemTech tools that focus on these areas struggle to gain traction. The lack of gender health content in educational curricula not only limits the potential impact of FemTech solutions but also reinforces outdated gender norms and reinforces the exclusion of women's health from the broader educational agenda. In many regions, educational reforms are needed to incorporate gender health education as a core component of the curriculum, enabling the integration of FemTech solutions in a way that is culturally relevant and academically meaningful.

Parental resistance to reproductive health content, reported by 39.8% of institutions, represents another significant barrier to FemTech integration, particularly in the Middle East, India, and parts of Latin America. In many of these regions, discussions about reproductive health are still viewed as taboo or inappropriate for young people. Parents often resist educational content related to reproductive health, fearing it may encourage early sexual activity or challenge traditional cultural norms. This resistance creates a significant obstacle for educational institutions seeking to implement FemTech solutions that address reproductive health. In environments where parental opposition to reproductive health education is strong, educational authorities may be reluctant to introduce FemTech tools into the classroom, fearing backlash from parents or the broader community. Overcoming this resistance requires a sensitive and culturally aware approach that balances the need for comprehensive health education with respect for local values.

Language and localization limitations are also a notable barrier, affecting 36.1% of educational institutions, particularly in Africa and Latin America. Language and cultural differences pose significant challenges to the effective deployment of FemTech tools in these regions. Many FemTech solutions are designed primarily for English-speaking audiences, which limits their accessibility and effectiveness in non-English-speaking countries. Additionally, even in regions where the tools are available in local languages, there may be issues related to cultural nuances, dialects, and local health practices that are not adequately addressed. For FemTech tools to be truly effective in these regions, they need to be localized not only in terms of language but also in terms of cultural and health-related contexts. This requires a deeper understanding of local health practices, beliefs, and attitudes, ensuring that FemTech tools are relevant and resonate with the communities they are intended to serve.

In conclusion, the cultural barriers to the integration of FemTech in educational institutions, as outlined in Table 3, reveal the multifaceted challenges that must be addressed to create a more inclusive and supportive educational environment for female learners. These barriers—ranging from cultural taboos around menstruation to parental resistance to reproductive health content—underscore the importance of cultural sensitivity and local context in the design and implementation of FemTech solutions. Overcoming these challenges requires collaborative efforts from educational institutions, governments, and FemTech developers to ensure that digital health solutions are not only accessible but also culturally relevant and supportive of the unique needs of female students. By addressing these cultural barriers, educational systems can unlock the full potential of FemTech in creating equitable, inclusive learning environments that empower female learners to thrive academically and personally.

Table 4. Impact of Culturally Integrated FemTech Solutions on Learning Outcomes (Pilot Programs, 2024)

Country	Group Sample	FemTech Feature Used	Learning Retention Improvement (%)	School Attendance Rise (%)
India (Rural)	520 girls	Menstrual tracking & health	+28.5	+31.2
Kenya	400 girls	SMS reproductive guidance	+21.6	+24.5
Brazil (Urban)	300 students	Mental health AI chatbot	+19.7	+11.3

continued on following page

Table 4. Continued

Country	Group Sample	FemTech Feature Used	Learning Retention Improvement (%)	School Attendance Rise (%)
Bangladesh	460 girls	Sanitation + app alerts	+26.9	+29.1
Jordan	250 girls	SafeSpace health platform	+23.2	+18.4

Source: UNICEF FemTech Integration Pilot Data Report, 2024

Table 4 presents data on the impact of culturally integrated FemTech solutions on learning outcomes, specifically focusing on pilot programs conducted in 2024. These programs, implemented in diverse geographic regions, aimed to assess the effectiveness of FemTech tools in improving educational outcomes such as learning retention and school attendance among girls. The data reveals significant improvements across multiple countries, demonstrating the potential of culturally adapted FemTech solutions to address gender-specific health barriers and enhance educational engagement, particularly for marginalized groups.

In India, particularly in rural areas, the use of menstrual tracking and health tools for 520 girls resulted in a notable increase in learning retention by 28.5% and a rise in school attendance by 31.2%. This outcome highlights the critical role of menstrual health management in improving educational outcomes. In many rural regions of India, menstruation is a significant barrier to school attendance, with girls often missing school due to menstrual discomfort or lack of proper sanitation facilities. By offering tools that track menstrual cycles and provide health information, FemTech solutions enable girls to manage their health more effectively, leading to fewer school absences and better retention of educational content. The significant rise in both learning retention and school attendance underscores the positive impact of addressing health-related challenges in educational settings, particularly in areas where such issues are often overlooked or stigmatized.

In Kenya, 400 girls participated in a program using SMS-based reproductive guidance, which resulted in a learning retention improvement of 21.6% and a school attendance rise of 24.5%. This program utilized mobile technology to provide reproductive health guidance, which is a critical area of concern in many African countries where access to sexual and reproductive health education is limited, especially for girls. The use of SMS technology is particularly beneficial in contexts where mobile phone penetration is high but internet access may be limited. The results from Kenya demonstrate that even simple mobile-based solutions can have a significant impact on educational outcomes by providing crucial information that empowers girls to take charge of their reproductive health, thereby enabling them to remain in school and engage more fully in their education.

In Brazil, a mental health AI chatbot was implemented among 300 students, leading to an improvement in learning retention by 19.7% and a more modest increase in school attendance by 11.3%. While the rise in school attendance is lower compared to other regions, the improvement in learning retention suggests that addressing mental health challenges can have a positive impact on academic performance. Mental health remains a significant barrier to educational success, especially in urban environments where stress, anxiety, and other mental health issues can significantly hinder students' ability to concentrate and retain information. The use of an AI-powered mental health chatbot to provide support to students highlights the potential of digital tools to provide accessible and anonymous mental health support, helping students manage stress and improve their academic outcomes.

In Bangladesh, 460 girls benefited from an intervention that combined sanitation and app alerts, resulting in an impressive 26.9% improvement in learning retention and a 29.1% increase in school attendance. This program addressed a fundamental barrier to education: access to sanitation facilities. In many developing countries, inadequate sanitation is a significant issue that disproportionately affects girls, particularly during menstruation. By integrating sanitation solutions with mobile app alerts, this FemTech solution not only provided timely reminders about menstrual health but also ensured that girls had access to the necessary sanitation facilities, which in turn allowed them to remain in school. The significant improvements in both learning retention and school attendance suggest that improving basic infrastructure, coupled with digital solutions, can have a transformative effect on girls' education, particularly in contexts where basic sanitation needs are not met.

In Jordan, the SafeSpace health platform was used by 250 girls, resulting in a 23.2% improvement in learning retention and an 18.4% rise in school attendance. The SafeSpace platform likely provided a range of health and safety information designed to empower girls and ensure their well-being while attending school. The platform's impact on learning retention is notable, indicating that addressing safety and health concerns in educational environments can improve students' ability to focus and perform academically. Although the increase in school attendance is somewhat lower than in other countries, the learning retention improvement suggests that the platform's impact was more pronounced in terms of cognitive engagement with the curriculum.

The data from these pilot programs clearly demonstrates the positive impact of culturally integrated FemTech solutions on educational outcomes. Across different regions, from rural India to urban Brazil, FemTech tools tailored to address specific health challenges faced by girls—such as menstrual health, reproductive health, sanitation, and mental health—showed marked improvements in both learning retention and school attendance. These outcomes highlight the importance of integrating health-related solutions into educational frameworks, particularly in regions where gender-specific barriers to education remain pervasive.

Furthermore, the variation in impact across countries suggests that the effectiveness of FemTech solutions is not only dependent on the specific health challenges they address but also on how well these tools are adapted to the local cultural and infrastructural context. In countries like India and Bangladesh, where menstrual health and sanitation are major barriers, the improvements in learning retention and attendance were particularly pronounced. In contrast, in more urbanized settings like Brazil, the focus on mental health yielded positive results in learning retention but a smaller effect on school attendance, indicating that mental health support can have a profound impact on cognitive engagement but may require additional interventions to address attendance issues.

In conclusion, the findings from these pilot programs provide strong evidence of the potential of FemTech solutions to enhance educational outcomes, especially for girls facing gender-specific challenges in accessing education. By addressing health-related barriers, these solutions not only promote well-being but also create a more supportive and inclusive learning environment, empowering girls to remain in school and achieve better academic results. The success of these programs underscores the need for further investment in culturally sensitive, health-focused FemTech solutions that can be scaled and adapted to different regional contexts to improve education for girls worldwide.

Table 5. Policy Adoption on FemTech and Cultural Digital Equity in Education (2024)

Country	National EdTech Policy Exists	FemTech Included in Curriculum	Gender-Sensitive Design Mandated	Local Language Integration (%)
Sweden	Yes	Yes	Yes	93.1
India	Yes	Partially	No	67.8
Nigeria	Yes	No	No	52.3
Brazil	Yes	Yes	Yes	89.6
Indonesia	Yes	Partially	Yes	75.4

Source: World Bank EdTech Readiness & Gender Policy Tracker, 2024

Table 5 provides a snapshot of the policy landscape surrounding FemTech integration and cultural digital equity in education across five countries in 2024. The data offers insights into the adoption of national EdTech policies, the inclusion of FemTech in educational curricula, the mandate for gender-sensitive design, and the integration of local languages in digital educational solutions. These factors are crucial in understanding how educational systems globally are addressing gender disparities and cultural nuances in the integration of digital technologies, particularly those related to FemTech.

Sweden stands out as a leader in both EdTech policy adoption and cultural digital equity. The country has a national EdTech policy in place, which explicitly includes FemTech in the curriculum and mandates gender-sensitive design in educational tools. Furthermore, Sweden boasts a remarkable 93.1% integration of local languages in its digital educational solutions, reflecting the country's commitment to ensuring that educational technology is both culturally relevant and inclusive. Sweden's progressive approach demonstrates how a comprehensive national policy can effectively address gender equity in education and the integration of health-focused technologies like FemTech, making them accessible and useful for all learners. This inclusive approach is essential for creating an equitable educational system, where every student, regardless of gender or cultural background, has access to tools that can enhance their learning and personal development.

India, while also having a national EdTech policy in place, shows a mixed approach to the integration of FemTech and gender-sensitive design. FemTech is only partially included in the curriculum, and gender-sensitive design is not mandated in the country's educational tools. Despite this, India has made significant progress with 67.8% local language integration in educational technologies. The partial inclusion of FemTech in the curriculum indicates a growing recognition of the importance of addressing women's health and well-being in educational settings. However, the lack of a mandate for gender-sensitive design suggests that there is still much work to be done to ensure that educational tools are fully adapted to the needs of female learners, particularly in rural and underserved areas. The moderate local language integration is a step in the right direction, as it ensures that digital education tools are more accessible to a wider range of students, particularly those who speak regional languages.

Nigeria presents a more challenging scenario with respect to FemTech integration and cultural digital equity. While Nigeria has a national EdTech policy, FemTech is not included in the curriculum, and there is no mandate for gender-sensitive design. Additionally, local language integration stands at only 52.3%, which is comparatively low. This data reflects the significant barriers that Nigeria faces in terms of addressing gender-specific needs in education and the integration of culturally relevant digital tools. In many parts of Nigeria, traditional gender roles and cultural attitudes toward women's health remain deeply entrenched, making the inclusion of FemTech solutions in the educational curriculum a challenging task. Moreover, the lack of local language integration suggests that digital education tools are not sufficiently tailored to Nigeria's diverse linguistic landscape, which further limits their effectiveness and accessibility. For Nigeria to foster gender equity in education through digital technologies, there will need to be a stronger focus on including

FemTech in the curriculum, implementing gender-sensitive design, and ensuring that digital tools are localized to meet the needs of its diverse population.

Brazil, in contrast, shows a more promising picture. The country has a national EdTech policy in place, and FemTech is included in the curriculum alongside a mandate for gender-sensitive design. Additionally, local language integration stands at 89.6%, demonstrating Brazil's commitment to ensuring that educational technologies are accessible and culturally relevant. The inclusion of FemTech in the curriculum and the mandate for gender-sensitive design indicate that Brazil recognizes the importance of addressing female health and well-being in educational contexts. This holistic approach ensures that FemTech solutions are not only integrated into the educational framework but also designed with gender equity in mind. The high level of local language integration further emphasizes the importance of making digital education tools accessible to a broad range of students, particularly those in remote or rural areas where local languages are predominantly spoken. Brazil's policies serve as an example of how a comprehensive and culturally sensitive approach to EdTech can promote gender equity and digital inclusion.

Indonesia, like India and Brazil, has a national EdTech policy, but the inclusion of FemTech in the curriculum is partial, and gender-sensitive design is mandated. Local language integration stands at 75.4%, which is higher than Nigeria but lower than Brazil. While Indonesia has made strides in ensuring that digital educational tools are culturally relevant, the partial integration of FemTech in the curriculum suggests that more work is needed to fully incorporate gender-focused health education into the country's educational system. The mandated gender-sensitive design is a positive step, indicating a recognition of the need to adapt educational technologies to the unique needs of female students. The relatively high level of local language integration also ensures that digital tools are more accessible to Indonesia's diverse population, which speaks a wide range of languages.

In conclusion, the data in Table 5 reveals varying levels of commitment to cultural digital equity and the integration of FemTech across different countries. While countries like Sweden and Brazil have adopted comprehensive policies that integrate FemTech into the curriculum and mandate gender-sensitive design, others like Nigeria still face significant challenges in this area. The integration of local languages in educational technologies is a crucial factor in ensuring that digital tools are accessible and effective, particularly in countries with diverse linguistic populations. As global efforts continue to address gender equity in education, the adoption of policies that include FemTech and prioritize culturally sensitive design will be essential for creating educational systems that support the well-being and success of all learners, regardless of gender or cultural background.

DISCUSSION

The integration of FemTech in culturally attuned digital transformation within education represents an important step toward creating more inclusive learning environments. This study explores how digital tools can be adapted to meet the diverse cultural and gender-specific needs of students, with a particular focus on addressing the challenges that female learners face in traditional and digital educational settings. The research emphasizes the intersectionality of culture and gender in education, asserting that technological solutions must be tailored to these dimensions to be effective. The findings suggest that while digital transformation has the potential to revolutionize education, the success of these initiatives largely depends on the cultural responsiveness and gender sensitivity of the tools being implemented.

One of the primary challenges identified in the discussion is the insufficient alignment of digital tools with the cultural contexts and lived experiences of students, especially female learners. Despite the increasing adoption of FemTech in educational settings, many platforms fail to consider the socio-cultural and gender-specific barriers that hinder the effective use of technology. For instance, in regions with deeply ingrained gender norms, female students may have limited access to technology or face societal resistance when engaging with digital platforms. Furthermore, the content provided by many digital learning tools often overlooks the cultural values and knowledge systems that are integral to the students' identities. This lack of cultural sensitivity can lead to disengagement, as students do not see themselves reflected in the digital content, reducing the potential impact of technology on their learning outcomes.

Another critical point discussed is the digital divide, which remains a significant barrier to equitable education, particularly in low-income and rural areas. While some urban schools may have access to advanced digital infrastructure, rural areas often suffer from inadequate internet connectivity, limited access to devices, and lack of proper training for educators. These infrastructural challenges not only hinder the integration of FemTech solutions but also exacerbate existing gender disparities in education. For instance, girls in rural areas may have limited opportunities to benefit from FemTech platforms due to the lack of technological resources and training.

Theoretical perspectives, particularly the Feminist Theory of Technology, provide valuable insights into these challenges. The feminist lens helps highlight how digital tools, including FemTech, can perpetuate or challenge gender inequalities in education. While the introduction of FemTech offers a promising avenue for addressing these issues, it also requires a critical examination of how gender biases are embedded in technology development. Ensuring that FemTech solutions are designed with a deep understanding of the cultural and gendered realities of female students is essential for their success. This study calls for greater representation of women in the development of educational technologies and a more inclusive design process that takes into account the specific needs of female learners from diverse cultural backgrounds.

Moreover, the discussion underscores the importance of teacher training in effectively integrating culturally attuned digital tools into the classroom. Teachers play a crucial role in facilitating the adoption of digital technologies, and their ability to adapt these tools to the cultural and gender-specific needs of students is paramount. Professional development programs that focus on culturally responsive teaching and gender-sensitive pedagogy are essential to empower educators to make the most of digital learning platforms. However, in many contexts, teachers lack the training and resources necessary to implement these tools effectively, which poses a significant challenge to the successful integration of FemTech in education.

In conclusion, this study contributes to the growing body of research on digital transformation in education by focusing on the intersection of culture, gender, and technology. It highlights the importance of integrating FemTech solutions that are both culturally sensitive and gender-responsive, ensuring that they meet the unique needs of female students across diverse educational contexts. By addressing the practical challenges and theoretical gaps identified in the discussion, this research provides valuable insights for future policymakers, educators, and technology developers. The study advocates for a more inclusive and contextually grounded approach to digital transformation, which can help bridge the gender and cultural divides in education, ultimately leading to more equitable learning opportunities for all students.

Political Implications of FemTech Integration in Education

The integration of FemTech into educational systems holds profound political implications that traverse the intersection of gender equality, technological policy, socio-economic development, and cultural transformation. FemTech, encompassing a broad range of digital solutions targeting women's health—such as menstrual health tracking, mental wellness apps, and reproductive health education—presents a unique avenue through which educational institutions can foster greater inclusivity, empowerment, and equity. However, the adoption and integration of these technologies in educational environments are shaped by political forces, particularly concerning the regulatory landscape, cultural attitudes, and socio-political agendas that influence policy-making in education and health sectors. These implications, when viewed through a political lens, shed light on the complex dynamics between technology, governance, and gender politics.

A critical aspect of the political discourse surrounding FemTech in education is the role of national governments in shaping educational and health policies. The incorporation of FemTech tools into educational curricula depends significantly on political will, governance structures, and the alignment of educational and health ministries. Countries with robust national EdTech policies that are gender-sensitive are more likely to facilitate the adoption of FemTech solutions in educational contexts. In this respect, the political commitment to gender equity becomes paramount, as educational systems are increasingly recognized not merely as institutions for academic knowledge dissemination but as vehicles for broader social change. Governments that prioritize gender equity and women's health, as well as those that promote digital literacy and health education, are more likely to implement policies that incorporate FemTech tools into schools, thus benefiting female students and advancing overall educational outcomes.

Furthermore, the integration of FemTech into education intersects with broader debates on the digital divide and equitable access to technology. While technological advancements have the potential to democratize access to education and health resources, the unequal distribution of these technologies across socio-economic and geographic boundaries remains a pressing issue. Political decisions regarding digital infrastructure development—such as internet access, mobile technology proliferation, and affordable devices—directly impact the effectiveness of FemTech tools in educational settings, especially in rural or underserved areas. Political leaders must address these disparities by ensuring that adequate resources are allocated to bridge the digital divide, facilitating equal access to FemTech tools for all students. Moreover, policies that support affordable access to technology for marginalized communities can significantly amplify the potential of FemTech in fostering inclusive education, especially for young women in remote areas where traditional education systems are often inaccessible.

The implementation of FemTech in educational institutions also raises significant concerns about data privacy, surveillance, and the regulation of digital health technologies. Given that FemTech tools often collect sensitive health data, including menstrual cycles, mental health information, and reproductive health status, there is an inherent risk of exploitation, misuse, or inadequate protection of this data. Governments must, therefore, enact stringent data protection laws and regulations to safeguard students' privacy and ensure ethical use of their personal information. The political discourse surrounding data privacy and the regulation of digital health tools involves a delicate balance between innovation and protection. While it is essential to promote the development and adoption of cutting-edge technologies like FemTech, it is equally crucial to implement frameworks that ensure data security and the prevention of abuse, particularly given the vulnerability of young women and girls in educational settings.

Additionally, the political implications of FemTech in education are shaped by the cultural and societal values that influence how technology is perceived and used.

In many countries, particularly in the Global South, cultural taboos surrounding menstruation, reproductive health, and mental well-being continue to shape public discourse and educational policies. The political resistance to addressing these issues in schools often stems from deeply ingrained cultural norms, religious beliefs, and traditional gender roles that restrict open discussions of female health. Governments must navigate these cultural sensitivities carefully when advocating for FemTech solutions in education. Political leaders who challenge these taboos and promote inclusive policies that recognize and address the specific health needs of female students are engaging in a form of cultural and political leadership that prioritizes gender equity and the health of young women.

In some regions, the adoption of FemTech in education also intersects with political struggles around gender rights, feminist movements, and women's empowerment. For instance, the introduction of menstrual health and reproductive education tools in schools can be seen as a political act of resistance against patriarchy and gender inequality. Governments that resist or delay the integration of FemTech tools in educational institutions may face backlash from women's rights activists and gender equality advocates who argue that access to FemTech is crucial for the empowerment and autonomy of young women. In this sense, the push for FemTech in education is not only a matter of technological integration but also a manifestation of the broader struggle for women's rights and gender justice. Thus, FemTech adoption becomes a political battleground where policies are contested, and the political climate surrounding gender equality in education can significantly influence the extent to which FemTech is embraced or opposed.

Moreover, the political economy of education plays a pivotal role in the integration of FemTech solutions. The funding and resources allocated to educational institutions directly impact their capacity to adopt and implement FemTech tools. Political decisions on budget allocation for educational technology and health education can either facilitate or hinder the introduction of FemTech in schools. In many developing countries, budget constraints and competing priorities often limit the scope of educational reforms, including the integration of digital health solutions. In these contexts, political advocacy for increased public spending on digital education infrastructure, including FemTech solutions, is necessary to overcome these financial barriers and ensure that all students, particularly female students, benefit from these innovations. Moreover, the role of international organizations, NGOs, and the private sector in funding and supporting FemTech initiatives also intersects with political dynamics, as governments may need to negotiate partnerships and agreements to bring these technologies into schools.

Finally, the global political environment, including international treaties and frameworks, can also influence the integration of FemTech in education. Multilateral organizations, such as the United Nations and the World Health Organization, have increasingly focused on the importance of digital health and education as key components of sustainable development goals (SDGs). These global frameworks provide both a mandate and a guideline for countries to adopt policies that promote gender equality and digital inclusion. In this way, international political pressure and cooperation can drive national governments to adopt policies that integrate FemTech into their educational systems. Furthermore, political negotiations at the global level regarding trade, technology transfer, and intellectual property rights may shape the availability and accessibility of FemTech tools in various regions, especially in low- and middle-income countries.

Managerial Implications

The findings of this study offer several important managerial implications for leaders in the education sector, particularly those involved in the implementation of digital transformation and the integration of FemTech in educational systems. First and foremost, managers must recognize the significance of cultural and gender sensitivity when designing and deploying digital tools in education. The successful adoption of these tools hinges on their ability to resonate with students from diverse cultural backgrounds and to address the unique needs of female learners. Therefore, managers in educational institutions, as well as those in technology companies developing FemTech solutions, must prioritize the development of culturally relevant content that aligns with the values and experiences of the target students. This approach not only enhances engagement but also fosters an environment where students feel seen, respected, and empowered.

Additionally, managers must consider the infrastructural challenges that many educational institutions face when attempting to integrate digital technologies. The digital divide remains a critical issue, particularly in rural and underserved areas. Managers should advocate for investments in the necessary infrastructure, such as improved internet connectivity, access to devices, and training programs for both teachers and students. This is particularly important for the successful implementation of FemTech, which can otherwise remain inaccessible to those who need it the most. Managers should also explore partnerships with governments, non-governmental organizations, and private sector players to facilitate the necessary investments in digital infrastructure and resources.

Furthermore, the role of educators cannot be overlooked in the successful integration of FemTech and culturally attuned digital tools. Managers must ensure that teachers are not only equipped with the technological tools but also with the pedagogical training necessary to use these tools effectively. This includes providing professional development opportunities that focus on culturally responsive teaching and gender-sensitive pedagogies. Managers should work closely with educational leaders to design training programs that enable educators to integrate digital technologies in ways that are culturally appropriate and gender-inclusive, ensuring that all students benefit from the digital transformation.

Finally, managers must recognize the importance of ongoing evaluation and feedback in the integration of FemTech in education. The process of digital transformation is dynamic, and it is essential to continuously assess the effectiveness of digital tools and platforms in meeting the needs of female students. Managers should implement systems for collecting feedback from students, teachers, and other stakeholders, using this information to refine and improve the technological solutions being used. By taking a data-driven approach to the implementation of digital technologies, managers can ensure that the tools are not only culturally and gender-sensitive but also effective in enhancing student learning outcomes.

Practical Implications

The practical implications of this study underscore the need for a holistic, culturally sensitive approach to integrating digital technologies, particularly FemTech, into educational environments. One of the primary takeaways is the importance of designing digital tools that are not only technologically advanced but also contextually relevant to the cultural and gender-specific needs of students. Educational institutions and tech developers should focus on creating platforms that acknowledge and integrate the unique cultural values and experiences of students, especially female learners. For instance, digital tools and content should reflect the cultural norms, languages, and traditions of the target demographic, ensuring that the technology resonates with the students and fosters meaningful engagement.

Another key implication is the need to address infrastructural limitations. In many regions, particularly rural and underserved areas, access to reliable internet, digital devices, and adequate power supply can severely limit the effectiveness of digital learning solutions. Therefore, practical efforts should focus on improving the digital infrastructure in these areas, ensuring that students, particularly girls, have the necessary tools to benefit from digital transformation. This includes not only providing access to devices but also ensuring reliable internet connectivity and supporting digital literacy programs that empower both teachers and students to navigate these tools effectively.

Furthermore, practical considerations also include the training and professional development of educators. Teachers are at the forefront of digital learning, and their ability to effectively incorporate digital tools into their teaching methods is critical for success. Practical initiatives should focus on training educators in culturally responsive teaching practices, as well as gender-sensitive pedagogies that consider the specific challenges faced by female students. Professional development should be an ongoing process, with opportunities for teachers to stay updated on the latest digital tools and strategies for inclusive learning.

Additionally, creating spaces for continuous feedback from students, teachers, and other stakeholders is essential for ensuring that FemTech solutions are meeting the desired outcomes. By collecting and analyzing feedback, educational institutions can make necessary adjustments to improve the design, delivery, and impact of digital tools. This practice ensures that the technologies are continuously evolving and adapting to the changing needs of the student population.

Finally, the study emphasizes the importance of collaboration between educational institutions, policymakers, and technology developers. A coordinated effort is needed to address the digital divide, improve access to resources, and create policies that support the integration of culturally attuned digital tools. This collaboration can help bridge the gap between technological innovation and practical application, ensuring that digital transformation in education is inclusive, equitable, and sustainable.

Theoretical Implications

The theoretical implications of this study highlight the importance of expanding existing educational and technological frameworks to integrate cultural and gender-sensitive perspectives, particularly in the context of FemTech and digital transformation in education. Traditionally, educational theories have focused on generic models that do not sufficiently account for the cultural and gendered realities of diverse student populations. This study challenges those traditional models by arguing for the need to include gendered and culturally responsive frameworks when designing and implementing digital educational tools. The integration of FemTech into educational settings underscores the necessity of revisiting and rethinking foundational educational theories to make them more inclusive and relevant to the evolving needs of a global, multicultural, and gender-diverse student body.

The study also brings attention to the limitations of existing theories in explaining how digital tools, particularly those focused on women's health and education, can be effectively integrated into diverse cultural contexts. For instance, feminist theories of technology, which focus on the gendered nature of technological development, provide a critical lens to examine the inequalities perpetuated by traditional educational technologies. By incorporating a feminist theoretical perspective, this study reveals how FemTech can not only address gender disparities but also foster empowerment and engagement among female students in underrepresented regions. Thus, the study extends feminist theory in technology by showing how these gendered technologies can be adapted to educational contexts, offering new insights into the role of FemTech in overcoming barriers to gender equity in education.

Furthermore, the study underscores the need for new theories or adaptations of existing models to address the complex intersectionality of culture, gender, and technology. While the Diffusion of Innovations Theory helps explain how new technologies are adopted, it falls short when addressing the nuances of cultural and gender barriers that inhibit adoption in certain regions. This study calls for the expansion of such theories to better account for the challenges faced by female students in particular, especially in societies where gender norms restrict access to technology. Theoretical frameworks should evolve to emphasize not just the technological adoption process but also the social and cultural barriers that may prevent full engagement with these tools.

In addition, the research suggests a gap in understanding how culturally attuned digital tools can promote meaningful learning experiences. The application of Vygotskian constructivism, which emphasizes the role of social interaction in learning, could be enhanced by incorporating a cultural lens that recognizes the diversity of student backgrounds and experiences. Constructivist theory, in its traditional form, tends to universalize the learning process, but by integrating cultural and gender considerations, the theory can be adapted to better explain how digital tools can promote active learning among students from different cultural contexts.

The study also proposes that the current theoretical landscape needs to better integrate the voices of marginalized groups, particularly women, in the design and implementation of educational technologies. Existing theories on digital transformation in education largely overlook the role that gender plays in shaping how technology is used, perceived, and adopted. By adding a gendered dimension to these theoretical models, the study pushes for a more comprehensive understanding of how FemTech can be integrated effectively into educational environments to create equitable and inclusive learning experiences.

Recommendation

Based on the findings of this study, several key recommendations emerge for policymakers, educational leaders, and technology developers to enhance the integration of culturally attuned digital tools and FemTech in education. First, it is crucial to prioritize the development of educational technologies that are culturally responsive and gender-inclusive. These tools must reflect the values, traditions, and socio-cultural contexts of diverse student populations, particularly female learners. Developers should engage with local communities to co-create content that resonates with students' lived experiences, ensuring that the technology is not only accessible but also engaging and relevant.

Moreover, improving digital infrastructure in underserved areas is essential to bridge the digital divide and ensure equitable access to educational technologies.

Policymakers should invest in better internet connectivity, the provision of digital devices, and the establishment of community-based learning hubs in rural and low-income regions. This infrastructure should also be accompanied by training programs to build digital literacy among both teachers and students, enabling them to navigate and utilize digital tools effectively.

In addition, there is an urgent need to train educators in culturally responsive and gender-sensitive pedagogies. Teachers should be equipped with the skills to integrate digital technologies into their teaching while being mindful of the cultural and gender-specific needs of their students. Professional development programs should focus on empowering educators to create inclusive learning environments where all students, regardless of gender or cultural background, feel supported and valued.

Finally, continuous monitoring and feedback mechanisms should be implemented to assess the effectiveness of FemTech and culturally attuned digital tools. Data collected from students, teachers, and other stakeholders can be used to refine and improve these technologies, ensuring they continue to meet the evolving needs of diverse learners. Collaborative efforts between educational institutions, technology developers, and policymakers will be crucial to drive long-term success in creating inclusive digital learning environments.

Future Directions

Future research should build upon the findings of this study by exploring the long-term impacts of culturally attuned digital transformation in education, particularly in the context of FemTech. Large-scale, longitudinal studies are needed to assess how the integration of these technologies affects learning outcomes, particularly for female students in culturally diverse settings. Such research would provide valuable insights into the sustainability and scalability of these initiatives, offering guidance for the widespread adoption of FemTech in educational systems.

Moreover, there is a need for further exploration into the development of inclusive and gender-sensitive curricula that incorporate FemTech solutions. Future studies could focus on how curricula can be designed to reflect not only the educational needs but also the cultural and gender-specific needs of students. Research could investigate how FemTech can be seamlessly integrated into various subject areas, from STEM to the humanities, to promote gender equity and empower female students.

Another promising direction for future research is to examine the role of policy in shaping the adoption and integration of digital technologies in education. Investigating the effectiveness of existing policies and identifying gaps in policy frameworks could inform future efforts to create supportive environments for the implementation of culturally attuned digital tools. This includes understanding the challenges faced by policymakers in addressing the digital divide, as well as the role of government and private sector partnerships in enhancing access to FemTech solutions.

Finally, there is an opportunity to further investigate the role of social and cultural factors in shaping the acceptance and use of educational technologies. Future research could explore the barriers faced by female students in different cultural contexts and how these barriers can be overcome through technology. This could include examining how gender norms, community attitudes, and socio-economic factors influence the adoption of digital tools, particularly FemTech, in educational settings.

CONCLUSION

In conclusion, the integration of FemTech into educational systems presents a transformative opportunity to address long-standing gender disparities in education, particularly in relation to women's health and well-being. The data and discussions surrounding the adoption of FemTech, from its impact on learning retention and school attendance to the cultural and policy barriers it faces, underscore its potential to revolutionize educational outcomes for female students. The varying levels of FemTech integration across regions, as well as the diverse cultural, political, and infrastructural challenges, highlight the complexity of implementing these technologies on a global scale.

The political implications of FemTech's adoption are significant, as they encompass a range of issues from digital equity and access to data privacy, as well as the broader gender equality movement. While countries like Sweden and Brazil demonstrate progressive approaches in integrating FemTech into educational curricula with gender-sensitive design, other nations like Nigeria and parts of South Asia still face substantial barriers rooted in cultural taboos, lack of infrastructure, and resistance to reproductive health education. These challenges point to the need for a multi-faceted approach, including robust policy frameworks, cultural sensitivity, and financial investments in digital infrastructure, to fully realize the potential of FemTech in education.

As we continue to explore the intersection of technology and education, the political, cultural, and economic factors influencing FemTech adoption will remain pivotal in determining its success. To ensure that the benefits of FemTech reach all students, particularly those in marginalized communities, it will be essential for governments, educational institutions, and stakeholders to prioritize gender equity, data protection, and cultural inclusivity. The success of FemTech in education can drive meaningful change, not only in improving educational outcomes for female students but also in advancing the broader goal of gender equality in society.

REFERENCES

Agrawal, A., McIntyre, B. B., Agg, C., & Zou, Y.-X. (2025). Diverse and Inclusive Learning and Working Environments. *Lecture Notes in Networks and Systems, 1097*, 333–352. DOI: 10.1007/978-3-031-68282-7_18

Akazawa, S. (2025). Women's Comprehensive Outpatient Clinic and Antiaging. In *Anti-Aging Medicine: Basics and Clinical Practice*. Springer Science+Business Media. DOI: 10.1007/978-981-97-8514-8_162

Alfawzan, N., & Christen, M. (2023). The future of FemTech ethics & privacy – a global perspective. *BMC Medical Ethics*, *24*(1), 88. Advance online publication. DOI: 10.1186/s12910-023-00976-z PMID: 37891591

Alzate, C. (2024). Learning from femtech to inform the design of healthcare technologies. In *Digital Transformation in Design: Processes and Practices*. Transcript-Verlag. DOI: 10.1515/9783839471425-008

Balfour, L. (2023a). FemTech: Intersectional Interventions in Women's Digital Health. In *FemTech: Intersectional Interventions in Women's Digital Health*. Springer Singapore. DOI: 10.1007/978-981-99-5605-0

Balfour, L. (2023b). Introduction: Who Is FemTech For? In *FemTech: Intersectional Interventions in Women's Digital Health*. Springer Singapore. DOI: 10.1007/978-981-99-5605-0_1

Baltzer, C., & Bonancina, S. (2023). Enhancing Women's Health: An Assessment of Data Privacy and Security of Menopause FemTech Applications. *Studies in Health Technology and Informatics*, *309*, 155–159. DOI: 10.3233/SHTI230765 PMID: 37869830

Callegari, L. S., Mosley, E. A., Borrero, S., Talabi, M. B., Kazmerski, T. M., Donley, G., & Krishnamurti, T. (2025). Implementing digital sexual and reproductive health tools: Challenges and recommendations post-Dobbs. *Contraception*, 110969. Advance online publication. DOI: 10.1016/j.contraception.2025.110969 PMID: 40412590

Canali, S., & Hesselbein, C. (2023). Using and Interpreting FemTech Data: (Self-) Knowledge, Empowerment, and Sovereignty. In *FemTech: Intersectional Interventions in Women's Digital Health*. Springer Singapore. DOI: 10.1007/978-981-99-5605-0_13

Carre-Skinner, H. (2024). The rise of FemTech and why compliance is key to its success. *Regulatory Rapporteur, 21*(2).

Chen, T. (2025). The new patriarchal digitality? Understanding gendered power dynamics through a systematic review of femtech apps in China. *Gender, Technology and Development*, *29*(2), 263–286. Advance online publication. DOI: 10.1080/09718524.2025.2503561

Cook, S., Mehrnezhad, M., & Toreini, E. (2024). Bluetooth security analysis of general and intimate health IoT devices and apps: The case of FemTech. *International Journal of Information Security*, *23*(6), 3547–3567. DOI: 10.1007/s10207-024-00883-3

Corso, S. (2023). ON FEMALE TECHNOLOGY OR FEMTECH. ARTIFICIAL INTELLIGENCE, WOMEN'S HEALTH AND THE WILL OF THE INDIVIDUAL; [Sulla female technology o Femtech. Intelligenza artificiale, salute della donna e volontà della persona]. *BioLaw Journal*, *3*, 81 – 112. DOI: 10.15168/2284-4503-2755

Cromack, S. C., & Walter, J. R. (2024). Consumer wearables and personal devices for tracking the fertile window. *American Journal of Obstetrics and Gynecology*, *231*(5), 516–523. DOI: 10.1016/j.ajog.2024.05.028 PMID: 38768799

Dahlman, S., Just, S. N., Pedersen, L. M., Lantz, P. M. V., & Kristiansen, N. W. (2023). Datafied female health Sociotechnical imaginaries of femtech in Danish public discourse. *MedieKultur*, *39*(74), 105–126. DOI: 10.7146/mk.v39i74.133900

Espíndola, L. N., Grisolia, A. M. M., & de Oliveira, G. M. M. (2025). Digital Health – A Tool of Empowerment and Gender Equality? *Arquivos Brasileiros de Cardiologia*, *121*(12), e20240739. Advance online publication. DOI: 10.36660/abc.20240739i PMID: 39813462

Farahani, N. Z., Faubion, S., Sundsbak, J., Bethke, S., & Enayati, M. (2025). FEMTECH SOLUTIONS AND DEVICES: TECHNOLOGICAL INNOVATIONS AND THEIR IMPACT ON WOMEN'S HEALTH OUTCOMES. *Proceedings of the 2025 Design of Medical Devices Conference, DMD 2025*. DOI: 10.1115/DMD2025-1107

Faubion, S. S. (2021). Femtech and midlife women's health: Good, bad, or ugly? *Menopause (New York, N.Y.)*, *28*(4), 347–348. DOI: 10.1097/GME.0000000000001742 PMID: 33534432

Gomes, M., Provaggi, E., Pembe, A. B., Olaitan, A., & Gentry-Maharaj, A. (2025). Advancing Cervical Cancer Prevention Equity: Innovations in Self-Sampling and Digital Health Technologies Across Healthcare Settings. *Diagnostics (Basel)*, *15*(9), 1176. Advance online publication. DOI: 10.3390/diagnostics15091176 PMID: 40361993

Grimme, S., Spoerl, S. M., Jung, F., & Koelle, M. (2025). Hidden in Plain Sight: a Structured Analysis of Privacy Policies in the Context of Body-worn "FemTech" Technologies. *Conference on Human Factors in Computing Systems - Proceedings*. DOI: 10.1145/3706598.3713702

Hajkova, A., & Doyle, T. A. (2024). Hacking the Cycle: Femtech, Internalized Surveillance, and Productivity. *Philosophy & Technology*, *37*(4), 123. Advance online publication. DOI: 10.1007/s13347-024-00801-4

Hendl, T., & Jansky, B. (2022). Tales of self-empowerment through digital health technologies: A closer look at 'Femtech.'. *Review of Social Economy*, *80*(1), 29–57. DOI: 10.1080/00346764.2021.2018027

Hod, M., Divakar, H., Kihara, A. B., & Geary, M. (2023). The femtech revolution—A new approach to pregnancy management: Digital transformation of maternity care—The hybrid e-health perinatal clinic addressing the unmet needs of low- and middle-income countries. *International Journal of Gynaecology and Obstetrics: the Official Organ of the International Federation of Gynaecology and Obstetrics*, *163*(1), 4–10. DOI: 10.1002/ijgo.15032 PMID: 37554042

Hofmann, D. (2024). FemTech: Empowering reproductive rights or FEM-TRAP for surveillance? *Medical Law Review*, *32*(4), 468–485. DOI: 10.1093/medlaw/fwae035 PMID: 39361867

Howes-Mischel, R., & Tracy, M. (2025). Interembodiment beyond kin: Leveraging partibility within microbial FemTech. *Social Science & Medicine*, *376*, 117742. Advance online publication. DOI: 10.1016/j.socscimed.2025.117742 PMID: 40279782

Jain, T., & Mudliar, P. (2024). Platforming PCOS Treatment Online: FemTech Logics of Care. *Conference on Human Factors in Computing Systems - Proceedings*. DOI: 10.1145/3613904.3642882

Jeswani, N., Jain, N., Sharma, A., & Roychowdhury, S. (2023). Comprehensive FemTech Solution for Feminine Health. *Proceedings of 2023 International Conference on Signal Processing, Computation, Electronics, Power and Telecommunication, IConSCEPT 2023*. DOI: 10.1109/IConSCEPT57958.2023.10170571

Kelly, B. G., Junchaya, O., Min, J., & Burdan, M. (2025). Safeguarding autonomy: Examining the complexities and implications of under-regulated period-tracking apps and paired devices in a post-Roe landscape. *Contraception*, 110981. Advance online publication. DOI: 10.1016/j.contraception.2025.110981 PMID: 40513932

Khan, K. L., & Azhar, F. (2023). FemTech and Taboo Topics: Raaji as a Tool for Educating Women in Pakistan. In *FemTech: Intersectional Interventions in Women's Digital Health*. Springer Singapore. DOI: 10.1007/978-981-99-5605-0_9

Krishnamurti, T., Talabi, M. B., Callegari, L. S., Kazmerski, T. M., & Borrero, S. (2022). A Framework for Femtech: Guiding Principles for Developing Digital Reproductive Health Tools in the United States. *Journal of Medical Internet Research, 24*(4), e36338. Advance online publication. DOI: 10.2196/36338 PMID: 35482371

Lanzing, M. (2025). Our Bodies, Our Data, Our Choices: The Value of Privacy for Female* Self- Determination in a Post- Roe Era. In *Beyond Privacy: People, Practices, Politics*. Bristol University Press., DOI: 10.2307/jj.12348234.7

Mathiason, J. L. (2023). Femtech: The "Smart" Business of Menstruation, Hormone Tracking, and the Corporate Construction of Risk. *Feminist Studies, 49*(1), 118–149. DOI: 10.1353/fem.2023.a901596

McMillan, C. (2022). MONITORING FEMALE FERTILITY THROUGH 'FEM-TECH': THE NEED FOR A WHOLE-SYSTEM APPROACH TO REGULATION. *Medical Law Review, 30*(3), 410–433. DOI: 10.1093/medlaw/fwac006 PMID: 35482289

McMillan, C. (2024). Gender, health and technology: The rise of femtech - periods, profit and power. In *A Research Agenda for Gender and Health*. Edward Elgar Publishing Ltd., DOI: 10.4337/9781802209228.00010

Mehrnezhad, M., Shipp, L., Almeida, T., & Toreini, E. (2022). Vision: Too Little too Late? Do the Risks of FemTech already Outweigh the Benefits? *ACM International Conference Proceeding Series*, 145 – 150. DOI: 10.1145/3549015.3554204

Mishra, P., Kaur, R., Vikram, S., & Sharma, P. (2024). Femtech apps and quantification of the reproductive body in India: Issues and concerns. *Current Sociology, 72*(7), 1340–1359. DOI: 10.1177/00113921231206491

Mishra, P., & Suresh, Y. (2021). Datafied body projects in India: Femtech and the rise of reproductive surveillance in the digital era. *Asian Journal of Women's Studies, 27*(4), 597–606. DOI: 10.1080/12259276.2021.2002010

Neiman, E., Bornstein, M., Turner, A. N., Kavanaugh, M. L., & Gallo, M. F. (2025). Use of period- or fertility-tracking technologies pre- and post-Dobbs. *Contraception*, 110812. Advance online publication. DOI: 10.1016/j.contraception.2025.110812 PMID: 39800282

Nellore, N., Mishra, T., & Zimmer, M. (2024). Unveiling User Perspectives: Exploring Themes in Femtech Mobile App Reviews for Enhanced Usability and Privacy. *Proceedings of the ACM on Human-Computer Interaction, 8*(MHCI). DOI: 10.1145/3676530

Ng, W. Y., Lau, N. Y., Lee, V. V., Vijayakumar, S., Leong, Q. Y., Ooi, S. Q. D., Su, L. L., Lee, Y. S., Chan, S.-Y., Blasiak, A., & Ho, D. (2024). Shaping Adoption and Sustained Use Across the Maternal Journey: Qualitative Study on Perceived Usability and Credibility in Digital Health Tools. *JMIR Human Factors, 11*, e59269. Advance online publication. DOI: 10.2196/59269 PMID: 39352732

Nishi, T., Aikawa, Y., Kato, K., Kaneko, M., & Kiyono, K. (2025). Menstruation-Related Physical Condition Management for Women Using an Underwear-Type Wearable Biosensor †. *Engineering Proceedings, 92*(1), 5. Advance online publication. DOI: 10.3390/engproc2025092005

O'Brien, B., & Iriarte, E. G. (2025). Periods, technology and identity: The experience of period-tracking app users. *Irish Journal of Sociology*, 07916035251338808. Advance online publication. DOI: 10.1177/07916035251338808

Park, J. Y., Hsueh, S., Woytuk, N. C., Huang, X., Felice, M. C., & Balaam, M. (2024). Critiquing Menstrual Pain Technologies through the Lens of Feminist Disability Studies. *Conference on Human Factors in Computing Systems - Proceedings*. DOI: 10.1145/3613904.3642691

Peter-Spiess, M.-H., & Hofmann, D. (2025). Navigating FemTech app regulation in Switzerland: Challenges and opportunities from a public health perspective. *Contraception*, 110975. Advance online publication. DOI: 10.1016/j.contraception.2025.110975 PMID: 40412592

Pybus, J., & Mir, M. (2025). Tracking menopause: An SDK Data Audit for intimate infrastructures of datafication with ChatGPT4o. *New Media & Society, 27*(4), 1888–1908. DOI: 10.1177/14614448251314401

Roberts, G. M. (2023). Providing Care When There Is No Cure: How FemTech Can Help Destigmatize Autoimmune Diseases. In *FemTech: Intersectional Interventions in Women's Digital Health*. Springer Singapore. DOI: 10.1007/978-981-99-5605-0_6

Siapka, A., Tzanou, M., & Nelson, A. (2024). Re-imagining data protection: Femtech and gendered risks in the GDPR. In *Critical Reflections on the EU's Data Protection Regime: GDPR in the Machine*. Bloomsbury Publishing Plc. DOI: 10.5040/9781509977871.ch-005

Siddiqui, F. (2024). The birth of femtech lays fertile grounds for pregnancy discrimination in the workplace. *Family Court Review*, *62*(2), 413–427. DOI: 10.1111/fcre.12787

Sillence, E., Osborne, A. K., Kemp, E., & McKellar, K. (2025). Menopause apps: Personal health tracking, empowerment and epistemic injustice. *Digital Health*, *11*, 20552076251330782. Advance online publication. DOI: 10.1177/20552076251330782 PMID: 40297381

Tjandraprawira, K. D., Armawan, E., Aziz, M. A., & Djuwantono, T. (2025). A Study on the Quality of Patient-Centred Endometriosis Mobile Applications: Analysis and Future Prospects. *Obstetrics and Gynecology International, 2025*(1). DOI: 10.1155/ogi/5582127

Westwood, H. L. (2023). Reinventing the Beauty Myth? FemTech's Cost to the Consumer. In *FemTech: Intersectional Interventions in Women's Digital Health*. Springer Singapore. DOI: 10.1007/978-981-99-5605-0_3

Yi, C. Q., Sin, S. H., & Sam, T. L. (2024). A Bibliometric Analysis of Female Technology (Femtech) Research: Trends and Gaps from 2013 to 2023. *Journal of Technology Management & Innovation*, *19*(4), 127–144. DOI: 10.4067/S0718-27242024000400127

Zokaityte, A. (2025). FemTech Assets. *Feminist Legal Studies*. Advance online publication. DOI: 10.1007/s10691-025-09570-7

Chapter 11
Cultural Sensitivity in Digital Learning Platforms:
A Global Perspective

Mustafa Kayyali
https://orcid.org/0000-0003-3300-262X
Maaref University of Applied Sciences, Syria

ABSTRACT

As digital learning platforms become central to education worldwide, the need for culturally sensitive design has moved from a marginal concern to a pressing imperative. This chapter examines how cultural assumptions—often embedded unconsciously into technology—can shape, limit, or empower learning experiences across global contexts. Drawing on interdisciplinary research and real-world examples, the chapter explores the intersection of culture, pedagogy, and platform design. It also highlights missteps that have alienated learners, as well as innovations that honor local norms and cognitive styles. The aim is not to universalize design, but to advocate for a mindset that is reflexive, adaptive, and respectful of cultural plurality in digital learning. In a world increasingly connected yet fractured, cultural sensitivity isn't just ethical—it's essential for meaningful, equitable education.

INTRODUCTION

The modern classroom no longer has walls. With the click of a button, a learner in rural Kenya can access the same platform as a student in urban Seoul. A teenager in Brazil might be enrolled in an online course developed by an institution in Canada,

DOI: 10.4018/979-8-3373-3673-2.ch011

using interface elements coded in Silicon Valley, translated into Portuguese by a freelancer in Spain. The digitalization of education has indeed democratized access in extraordinary ways (Walls, 2021). But alongside this opportunity comes an urgent question: **Whose culture is embedded in the design of these platforms—and at what cost?**

The digital tools we use to teach and learn are not culturally neutral. Every font choice, feedback tone, navigation logic, icon, color scheme, and even the metaphor used to explain a concept, reflects a worldview—often unexamined. Educational technology, especially when designed for scale, frequently draws from dominant cultural and pedagogical paradigms—most often Western, linear, individualistic, and English-centric. In doing so, it unintentionally flattens the rich, diverse terrain of global learning traditions, epistemologies, and communication styles. This silent erasure rarely makes it into design sprints or code review meetings, yet its impact on learners can be profound, ranging from cognitive dissonance and disengagement to outright cultural alienation.

The problem lies not just in overt content but in the hidden architecture of digital learning platforms—the assumptions about what good learning looks like, how learners should behave, and what success means. For instance, a platform designed around independent, self-paced modules may work well for learners in cultures that value individual autonomy. But what about learners from collectivist societies, where interdependence and group learning are central to knowledge-building? What about those whose oral traditions and narrative-based reasoning are disrupted by rigid multiple-choice assessments or gamified badges?

Moreover, the global distribution of technology has not equated to the global representation of cultures. While tech infrastructure spreads rapidly, the cultural imagination embedded in these tools often remains narrow. This is particularly true in educational settings where standardized solutions are exported to diverse communities with little regard for local pedagogical traditions, spiritual beliefs, or social norms. When this happens, the digital classroom doesn't just ignore culture—it actively reshapes it, often in subtle but consequential ways.

This chapter does not argue against digital education—far from it. Technology, when harnessed thoughtfully, can support inclusive, context-sensitive learning and open up pedagogical possibilities that were once unimaginable. But to achieve this, we must move beyond the illusion of universality in digital design and confront the cultural blind spots embedded in our platforms. We must stop thinking of "global reach" as a technical problem and begin to understand it as an ethical, cultural, and pedagogical challenge. In this chapter, we explore what cultural sensitivity in digital learning truly means—not as a checklist of do's and don'ts, but as a philosophy of design and engagement. We examine real-world examples of both success and failure, unpack the hidden layers of cultural coding in digital environments, and propose a framework for culturally responsive edtech. Our approach is grounded in humility and curiosity: acknowledging that culture is not static or neatly bounded, but fluid, layered, and deeply personal.

Ultimately, this chapter is a call to action—not only for designers and developers, but for educators, policymakers, and learners themselves. As digital education continues to evolve and expand, it is time to ask: **Are we building platforms that respect the plurality of human experience—or are we exporting a single model under the guise of innovation?** The answer to this question will shape the future of learning more than any new feature or algorithm ever could.

The Cultural Lens in a Digital Age: Why It Matters More Than Ever

It begins quietly, almost imperceptibly. You sign into a learning platform. A tidy dashboard greets you with its clean lines, cool color palette, and friendly icons. Everything feels familiar, professional, efficient. But pause for a moment. Whose idea of "friendly" is that soft blue hue? Why does the feedback button look like a speech bubble? Why is the course structured around milestones, deadlines, and badges? What unspoken values—what silent assumptions—are stitched into this experience?

Culture doesn't knock. It seeps in. In a time when education is being digitized at breakneck speed, the cultural lens through which we design and experience learning platforms has never been more relevant, or more invisible (McHaney, 2023). We speak about scalability, user-friendliness, gamification—but rarely do we ask: scalable for whom? User-friendly by whose standards? Gamified in what cultural context?

Let's not kid ourselves—technology, no matter how elegant or efficient, is never neutral. It is made by people with stories, biases, traditions, preferences, and blind spots. Every drop-down menu, every default setting, every AI-generated quiz question is shaped by someone's worldview (Korinek, 2024). And yet, as learners from radically different cultural, linguistic, and epistemological backgrounds interact with these platforms, they are expected to conform to a single mold—a mold that often doesn't fit. And when it doesn't, the learner is the one who's labeled slow, disengaged, or underperforming.

Let's call this what it is: a quiet violence. Not the kind that wounds with sharp edges, but the kind that slowly dulls a learner's sense of self. The kind that tells a student in Indonesia that their collaborative instincts are less valid than the platform's preference for solitary tasks. The kind that subtly suggests to a girl in Ghana that her storytelling flair must yield to bullet-point summaries. The kind that makes a Syrian refugee child feel like their entire cultural frame is an error message.

We live in a paradox. On the one hand, we are more globally connected than ever. On the other, the digital spaces we inhabit are often culturally narrow—flattened into sameness under the guise of universality. But what we call universal is usually just familiar to the dominant culture in which the product was made. What's marketed as "intuitive design" is often nothing more than Western logic dressed up as objectivity. And what's praised as global reach too often comes without global depth.

The cultural lens matters because education is not just about transferring knowledge—it's about shaping identity, belonging, voice (Owens et al, 2024). When platforms disregard cultural context, they don't just risk being ineffective; they risk being alienating. The learner doesn't just struggle with the content—they begin to question whether their way of knowing, speaking, thinking, or being even belongs in this new digital world. And that's not just unfortunate—it's profoundly unjust.

Let's step back for a moment. What even *is* culture in the context of digital learning? It's not just about language or national identity. It's a complex web of values, social norms, learning preferences, power dynamics, communication styles, and assumptions about what knowledge is and how it should be acquired. In some cultures, asking questions is a sign of curiosity. In others, it may be seen as challenging authority. In some classrooms, the teacher is a guide; in others, a figure of reverence. These distinctions don't disappear when the classroom moves online. In fact, they often become more pronounced.

Take feedback, for example. In a U.S.-centric platform, direct and immediate feedback may be seen as helpful, even motivational. But in many Asian contexts, especially those influenced by Confucian ideals, blunt feedback can feel disrespectful or shaming. Similarly, a student from a high-context culture, where meaning is derived from relationships and subtext, might find a literal, step-by-step platform experience barren or robotic. The platform might be "working"—technically—but it is failing to connect. And that's a failure that algorithms don't catch.

There's another layer here: the commodification of education. As learning platforms become products, and students become users, the cultural lens is often seen as a market segmentation issue, not a human dignity issue (Kayyali, 2025 A). Localization becomes a business strategy rather than a pedagogical one. Translate the text, swap a few icons, and call it global. But cultural sensitivity isn't cosmetic. It's foundational.

I remember sitting in a workshop once, watching a designer walk through a prototype for a global literacy app. The interface was slick, modern. The content was vetted. But something felt off. The avatars used Western names and wore clothing that didn't match the regions the app was intended for. The voiceover had an accent foreign to the target audience. And the reward system—based on points and badges—reflected a distinctly competitive, individualistic ethos. I asked if they had tested it with kids from the intended regions. The answer: not yet. They were planning to roll out globally first, then iterate based on feedback.

That moment stayed with me. It crystallized how easy it is, even with good intentions, to treat cultural identity as an afterthought—something to patch, not to anchor. It reminded me that speed is often the enemy of reflection. That efficiency can undermine empathy. That when education becomes a product, cultural nuance becomes collateral damage (Jia, 2025). But it doesn't have to be this way.

Cultural sensitivity in digital learning platforms is not about exoticizing difference (Jafarov, 2024). It's about designing with cultural humility. It's about sitting with the discomfort of not knowing, of realizing that your mental model of what "good learning" looks like may not apply everywhere. It's about involving local educators and learners from the beginning—not as testers, but as co-creators. It's about moving beyond "user personas" and engaging with real people, in real places, with real stories. And yes, it's hard. It's messy. It's slow. But it's also deeply necessary. Because when we don't account for culture, we don't just risk building ineffective tools. We risk reinforcing the very inequities that digital education was supposed to dissolve. We risk creating platforms that are technically inclusive but emotionally alienating. We risk widening the gap between access and belonging.

Table 1. Challenges in Implementing Cultural Sensitivity in Global EdTech

Challenge	Description
Scalability	Balancing global reach with local relevance in platform design.
Cultural Misrepresentation	Inaccurate or stereotypical depictions of cultures.
Bias in Algorithms	Embedded biases affecting learning recommendations.
Technical Constraints	Inadequate infrastructure in marginalized regions.
Lack of Cultural Expertise	Limited input from culturally diverse stakeholders.

Let's talk about belonging. It's a strange thing in digital spaces—so intangible, yet so vital. A student can have high-speed internet, a sleek tablet, and a full library of content, and still feel like an outsider. Belonging isn't just about having access. It's about being seen. Heard. Respected. And culture is the lens through which we offer—or withhold—that sense of recognition.

Designers often say, "Good design is invisible." But maybe, when it comes to education, we need visible design. Culturally visible design. Design that signals to the learner: *We see you. We understand where you're coming from. Your way of knowing matters here.*

That doesn't mean pandering. It means being radically intentional. What would it look like if platforms were designed not just to scale, but to adapt? What if the learning environment responded not just to a student's performance metrics, but to their cultural background, language style, and cognitive preferences? What if "personalized learning" wasn't just about algorithmic pacing, but about cultural alignment?

Imagine a learning module on storytelling that offers different paths: one rooted in Western linear narrative, another in circular Indigenous storytelling, another in African oral tradition. Imagine an assessment system that doesn't assume written text as the default, but allows spoken word, dance, or image-based expression as valid forms of knowledge demonstration (Kim & Li, 2021). Imagine a feedback system that adapts its tone based on cultural expectations around authority and face-saving. These aren't pipe dreams. These are possibilities—if we're willing to ask better questions and center better values.

Of course, culture isn't static. It evolves. It overlaps. It surprises. No learner fits neatly into a single box, and not every individual from a cultural group will conform to its dominant patterns. That's why cultural sensitivity is not about stereotyping; it's about awareness. Attunement. Curiosity. It's about designing for flexibility, not fixity. It's also about confronting power. Because at the end of the day, cultural erasure in digital learning platforms isn't just a design flaw—it's a power imbalance. The power to define what counts as knowledge. The power to shape how learners engage. The power to decide who gets to feel at home in a digital space, and who has to navigate it as a guest.

So, here's the provocation: What if we treated culture not as a constraint, but as a compass? What if we allowed it to guide—not limit—our design choices? What if the measure of success wasn't how many countries a platform reaches, but how many cultures it honors? This is not romantic idealism. It's a call for pedagogical integrity. For design justice. For digital spaces that don't just teach, but also affirm. Because when learners see themselves reflected in the tools they use—when their languages, histories, traditions, and ways of thinking are not just tolerated but celebrated—they don't just learn better. They belong deeper. They become co-authors of their own learning journey. And that, in a fractured world, might be the most powerful kind of education there is.

Designing for Diversity: Navigating Norms, Values, and Learning Styles

Let's start with a simple truth: no two learners are the same. It sounds cliché—obvious, even—but the depth of what that means is often lost in the churn of edtech innovation (Weller, 2022). We nod politely at the idea of "learner diversity," then turn around and feed everyone the same platform logic, the same feedback mechanisms, the same sterile UI that assumes cognition happens in neatly structured boxes.

What's worse is that we often congratulate ourselves for adding language support or customizable avatars, imagining that we've somehow accommodated the world.

We haven't. Not even close. Diversity isn't a skin you slap onto a system. It's the soul of learning. It's messy, layered, volatile—full of contradictions, tensions, and beauty (Kayyali, 2022). And when we design digital platforms that ignore that, we're not just missing the mark. We're flattening the entire human experience into something machine-readable.

So, what does it really mean to design for diversity? It means asking uncomfortable questions. About whose values are encoded in the platform. About which norms get privileged. About what "good learning" looks like to different people, in different places, shaped by different histories and hopes. Because norms are not just customs—they are power in disguise. And when a platform tells a learner how to learn, it's also—quietly—telling them how to be.

Let's take an example that seems innocuous: time. In many Western-designed platforms, learning is structured around time-efficiency. Modules are broken into 20-minute tasks. Pacing is prized. Progress bars demand forward motion. There's a built-in assumption that time is linear, measurable, something to be optimized. But not all cultures see time that way. For many Indigenous communities, time is cyclical. Learning unfolds in rhythm with nature, story, and silence. It's not about checkpoints—it's about depth, context, relation. So what happens when you force that worldview into a platform that celebrates speed over reflection?

You don't just create friction. You create erasure. Or consider the concept of voice. In many Western pedagogical models, having a voice means speaking up, participating actively, showing confidence (Sekhar, 2024). But in other cultures, deference and silence are signs of respect—not disengagement. A learner might remain quiet not because they lack ideas, but because their culture teaches them to listen first. Yet digital discussion boards, video submissions, and participation scores often penalize this very approach. The result? A learner who begins to doubt their own instincts, who feels pressure to perform inauthentically just to "succeed." And then there's feedback.

The way we give and receive feedback is deeply cultural. In some places, directness is seen as honesty—a mark of respect. In others, it's perceived as rude or even hostile. Yet many platforms use automated feedback loops that are blunt, transactional, and tone-deaf. "Incorrect. Try again." "Incomplete. Please revise." Imagine receiving that in a culture where maintaining face is paramount, where critique is delivered obliquely, often wrapped in praise. The platform might be doing its job, technically—but it's also bruising a learner's sense of self.

These are not minor issues. They strike at the core of what it means to feel safe in a learning space. And safety—let's be clear—is not just physical. It's emotional. Psychological. Cultural. If a learner doesn't feel like they belong, if their way of thinking is subtly undermined at every turn, they won't engage (Allen, 2022). Or worse, they'll perform compliance while disconnecting internally. That's not learning. That's survival. So how do we do better?

Well, the first step is to stop pretending there's a neutral baseline. There isn't. Every interface, every interaction, every instructional choice is steeped in assumptions. Recognizing that doesn't mean we abandon structure or standards. It means we make space for plurality within them (Reus-Smit, 2021). It means we shift from designing for the average to designing for the edge.

It also means thinking beyond demographics. Cultural sensitivity is not about checking a box for every ethnicity, religion, or language group (Gove et al, 2021). It's about understanding deeper currents—epistemologies, worldviews, communication norms, cognitive preferences. For instance, does the platform favor visual over auditory processing? Does it assume a high level of digital literacy? Does it require fast internet or frequent typing? These choices may seem technical, but they have cultural and economic implications (Kayyali, 2025 B). And then there's learning style—another dimension we love to generalize, even when the science is fuzzy. But what if we thought of learning style not as a rigid category, but as a dynamic interplay between culture and cognition?

Let's take a learner from a culture steeped in oral tradition. Their strength may lie in storytelling, rhythm, voice, memory. But if the platform offers only multiple-choice quizzes and drag-and-drop diagrams, how do they shine? Or consider a student whose culture values group achievement over individual performance. They may excel in collaborative environments, but struggle with platforms that rank learners against each other on leaderboards. Are they underachieving—or just underserved?

We often talk about "engagement" in digital learning as if it's a one-size-fits-all metric. But engagement looks different in different places. In some contexts, it's lively debate. In others, it's silent reflection. In some, it's visible enthusiasm. In others, it's quiet perseverance. If we measure engagement by a single yardstick, we risk misreading the very signals we're trying to capture.

The hard part? You can't solve any of this with a plugin or a patch. Designing for diversity means slowing down. Listening more. Bringing in cultural consultants, local educators, anthropologists (Stein, 2021). It means giving learners the tools to shape their own path through the material—not just in pacing, but in expression, interpretation, feedback, and form. It means creating space not just for access, but for agency. And yes, this kind of design is harder. It's slower. It's more expensive. But the cost of *not* doing it is higher: alienated learners, missed potential, education that replicates the very inequities it claims to dismantle.

Sometimes I think about what it would mean to design a learning platform with no default. No assumed norm. A platform that begins not with a model, but with a question: *Who are you, and how do you learn best?* What if instead of segmenting users by geography or age, we asked about values? Do you prefer to learn through stories or steps? Do you like to work alone or in a group? Do you need quiet or dialogue? Do you want feedback that's direct or gentle, immediate or reflective? Imagine a platform that flexes, shifts, adapts—not just cosmetically, but at its core. We're not there yet. But we can get closer (McHaney, 2023). And part of getting closer means grappling with contradictions. Because designing for diversity isn't clean. It's contradictory, paradoxical, and often uncomfortable. You'll make mistakes. You'll offend someone, somewhere. You'll try to honor one culture and find yourself clashing with another. That's okay. The goal isn't perfection—it's intentionality. It's making the effort, over and over again, to do less harm and more good.

It's also about honoring complexity. Because culture isn't just external—it lives inside each of us, in messy, overlapping layers. I might be Arab, raised in the Middle East, but schooled in American-style debate. I might prefer group learning in one context and quiet study in another. Culture isn't fixed. It's fluid, dynamic, contextual. And our designs should reflect that. Which brings me to a final point: humility.

Designing for diversity requires a kind of epistemic humility—a willingness to admit what we don't know. A readiness to listen. A commitment to iteration. It's about replacing the designer's ego with the learner's voice. It's about co-creating, not dictating. About asking: *What does this mean to you?* and *How can we do it better?*

I've seen small teams do this beautifully. A group of educators in rural India working with coders to create math modules that include traditional games and local metaphors. A platform in South Africa that lets learners submit voice notes instead of typed answers. A university in Finland partnering with Sámi communities to integrate Indigenous knowledge into online science courses. These aren't perfect systems. But they're brave ones. And they remind us that diversity isn't a burden—it's a source of innovation, creativity, resilience. So, let's stop designing for compliance. For performance. For some mythical "global user." Let's start designing for presence. For humanity. For the wild, beautiful diversity of how we think, speak, learn, and make meaning in this world. Because at the end of the day, education—real education—is not about conformity. It's about becoming. And if our platforms can't hold that, then what are we building them for?

Case Studies Across Borders: What Works, What Offends, What's Missed

It's one thing to speak in theories, frameworks, and polished abstractions. It's another thing entirely to sit across from a learner—a real person with a history, a language, a sense of self—and realize that the platform meant to help them grow is, in subtle ways, pushing them to shrink. So, let's put away the rhetoric for a moment and turn to the stories. Stories of platforms launched with optimism, some with grace, others with cultural blind spots so glaring they almost read like satire. Let's sift through what's worked, what's offended, and what has—despite best intentions—been entirely missed. Because in these messy, honest case studies, we don't just find data. We find patterns. And more importantly, we find people.

1. **South Korea and the Silence that Speaks Volumes:** Start with Seoul. A bustling metropolis where students are known globally for their academic rigor and test performance. A U.S.-based edtech company, eager to break into the East Asian market, rolled out its math platform in South Korea with high hopes. Everything was technically sound: smooth UX, gamified progression, polished animations, bright leaderboards that ranked students globally in real time. What could go wrong? Everything, it turns out. The first round of feedback revealed something that caught the developers off guard: Korean students were uncomfortable with the competitive design. Not because they didn't like challenges, but because the leaderboard made their scores public—and in a culture where social harmony and modesty are core values, being ranked in public (especially below peers) wasn't just unpleasant (Kayyali, 2026 B). It was shaming. The result? Many students disengaged entirely. Some used fake names to avoid embarrassment. Others refused to log in during class time. Teachers, too, were uneasy—feeling that the platform undermined their relational authority in favor of a cold algorithm that didn't understand the nuance of the Korean classroom. What the company had missed was this: visibility isn't always empowering. In some contexts, it can be a form of coercion. A spotlight doesn't always feel like praise—it can feel like exposure.
2. **Kenya: The Voice of the Mother Tongue:** Now picture a dusty classroom in Nakuru County, Kenya. Tablets have just been distributed through a pilot program aimed at improving literacy in rural areas (Kayyali, 2024). The interface is in English, and the lessons are built around short, phonics-based exercises designed for rapid decoding. It's the kind of content that tested well in classrooms in Chicago and London. But the kids in Nakuru speak Kikuyu at home. English is their third language, sometimes fourth. Their cognitive world is rich with oral storytelling, folk songs, call-and-response patterns, communal chants. The app, with its solitary reading modules and sterile clip art, didn't just confuse them—it bored them. One teacher, Miriam, shared this with researchers: *"They don't see their world in this screen. It feels like something from a faraway place that doesn't belong to them."* Eventually, local developers stepped in. They built a parallel platform featuring bilingual storybooks rooted in Kenyan fables and translated by elders. Suddenly, the same children who had sat disengaged lit up. They laughed. They argued about characters. They asked to read more. It wasn't

a miracle. It was just resonance. The original platform hadn't failed because it lacked technical merit. It had failed because it had no ears.

3. **Saudi Arabia: Gender Norms in the Virtual Classroom:** Next, drift to the Gulf. In Saudi Arabia, a global edtech company partnered with a national university to roll out a remote-learning platform during the COVID-19 lockdown. It was a rushed, urgent deployment—like many during that time—and the default settings were based on Western classroom dynamics: camera on, voice on, faces visible. Within days, complaints started rolling in—not about the tech, but the cultural implications. Many female students, due to deeply held religious and cultural norms around modesty and gender separation, were uncomfortable turning on their cameras in mixed-gender classes. Some dropped out. Others covered their webcams with tape or simply stayed silent, fearing exposure or judgment. Here, the issue wasn't technological—it was architectural. The platform architecture presumed that visibility equaled participation. That assumption, when ported into a context where privacy is sacred, became deeply problematic. Eventually, accommodations were made. Voice-only options. Gender-separated virtual classrooms. Interfaces that respected modesty. But trust had already eroded. This case reveals something fundamental: dignity is not a universal template. It is context-dependent, sacred, and too often ignored in favor of convenience.
4. **Brazil: Humor as a Learning Bridge:** Now let's head to Rio. A local startup launched a digital science platform tailored for secondary students in public schools (Paul et al, 2025). But instead of importing a global model, they did something radical—they leaned into humor. Not generic fun, but Brazilian humor: memes, slang, irreverent jokes, characters that resembled students' older cousins. They consulted comedians, linguists, and teenage focus groups. The result? A wildly successful platform where learning felt less like compliance and more like cultural celebration. Students didn't just learn. They laughed. They shared clips with friends. They made up songs about photosynthesis and reenacted biology skits for TikTok. Critics scoffed at the informality. But the metrics spoke for themselves: higher retention, more voluntary usage, and teachers reporting increased classroom enthusiasm. Sometimes, what works isn't what looks respectable on paper. Sometimes, irreverence is the secret language of engagement.
5. **Finland: The Beauty of Silence:** Meanwhile, in the Nordic North, a different lesson unfolded. In Finland—a country with one of the world's most lauded education systems—platform designers had a different challenge. How do you digitize inquiry-based, minimalist learning without crowding it with noise? A global platform that had succeeded elsewhere—complete with pop-ups, notifications, interactive elements, and constant prompts—was tested in Helsinki (Zindulka, 2025). It failed. Students described it as "stressful," "chaotic," "too

busy." Teachers said it disrupted the calm, slow-paced rhythm of their classrooms. One principal likened it to "a mall inside a monastery." Eventually, Finnish developers reimagined the interface. They removed non-essential animations, muted the color palette, added whitespace, and allowed students to toggle between different levels of stimulation. They even included a "silence mode" where all interaction could pause for a reflection break. And guess what? The platform flourished—not by adding, but by subtracting. What's often missed in digital learning design is the power of stillness. Not every culture wants more. Some want less. Less noise. Less push. More space to breathe.

6. **Indigenous Australia: Whose Knowledge Counts?:** And then there's the Australian outback. An educational initiative sought to bring STEM content to Aboriginal communities. But the platform—while designed with rural access in mind—was steeped in Western scientific paradigms: empirical observation, linear progression, objective truth. Community members pushed back. They argued that the platform didn't reflect their holistic worldview, where knowledge is often spiritual, ecological, relational. Where the land itself is a living text. Where science is not separate from story, myth, or ancestry. The designers—thankfully—listened. Together, they built modules that wove in Dreamtime narratives, integrated land-based learning, and acknowledged Indigenous ways of knowing not as folklore, but as science. It wasn't perfect. But it was respectful. And that mattered. This case reminds us of a hard truth: digital education often presumes the supremacy of Western knowledge systems. If we're serious about inclusion, we have to rethink not just *how* we teach—but *what* we teach, and who decides. What works is not always what's high-tech. What offends is often unintentional. What's missed—repeatedly—is nuance. The best platforms don't just translate language. They translate *experience*. They don't ask, "Can it scale?" They ask, "Does it fit?" And the worst offenders? They're not malicious. They're just deaf. Deaf to context. Deaf to rhythm. Deaf to the whisper of difference.

The case studies above aren't just cautionary tales. They're invitations. To pay attention. To go slower. To make fewer assumptions. To ask more questions. When we design with cultural humility, we open ourselves to richness we never could have imagined. We stop trying to export a solution and start co-creating one. We stop seeing learners as "users" and start seeing them as collaborators. So let's end this section not with a summary, but a provocation:

What would happen if we stopped designing for "the world"—and started designing *with* it?

Because the difference between what works and what wounds often comes down to that one simple thing: *listening*.

BARRIERS TO CULTURAL INCLUSION IN EDTECH: FROM ALGORITHMS TO AESTHETICS

Try this: open your favorite digital learning platform and sit with it—not as yourself, but as a child from a fishing village in the Philippines. Or as a teenage girl in a conservative Saudi town. Or maybe a first-generation college student in Bolivia. Look at the fonts, the navigation, the avatars, the tone of instructions, the implied assumptions in every piece of "content." How long does it take before you feel like a guest in someone else's house? It's one thing to preach global access. It's quite another to embody cultural inclusion. Too often, EdTech dreams big and listens small. Behind the polished dashboards and codebase bravado, you'll find barriers—sometimes visible, but more often baked in so subtly they're mistaken for universal truth. From the math of the algorithm to the curve of a button's edge, these platforms carry cultural freight. And the heavier the cargo, the more likely someone gets left behind. Let's unravel the tangle (Kayyali, 2026 A). Because when we say "barriers to inclusion," we're not just talking about technical glitches or internet access. We're talking about deep, infrastructural blindness. The kind that wears a user-friendly face but whispers a monocultural gospel underneath.

The Algorithm Knows Best... Or Does It?

Start with the algorithm. That unseen gatekeeper of modern learning platforms (Potnis et al, 2025). The one that recommends, personalizes, nudges. It seems so objective, so smart. But every algorithm is, at its core, a reflection of someone's values encoded into math. Who trained it? On whose data? Using what assumptions about "success"? Take adaptive learning systems. They promise personalized journeys—but often personalize based on Western pedagogical norms. Quick responses are rewarded. Linear progression is assumed. Deviation is flagged as error (Amo et al, 2022). But what if a learner moves in spirals, lingers on ideas, jumps between related topics? The system might interpret that as inefficiency or confusion when it's actually exploration, curiosity, cultural rhythm. Even worse, algorithms can reinforce existing inequities. If students from underrepresented backgrounds historically perform lower—due to systemic issues, not intelligence—the data may label them as "high risk" and feed them watered-down content. Less challenge. Less opportunity. All in the name of "helping." We don't need smarter algorithms. We need wiser ones. Ones that recognize cultural learning styles, not just behavioral patterns. Ones that see complexity as richness, not noise.

Language: More Than Words

Let's talk language—and not just the words on the screen. It's tone, cadence, idiom, subtext. Most platforms default to "neutral English." But that neutrality is a myth (KANİ, 2021). It's often Americanized, informal, cheerful in a vaguely corporate way. "Awesome job!" "Oops, not quite!" "Try again—you're so close!" Harmless? Maybe. But imagine translating that tone into a culture where learning is serious business. Where mistakes are private. Where exuberance feels out of place. That chirpy encouragement can land as condescension. Or worse, alienation. And then there's the issue of multilingual learners. Many platforms offer translations—but do so with mechanical coldness, stripping cultural nuance. A translated sentence might be grammatically correct but emotionally tone-deaf. Or it might use regional terms inappropriate for the target audience. Worse, platforms may offer no translation at all, assuming that learners will adapt. But why should they? Cultural inclusion means speaking not just *to* learners but *with* them—in their linguistic and emotional vernacular.

Visual Aesthetics: The Quiet Language of Inclusion

Now pause and look at the aesthetics. Color palettes. Facial expressions. Clothing styles. Even the angle of a cartoon character's eyes. These things don't scream meaning—but they whisper it. Loudly. Consider a math platform that uses avatars wearing baseball caps, jeans, and sneakers. Innocent enough. But for learners in conservative cultures, that's not just unfamiliar—it's alien. Or think about female avatars that all have visible hair, Western beauty features, and exposed shoulders. That image—again, accidental—excludes entire populations of girls who can't see themselves in that mirror. Then there's architecture. Western interfaces often privilege left-to-right reading, bold colors, minimalism. But in other cultures, design is ornate, layered, nonlinear. What feels "cluttered" to a Silicon Valley designer may feel rich and beautiful to someone in Rajasthan or Morocco. Icons, too, carry bias. A trash can to delete? A lightbulb for ideas? These metaphors assume a cultural familiarity that doesn't always translate. In some cultures, a lightbulb doesn't represent "idea"—it's just a household object. Design is not neutral. Every pixel participates in cultural storytelling. We ignore that at our peril.

Normative Behavior: Who Gets to Be a "Good Learner"?

Let's dive into something thornier: behavioral norms. What does a "good learner" look like on a platform? They complete tasks on time (Hattie, 2021). They interact regularly. They give feedback, express opinions, take initiative. But guess what? That learner is modeled after Western educational values: independence, assertiveness, self-promotion. In many cultures, learning is relational, deferential, patient. A student may wait to be invited to speak. May prefer group harmony over personal opinion. May avoid direct confrontation with peers or teachers. But the platform might read that as passivity. As a red flag. And that's how we end up punishing cultural difference under the guise of performance metrics. It goes further. Group work tools, discussion forums, breakout rooms—all presume comfort with collaboration. But collaboration looks different across cultures. In some places, hierarchies matter. Age matters. Gender matters. Mixing them without consent can feel disruptive, even unsafe. If platforms don't account for these dynamics, they don't just miss the mark—they replicate exclusion.

Content Curation: Whose Knowledge Gets Center Stage?

Then comes content. The stories we tell. The examples we give. The history we frame. Many platforms are filled with Western narratives. They teach Shakespeare but not Tagore (Mukherjee, 2022). They explain economics through Wall Street but ignore informal economies in Lagos. They showcase scientific innovation through Newton and Darwin but omit Ibn al-Haytham, Hypatia, or Chinese alchemy. Even when localized, the localization is often superficial. A few names changed. A festival mentioned. But the underlying epistemology—the way knowledge is structured—remains the same. Linear. Fact-based. Disconnected from land, story, and ritual. This isn't just exclusion. It's epistemic violence. It tells learners: *Your way of knowing doesn't count.* Real cultural inclusion demands a reimagining of content—not just its packaging. It asks us to center Indigenous knowledge, oral traditions, spiritual philosophies—not as exotic sidebars, but as valid, rigorous, transformative.

Access and Infrastructure: The Hidden Privilege

Let's not forget the basics. Inclusion starts with access. Many EdTech platforms assume stable internet, up-to-date devices, quiet homes, literate caregivers (Burns, 2023). That's a middle-class fantasy. In large parts of the world, students access platforms on shared phones. Or in community centers with irregular electricity. Or while working jobs to support their families. When a platform auto-updates at 300MB, that's not progress—it's exclusion. When an interface requires a mouse, it shuts out mobile users. When learning assumes parents can help with homework, it marginalizes first-generation learners. True cultural inclusion means designing for constraint. Offline options. Audio-first interfaces. Text-light design. Low-bandwidth modes. It means building for the real world, not the imagined one.

Data Ethics and Surveillance: Who's Watching Whom?

Here's a final, often-ignored piece: surveillance. Many platforms track students obsessively—clicks, pauses, time spent, even facial expressions (McHaney, 2023). This is sold as engagement data. But in some cultures, being observed—especially by unknown authorities—feels invasive. Traumatizing, even. A refugee child who's fled war may feel deep anxiety when prompted to turn on a webcam. A girl in a conservative setting may feel exposed. A student from a mistrustful society may assume the platform is spying. And sometimes, they're not wrong. Data privacy is not just a legal issue. It's a cultural one. Trust, transparency, consent—all look different across cultures. Platforms that ignore that don't just break laws. They break trust.

So Why Does All This Keep Happening?

Because inclusion is inconvenient. It slows down production. It complicates funding. It demands uncomfortable questions. It forces teams to admit their worldview isn't universal. But it also unlocks deeper beauty. When we challenge the default, we find richness. When we question the assumptions, we find better questions. When we let the learner—not the engineer—lead, we build platforms that feel less like systems and more like sanctuaries.

What if algorithms were co-trained by culturally diverse educators? What if aesthetics were rooted in local design languages? What if behavioral norms were set by communities, not by software architects? What if inclusion wasn't a feature but the foundation? Barriers aren't always built with malice (Khan, 2025). Sometimes they're built with ignorance, haste, or hubris. But their impact is the same: learners who feel out of place. Who feel like guests. Who learn to translate themselves to fit the system, rather than the other way around. It doesn't have to be this way. Inclusion is possible. But only if we're willing to look closely. At every layer. Every choice. Every assumption. From algorithms to aesthetics. Because somewhere out there, a child logs into a platform and asks a silent question:

Is there room for me here?

And our answer should not be "yes" in theory. It should be felt. Deeply. Viscerally. In every pixel, prompt, and pause.

TOWARD EQUITABLE DIGITAL LEARNING: FRAMEWORKS FOR CULTURALLY RESPONSIVE DESIGN

So here we are. After all the case studies, the stories, the missteps, the missed signals, the glimpses of what *could* be—we arrive at the hard part: building something better. Not hypothetically. Not one day. But now. And with care. Because cultural responsiveness in digital learning isn't a destination. It's a discipline. A framework. A way of thinking that must sit beneath the code, the curriculum, the user interface, the pedagogy (Tham et al, 2022). And it starts—let's be honest—not with technology, but with humility. Before anything is sketched, scripted, or scaled, we have to admit something many designers, developers, and educators don't like to say out loud: *We don't know everything.* Our mental models are shaped by our own upbringings, assumptions, and pedagogical histories. And if we don't pause to interrogate those before we build, we risk designing platforms that are technically brilliant but culturally barren. So, what does a framework for equitable digital learning actually look like? It's not a blueprint. It can't be. Culture doesn't sit still. It flexes, it pulses, it argues with itself.

Table 2. Key Design Elements for Culturally Sensitive Digital Platforms

Design Element	Purpose
Language Options	Provide multilingual support for accessibility.
Visual Representation	Reflect diverse identities and cultural markers.
Cultural Examples	Include region-specific case studies and stories.
Navigation Norms	Respect cultural preferences in interface design.
Content Neutrality	Avoid culturally biased or exclusionary content.

A rigid system pretending to accommodate fluid identities will always fail. Instead, what we need are guiding pillars—principles, if you will—that hold space for complexity. Let's walk through them. Slowly. Honestly.

1. **Begin with Positionality, Not Product:** Before you even think about functionality, think about *who's in the room*—and who isn't. Whose culture is shaping the architecture? Whose definitions of "success," "engagement," or "efficiency" are guiding the metrics? You can't design a platform that honors diverse ways of knowing if your team all comes from the same educational tradition. A culturally responsive framework demands pluralism at its core—at the whiteboard, in the codebase, on the research team. Not as token representation, but as epistemic breadth (Gilbert & Pasque, 2023). If your UX designer sees education as a competitive, time-boxed sprint, and your target users come from communities that value intergenerational dialogue and slow learning, you've already built the wrong house. Ask hard questions: Where were we educated? What learning styles were we taught to value? What does "smart" look like in our culture—and

how might that limit our imagination? This work is unsettling. But it's necessary. Because positionality isn't a confession—it's a compass.

2. **Design *with*, not *for*:** This one's been said so many times, it risks sounding empty. But most EdTech still doesn't do it. Not really. Co-design means handing over some of the brush. It means involving learners and educators from the communities you hope to serve—early, honestly, and with actual power. Not as focus group participants. As architects. Collaborators. If you're designing for rural Indigenous learners, invite elders into the design studio (Gajendran et al, 2022). If you're building for migrant students, make space for their families' voices—not just translated interfaces, but their lived rhythms and fears and hopes. Co-design also means listening without agenda. It means being willing to throw away your favorite feature because it doesn't resonate. It means learning to love friction, not avoid it. Platforms born in collaboration feel different. They breathe differently. Because they're not imposed. They're invited.
3. **Decenter the Western Canon:** Let's say it plainly: the dominance of Western epistemology in EdTech is a form of soft colonization (Koole et al, 2024). When only Western texts, metaphors, pedagogies, and aesthetics are embedded into platforms, we send a message—unspoken but loud: *Other knowledge is secondary. Decorative. Optional.* A responsive framework actively works to disrupt that. This doesn't mean discarding all Western content. It means *making room.* Room for oral traditions. For mythologies. For alternate forms of logic. For cyclical rather than linear structures. For learning that happens through song, ceremony, silence. It means building templates that don't assume a five-paragraph essay is the gold standard. That don't reduce comprehension to multiple-choice quizzes. That allow a student to demonstrate understanding through storytelling, visual design, dialogue, performance. A platform that treats Indigenous astronomy as equally valid as Copernican astronomy is not being generous—it's being just. Equity is not about kindness. It's about undoing erasure.
4. **Flex the Interface:** Design should never be static. Especially not in education. A culturally responsive platform needs multiple faces (Lachney et al, 2021). Not in a performative way—where themes and skins are just aesthetic swaps—but in deep structure. Think of it like a language with dialects. The core message stays, but the way it's spoken shifts. Allow learners to customize tone. Some cultures prefer formality. Others, warmth. Some like humor. Others, restraint. Why assume one-size-fits-all feedback will work? Give options for visual density. Some users want minimalism. Others find whitespace unnerving. Let them choose. Even pacing: allow learners to slow down or loop back without being penalized. Let them pause, linger, reflect. Not every culture views speed as intelligence. Design that flexes affirms difference. It tells the learner: *There's room here for how you move through the world.*

5. **Build for Low Infrastructure by Default:** Equity doesn't mean designing for the best-connected. It means designing for the margins. Too many platforms require high bandwidth, stable electricity, or the latest devices (Schwidtal, 2022). That's not a learning platform. That's a luxury product. Responsive design means offline modes. Lightweight data loads. SMS-based access for mobile-first communities. Audio-first learning for low-literacy users. Downloadable content for asynchronous review. No auto-play. No mandatory video. And please, don't build a brilliant interface that can only function on a tablet that costs half a family's monthly income. Accessibility is not an afterthought. It's a first principle. Because you cannot include someone you've already priced out.
6. **Redefine Engagement:** Ask most EdTech platforms what engagement means, and they'll give you metrics: time-on-task, click rates, forum posts (Caspari-Sadeghi, 2022). But cultural engagement is not just behavioral. It's emotional. It's relational. It's sometimes invisible. A silent learner may be fully immersed. A slow one may be wrestling deeply. A group that doesn't "interact" might be working collaboratively offline. So, stop measuring attention. Start asking better questions: Did the learner feel seen? Did the platform honor their story? Did it meet them where they were, or did it demand translation? Engagement, redefined, is about resonance. Not just reaction.
7. **Practice Consent, Not Surveillance:** Too many platforms surveil. They say it's for improvement. For personalization (Gordon-Tapiero et al, 2022). But for many learners—especially from marginalized or traumatized communities—being watched is not comforting. It's triggering. Culturally responsive design means asking: What does safety look like here? What does consent feel like? Can a learner opt out of camera use without penalty? Can they choose what data is collected—and when? Transparency matters. So does restraint. Just because you *can* track doesn't mean you *should*. Trust isn't built through data. It's built through respect.
8. **Ritualize Reflection:** In many cultures, learning isn't just consumption. It's integration. And integration takes time (Djafarova & Foots, 2022). Build in moments of stillness. Not just end-of-unit tests, but reflective prompts. Journaling space. Opportunities for learners to ask *Why does this matter to me? How does this connect to my world?* Encourage teachers to pause the platform. To contextualize. To slow the tempo. Add a "sacred space" feature—no notifications, no scores—just breath. Learning is not just output. It's becoming. And becoming is not fast.
9. **Audit for Bias—Relentlessly:** Bias hides in defaults. In suggested answers. In the images used. In the names that show up in case studies. In who's quoted and who's invisible (Tartaglione et al, 2021). Build tools to audit your platform.

Not once. Continuously. Hire cultural reviewers. Let learners flag content that doesn't feel right. Update quickly. Own mistakes. Bias isn't just offensive. It's pedagogically damaging. A student who never sees their culture reflected starts to believe their story has no place in knowledge. That is not inclusion. That is intellectual colonization.

10. **Leave Room for the Sacred:** Not everything must be explained. Not everything can be. Some cultures hold mystery as central to learning. Not as ignorance—but as reverence. Let your platform honor that. Leave space for silence. For things not said. Don't require articulation when reflection is more powerful. Don't reduce spirituality to superstition. Recognize that for many, learning is intertwined with the divine. Make room for it. Not because it's trendy. But because it's true.

CONCLUSION

As we reach the end of this inquiry, the question lingers: **What does it truly mean to build culturally sensitive digital learning platforms in a world so vast, so intricate, so layered with difference?** If we have learned anything throughout this chapter, it is that cultural sensitivity is not a technical feature to toggle on or off—it is a mindset, a posture, and a sustained commitment to empathy, inclusion, and humility in the face of complexity.

Digital learning platforms are often praised for their neutrality, their efficiency, their ability to scale. But neutrality is a myth. Every digital space is infused with human choices—choices that are shaped by specific histories, power structures, biases, and cultural frameworks. Pretending otherwise only deepens the distance between those who build platforms and those who use them. The illusion of objectivity masks a very real imbalance: the majority of digital learning environments are designed in places with disproportionate technological privilege, then disseminated to audiences whose voices were never part of the conversation. In the process, global learners are often expected to conform, adapt, and assimilate—to learn not just the curriculum, but the culture embedded within the platform itself.

This dynamic must be disrupted. And not just through tokenistic efforts—like translating the interface into multiple languages or adding a few regionally relevant images. True cultural sensitivity requires deeper structural change. It requires that design teams become more globally representative, that user testing involves communities from varied backgrounds, that pedagogical assumptions are constantly challenged and reexamined. It means asking difficult questions: Is this feedback style appropriate across cultures? Does this visual metaphor hold meaning beyond a Western audience? Are we privileging certain learning styles while marginalizing others?

Moreover, cultural sensitivity cannot stop at representation. It must evolve into **cultural solidarity**—an ethos that recognizes the interdependence of learners worldwide and seeks to co-create educational experiences that are as diverse and dynamic as the people they serve. This shift moves us from merely avoiding offense to actively cultivating connection; from minimizing harm to maximizing belonging.

Some of the most promising examples in this space have emerged not from large-scale commercial platforms, but from community-based projects, grassroots innovation, and hybrid models that blend local wisdom with digital infrastructure. In places where technology is co-developed with educators, elders, students, and designers working side-by-side, the results are often more attuned to real needs—and more powerful in their impact.

Still, the road ahead is not simple. Cultural sensitivity is not a one-time fix or an endpoint to be reached. It is an ongoing, iterative process of listening, learning, and unlearning. It will require institutions to abandon one-size-fits-all thinking and embrace the uncomfortable truth that equity cannot be engineered in a vacuum. It will ask us to slow down, to think relationally rather than transactionally, and to make room for voices that have too long been sidelined.

We must also acknowledge that cultural sensitivity exists within broader questions of justice, identity, and power. As such, the work of inclusive digital education must go hand in hand with efforts to decolonize knowledge systems, confront algorithmic bias, and resist the commodification of education. Only then can we hope to build platforms that don't just deliver content, but also nourish the human spirit and affirm the learner's place in the world.

In closing, the call is clear: Let us reimagine digital education not as a homogenized product for mass consumption, but as a global conversation—messy, multilingual, multicultural, and deeply human. Let us make space for difference not just as a challenge to be managed, but as a gift to be honored. And let us commit, together, to shaping digital spaces where every learner—regardless of culture, language, or location—feels seen, respected, and empowered to grow.

REFERENCES

Allen, K. A., Gray, D. L., Baumeister, R. F., & Leary, M. R. (2022). The need to belong: A deep dive into the origins, implications, and future of a foundational construct. *Educational Psychology Review*, *34*(2), 1133–1156. DOI: 10.1007/s10648-021-09633-6

Amo, R., Matias, S., Yamanaka, A., Tanaka, K. F., Uchida, N., & Watabe-Uchida, M. (2022). A gradual temporal shift of dopamine responses mirrors the progression of temporal difference error in machine learning. *Nature Neuroscience*, *25*(8), 1082–1092. DOI: 10.1038/s41593-022-01109-2

Burns, M. A. R. Y. (2023). Technology in education. Paper commissioned for the.

Caspari-Sadeghi, S. (2022, January). Applying learning analytics in online environments: Measuring learners' engagement unobtrusively. [). Frontiers Media SA.]. *Frontiers in Education*, *7*, 840947. DOI: 10.3389/feduc.2022.840947

Djafarova, E., & Foots, S. (2022). Exploring ethical consumption of generation Z: Theory of planned behaviour. *Young Consumers*, *23*(3), 413–431. DOI: 10.1108/YC-10-2021-1405

Gajendran, T., Tucker, C., Ware, S., & Tose, H. S. (2022). Integrating Indigenous, Western and Inclusive Pedagogies for Work-Integrated Learning Partnerships in Architecture and Design Disciplines. *International Journal of Work-Integrated Learning*, *23*(2), 259–277.

Gilbert, C., & Pasque, P. A. (2023). Defining culturally responsive research: Learnings and tensions in minoritized researcher perspectives. *Journal of Diversity in Higher Education.*

Gordon-Tapiero, A., Wood, A., & Ligett, K. (2022, November). The case for establishing a collective perspective to address the harms of platform personalization. In *Proceedings of the 2022 Symposium on Computer Science and Law* (pp. 119-130). DOI: 10.1145/3511265.3550450

Gove, D., Nielsen, T. R., Smits, C., Plejert, C., Rauf, M. A., Parveen, S., Jaakson, S., Golan-Shemesh, D., Lahav, D., Kaur, R., Herz, M. K., Monsees, J., Thyrian, J. R., & Georges, J. (2021). The challenges of achieving timely diagnosis and culturally appropriate care of people with dementia from minority ethnic groups in Europe. *International Journal of Geriatric Psychiatry*, *36*(12), 1823–1828. DOI: 10.1002/gps.5614

Hattie, K. (2021). Building a language of learning: The harvest home learner. *Connect*, (248), 7–10.

Jafarov, S. (2024). Internationalisation and Cultural Aspects of Online Learning, Training, and Research. *Pakistan Journal of Life and Social Sciences*, *22*(2), 6437–6452. DOI: 10.57239/PJLSS-2024-22.2.00486

Jia, K., Kang, R., Wang, Y., Ma, L., & Liu, X. (2025). Constructing an empathy education system: Values, principles, and approaches. *Journal of Moral Education*, •••, 1–29.

KANİ, Z. G. (2021). How (un) critically oriented is english language teaching?: Perspectives from the turkish efl context1. Research & reviews in educational sciences, 87.

Kayyali, M. (2022). Equity, Equality, Diversity, and Inclusion as Key Performance Indicators in Higher Education. *Online Submission*, *3*(5), 1–3.

Kayyali, M. (2024). Digital literacy in higher education: Preparing students for the workforce of the future. *International Journal of Information Science and Computing*, *11*(1). Advance online publication. DOI: 10.30954/2348-7437.1.2024.6

Kayyali, M. (2025a). E-Learning Platforms and Their Influence on Lifelong Learning. In Impact of Digitalization on Education and Social Sustainability (pp. 155-176). IGI Global.

Kayyali, M. (2025b). Digital Literacy for Sustainability: Preparing Students for the AI-Driven World. In Rethinking the Pedagogy of Sustainable Development in the AI Era (pp. 197-224). IGI Global Scientific Publishing.

Kayyali, M. (2026a). The Role of Digital Platforms in Shaping Competitive Intelligence Strategies. In Competitive Intelligence in the Digital Age: Strategies for Business and Technology Leadership (pp. 241-264). IGI Global Scientific Publishing.

Kayyali, M. (2026b). The Digital Transformation of Education: Opportunities and Challenges for Communication. Effects of Education Communication in Digital Learning Environments, 433-472.

Khan, N. (2025). Deep acting attraction: Predation, masculinity and erotic labour in algorithmic romance. *New Media & Society*, •••, 14614448251336419. DOI: 10.1177/14614448251336419

Kim, D., & Li, M. (2021). Digital storytelling: Facilitating learning and identity development. *Journal of Computers in Education*, *8*(1), 33–61. DOI: 10.1007/s40692-020-00170-9

Koole, M., Smith, M., Traxler, J., Adam, T., & Footring, S. (2024). Decolonising educational technology. *Education Sciences, 14*(10), 1070. DOI: 10.3390/educsci14101070

Korinek, A. (2024). *Generative AI for economic research: LLMs learn to collaborate and reason (No. w33198)*. National Bureau of Economic Research. DOI: 10.3386/w33198

Lachney, M., Bennett, A. G., Eglash, R., Yadav, A., & Moudgalya, S. (2021). Teaching in an open village: A case study on culturally responsive computing in compulsory education. *Computer Science Education, 31*(4), 462–488. DOI: 10.1080/08993408.2021.1874228

McHaney, R. (2023). *The new digital shoreline: How Web 2.0 and millennials are revolutionizing higher education*. Taylor & Francis. DOI: 10.4324/9781003447979

Mukherjee, S. (2022). Teaching Shakespeare in the Indian (Google) Classroom: The Digital Promise and the Digital Divide. In *Digital Shakespeares from the Global South* (pp. 73–92). Springer International Publishing. DOI: 10.1007/978-3-031-04787-9_5

Owens, A., Zeek, H., & Oye, E. (2024). The Role of Cultural Identity in Shaping Educational Experiences.

Paul, P. K., Bommali, T., Kayyali, M., Chakraborty, S., Debnath, D., Gupta, S. K., & Sharma, S. K. (2025). Demystifying Issues and Concerns of AI and Allied Technologies in Digital Education and Learning: A Scientific Study. In AI-Enabled Sustainable Innovations in Education and Business (pp. 1-32). IGI Global Scientific Publishing. DOI: 10.4018/979-8-3373-3952-8.ch001

Potnis, D., Tahamtan, I., & McDonald, L. (2025). Negative consequences of information gatekeeping through algorithmic technologies: An Annual Review of Information Science and Technology (ARIST) paper. *Journal of the Association for Information Science and Technology, 76*(1), 262–288. DOI: 10.1002/asi.24955

Reus-Smit, C. (2021). The end of global pluralism? *European Journal of International Relations, 27*(4), 1249–1273. DOI: 10.1177/13540661211017273

Schwidtal, J. A. N. (2022). Comprehensive Evaluation of Electricity Market Design Elements for the Strategic Integration of Renewable Energies.

Sekhar, A. (2024). How transformation from traditional to participatory learning and teaching pedagogy helps build confidence and communication skills in international students-a reflective analysis. *Journal of Global Business & Technology, 20*(2).

Stein, H. F. (2021). *Listening deeply: An approach to understanding and consulting in organizational culture*. Routledge. DOI: 10.4324/9780429034190

Tartaglione, E., Barbano, C. A., & Grangetto, M. (2021). End: Entangling and disentangling deep representations for bias correction. In Proceedings of the IEEE/CVF conference on computer vision and pattern recognition (pp. 13508-13517).

Tham, J., Howard, T., & Verhulsdonck, G. (2022). Extending design thinking, content strategy, and artificial intelligence into technical communication and user experience design programs: Further pedagogical implications. *Journal of Technical Writing and Communication*, *52*(4), 428–459. DOI: 10.1177/00472816211072533

Walls, J. (2021). Tensions in care and control in the middle school classroom: Lessons for equitable social-emotional learning. *Middle School Journal*, *52*(3), 25–34. DOI: 10.1080/00940771.2021.1893591

Weller, M. (2022). Metaphors of ed tech. Athabasca University Press.

Zindulka, T., Sekowski, J. M., Lehmann, F., & Buschek, D. (2025, April). Exploring Mobile Touch Interaction with Large Language Models. In *Proceedings of the 2025 CHI Conference on Human Factors in Computing Systems* (pp. 1-21). DOI: 10.1145/3706598.3713554

KEY TERMS AND DEFINITIONS

Cultural Sensitivity: The awareness and respectful consideration of different cultural values, beliefs, and practices in educational environments.

Localization: The adaptation of content and interfaces in digital platforms to reflect the cultural and linguistic context of users.

Digital Inclusivity: Ensuring all learners, regardless of background, can access, understand, and benefit from digital learning tools.

Cross-Cultural Communication: The process of understanding and effectively interacting with individuals from diverse cultural backgrounds.

Equity in EdTech: The principle of providing fair digital learning experiences that accommodate cultural, linguistic, and socioeconomic diversity.

Global Learning Design: An instructional approach that intentionally integrates multicultural perspectives into digital content and pedagogy.

Ethical AI in Education: The responsible use of artificial intelligence to support fair, unbiased, and culturally respectful learning experiences.

Chapter 12
Cultural Diversity in Gamified Learning:
Leveraging Multinational Teamwork in Business Simulations

Hélder Fanha Martins
https://orcid.org/0000-0003-3544-0703
Polytechnic University of Lisbon, Portugal

ABSTRACT

This chapter investigates how cultural diversity influences collaboration, decision-making, and learning outcomes in a multinational business simulation at the Lisbon Accounting and Business School. Drawing from reflective journals, surveys, team reports, and debriefing sessions, it explores how cross-cultural factors such as leadership expectations, communication norms, and risk tolerance shape teamwork dynamics. Findings reveal that teams initially experience tension due to divergent cultural values but gradually develop adaptive strategies, like rotating leadership and explicit conflict protocols, that leverage diversity as a source of creativity and resilience. Although cultural variety can prolong decision cycles, it also enriches problem-solving perspectives and fosters heightened intercultural competence. The chapter concludes by offering pedagogical implications and practical recommendations on facilitating culturally inclusive simulations, underscoring how purposefully designed gamified experiences can transform cultural differences into powerful drivers of global readiness.

DOI: 10.4018/979-8-3373-3673-2.ch012

1. INTRODUCTION

Higher education institutions across the globe have been challenged like never before to reimagine their conventional teaching and learning approaches in ways that would enable graduates to more effectively address mounting global, technology-rich, and rapidly changing workplace demands. Digital transformation in higher education has spearheaded institutional initiatives intended to advance engagement, relevance, and skills-in-use among learners. At the center of this shift is a heightened emphasis on using digital tools and approaches that not only facilitate knowledge learning but also the application of such knowledge in practical, collaborative, and dynamic contexts.

Over the past decade, digital transformation has accelerated the adoption of technology-mediated pedagogies that promise higher engagement and authentic skill development in business education. Within this movement, gamified learning and high-fidelity business simulations have emerged as signature practices, allowing students to experiment with strategic choices, receive instant feedback, and cycle through decision rounds that mirror real-world volatility (Ahuja 2024; Polydorou, 2025). Meta-analytic evidence confirms their positive effects on motivation and learning outcomes, particularly when game mechanics align with self-determination principles of autonomy, competence, and relatedness (Sailer & Homner 2019).

Concurrently, internationalization policies have turned many classrooms into culturally heterogeneous spaces, where learners bring diverse communication norms, leadership preferences, and attitudes toward risk. Although this diversity can spark creativity, it also introduces coordination costs, stereotype threat, and unequal participation when not deliberately managed (Taras et al 2016; Wang et al 2019). Educators therefore face a dual imperative: harness the motivational power of gamification and design for intercultural inclusivity.

A review of 2014-2024 research studies reveals a striking gap: while more than 200 studies analyze game elements or learning analytics ((Tegon, 2024; Ramírez Ruiz et al., 2024), fewer than a dozen examine how cultural diversity shapes team processes inside simulations, and most of those focus on surface-level outcomes such as grades or satisfaction rather than the mechanisms of cross-cultural collaboration (Foronda et al., 2018; Pimentel et al., 2020). As a result, instructors lack evidence-based guidance on questions like: Which cultural factors most influence decision speed? How do power-distance norms affect leadership emergence? and What facilitation moves help teams convert friction into learning?

Also, existing gamified-learning research does not yet explain how cultural diversity influences – and is influenced by – team dynamics within business simulations, leaving educators without a validated framework for designing inclusive, high-impact experiences.

Although gamified business simulations are now widespread in international business curricula, empirical research has not yet explained how cultural diversity within student teams shapes, and is shaped by, communication patterns, leadership emergence, conflict management, and ultimately performance outcomes. This knowledge gap leaves instructors without evidence-based design principles for turning cultural heterogeneity from a potential friction point into a strategic learning resource.

Responding to this gap, the present chapter investigates multinational student teams participating in the Marketplace Live: International Corporate Management simulation, asking how cultural values intersect with communication, leadership, and conflict-management patterns over a semester-long competitive exercise. By foregrounding these dynamics, the chapter advances both theoretical understanding of intercultural teamwork in digital environments and practical guidelines for instructors seeking to transform cultural diversity from a potential stressor into a strategic learning resource.

Among the most prominent trends within the overall digital transformation project has been the increased application of gamification and business simulations in university and college settings. These methods, which blend aspects of fun and competition with more structured pedagogies, have been taken up quickly as mechanisms for facilitating richer and more profound learning experiences. By creating immersive and interactive environments that require active participation in both the content and the students themselves, gamified learning contexts mimic real professional settings, thus making students better prepared for actual employment prospects. Business simulations, specifically, have been shown to be very successful in management, economics, and finance disciplines, as they provide students with an opportunity to test decision-making approaches, observe the immediate consequences of their actions, and reflectively ponder the complexity and interdependence of modern organizational issues.

The effectiveness of gamified and simulation-based pedagogies is not only a function of their structural or technological sophistication. Equally important is whether they can be responsive and sensitive to the growing cultural diversity of the cohorts of students. In modern higher education settings, the composition of student bodies tends to be a vibrant tapestry of various nationalities, cultures, and socio-cultural backgrounds. Cultural diversity plays a crucial role in influencing students' attitude towards teamwork activities, leadership assignments, communication patterns, and conflict resolution strategies. Therefore, the effectiveness and inclusiveness of learning interventions, such as simulations and gamification, heavily rely on the deliberate integration and inclusion of cultural awareness and intercultural competences in their planning and execution. Although the value of culture as a determinant of learning processes and collaborative interactions has been acknowledged, there is limited scholarly research that explicitly examines the impact of cultural diversity on engagement, collaboration, and learning outcomes in gamified contexts like business simulations. The purpose of this chapter is to explicitly fill this research gap.

The specific focus of this chapter is on analyzing cultural diversity within multinational student teams taking part in a virtual business simulation. Drawing insights from a semester-long experience of students from ten European countries participating in Marketplace Live: International Corporate Management at the Lisbon Accounting and Business School, Polytechnic University of Lisbon, this chapter investigates how cultural differences among team members influence their collaborative behaviors, communication practices, decision-making processes, and overall performance within this competitive yet collaborative game-based setting. The business simulation employed provides a dynamic, rich, and highly interactive digital context wherein students assume executive roles, make complex strategic decisions, and actively collaborate and compete, mirroring real-world corporate settings.

By examining the interaction of cultural background and teamwork processes in such gamified settings, this chapter seeks to accomplish a few different goals. First and foremost, it tries to illustrate the practical expressions of cultural diversity within team interaction, influencing roles, leadership emergence, and teamwork processes in the context of business simulations. Second, the objective is to identify and express key opportunities and shared challenges related to cultural diversity in gamified settings, offering a differentiated understanding of how culturally diverse groups engage with tasks and manage interpersonal relations. Third, the study aims to offer actionable knowledge and concrete strategies for educators, trainers, and instructional designers who seek to use cultural diversity as a resource in learning settings that are defined by digitalization and gamification.

The guiding questions explored throughout this chapter are as follows:

1. How does cultural diversity among multinational student teams impact collaboration and communication processes within virtual business simulations?
2. In what ways does cultural diversity affect leadership dynamics, decision-making processes, and conflict resolution strategies in these gamified educational settings?
3. What are the key challenges faced by culturally diverse teams participating in a competitive business simulation, and how are these challenges overcome or managed?
4. What opportunities for enhancing intercultural competence and global readiness can be derived from purposeful integration of cultural considerations into gamified learning experiences?

Ultimately, this chapter contributes to both theoretical understandings and practical applications within the fields of educational innovation, intercultural education, and digital transformation in higher education. By identifying the pedagogical implications associated with the integration of cultural diversity in gamified learning contexts, the insights and recommendations presented offer guidance to educational institutions seeking to maximize the benefits of digital transformation initiatives while responding effectively to the global and multicultural composition of contemporary student populations.

Following this introduction, the chapter will provide a review of existing literature on gamification and cultural diversity in educational contexts, illustrating how the interplay between culture and game mechanics offers a window into student behavior and outcomes. Subsequently, a detailed methodological explanation will present how data was collected, analyzed, and interpreted to better understand the interplay of cultural differences and game-based learning dynamics.

The results and discussion section, which analyzes how cultural diversity affected collaboration, decision-making, and conflict resolution among multinational teams in a high-stakes simulation, forms the core of the chapter. Concrete examples and participant reflections will help translate theoretical notions of cultural dimensions into tangible, practice-based insights. The chapter will then consider pedagogical and institutional implications: how educators and administrators can deliberately design and facilitate such gamified experiences to harness the full value of cultural diversity. The conclusion will synthesize key findings, acknowledge methodological constraints, and propose future directions for research, especially important as technology continues to evolve rapidly in higher education. In this way, the chapter offers a comprehensive roadmap, touching on literature, research design, empirical examples, and recommendations, for capitalizing on the transformative potential of cultural diversity in gamified learning environments.

2. LITERATURE REVIEW

2.1. Gamification and Learning Theories

A foundational premise behind gamified learning is rooted in constructivist theory, which posits that learners construct knowledge through active engagement and interpretation of experiences rather than mere passive reception (Piaget, 1970; Machmud et al, 2023). Building upon the constructivist perspective, Kolb's experiential learning model emphasizes the cyclical process of concrete experience, reflective observation, abstract conceptualization, and active experimentation (Kolb, 2015). In digital education, these theoretical underpinnings suggest that immersive, interactive experiences, such as those found in games and simulations, lead to deeper learning outcomes because learners are required to make decisions, reflect on results, and adapt strategies.

Game-based learning frameworks similarly highlight the importance of engagement and interactivity, arguing that learners benefit most when the tasks are meaningful, scaffolded, and enjoyable (Nadeem et al., 2023; Martins, 2023; Shu & Liu, 2019). These approaches also promote social constructivist principles when games facilitate collaborative interaction, peer learning, and active knowledge co-construction. Within higher education, gamified learning experiences often adopt a problem-based structure, where learners navigate authentic tasks that mirror real-life professional challenges. By doing so, students develop not just disciplinary knowledge but also transferable skills in critical thinking, communication, and problem-solving.

While "gamification," "serious games," and "simulations" are interrelated concepts, they differ slightly in their design and implementation. Gamification typically involves adding game elements, such as points, badges, levels, or leaderboards, to non-game settings (Sailer & Homner, 2019). A classic example is awarding badges for completing specific learning modules. Serious games, conversely, are digital games intentionally designed with educational outcomes in mind and typically feature storyline, characters, and explicit learning objectives integrated into the gameplay itself (Lameras et al., 2017). An example might be a role-playing game in which learners must navigate historical events to understand complex social, economic, or political dynamics.

Simulations, although often labeled under the umbrella of serious games, tend to be more focused on realism, modeling real-world systems or processes in order to let learners experiment with variables and see how outcomes change (Martins, 2023). Within management and business education, simulations such as Marketplace Live or other corporate strategy platforms mimic actual market forces, competition, financial constraints, and consumer behaviors (Aila, 2024; Martins, 2012). In these environments, students can apply theoretical concepts to practice, while receiving immediate or near-immediate feedback on their decisions. Although gamified features, like points or dashboards, may be included, the primary design aim of simulations is to authentically replicate business scenarios.

Together, these three constructs, gamification, serious games, and simulations, can serve distinct but overlapping pedagogical functions. Gamification might be used to motivate completion of tasks, serious games can be used to explore rich narratives or ethical dilemmas, and simulations provide a sandbox-like arena where learners can engage in trial-and-error within a faithful representation of a system. In the field of cross-cultural education, business simulations are particularly valuable because they allow diverse student teams to work on realistic tasks that test not just knowledge or skills, but also communication styles, leadership tendencies, and conflict resolution approaches.

A prominent argument for introducing gamified or simulation-based approaches is their promise to enhance student motivation and engagement. According to self-determination theory, learning environments that satisfy students' needs for autonomy, competence, and relatedness facilitate intrinsic motivation (Ameloot et al., 2024; Deci & Ryan, 2000). In a gamified setting, the idea of autonomy can be developed by giving students choices about how they tackle difficulty; the feeling of competence is developed through progressively harder levels; and the quality of relatedness is maintained through collaborative or competitive dynamics that bring students together.

The concept of flow, an optimal state of immersion and focus, further reinforces the idea that a well-designed game or simulation can significantly boost engagement (Heutte et al., 2021). When challenges are matched to skill levels, learners can experience flow states, during which they are highly motivated to persist despite difficulty or setbacks. This heightened motivation is particularly relevant to business simulations, as they often escalate in complexity over time, requiring learners to apply not just theoretical knowledge but also creativity, collaboration, and tenacity.

Overall, the literature underscores that gamified designs can revitalize learning experiences across a range of disciplines. For educators working with culturally diverse cohorts, these mechanisms of engagement can help equalize participation and encourage peer-to-peer collaboration, even though cultural variations in communication and leadership preferences may add layers of complexity to the learning environment.

2.2. Business Simulations in Management Education

Simulation games have consequently gained recognition as an effective pedagogical strategy in business education, offering students an immersive, "hands-on" environment that connects academic concepts to real-world problem-solving (Polydorou, 2025). Such gamified learning tools not only increase student motivation and engagement but also allow business students to practice decision-making in a risk-free setting, closely simulating the complexities of modern marketplaces.

Business simulations represent a synthesis of experiential, problem-based, and team-based learning (Polydorou, 2025; Martins, 2023). Designed to replicate market dynamics and internal corporate structures, they provide a safe yet realistic environment for students to exercise managerial decision-making. For example, in marketing-focused simulations, participants might select product prices, allocate advertising budgets, and negotiate channel strategies, while finance-oriented simulations task students with raising capital, managing cash flow, and analyzing risk.

A major pedagogical advantage is the immediacy and authenticity of feedback. Instead of waiting until the end of a course to see the impact of strategic choices, learners see how decisions reverberate in subsequent "quarters" or "rounds" of the simulation (Ahuja, 2024). This cyclical process of decision-action-feedback-reflection is integral to Kolb's experiential learning model, reinforcing theoretical principles with practical application. Instructors can facilitate debriefing sessions where students discuss what happened and why, linking simulation outcomes back to business concepts such as market segmentation, product life cycles, supply chain constraints, or leadership theories. The result is an integrative, situated learning experience far removed from traditional textbook-based exercises (Martins, 2023).

The learning outcomes frequently attributed to the use of business simulations are broad. Foremost, simulations deepen decision-making skills. Because learners must make and justify strategic choices under uncertainty, often lacking complete information, they cultivate analytical thinking, risk assessment, and scenario planning capabilities (Ahuja, 2024). Students also encounter the necessity of agility in responding to market changes or competitive moves, which mirrors real business volatility.

Second, simulations can serve as a crucible for leadership development. In collaborative settings, natural leaders often emerge to coordinate tasks, frame the vision, or navigate team tensions. Students who might be less vocal in standard classroom settings can assume leadership responsibilities in simulation teams, offering them a supportive environment to experiment with different leadership and communication styles. This leadership dimension has an added significance in multicultural teams, where students learn how to adapt leadership approaches to accommodate diverse cultural expectations about power distance or communication norms.

By design, business simulations foster team collaboration. Cross-functional roles, finance, marketing, operations, must align their decisions and priorities to optimize overall performance. Such collaborative interdependence not only mirrors corporate teamwork but also reveals interpersonal differences in conflict management, motivation, and communication style. For culturally diverse teams, these differences may be magnified yet can also lead to richer, more creative decision-making if managed effectively (Kourgiantakis et al., 2019).

Finally, simulations promote systems thinking, as students must understand how various parts of a simulated organization, production, finance, marketing, human resources, fit together (Ahuja, 2024; Sitzmann, 2011). They learn to see the enterprise as an interconnected whole, where one decision can have cascading effects throughout the system. This holistic perspective on cause-and-effect relationships parallels the complexity of global enterprises and underscores the integral role each functional area plays in organizational success.

2.3. Cultural Dimensions in Education

Effective teamwork in any learning context often depends on how well students navigate and respect culturally derived expectations, communication styles, and social norms. Pioneering frameworks such as Hofstede's Cultural Dimensions (Hofstede, Hofstede, & Minkov, 2010) and Hall's High vs. Low Context Communication (Hall, 1976) offer insights into how cultural orientations differ across national or regional groups. Hofstede's model, for instance, includes dimensions like Power Distance, Individualism vs. Collectivism, Masculinity vs. Femininity, Uncertainty Avoidance, Long-term Orientation, and Indulgence vs. Restraint. In a classroom or simulated business setting, these dimensions can help understand why some students might prefer hierarchical structures, why others respond better to collaborative or egalitarian team models, or how certain cultures handle uncertainty or risk.

Hall's (1976) distinction between high-context and low-context cultures has also been instrumental in explaining communication differences. Students from high-context cultures often rely on implicit cues, nonverbal communication, and context to interpret messages, whereas low-context cultures tend to value direct, explicit communication. When student teams gather in virtual or face-to-face simulations, awareness of these differences can be critical for resolving misunderstandings or preventing conflict. Research shows that unrecognized cultural assumptions can result in perceived disrespect or lack of cooperation (Karlsen & Nazar, 2024; Iskhakova & Ott, 2020).

Beyond Hofstede and Hall, other cross-cultural models and typologies examine how societal norms influence behavior. The GLOBE study expands on Hofstede's dimensions by adding more granular cultural attributes related to leadership (House et al., 2004). Trompenaars and Hampden-Turner (2012) emphasize universalism vs. particularism, specific vs. diffuse relationships, and time orientation, among others. Although each theory or framework offers distinct lenses, they converge on the understanding that cultural values underlie people's communication styles, attitudes, and problem-solving approaches.

Student teams frequently reflect the complexity of these cultural values, especially when composed of diverse nationalities. For instance, a student from a high power-distance culture may be more comfortable with a single, clearly designated leader, while a teammate from a low power-distance culture could expect egalitarian, consensus-based decision-making (Paulus et al., 2005). Such divergences in leadership expectation can give rise to tension if left unspoken, yet can also facilitate creativity and mutual learning when addressed positively.

Communication processes are similarly influenced. High-context communicators might emphasize harmony and implicit signals, whereas low-context communicators favor open critique and explicit statements (Liu, 2025). These distinctions can affect how swiftly teams reach decisions, how directly they confront disagreements, and how they perceive "respectful" behavior. Further complexity arises in written communication, a common medium in blended or remote courses, where nuance, tone, and real-time feedback are reduced compared to face-to-face meetings.

Decision-making itself is also rooted in cultural traits. Teams that exhibit more individualistic norms may celebrate strong personal initiative and open debate, whereas collectivist-oriented teams may focus on achieving group consensus and maintaining relational harmony (Taras et al., 2016). In fast-paced simulated competitions, these differences in approach can translate to significant variances in outcomes. Certain cultures might emphasize strategic risk-taking and experimentation, while others prioritize thorough planning and careful consensus-building. It becomes apparent that recognizing, reconciling, and leveraging cultural diversity can be a formidable asset for teams seeking innovative solutions, providing a wider range of perspectives and avoiding homogeneous thinking.

Many international institutions adopt frameworks for integrating intercultural competence into their curricula, viewing cultural literacy as a critical 21st-century skill (Deardorff, 2009). Intercultural competence involves not only knowledge of cultural norms but also the attitudes, skills, and self-awareness to engage effectively and ethically with individuals from various cultural backgrounds. In management simulations, students can practice these competencies in real time, negotiating meaning, communicating respectfully, and adapting their behavior to the culturally diverse team context.

Global education initiatives, sometimes referred to as "internationalization at home," similarly push for incorporating cultural and global perspectives in curricula (Yang & Zhong, 2024; Leask, 2015). Business simulations that assemble virtual multinational teams are a promising expression of this trend, reflecting both the realities of globalized workplaces and the desire to foster intercultural communication skills. When facilitated carefully, these initiatives can simultaneously build subject-area expertise and intercultural competence, contributing to greater employability and social cohesion in modern workplaces.

2.4. Multinational Teamwork and Virtual Collaboration

Higher education now prioritizes multinational and multicultural teamwork because these practices mirror current labor market demands and the capabilities of technological learning platforms. Remote collaboration technologies have become crucial tools for connecting students worldwide who work together on common projects despite geographic and time differences (Weissker et al., 2020). Since digital adoption became dominant in global education virtual teamwork has transitioned from experimental practice to fundamental academic standard.

Culturally diverse teams, whether physically co-located or meeting entirely online, face unique dynamics. On the one hand, diversity can enrich the team with broader perspectives, encourage greater creativity, and foster inclusive problem-solving strategies (Lauring & Selmer, 2018). On the other hand, misunderstandings stemming from language barriers or differences in communication etiquette can hamper trust-building. Students might struggle to calibrate tone and directness in emails or chat messages, raising the potential for conflict escalation. The intangible cues of team morale and group cohesion can be more challenging to sense in a virtual space, especially for team members accustomed to more "collectivist" or face-to-face learning norms.

Research on global teams confirms that certain dynamics strongly influence effectiveness in culturally diverse groups. In particular, high cultural intelligence and a transformational leadership style can enhance decision-making in multicultural teams, even turning task disagreements into productive discussion. By contrast, unaddressed interpersonal frictions, or "relationship conflicts", have been shown to undermine communication and, ultimately, team performance in virtual cross-cultural settings (Davidavičienė & Al-Majzoub, 2022), underscoring the need for leaders to foster an open, respectful team climate.

Miscommunication remains a primary challenge, particularly when multiple languages converge. This can manifest in everything from unintentional interruptions on video calls to ambiguous instructions in a project brief. Cultural assumptions regarding punctuality, attitudes toward hierarchy, and negotiation styles further complicate interactions (Harzing & Pudelko, 2016). Culturally influenced leadership conflicts might arise if two or more team members have competing notions of what constitutes an effective leader, or if certain cultures place higher value on relational harmony versus direct confrontation of issues.

Despite these potential pitfalls, multinational teams also yield distinct benefits. Exposure to new approaches can spur higher-level creativity (Wang et al., 2019). Differences in problem-solving can help teams avoid groupthink, pushing members to question each other's assumptions. Also, the very act of navigating cultural contrasts can build empathy, adaptability, and intercultural competence. Students experience, in real time, how to negotiate meaning and reach shared understandings, gaining skills transferrable to globally distributed workplaces. Research also suggests that with proper facilitation, culturally diverse teams often outperform more homogeneous groups in tasks requiring innovation and lateral thinking (Choi, 2024; Howard et al., 2023).

As digital transformation accelerates, reliance on tools such as videoconferencing, project management software, instant messaging and artificial intelligence has become commonplace in business simulations. The ability to leverage these platforms effectively is integral to team success in virtual collaboration (Martins, 2024; Aparicio et al., 2016). Digital competence, the savvy use of online environments, information retrieval, data handling, and e-collaboration, thus emerges as another skill dimension enhanced by the simulation experience.

Selecting appropriate platforms helps to alleviate intercultural tensions through clear task visibility and timeline management. Through the use of collaborative documentation tools members can edit documents at the same time while tracking versions to understand individual contributions. Simulations which integrate uninterrupted communication cycles or mandatory reflection moments help prevent misunderstandings while allowing all participants to express themselves despite cultural norms that typically prevent open discussion. Although technology cannot fully align varied communication styles, supportive digital infrastructures help achieve equitable participation and organized decision-making in diverse team settings.

Recent advances in artificial intelligence have introduced real-time translation engines (e.g., Zoom AI Companion, Microsoft Translate) and data-rich collaboration dashboards (e.g., Miro, Trello, Notion AI) that promise to reduce language friction and surface implicit assumptions in multicultural teams. Grounded in sociomaterial theory, these tools act not merely as neutral conduits but as active mediators that shape discourse, power, and inclusion (Martins, 2024).

Early evidence is mixed. In a quasi-experiment with 142 globally distributed students, Aparicio et al. (2016) found that groups equipped with a bilingual chat interface plus shared annotation board reported 31% fewer culture-based misunderstandings and completed tasks 18% faster than control groups using e-mail alone. However, the same study warned that low digital-literacy participants defaulted to monolingual "safe zones," limiting the tool's integrative potential. Extending this line of inquiry, Jony and Hamim (2024) show how real-time performance dashboards that blend predictive analytics with sentiment analysis help multicultural virtual teams reframe emerging conflicts as task-focused rather than personal, thereby preserving psychological safety.

Taken together, these studies suggest that AI affordances can convert latent relationship conflict into constructive task conflict, but only when users possess sufficient digital literacy and when facilitators set explicit norms for inclusive use. The present chapter's focus on face-to-face simulation teams complements this stream by identifying which moments in a competitive game cycle are most prone to culture-triggered tensions, thereby pinpointing where technology could be strategically inserted to sustain inclusive collaboration.

The foregoing review revealed two consistent gaps: (1) scant empirical evidence on the mechanisms linking cultural values to simulation-team performance, and (2) a lack of practical guidance for instructors seeking to leverage diversity as a resource. To address these gaps, we designed a mixed-methods study centered on multinational student teams competing in the Marketplace Live 'International Corporate Management' simulation. The methodological framework below explains the research setting, data-collection procedures, and analytic strategies adopted

3. METHODOLOGICAL FRAMEWORK

This chapter adopts a qualitative methodology designed to investigate how cultural diversity influences learning dynamics and collaboration within a multinational business simulation. The following sections elaborate on the context of the study, the research design, and the analytical approach, including ethical considerations and validation strategies. By explaining these methodological foundations, the chapter aims to ensure rigor, transparency, and credibility in the examination of intercultural processes observed within the simulation environment.

3.1. Context of the Study

Overview of the International Corporate Management (ICM) Simulation

The International Corporate Management (ICM) simulation is a semester-long, computer-mediated exercise in which participants form virtual companies and compete in a global marketplace. This simulation challenges students to make decisions in areas such as product development, pricing, marketing, finance, and strategic planning. Each decision represents a "quarter" in the simulated corporate calendar, with immediate or near-immediate feedback provided through game dashboards and performance metrics (Martins, 2012).

The immersive, context-rich environment of the ICM simulation serves as a microcosm of real-world corporate conditions. Students navigate market competition, scarcity of resources, and internal team negotiations that require compromise and mutual understanding. This environment also accentuates how cultural assumptions and communication preferences influence strategy development and execution.

Key features of the ICM simulation include:

1. Multinational Virtual Teams: Students from varied cultural backgrounds collaboratively manage their simulated company.
2. Sequential Rounds (Quarters): Decisions are processed, results are published, and teams then adapt their strategies for subsequent quarters.

3. Complex Performance Metrics: Revenue, market share, brand loyalty, stock price, and other key indicators provide tangible outcomes that participants analyze and discuss.

In line with course learning objectives, the ICM simulation encourages iterative learning, reflection, and knowledge construction through experiential tasks. Its high fidelity to real-world business processes has made it an ideal context for investigating how culture shapes group dynamics and decision-making under competitive conditions.

Participant Demographics

The participants in this study were 32 business major students enrolled in an international management program at the Lisbon Accounting and Business School, Polytechnic University of Lisbon. They represented ten different European countries, such as Portugal, Spain, Germany, France, Italy, Poland, Norway, Finland, Romania, and the Czech Republic. Some students also brought additional diversity through bicultural or multilingual backgrounds.

Most participants were in their early to mid-twenties, though there were a few mature students with prior work experience. Fields of specialization included marketing, finance, accounting, operations, and international management. The cohort's multifaceted demographic composition yielded a complex mix of cultural values, communication styles, and expectations, which were accentuated in the intense environment of the simulation. On average, each team comprised four to six students from at least three different countries, making intercultural interaction an inherent part of their day-to-day collaboration.

Institutional Context and Teaching Goals

The Lisbon Accounting and Business School has been actively promoting internationalization in its curriculum, recognizing the importance of preparing graduates for a globalized workforce. Within this institutional climate, the ICM course was developed as a capstone experience that integrates theoretical knowledge from earlier coursework, strategic management, finance, marketing, and organizational behavior, with practical decision-making in a controlled yet evolving simulation environment.

Faculty members who facilitate the ICM simulation underscore several pedagogical goals:

1. Integration of Functional Knowledge: Students are expected to connect concepts from different business disciplines to formulate coherent strategies.

2. Development of Soft Skills: The simulation emphasizes leadership, team building, conflict resolution, and cross-cultural communication.
3. Experiential Learning: By replicating authentic market forces and organizational structures, the simulation allows students to "learn by doing" and to reflect on outcomes for continual improvement.
4. Cultivation of Intercultural Competence: The instructors explicitly encourage students to explore how cultural backgrounds inform their assumptions and behaviors within a competitive yet collaborative setting.

The institutional mandate for global readiness and intercultural collaboration informed both the design of the course and the decision to undertake a research study analyzing cultural diversity in this simulated context.

3.2. Research Design

Qualitative Case Study Approach

A qualitative case study approach was selected to capture the depth and richness of students' experiences and perceptions as they navigated the ICM simulation (Yin, 2018). Given the complexity of cultural interactions, a case study methodology is well suited for investigating context-dependent processes and uncovering underlying meanings behind participants' decisions and behaviors. While a mixed-method design might have yielded additional quantitative insights, this study prioritized the subjective, interpretive dimensions of intercultural dynamics, focusing on how students themselves articulated, interpreted, and addressed cultural influences in team-based work.

The study can be characterized as a single-case design with embedded sub-cases (i.e., each team is considered a sub-unit of analysis within the overarching context of the ICM course). This multi-layered design highlights both individual perspectives (e.g., how a specific student perceives cultural conflict) and group-level phenomena (e.g., how a team negotiates differences in communication style).

Data Collection Methods

Reflective Journals: Each student was asked to maintain a reflective journal, updated after each simulation round. Journal prompts included open-ended questions on challenges faced, team communication strategies, leadership dynamics, and personal reflections on cultural impact. Reflective journals provided candid, real-time insights into the evolving group processes and participants' self-assessment of learning.

Team Reports: Throughout the simulation, teams submitted collective strategy reports and interim evaluations to their instructor, describing decision rationales, role assignments, and perceived successes or failures. While these documents primarily focused on business outcomes, they often contained narrative sections on teamwork processes, conflicts, and synergy, highlighting how cultural diversity shaped strategic choices.

Surveys: Midway through the semester and again at its conclusion, short anonymous surveys were administered to gauge participants' perceptions of intercultural collaboration. Items probed the frequency of misunderstandings, conflict resolution strategies, satisfaction levels with team functioning, and perceived gains in intercultural competence. Closed-ended Likert-scale items were balanced with open-ended prompts.

Debriefings: At the end of each simulation round, the instructor conducted debriefing sessions during which teams and individuals articulated their experiences and posed questions. These sessions revealed dynamic group processes and occasionally touched on cultural values. With participant consent, the sessions were recorded and later transcribed for analysis.

Collectively, these qualitative data sources delivered a multifaceted view of how cultural factors, such as communication norms, leadership styles, risk appetite, and time orientation, shaped the interactions and decisions within the ICM simulation environment. Triangulating data across journals, reports, surveys, and debriefings mitigated the risk of relying solely on one data type and increased the robustness of the study's findings.

Ethical Considerations

All data collection procedures complied with institutional ethics guidelines for educational research involving human subjects. Prior to the start of the simulation, participants received an information sheet detailing the study's purpose, the voluntary nature of their involvement, and their right to withdraw at any time without academic penalty. Informed consent was obtained verbally from all students.

To protect participant privacy, each student was assigned a pseudonym in all study documents and publications. Team names were similarly anonymized, and any quotes from journals or debriefings were carefully reviewed to remove identifying details. In addition, while many students were comfortable writing in English, some texts contained minor spelling or grammar issues. To ensure clarity, brief quotations cited in the manuscript have been lightly edited for English usage. These edits did not alter the content or meaning of participants' statements, respecting the integrity of their reflections. Survey data was aggregated; any references to individual or team performance were reported in ways that preserved confidentiality. These steps helped maintain trust, encouraging frank and honest reflection from participants.

3.3. Analytical Approach

Thematic Analysis

To interpret the interplay between cultural diversity and learning dynamics in the International Corporate Management (ICM) simulation, this study employed thematic analysis. Defined as a method for identifying, analyzing, and reporting patterns (themes) within data (Braun & Clarke, 2006), thematic analysis offers a flexible yet systematic approach to handle complex, qualitative datasets. While other qualitative methods (e.g., grounded theory, discourse analysis) could be used, thematic analysis was chosen for its adaptability to multiple data sources, reflective journals, team reports, surveys, and debriefings, while allowing the researcher to focus specifically on issues of culture, collaboration, and learning.

A six-phase process guided the thematic analysis (Alhojailan, 2012; Braun & Clarke, 2006). First, the researcher familiarized himself with the data by reading the journals, reports, and debriefing transcripts repeatedly and taking initial notes. Second, preliminary codes were generated to represent interesting elements relevant to cultural interplay, such as "conflict resolution," "leadership emergence," or "language barriers." Third, these initial codes were grouped into overarching themes (e.g., "communication styles," "decision-making tensions," "team cohesion," "cultural adaptation strategies"). Fourth, the themes were reviewed and refined, ensuring coherence within each theme and clear distinctions among them. Fifth, the themes were labeled and defined in relation to relevant theoretical constructs on intercultural collaboration and learning. Finally, the results were translated into a narrative account, providing illustrative quotes and situating each finding in the context of existing literature.

Coding Framework for Intercultural Collaboration and Learning Dynamics

Building on the thematic analysis structure, a more specific coding framework was developed to systematically capture how intercultural interactions shaped participants' experiences. This framework comprised three principal categories: (1) Cultural Dynamics, (2) Team Dynamics and Interaction, and (3) Learning Outcomes and Reflections. Each category contained sub-codes reflecting the patterns that emerged across participant data. For instance, under Cultural Dynamics, sub-codes such as "Cultural Values," "Cultural Awareness," and "Cultural Conflicts" were used to label segments of text where students directly mentioned how their national or personal cultural backgrounds influenced team behavior.

A portion of the coding framework was informed by existing cross-cultural theories (Hofstede et al., 2010) and prior research on global virtual teams (Cramton & Webber, 2005). However, in vivo codes, terms participants themselves used, were also incorporated to maintain fidelity to the students' lived experiences. For example, some participants described "hesitancy to disagree in a group" or "needing an explicit process for feedback" in ways that did not perfectly align with standard theoretical labels. These in vivo codes were integrated into the coding structure to preserve contextual nuances.

During coding, each reflective journal entry or team report was read carefully, with relevant text passages (e.g., quotes, descriptions of events) highlighted and assigned to one or more codes. The same process was applied to transcripts from debriefing sessions. This systematic coding ensured that even minor references to cultural influences were captured. After individual coding, the researcher compared notes to confirm consistency. Any discrepancies were resolved through discussion, refining definitions of codes or adjusting code boundaries. This iterative refinement resulted in a framework that captured critical episodes of cultural negotiation, moments of learning, and evidence of intercultural competence development.

Validation Strategies

Ensuring trustworthiness and credibility in qualitative research requires multiple validation measures (Creswell & Poth, 2018; Nowell et al., 2017). In this study, several strategies were employed:

1. Triangulation of Data Sources

By drawing on reflective journals, team reports, surveys, and debriefing transcripts, the study triangulated evidence regarding cultural influences on teamwork. If a certain challenge, say, disagreements arising from varying power-distance expectations, appeared both in journals and in team debriefings, it was considered a stronger indication of genuine intercultural tension rather than a singular or isolated perception.

2. Peer Debriefing

Draft analyses were regularly shared with fellow faculty and advanced doctoral researchers experienced in management education and qualitative methods. Through these debriefing sessions, the study's interpretations were challenged, prompting clarifications and ensuring that emerging themes remained grounded in the data.

3. Member Checking

Near the end of the semester, a summary of preliminary findings was presented to participating students in a dedicated session. They were invited to respond and clarify whether the themes and interpretations resonated with their personal experiences. Member checking was voluntary and anonymous, ensuring students felt free to verify or contest the interpretations without repercussions. This feedback not only strengthened the credibility of the findings but also highlighted nuances that researchers might have overlooked.

4. Reflexivity

Given that cultural studies are particularly prone to researcher bias, the researcher engaged in reflexive practices by keeping memos on their backgrounds, assumptions, and evolving interpretations throughout the analysis (Lincoln & Guba, 1985). This self-awareness helped mitigate the risk of imposing unwarranted cultural stereotypes or overinterpreting certain responses. Transparent documentation of any biases in daily memos made the final interpretation more credible.

5. Thick Description

In the final narrative, the study provides contextual detail about the nature of the simulation tasks, the timeline of decisions, and the cultural backgrounds of participants. Such detail enables to determine whether and how the findings may transfer to other contexts. By offering multiple participant quotes, the study captures the richness and complexity of intercultural negotiation and conflict resolution.

Ethical and Contextual Constraints

Though the multi-method approach and validation procedures aimed to ensure consistent findings, certain limitations are acknowledged. First, the participants were drawn from a single educational institution specializing in business, which may limit generalizability to other disciplinary contexts. Second, the study did not gather formal data on participants' prior intercultural exposure or language proficiency, although these factors may have significantly influenced how readily students adapted to multicultural settings.

Although the participating students represented European countries, the absence of Asian and African learners restricts the cultural breadth of the study. Some team-process dynamics, particularly high-context communication norms or hierarchical deference, may manifest differently in non-Western cohorts. We therefore advise a view of the present findings as exploratory and to triangulate them with local pilot data. Future research should replicate the design with balanced regional representation or employ matched-cohort comparisons to test cultural moderation effects."

While debriefings were comprehensive, time constraints in the course schedule sometimes limited deeper probing into issues of culture and collaboration. Some participants may have filtered their reflections knowing that instructors and peers would have access to certain documents, creating a potential "courtesy bias." However, the anonymity of surveys and reflective journals and the repeated emphasis on the non-evaluative nature of this study attempted to mitigate such risks.

Overall, the methodology reflects a conscious effort to explain how cultural factors intersect with team-based decision-making in an experiential simulation. By integrating multiple forms of qualitative data, employing thematic analysis with a clear coding framework, and incorporating validation strategies, the study aspires to present trustworthy insights into the benefits and challenges of leveraging cultural diversity in gamified educational contexts.

4. RESULTS AND DISCUSSION

4.1. Team Formation and Cultural Dynamics

This section explores how students in the International Corporate Management (ICM) simulation navigated cultural differences during their initial team setup and how these differences shaped emerging team roles and leadership styles. Data for this section come primarily from reflective journals documenting students' first impressions, early teamwork experiences, and strategies for handling cultural diversity. These reflections are complemented by initial team reports submitted at the simulation's outset, as well as instructor-led debriefing sessions focused on group formation.

Navigating Cultural Differences: Early Impressions and Adaptation

From the start of the simulation, participants found themselves grouped into teams typically comprising four to six individuals of at least three different nationalities.

Students noted various reactions to this deliberate cultural mixing. In her reflective journal, Gabriela (Poland) wrote:

"Our team first met online to discuss who would take which role, finance, marketing, etc. At first, it felt awkward because we all came with different ideas about how to begin. The Norwegian students said, 'Let's make a step-by-step plan in Google Docs,' while my friend from Italy wanted to talk everything through face-to-face (on Zoom) before writing anything. We needed some time to see the value in each approach."

Such accounts illustrate the initial uncertainty and negotiation processes typical of diverse teams. Students found that culture-specific communication norms, direct, structured planning vs. flexible, discussion-driven brainstorming, shaped how tasks were proposed, accepted, or challenged. In an early debriefing, the instructor prompted each team to describe their approach to orientation and role assignment. Team Alpha's spokesperson explained:

"We decided not to jump straight into roles. Instead, we spent almost an hour chatting about backgrounds, what we study, why we chose Lisbon. It felt like we needed trust first. But I know some of us were like, 'Wait, why aren't we deciding the roles yet?' It was interesting to see how certain cultures prefer diving right into the task, while others want more personal rapport first."

Survey responses at mid-semester echoed this theme of "negotiating differences," with over 70% of respondents indicating that they "often" or "very often" encountered at least one cultural misunderstanding in the first two weeks of collaboration. Yet, just as many participants rated these misunderstandings as "moderately easy" to resolve, citing open discussion and instructor-led reflection prompts as beneficial.

Emerging Team Roles: Cultural Preferences and Negotiated Leadership

The next stage in team formation involved deciding on roles such as Chief Executive Officer (CEO), Chief Financial Officer (CFO), Chief Marketing Officer (CMO), and so forth. While some teams assigned these roles swiftly, often basing decisions on pre-existing expertise or personal interests, others took more time, reflecting cultural nuances around leadership emergence and power distance (Hofstede et al., 2010).

For instance, a reflective journal from Simon (Finland) recounted how an Italian teammate informally stepped into a CEO-like role:

"Alessandra naturally started organizing tasks and setting deadlines. I think many of us were relieved because we needed direction. But then Li (China) was hesitant, maybe because in her culture, you wait for a formal agreement to name a leader. It wasn't conflict, just confusion: Do we want a single leader, or do we share leadership? We eventually agreed Alessandra would be CEO if we all had input. So, it was a compromise."

This anecdote underscores how certain cultures, especially those more comfortable with explicit authority, took initiative in leading, while others expected a group mandate. Students also noted that "leading" did not always align with a formal title. Some team members from low power-distance backgrounds (e.g., Northern Europe) actively contributed to decision-making without identifying as "leaders." Meanwhile, individuals from cultures with higher power-distance norms reported feeling more comfortable when a single person was visibly "in charge," as it minimized uncertainty or the potential for messy consensus-seeking.

Teams that recognized and discussed these divergent leadership preferences early on tended to develop more stable structures. For example, Team Delta's first written report explicitly addressed the topic of leadership:

"We come from four different countries with different ways of making decisions. After discussing our experiences, we agreed on a rotating model where each round (quarter) a different person leads the main strategic meeting. This way, we share responsibility and learn from each other's style."

Observations from the instructor's notes confirmed that Team Delta's approach fostered active participation and minimized friction. By contrast, Team Echo initially had a self-appointed leader who dominated discussions; survey data and debriefing feedback suggested that some team members felt overshadowed. Following an instructor prompt, they revisited their leadership structure and integrated more inclusive decision-making in subsequent rounds, yielding higher reported satisfaction.

Cultural Leadership Styles: Collaboration and Conflict Avoidance

Teams also expressed differences in how leadership was enacted. For instance, members from more collectivist cultures placed a strong emphasis on preserving group harmony. In interviews, they described their reluctance to confront mistakes or express dissent publicly. Conversely, students from individualist or low-context cultures indicated frustration when direct feedback was withheld, fearing the team might repeat errors. This tension sometimes surfaced in reflective journals. Adrien (France) commented:

"I expected that if we made a financial mistake, someone would just say so. But Maria and Peter were so polite that we found out too late we'd messed up our budget assumptions. Now I understand it's a respect thing, maybe they didn't want to embarrass me."

Such episodes highlight the role of cultural norms in shaping leadership styles that balance assertiveness and deference. In multiple teams, once these communication preferences were acknowledged, students adapted. Some instituted a short "check-out" at the end of each meeting: a structured round where each person had to voice at least one concern, normalizing constructive criticism. As a result, emergent leaders learned to encourage quieter voices without being perceived as confrontational.

Summary of Team Formation and Cultural Dynamics

Overall, the data indicate that cultural diversity strongly influenced how teams formed initial bonds, negotiated roles, and established leadership structures. While some students gravitated toward clear hierarchical roles, others prioritized an egalitarian approach. Early tensions often revolved around varying assumptions regarding power distance, collectivism vs. individualism, and direct vs. indirect communication. Teams that allocated time to discussing these differences, either prompted by the instructor or by self-awareness, tended to experience smoother role transitions and higher satisfaction with team structure.

Survey findings corroborate this pattern of early-stage tensions and subsequent alignment. In the mid-semester survey, 59% of respondents reported feeling "uncertain or uncomfortable" about their role assignments during the first two weeks, attributing confusion to divergent cultural expectations about leadership. By the time of the final survey, that percentage had dropped to just 24%, indicating that most teams successfully negotiated clearer role structures as they advanced in the simulation. This shift aligns with the qualitative reflections where participants described the evolving comfort around their newly established norms, such as rotating leadership or designated conflict mediators.

These findings align with cross-cultural models (Hofstede et al., 2010) showing that understanding and adapting to different cultural expectations can facilitate more harmonious collaboration and help leaders emerge in ways that all team members perceive as fair and respectful.

In the following section, we explore deeper the specific communication and collaboration processes that unfolded once roles were in place. We examine how language challenges, digital communication norms, and ongoing negotiation shaped each team's capacity to function effectively within the high-pressure environment of a multinational business simulation.

4.2. Communication and Collaboration

Cultural diversity was particularly evident in the communication and collaboration patterns that emerged throughout the International Corporate Management (ICM) simulation. This section focuses on two key aspects of these processes: the language challenges and digital communication norms teams encountered, and the ways cultural misunderstandings were negotiated and resolved through adaptive strategies.

Language Challenges and Digital Communication Norms

Although most participants possessed at least an intermediate command of English (the designated lingua franca for the simulation), they varied widely in their comfort levels with academic and business terminology. Early reflective journal entries often voiced concerns about accidental misinterpretations. Helena (Romania) wrote:

"Sometimes I had trouble keeping up with the conversation when people spoke very fast or used specific marketing terms I didn't know in English. I felt embarrassed to interrupt and ask for clarification."

Similarly, Jonas (Germany) mentioned that he found himself "softening" his speech to avoid sounding too direct, explaining that *"in my home culture, you can just say you disagree. But I worried it might come across as rude in a group with people from more indirect communication styles."*

Beyond oral comprehension, written communication posed additional challenges. Teams relied on shared documents, chat apps, and email. Slight differences in wording sometimes led to confusion about responsibilities or deadlines. In mid-semester surveys, over half the respondents acknowledged that phrasing issues or vocabulary gaps had caused them to miss key points at least once. Several teams adopted a "Plain English" policy to mitigate these problems, agreeing to limit jargon and use bullet points for clarity. They also created a shared glossary of frequently used business terms. This initiative, reported in multiple team documents, proved particularly helpful for members whose second or third language was English.

In addition to language hurdles, teams navigated divergent communication norms regarding synchronous vs. asynchronous tools. Students from higher-context cultural backgrounds often favored video calls to grasp subtle cues, while others from more direct cultures preferred short, structured text updates on project management platforms. Team Omega's report noted:

"We had conflict over scheduling real-time calls. Our Spanish and Brazilian members felt it was essential to see facial expressions to sense agreement or disagreement. Our Dutch teammate, though, insisted on using Slack or email because she found calls too time-consuming. After a short tension, we settled on a compromise: one mandatory Zoom call per round, plus daily Slack check-ins."

These negotiated solutions balanced the real-time, relational benefits of voice or video interaction with the efficiency and clarity of textual updates. By mid-semester, many teams had evolved a blended communication ecosystem: quick chats for daily coordination, weekly video conferences for strategic alignment, and structured decision-tracking documents to ensure accountability. Such multi-channel approaches reflected teams' attempts to accommodate varied cultural preferences for directness, formality, and synchronous contact.

A mid-semester survey item asked students to rate on a five-point scale how frequently language barriers or ambiguous phrasing caused misunderstandings within their teams. Results revealed that 52% selected either "often" or "very often," a figure that dropped to 22% by the final survey. In their open-ended responses, students credited structured 'plain English' agreements, shared glossaries, and regularly scheduled check-ins for improving clarity. As one participant put it in the final survey, *"We gradually learned which communication style each person preferred, and we used that to reduce misinterpretations."*

Cultural Misunderstandings vs. Negotiation and Adaptation

Misinterpretations often arose from indirectness, perceived "tone," or the assumption that silence implied agreement. In one debriefing, a student from Eastern Europe confessed she would remain quiet when unsure how to phrase criticism politely, while her teammate from the UK read this silence as consent to move forward. Both admitted that neither viewpoint had been openly articulated until a near-crisis in the second simulation round, when the team discovered they had allocated an incorrect advertising budget.

Such episodes highlighted the role of "face-saving" in certain cultures vs. more outspoken norms in others. High-context communicators expected nuances to be inferred, whereas low-context members felt uncertain when explicit statements were lacking. Survey data revealed that 43% of students cited *"not knowing if a teammate disagreed"* as a recurring issue. However, many also noted that learning to probe for silent dissent became a vital skill that improved overall collaboration.

By the final round, only 19% of respondents still reported ongoing confusion about "unspoken disagreements." This decline suggests that explicit feedback loops, like the 'check-back' or paraphrasing tactic, significantly reduced the uncertainty about whether teammates silently opposed a course of action.

In reflective journals, participants described various tactics to address and overcome cultural barriers. One frequently cited technique was the practice of "check-back" or paraphrasing. After a group discussion, the acting team leader or note-taker would restate the key points and invite corrections. Mariana (Portugal) shared:

"We learned to say, 'So, if I understand you correctly…' and then wait for feedback. This helps catch misunderstandings early. If someone was too shy to speak before, they have a second chance to say, 'No, that's not what I meant.'"

Another common adaptation involved implementing scheduled "round-robin" updates, ensuring everyone's viewpoint was solicited, regardless of cultural predispositions toward speaking up. This structured form of dialogue was especially effective for quieter members who, according to a Spanish student's journal, *"wouldn't volunteer opinions but actually had great ideas when asked directly."*

Teams also engaged in iterative reflection. After major simulation rounds, some groups held mini-debriefs specifically on communication: What went well this round? Where did we misunderstand each other? As Team Gamma's report explained:

"We realized a misunderstanding about pricing strategy could've been avoided if we'd asked direct follow-up questions earlier. Now we reflect each week on how we're communicating, not just on the business results."

Collectively, these measures gradually reduced cultural friction and enabled more precise coordination. By the final simulation rounds, the majority of teams reported smoother interactions and a higher sense of shared purpose, suggesting that the tension inherent in cross-cultural collaboration can be alleviated by deliberate, reflective effort.

Summary of Communication and Collaboration

Overall, while language barriers and diverse communication norms did generate misunderstandings, teams in the ICM simulation demonstrated remarkable adaptability by instituting strategies like shared glossaries, structured check-ins, and explicit follow-up questions. Students learned to recognize when cultural assumptions (about directness, politeness, or consent) were impeding clarity and collaboratively sought ways to address them. In essence, rather than hindering performance, the negotiation of communication norms became a critical driver of intercultural competence. These findings underscore the dynamic interplay of language, technology, and cultural values and reveal how open dialogue, combined with practical tools, can transform potential obstacles into rich opportunities for collaboration and learning.

Next, we examine how these communication and collaboration processes intersect with student learning outcomes and perceptions, particularly in terms of soft skill development, global mindset cultivation, and overall engagement in the simulation.

4.3. Learning Outcomes and Perceptions

In addition to reshaping communication and collaboration practices, the multicultural environment of the ICM simulation impacted participants' learning outcomes and self-perceptions in meaningful ways. This section explores students' reflections on intercultural learning, the development of soft skills such as empathy and a global mindset, and how cultural diversity ultimately influenced the simulation's performance metrics and overall engagement levels.

Student Reflections on Intercultural Learning

From the early weeks of the course, a majority of students expressed a growing awareness of how cultural backgrounds influence behavior and decision-making. In their final reflective journals, many highlighted newfound appreciation for the complexity of global teamwork. Sara (Italy) wrote:

"Before this simulation, I took for granted that everyone would just adapt to my straightforward style of problem-solving. But working with colleagues from Poland and Turkey taught me that direct confrontation sometimes needs softening. Now I see that adjusting communication can lead to better solutions and fewer hurt feelings."

Several participants noted that encountering diverse assumptions made the learning experience more impactful than conventional group projects. A Spanish student, Carlos, observed:

"Usually I work with classmates from Spain or Latin America. This time, because our group had a Lithuanian and a Finnish member, I realized how differently we handle conflict. We eventually created a conflict protocol to ensure fairness and clarity."

These reflections underscore how the simulation, by design, compelled students to reflect on their cultural norms rather than see them as universal or "correct." Alongside domain-specific skills like budgeting or marketing analysis, participants consistently cited intercultural communication as an unexpected yet vital dimension of their learning.

Development of Soft Skills: Empathy and Global Mindset

A key soft skill enhanced by the ICM simulation was empathy, which emerged organically as students worked to accommodate teammates' communication styles, leadership preferences, and work rhythms. In multiple surveys, respondents rated higher self-awareness of their personal biases and a greater inclination to "step into teammates' shoes" after the simulation. Markus (Germany) noted in a journal entry:

"At first, I was frustrated whenever colleagues didn't answer Slack messages promptly. Then I realized they might be juggling a different set of constraints or time zones. I became more patient and tried to schedule tasks in ways that respected everyone's schedule."

Such adaptations reflect empathy in practice, as students began to appreciate contexts different from their own. Instructor-led debriefings reinforced this by prompting teams to share not just what decisions they made, but also why certain teammates may have felt anxious, impatient, or unheard. Over time, these reflective cycles promoted more considerate behavior and a deeper sense of collective responsibility.

The notion of a "global mindset," typically associated with openness to new ideas, cultural adaptability, and an understanding of interconnected markets, was a recurring theme in end-of-semester narratives. In final debriefings, several students voiced how the simulation prepared them for real-world, cross-border collaborations. A Portuguese student, Mariana, remarked:

"I'm so used to Portuguese ways of doing business, now I see how quickly we have to adapt when working with people from different cultural backgrounds. The big takeaway is that no single approach is automatically 'best'; it's about mutual respect and synergy."

This growing sense of global readiness was evidenced by an overall rise in participants' confidence in tackling international projects or internships. Survey data showed that, at the course's conclusion, 88% of respondents felt "somewhat more" or "significantly more" prepared to work with diverse teams than they had at the beginning of the semester, an indicator that the ICM experience had nurtured both cultural awareness and a willingness to engage with global complexity.

In addition to general preparedness, the final survey probed perceived gains in specific intercultural competencies. For instance, 65% of students strongly agreed with the statement "I am better able to adapt my communication style for teammates from different cultural backgrounds," up from only 36% in the mid-semester survey. Meanwhile, 72% indicated improved confidence in addressing conflicts that arise from cultural misunderstandings, a substantial jump from the 41% reported earlier.

Impact of Cultural Diversity on Simulation Outcomes and Engagement

Students often grappled with bridging different cultural approaches to risk, hierarchy, and consensus, which shaped their strategic moves within the simulation. In final team reports, many cited diversity of viewpoints as a factor in more robust decision-making. Team Beta, which comprised members from four distinct cultural clusters, attributed their competitive advantage to an "active debate culture" where no single viewpoint dominated. Their final report stated:

"We rarely rushed decisions. Even though it meant longer discussions, we felt the synergy from combining a risk-taking perspective (from our UK rep) with a more cautious approach (from our Hungarian teammate). The balanced outcome usually led to fewer mistakes in the next quarter."

Interestingly, Team Beta's approach also reflected in their survey satisfaction scores: their average "team functioning" rating (on a 1–5 Likert scale) rose from 3.2 at mid-semester to 4.5 in the final survey, underscoring that embracing debate contributed not only to market success but also to positive team morale.

Not all teams found this process seamless, however. Some encountered analysis paralysis, particularly when collectivist-oriented members hesitated to finalize decisions without unanimous agreement. Yet, in retrospective reflections, even these teams recognized that protracted discussions often sparked more creative or carefully vetted solutions. Thus, cultural diversity, while occasionally lengthening decision cycles, served as both a catalyst for innovation and a safeguard against narrow thinking.

Cultural diversity also played a salient role in overall team engagement. Teams that openly acknowledged cultural differences and attempted to accommodate diverse views generally exhibited higher morale, frequent communication, and proactive problem-solving. They reported fewer instances of disengagement or "social loafing." In contrast, teams that overlooked cultural dynamics tended to fragment, with some members feeling marginalized. One debriefing transcript captured this phenomenon:

Instructor: *"What contributed to your team's dip in performance this round?"*

Team Representative: *"Honestly, some of us felt overshadowed and stopped contributing. It might be a cultural or language thing, people with stronger English or more direct styles ended up dominating."*

Nevertheless, by the simulation's final phase, most teams had identified workable strategies to maintain inclusive participation. The very fact that the ICM simulation included repeated rounds allowed students to learn from earlier missteps and refine their collaborative approach. This iterative process helped transform initial cultural friction into more harmonious group interactions.

Reflections on Personal Growth

In concluding surveys, a dominant theme was students' sense of personal growth in dealing with global challenges. As Elena (Czech Republic) succinctly wrote:

"If this was a real company, we'd have to face these issues daily. Now I know how beneficial it is to talk openly about differences. It saved our team from making big mistakes."

Such commentary points to a shift from viewing cultural diversity as an external obstacle toward embracing it as a strategic resource. The resulting sense of collective achievement helped bolster engagement and motivation, confirming that cultural diversity, when managed with awareness and empathy, can elevate both the learning process and the quality of performance outcomes.

Summary of Learning Outcomes and Perceptions

Taken together, these findings highlight that the ICM simulation not only advanced participants' technical and managerial skills, but also fostered significant growth in intercultural competence. Students reported greater empathy, broader global mindsets, and a deeper understanding of how culture shapes business decision-making. Culturally diverse teams, though occasionally slowed by communication issues or consensus-building requirements, often developed more nuanced strategies and showed higher long-term engagement. These insights reinforce the pedagogical value of designing gamified interventions that systematically incorporate and reflect on cultural variation, expanding the scope of student learning well beyond traditional classroom boundaries.

In the next section, we turn to the specific tensions and opportunities that arose in this multicultural environment, addressing common conflict areas, highlighting how diversity served as a catalyst for creativity and resilience, and examining the conditions under which teams leveraged rather than suffered from these cultural differences.

4.4. Tensions and Opportunities

Throughout the ICM simulation, cultural diversity served as both a source of friction and a wellspring of innovation. This section explores the key conflict areas students encountered and the strategies they employed to resolve them, followed by an examination of how cultural differences acted as catalysts for creativity and resilience within the simulation environment.

Identifying Conflict Areas and Resolution Strategies

One frequently cited tension revolved around differing leadership styles and hierarchical expectations. Students from more egalitarian or low power-distance cultures were often eager to distribute responsibilities evenly, expecting everyone to voice opinions freely. In contrast, those from high power-distance backgrounds appeared more at ease with a designated leader who set the direction. Several teams experienced friction when one or two members assumed authority without explicit group consent. Team Sigma's debriefing notes revealed:

"Our French teammate and Spanish teammate wanted a single leader to streamline decisions, while our Finnish member strongly believed in consensus. We struggled until we created a system where one coordinator facilitated discussions but final decisions needed majority agreement."

This agreement balanced clarity of leadership with collective input. Eventually, Team Sigma reported fewer disagreements and smoother decision-making processes. Reflective journals corroborated the importance of clarifying role expectations early. Students noted that acknowledging cultural preferences for leadership, rather than ignoring them, led to more equitable participation over time.

A second notable conflict area concerned pacing and deadline expectations. Individuals from cultures that emphasized punctuality and strict timelines (e.g., Germany, Finland) sometimes clashed with teammates more comfortable with flexible deadlines (e.g., Spain, Portugal). Johanna (Finland) wrote in her journal:

"I was stressed because after two days, we still hadn't finalized our product design or marketing budget. I felt we were behind, but my Spanish teammate said, 'We still have time, let's not rush a bad decision.' It took compromise to recognize both styles have merit."

Teams that recognized this contrast early typically instituted explicit schedules, with defined milestones and accountability checks. This brought structure for those who prized timeliness yet included built-in "reflection windows" for more deliberative members. Over time, the synergy of combining urgency with thoroughness benefited overall performance. In multiple team reports, students remarked that learning to negotiate schedules in a culturally diverse setting helped them appreciate alternative definitions of "on time" and "quality work."

Risk tolerance, whether financial, strategic, or interpersonal, surfaced as another stress point. Some participants were accustomed to bold moves and aggressive strategies in the simulation's competitive marketplace, while others advised caution and incremental adjustments. These disagreements occasionally escalated into conflict when perceived "recklessness" or "inertia" was blamed for underperformance. In one debriefing, a Czech student expressed frustration that her Swedish teammates vetoed an ambitious R&D investment:

"I felt they were too cautious, missing a big market opportunity. They said they didn't want to jeopardize stability. It became heated because we were both convinced we were 'right.'"

Teams that navigated these tensions effectively employed structured conflict-resolution approaches, such as devoting a separate meeting to weigh pros and cons or using simulation data to model best- and worst-case scenarios. Notably, 58% of participants in the final survey specifically mentioned 'conflict over strategic risk decisions' as their primary challenge in the early rounds. However, in final reflections, 71% agreed or strongly agreed that 'our team learned to balance different risk perspectives to create better strategies by the end of the simulation.' This aligns with participant testimonies describing more nuanced decision-making processes after each conflict incident. In final reflections, many students recognized that exposure to different risk appetites actually enhanced the depth of their strategic reasoning, pushing them to see both potential gains and pitfalls more clearly.

While each team devised its own solutions, several core strategies recurred:

1. Open Dialogues: Setting aside time explicitly to discuss and normalize cultural differences, often during post-round debriefings.

2. Protocol Checklists: Creating guidelines for decision-making, leadership rotation, or conflict escalation to defuse personal tensions.
3. Third-Party Facilitation: Occasionally, the instructor served as a neutral mediator, urging teams to articulate specific concerns rather than general frustrations.

Used together, these tactics helped convert cultural tensions into teachable moments. Even teams that reported early hostility discovered that structured conversations built trust and prevented ongoing resentments.

Cultural Diversity as a Catalyst for Creativity and Resilience

A recurring theme in journals and survey responses was that diversity enriched brainstorming. Students often contrasted the simulation to past group projects composed of culturally similar peers. One Portuguese student, Ana, highlighted how her team's variety of cultural experiences sparked original marketing campaigns:

"Our brand positioning combined Scandinavian minimalism with Southern European flair. Honestly, I'd never have thought of that angle on my own. The diverse feedback pushed us to be more inventive."

Such feedback echoes established research linking multicultural teams to higher levels of creativity, provided they learn to harness differences constructively rather than let them fracture group cohesion. While friction occasionally surfaced, it also forced students to re-examine their assumptions and refine their strategies.

Beyond creativity, cultural diversity appeared to foster resilience. When confronted with unexpected simulation outcomes, like underperforming brands or stock price drops, teams with heterogeneous cultural backgrounds seemed more flexible in pivoting strategies. Participant accounts suggest that group diversity supplied a reservoir of alternative viewpoints and coping mechanisms. In Team Nu's survey response, members recounted:

"In Q6, our market share plummeted. Instead of panicking, we tapped into each other's strengths, our French CFO proposed re-budgeting, our Polish marketer recommended an e-commerce pivot, and our German analyst analyzed competitor moves. Sharing these multi-faceted insights helped us bounce back."

In this sense, resilience stemmed not merely from technical skill but from the capacity to reframe problems through multiple cultural lenses. Once teams recognized these varied perspectives as assets, they learned to respond to losses with adaptive strategies rather than defeatism.

Summary of Tensions and Opportunities

Cultural diversity within the ICM simulation simultaneously generated areas of conflict and significant prospects for growth. Divergent leadership expectations, time orientations, and risk tolerances tested the equilibrium of many teams, sometimes resulting in misunderstandings and tension. Yet, the very friction these differences created also spurred creative approaches to marketing, finance, and strategic planning. By employing explicit communication protocols, shared rules for conflict resolution, and reflective debriefings, most groups transformed initial challenges into deeper mutual understanding.

Moreover, the culturally varied experiences within each team expanded collective problem-solving and bolstered resilience. As teams encountered simulation setbacks, they were able to draw on a broader palette of insights, fueling innovative pivots. The ICM course thus highlights how actively managed cultural diversity can turn latent tensions into tangible learning opportunities. In the following section, we consider how these findings align with or challenge existing theoretical models, such as Hofstede's cultural dimensions and Kolb's experiential learning cycle, and what implications emerge for future gamified educational designs.

4.5. Integration with Theoretical Insights

This final section of the results and discussion situates the findings from the ICM simulation within broader theoretical frameworks on culture and experiential learning. By revisiting Hofstede's cultural dimensions (Hofstede et al., 2010), Hall's high- vs. low-context communication theory (Hall, 1976), and Kolb's experiential learning cycle (Kolb, 2015), we can better understand how the observed patterns align with, extend, or challenge existing scholarly models.

Cross-Analysis with Hofstede's Cultural Dimensions

As demonstrated in Sections 4.1 and 4.4, teams composed of students from high power-distance cultures (e.g., parts of Southern Europe or Latin America) often preferred clear leadership structures. By contrast, those from lower power-distance backgrounds (e.g., Scandinavian countries) tended to distribute leadership more diffusely. This dynamic confirms Hofstede's (2010) assertion that power distance significantly influences decision-making processes and role expectations. Yet, the ICM simulation also highlights how flexible, adaptive approaches can transcend these initial preferences. Several teams successfully integrated structured leadership (satisfying high power-distance members) with consensus-building (appealing to low power-distance members). In effect, the simulation environment allowed participants to renegotiate cultural defaults in favor of a blended leadership model.

Hofstede's individualism-collectivism dimension was evident in how participants approached disagreement and personal responsibility. Students from more collectivist cultures often expressed concern for group harmony and showed reluctance to voice open criticism, initially leading to misunderstandings. However, as revealed in Sections 4.2 and 4.3, explicit communication protocols (e.g., round-robin feedback) helped collectivist-oriented members feel comfortable sharing ideas. Over time, some teams reported a hybrid approach that balanced consensus with direct feedback, underscoring that while cultural dimensions provide a useful starting framework, real-life teams can negotiate new norms that deviate from classic cultural scripts.

Hofstede's uncertainty avoidance dimension was frequently observed in the varying degrees of strategic caution or boldness. Students from high uncertainty-avoidance contexts displayed a preference for detailed planning and incremental decision-making, while those from lower uncertainty-avoidance cultures leaned toward experimentation and faster pivots. The simulation's iterative nature gave teams the opportunity to experiment with both approaches and find common ground. Interestingly, those that embraced a combination of cautious planning and risk-taking reported more balanced and stable performance, suggesting that mixing cultural preferences can enhance adaptability, an insight that refines Hofstede's model by showcasing the benefits of cross-cultural synergy in real-time practice.

Connections to Hall's High- vs. Low-Context Communication Theory

Hall's (1976) distinction between high-context (reliance on implicit cues, nonverbal signals, and shared assumptions) and low-context (dependence on explicit, direct communication) was evident in many teams' struggles with language, tone, and inferred meaning (Section 4.2). Participants from high-context backgrounds sometimes felt that excessive directness risked offense, while those from low-context cultures found indirect speech ambiguous. Consistent with Hall's theory, tension often emerged at the juncture of these contrasting norms, particularly around providing feedback or disagreeing with proposed strategies.

However, the ICM context also demonstrated how purposeful metacommunication, discussing how the team should communicate, bridged the gap between high- and low-context styles. Rather than one style dominating, successful teams adapted practices such as paraphrasing or structured clarifications, effectively creating a "mixed-context" environment. This approach supports Hall's core premise that context deeply influences messaging, while showing that team members can jointly craft new interactional norms that transcend their default cultural backgrounds.

Experiential Learning (Kolb) and the Gamified Context

Kolb's experiential learning cycle (2015) emphasizes that learners progress through concrete experience, reflective observation, abstract conceptualization, and active experimentation. The ICM simulation provided concrete experiences, making high-stakes decisions under time pressure, and active experimentation, as teams adjusted strategies each subsequent "quarter." The distinct value added by the multinational aspect lies in reflective observation and abstract conceptualization: after each round, students were compelled to interpret results not just in functional (marketing, finance) terms, but also in intercultural terms. Debriefing sessions and reflective journals frequently highlighted how cultural misalignments or synergies shaped outcomes, thus catalyzing deeper conceptual learning about cross-cultural collaboration.

Kolb's model also posits that true learning occurs when individuals integrate abstract ideas into concrete action. Evidence of this integration can be seen in how teams refined their communication norms, leadership structures, and conflict resolution methods over the simulation's lifespan (Sections 4.2 and 4.4). For instance, a team might initially face confusion stemming from cultural differences in directness but then consciously adopt new protocols, round-robin feedback, paraphrasing, to address these issues. This cycle of experience → reflection → conceptualization → reapplication aligns closely with Kolb's theoretical framework, highlighting that the interplay of cultural diversity multiplied the depth of experiential learning, urging participants to expand not only their managerial acumen but also their intercultural skill set.

Confirmations and Challenges to Existing Models

Overall, the ICM simulation largely confirms that Hofstede's and Hall's cultural dimensions, and Kolb's experiential cycle, remain strong lenses for interpreting intercultural dynamics. Students' behaviors often followed predicted patterns regarding power distance, context dependence, and uncertainty avoidance. Likewise, Kolb's emphasis on iterative learning and reflection appears instrumental in enabling cross-cultural adaptation.

However, the empirical data also suggest that these models, though instructive, may oversimplify certain realities. The repeated theme of negotiated or blended communication styles reveals that cultural identities are not static categories. Instead, participants selectively adopted or discarded cultural norms based on situational needs, generational influences, or personal preferences. Moreover, some participants identified with multiple cultural backgrounds, indicating that their behavior could not be neatly mapped onto a single set of cultural dimensions.

Finally, the simulation context itself, marked by repeated decision cycles, continuous feedback, and the instructor's facilitation, provides a unique environment where cultural boundaries can be transcended faster than in typical organizational settings. Hence, while Hofstede's and Hall's frameworks accurately diagnose early-stage team friction, the deeper takeaway is that learners can rapidly reconfigure cultural assumptions through reflection and practice, challenging the notion that culture imposes fixed constraints on collaboration.

Conclusion of Results and Discussion

By integrating the findings with classical cultural frameworks and experiential learning theory, this section underscores the dynamic and evolving nature of culture in a gamified educational setting. Students' capacity to blend or adapt cultural norms, experiment with leadership and communication styles, and reflect on both successes and setbacks demonstrates an active negotiation of cultural identity within the ICM simulation. The results show how theoretical insights can be both confirmed and nuanced by on-the-ground experiences of multinational teamwork, highlighting the transformative potential of well-structured simulations in preparing learners for a diverse, interconnected world.

5. PEDAGOGICAL IMPLICATIONS

Building on the empirical insights presented thus far, this section outlines the pedagogical implications of using multinational business simulations, particularly in contexts where cultural diversity is both a challenge and a potential asset. Specifically, we focus on four areas: designing gamified education for cultural diversity, the role of instructors in supporting multicultural teams, strategies for inclusive team formation and conflict mediation, and recommendations for systematically enhancing intercultural competence through such simulations.

5.1. Designing for Cultural Diversity in Gamified Education

Traditional gamified learning experiences frequently emphasize skill acquisition in areas like finance, marketing, or strategic planning. However, for courses that deliberately aim to foster intercultural competence, the simulation mechanics should be equally attuned to cultural learning objectives (Deardorff, 2009). This can involve designing simulation tasks that explicitly require cross-cultural negotiation, e.g., marketing products to diverse customer segments, each reflecting distinct cultural preferences, or creating scenarios where teams must integrate multiple cultural perspectives to succeed. By embedding intercultural triggers directly into the gameplay, educators can ensure that cultural diversity isn't merely an incidental factor but a core learning driver.

To mitigate the risk of cultural clashes or superficial engagement, simulations can incorporate structured reflective checkpoints (Kolb, 2015). For instance, after each "quarter" or decision cycle, participants might complete a brief reflection on how cultural dynamics influenced decisions or shaped communication outcomes. These reflections can be guided by prompt questions, such as: "What assumptions did you notice about leadership or risk-taking?" or "How did cultural norms affect conflict resolution in this round?" Such scaffolded reflection allows students to move beyond reactive impressions and develop deeper insights into how cultural dimensions underlie team processes.

Educational technology can further support cultural learning. Digital dashboards and analytics can track not just financial performance but also measure variables like communication frequency or distribution of speaking time across team members (Aparicio et al., 2016). While these tools require careful calibration, they can offer objective feedback that sparks conversation around equitable participation. For instance, if data show that half of the team rarely speaks during synchronous meetings, the instructor can facilitate a debrief on potential cultural or linguistic barriers and invite the team to adjust their collaboration methods accordingly.

5.2. Role of Instructors/Facilitators in Multicultural Team Support

Instructors play a pivotal role in shaping how cultural diversity is perceived and leveraged. At the outset of the simulation, faculty can set explicit norms emphasizing respect for different communication styles, risk appetites, and leadership preferences (Iskhakova & Ott, 2020). By demonstrating genuine curiosity about cultural variations, asking students to share experiences from their home contexts or highlighting the value of diverse viewpoints, facilitators set a positive tone that can reduce early misunderstandings. They can also model inclusive behaviors, such as paraphrasing for clarity, inviting quieter voices to speak, and affirming that no single approach is inherently superior.

While a hands-off approach may allow students to "learn from failure," the complexities of cross-cultural friction can sometimes overwhelm or alienate participants if left unchecked. Facilitators should monitor team dynamics and interject strategically when conflicts appear to escalate (Creswell & Poth, 2018). Guided debriefings after each simulation round can be structured around cultural themes, leadership distribution, communication styles, negotiation challenges, rather than purely financial or strategic outcomes. By prompting teams to articulate how cultural factors shaped successes or struggles, instructors help students make explicit connections between theory (e.g., Hofstede's dimensions, Hall's context orientation) and everyday interactions in the simulation.

Instructors can also encourage reflexivity by reminding students of their own cultural lenses. This might involve short reflective exercises or journaling activities focused on self-awareness: "What cultural assumptions do I bring to teamwork?" "How might others perceive my style of giving feedback?" By normalizing such introspection, facilitators reinforce the message that cultural competence is an evolving skill set, not a static trait. These reflections lay the groundwork for empathy, as students begin to recognize that peers who behave differently aren't necessarily "difficult" or "inefficient," but are acting within their own cultural logic (Hofstede et al., 2010).

5.3. Strategies for Inclusive Team Formation and Conflict Mediation

Given that cultural diversity can amplify both benefits and challenges, educators should form teams that are culturally heterogeneous yet balanced in terms of language fluency, prior international exposure, or academic backgrounds (Taras et al., 2016). This avoids isolating minority-language speakers or creating large majorities from a single culture. Additionally, distributing students with stronger English proficiency across teams can reduce language-based bottlenecks. If possible, instructors might request brief student profiles at the course's onset, capturing linguistic competence, cultural backgrounds, and learning goals, to inform the composition of each simulation team.

Early in the simulation, having each team draft a "team charter" or collaborative agreement can proactively address cultural friction. This document, created collectively, sets out norms for communication (e.g., frequency, channels), decision-making (e.g., how final consensus is achieved), and conflict resolution (e.g., guidelines for raising concerns). In culturally diverse settings, charters can specify how members with different time orientations or leadership expectations will compromise on schedules or role allocations (Paulus et al., 2005). Teams can revisit and revise this charter as they learn from each simulation round, ensuring a living framework that evolves along with team dynamics.

To handle conflicts internally without constant instructor intervention, some teams use peer mediation or rotating leadership (Howard et al., 2023). Assigning a mediator, a team member trained or self-selected for that role, can diffuse tensions by providing a neutral voice that restates positions, checks for understanding, and proposes solutions. Rotating leadership, on the other hand, ensures that no single cultural perspective dominates for the entire course. Each round, a different individual orchestrates the strategy discussion, harnessing the group's diverse strengths and reinforcing the idea that leadership style can, and should, adapt to shifting circumstances.

5.4. Recommendations for Enhancing Intercultural Competence Through Simulations

If the course design prioritizes developing intercultural competence, this objective should be formally assessed. Beyond evaluating financial outcomes or strategic insight, instructors can integrate reflection papers, short presentations on cultural conflict resolution, or peer evaluations that highlight intercultural learning (Deardorff, 2009). Such assessments encourage students to take cultural considerations seriously, reinforcing that the simulation's value extends beyond traditional business metrics.

Post-simulation coaching or reflection sessions can further solidify learning. This may involve meeting with smaller groups or individual students to review not only performance data but also feedback from teammates regarding intercultural interactions (Nowell et al., 2017). Personalized guidance helps students recognize persistent blind spots, such as dominating the conversation or disengaging during conflict, and craft specific action plans for future collaborations.

Many participants noted that the ICM experience felt authentic, mirroring global business conditions. Instructors can capitalize on this realism by inviting guest speakers from international organizations or by highlighting actual cross-cultural case studies in synergy with the simulation. If students see how the behaviors they practiced in the game translate into workplace effectiveness, they become more motivated to refine and retain their intercultural competencies (Leask, 2015). In addition, bridging classroom experiences to career contexts validates the importance of cultural literacy in a globally connected job market.

Finally, institutions might consider running successive cohorts through similar or evolving simulations, while tracking changes in intercultural communication proficiency. Surveys or standardized measures of cultural intelligence (Ang & Van Dyne, 2015) can be administered at multiple points throughout a program. These data can inform curriculum adjustments, identify which simulation elements most effectively promote intercultural growth, and reveal best practices for diverse cohorts. The iterative refining of simulation design, incorporating consistent feedback from instructors, students, and external collaborators, ensures that the approach to cultural diversity remains current, evidence-based, and responsive to evolving educational goals.

Designing and facilitating a gamified learning environment that fully leverages cultural diversity requires intentional planning, sensitive facilitation, and ongoing reflection. By embedding cultural triggers into simulation mechanics, promoting inclusive team formation, and employing proactive conflict mediation strategies, educators can transform cultural differences into key learning opportunities. Likewise, aligning these efforts with explicit assessment and continual coaching ensures that intercultural competence becomes an integral facet of students' academic development. Ultimately, such approaches underscore the transformative power of well-crafted simulations to prepare learners not just for specialized professional roles, but for global collaboration and cultural fluency in an increasingly interconnected world.

6. CONCLUSION

This chapter set out to examine how cultural diversity shapes collaboration, communication, and learning outcomes in a digital business simulation known as the International Corporate Management (ICM). Drawing on data from reflective journals, team reports, surveys, and debriefings, we explored how students from diverse cultural backgrounds formed teams, navigated differences in leadership and communication styles, negotiated conflicts, and ultimately leveraged their varied perspectives to enhance both strategic decision-making and intercultural competence. The findings highlight a complex interplay between culture-specific behaviors and the adaptive strategies students devised to build more inclusive, resilient teams.

The results suggest that cultural diversity in gamified educational contexts can function simultaneously as a stressor and a powerful driver of innovation. In early phases, teams often struggled with contrasting leadership expectations, linguistic barriers, and communication norms, challenges that aligned with Hofstede's power distance and uncertainty avoidance dimensions, as well as Hall's notions of high- and low-context communication. However, guided reflection, conscious norm-setting, and instructor facilitation frequently transformed these initial difficulties into opportunities for growth.

From a pedagogical standpoint, culturally mixed teams benefited from iterative cycles of experience, reflection, and adaptation, consistent with Kolb's experiential learning model. When students actively addressed cultural assumptions, they reported heightened empathy, broader global mindsets, and stronger interpersonal skills. The high-pressure simulation environment forced them to reconcile differing views on risk-taking, time orientation, and direct vs. indirect feedback. Over time, teams that integrated these diverse styles into coherent processes demonstrated higher resilience and more inventive strategic choices, suggesting that well-managed multicultural settings can yield superior learning outcomes.

Several constraints temper the generalizability of these findings. First, participants were drawn from a single educational institution in Europe, albeit with exchange students from beyond Europe. Although this cohort was culturally varied, broader global contexts, including non-Western regions, may present different dynamics. Second, while the multi-method qualitative approach proved useful for capturing nuances, it did not incorporate formal quantitative measures of intercultural competence, leaving some aspects of attitudinal shifts open to self-reporting biases. Third, the intensity and semester-long structure of the simulation may not reflect shorter or less immersive gamified activities, where cultural adjustment might unfold more slowly or remain superficial. Finally, instructor interventions, designed to facilitate reflective practice, played a notable role in guiding cross-cultural negotiation. In more hands-off environments, some teams might struggle to translate tension into positive outcomes.

There are multiple paths to extend this line of inquiry. First, comparative studies across different institutions or continents could reveal how cultural diversity functions in simulations involving, for instance, larger proportions of non-European or non-Western students. Second, integrating validated psychometric instruments, for example, cultural intelligence (CQ) scales or other quantitative measures, might triangulate self-reported growth in intercultural competence with more objective metrics. Third, future research could experiment with varying levels of instructor facilitation. Researchers might investigate whether highly structured reflection prompts yield better intercultural outcomes than a minimal-guidance approach. Finally, longitudinal studies could track students' intercultural skills beyond the course, assessing whether the collaboration patterns learned in simulation transfer to workplace or international internship settings.

As cultural intelligence becomes a critical competency for global business, educators are pressed to adopt innovative methods to cultivate it. Studies show that moving learning beyond a mono-cultural setting can markedly enhance students' cultural intelligence and overall learning experience. For example, accounting students who engaged in guided virtual collaborations with international peers saw significant improvements in all facets of their CQ, confirming the value of embedding intercultural teamwork into business education (Key et al., 2022)

The ICM experience illustrates that cultural diversity, when woven into a well-designed digital simulation, can deepen and broaden learning in ways that transcend traditional classroom paradigms. Rather than avoiding or downplaying differences, actively highlighting and reflecting upon them can stimulate critical thinking, creativity, and empathy, essential skills for thriving in globalized workplaces. The simulation's cyclical structure, with repeated decision rounds and built-in performance feedback, encourages students to confront the effects of cultural assumptions on everyday teamwork processes. This iterative process not only strengthens domain-specific abilities (finance, marketing, strategy), but also fosters nuanced intercultural awareness that classic lectures or homogenous group work seldom achieve.

In essence, cultural diversity emerges not as an optional add-on but as a fundamental element of transformative digital learning. By designing simulations that explicitly prompt students to reconcile competing worldviews, educators can mirror the complexities of real-world international collaboration. The synergy of diverse teams, once friction is addressed through conscious norm-setting and reflective dialogue, can propel learners toward innovative solutions and strong interpersonal skill development. As higher education institutions continue embracing digital transformation, the lessons from this chapter underscore the need to keep cultural responsiveness at the forefront of pedagogical design. Doing so not only prepares students for cross-border professional endeavors but also enriches the learning environment by valuing every student's cultural lens as a resource rather than a hurdle.

REFERENCES

Ahuja, V. (2024). Simulations in business education: Unlocking experiential learning. Practices and implementation of gamification in higher education, 1-21. DOI: 10.4018/979-8-3693-0716-8.ch001

Aila, A. (2024). Developing an End-to-End Scenario Simulation Tool for Strategic Decision-Making in a Large Cap OEM - Simulating Multiple Futures to Understand Business Implications of Key Strategic Variables.

Alhojailan, M. I. (2012, October). Thematic analysis: a critical review ofits process and evaluation. In *WEI international European academic conference proceedings*, Zagreb, Croatia.

Ameloot, E., Rotsaert, T., Ameloot, T., Rienties, B., & Schellens, T. (2024). Supporting students' basic psychological needs and satisfaction in a blended learning environment through learning analytics. *Computers & Education, 209*, 104949. DOI: 10.1016/j.compedu.2023.104949

Ang, S., & Van Dyne, L. (2015). *Handbook of cultural intelligence: Theory, measurement, and applications.* Routledge., DOI: 10.4324/9781315703855

Aparicio, M., Bacao, F., & Oliveira, T. (2016). Cultural impacts on e-learning systems' success. *The Internet and Higher Education, 92*, 95–110. DOI: 10.1016/j.iheduc.2016.06.003

Braun, V., & Clarke, V. (2006). Using thematic analysis in psychology. *Qualitative Research in Psychology, 3*(2), 77–101. DOI: 10.1191/1478088706qp063oa

Choi, H. M. (2024). To What Extent Does the Cultural Diversity within Organizations Impact and Contribute to Creative Problem-Solving Capabilities and Innovation? (Master's thesis, UIS).

Cramton, C. D., & Webber, S. S. (2005). Relationships among geographic dispersion, team processes, and effectiveness in software development work teams. *Journal of Business Research, 58*(6), 758–765. DOI: 10.1016/j.jbusres.2003.10.006

Creswell, J. W., & Poth, C. N. (2018). *Qualitative inquiry and research design: Choosing among five approaches* (4th ed.). SAGE.

Davidavičienė, V., & Al-Majzoub, K. (2022). The effect of cultural intelligence, conflict, and transformational leadership on decision-making processes in virtual teams. *Social Sciences (Basel, Switzerland), 11*(2), 64. DOI: 10.3390/socsci11020064

Deardorff, D. K. (2009). Implementing intercultural competence assessment. In Deardorff, D. K. (Ed.), *The Sage handbook of intercultural competence* (pp. 477–491). SAGE., DOI: 10.4135/9781071872987.n28

Deci, E. L., & Ryan, R. M. (2000). The "what" and "why" of goal pursuits: Human needs and the self-determination of behavior. *Psychological Inquiry, 11*(4), 227–268. DOI: 10.1207/S15327965PLI1104_01

Foronda, C. L., Baptiste, D.-L., Pfaff, T., Velez, R., Reinholdt, M., & Hudson, K. W. (2018). Cultural competency and cultural humility in simulation-based education: An integrative review. *Clinical Simulation in Nursing, 15*, 42–60. DOI: 10.1016/j.ecns.2017.09.006

Hall, E. T. (1976). *Beyond culture*. Doubleday.

Harzing, A.-W., & Pudelko, M. (2016). Do we need to distance ourselves from the distance concept? Why home and host country context might matter more than (cultural) distance. *MIR. Management International Review, 56*(1), 1–34. DOI: 10.1007/s11575-015-0265-4

Heutte, J., Fenouillet, F., Martin-Krumm, C., Gute, G., Raes, A., Gute, D., Bachelet, R., & Csikszentmihalyi, M. (2021). Optimal experience in adult learning: Conception and validation of the flow in education scale (EduFlow-2). *Frontiers in Psychology, 12*, 828027. Advance online publication. DOI: 10.3389/fpsyg.2021.828027 PMID: 35069401

Hofstede, G., Hofstede, G. J., & Minkov, M. (2010). *Cultures and organizations: Software of the mind* (3rd ed.). McGraw-Hill.

House, R. J., Hanges, P. J., Javidan, M., Dorfman, P. W., & Gupta, V. (Eds.). (2004). *Culture, leadership, and organizations: The GLOBE study of 62 societies*. SAGE., DOI: 10.5465/ame.2005.16965495

Howard, B., Ilyashenko, N., & Jacobs, L. (2023). Cross-cultural collaboration through virtual teaming in higher education. *Perspectives in Education, 41*(1), 74–87. DOI: 10.38140/pie.v41i1.6319

Iskhakova, M., & Ott, D. L. (2020). Working in culturally diverse teams: Team-level cultural intelligence (CQ) development and team performance. *Journal of International Education in Business, 13*(1), 37–54. DOI: 10.1108/JIEB-11-2019-0052

Jony, A. I., & Hamim, S. A. (2024). Empowering virtual collaboration: Harnessing AI for enhanced teamwork in higher education. *Educational Technology Quarterly, 2024*(3), 337–359. DOI: 10.55056/etq.746

Karlsen, E. H., & Nazar, M. (2024). How cultural diversity affects communication and collaboration within global high-performance project teams? *Procedia Computer Science, 239*, 491–497. DOI: 10.1016/j.procs.2024.06.197

Key, K., Healy, M., & Mulligan, E. (2022). Closing the cultural intelligence skills gap in accounting students: An action research approach to cross-cultural teamwork. *The British Accounting Review, 54*(6), 101034. DOI: 10.1016/j.bar.2021.101034

Kolb, D. A. (2015). *Experiential learning: Experience as the source of learning and development* (2nd ed.). Pearson.

Kourgiantakis, T., Bogo, M., & Sewell, K. M. (2019). Practice Fridays: Using simulation to develop holistic competence. *Journal of Social Work Education, 55*(3), 551–564. DOI: 10.1080/10437797.2018.1548989

Lameras, P., Arnab, S., Dunwell, I., Stewart, C., Clarke, S., & Petridis, P. (2017). Essential features of serious games design in higher education: Linking learning attributes to game mechanics. *British Journal of Educational Technology, 48*(4), 972–994. DOI: 10.1111/bjet.12467

Lauring, J., & Selmer, J. (2018). Person-environment fit and emotional control: Assigned expatriates vs. self-initiated expatriates. *International Business Review, 27*(5), 982–992. DOI: 10.1016/j.ibusrev.2018.02.010

Leask, B. (2015). *Internationalizing the curriculum*. Routledge., DOI: 10.4324/9781315716954

Lincoln, Y. S., & Guba, E. G. (1985). Naturalistic inquiry. *Sage (Atlanta, Ga.).*

Liu, X. (2025). Bridging Cultures in Virtual Workplaces: A Communication-Focused Review of Global Virtual Teams. *Business and Professional Communication Quarterly*, 23294906251327747. Advance online publication. DOI: 10.1177/23294906251327747

Machmud, M. T., Wattanachai, S., & Samat, C. (2023). Constructivist gamification environment model designing framework to improve ill-structured problem solving in learning sciences. *Educational Technology Research and Development, 71*(6), 2413–2429. DOI: 10.1007/s11423-023-10279-0

Martins, H. F. (2012). The Use of a Business Simulation Game in a Management Course. In Cruz-Cunha, M. (Ed.), *Handbook of Research on Serious Games as Educational, Business and Research Tools* (pp. 693–707). IGI Global Scientific Publishing., DOI: 10.4018/978-1-4666-0149-9.ch035

Martins, H. F. (2023). *Mastering the Game: A Reference Handbook On Business Simulations*. LABS - Information and Communication Sciences.

Martins, H. F. (2024). The Impact and Future of AI-Enhanced Teaching Methods in the Use of Business Simulations. In Ahmed, Z., Hassan, A., & Saeed, R. (Eds.), *AI-Enhanced Teaching Methods* (pp. 305–321). IGI Global Scientific Publishing., DOI: 10.4018/979-8-3693-2728-9.ch014

Nadeem, M., Oroszlanyova, M., & Farag, W. (2023). Effect of digital game-based learning on student engagement and motivation. *Computers*, *12*(9), 177. DOI: 10.3390/computers12090177

Nowell, L. S., Norris, J. M., White, D. E., & Moules, N. J. (2017). Thematic analysis: Striving to meet the trustworthiness criteria. *International Journal of Qualitative Methods*, *16*(1), 1–13. DOI: 10.1177/1609406917733847

Paulus, T., Bichelmeyer, B., Malopinsky, L., Pereira-Leon, M., & Rastogi, P. (2005). Power distance and group dynamics of an international project team: A case study. *Teaching in Higher Education*, *10*(1), 43–55. Advance online publication. DOI: 10.1080/1356251052000305525

Piaget, J. (1970). *Science of education and the psychology of the child*. Viking.

Pimentel, J., Arias, A., Ramírez, D., Molina, A., Cockcroft, A., Chomat, A. M., & Andersson, N. (2020). Game-based learning interventions to foster cross-cultural care training: A scoping review. *Games for Health Journal*, *9*(3), 1–18. DOI: 10.1089/g4h.2019.0078 PMID: 32027184

Polydorou, E. (2025). The Effect of Simulation Games in Entrepreneurship Education. In *Integrating Simulation Tools Into Entrepreneurship Education* (pp. 445–468). IGI Global Scientific Publishing., DOI: 10.4018/979-8-3693-9040-5.ch020

Ramírez Ruiz, J. J., Vargas Sanchez, A. D., & Boude Figueredo, O. R. (2024). Impact of gamification on school engagement: A systematic review. *Frontiers in Education*, *9*, 1466926. Advance online publication. DOI: 10.3389/feduc.2024.1466926

Sailer, M., & Homner, L. (2019). The gamification of learning: A meta-analysis. *Educational Psychology Review*, *31*(4), 1191–1220. DOI: 10.1007/s10648-019-09498-w

Shu, L., & Liu, M. (2019). Student engagement in game-based learning: A literature review from 2008 to 2018. *Journal of Educational Multimedia and Hypermedia*, *28*(2), 193–215. DOI: 10.3102/1442816

Sitzmann, T. (2011). A meta-analytic examination of the instructional effectiveness of computer-based simulation games. *Personnel Psychology*, *64*(2), 489–528. DOI: 10.1111/j.1744-6570.2011.01190.x

Taras, V., Steel, P., & Kirkman, B. L. (2016). Does country equate with culture? Beyond geography in the search for cultural boundaries. *MIR. Management International Review*, *56*(4), 455–487. DOI: 10.1007/s11575-016-0283-x

Tegon, R. (2024). An updated systematic review on the impact of gamification in education: Insights from early 2024. In Martínez-Roig, R., Pulido-Montes, C., & Mateu-Luján, B. (Eds.), *Nuevas investigaciones educativas para definir la enseñanza y el aprendizaje* (pp. 318–330). Octaedro.

Trompenaars, F., & Hampden-Turner, C. (2012). *Riding the waves of culture: Understanding diversity in global business* (3rd ed.). McGraw-Hill.

Wang, J., Cheng, G. H. L., Chen, T., & Leung, K. (2019). Team creativity/innovation in culturally diverse teams: A meta-analysis. *Journal of Organizational Behavior*, *40*(6), 693–708. DOI: 10.1002/job.2362

Weissker, T., Bimberg, P., & Froehlich, B. (2020). Getting there together: Group navigation in distributed virtual environments. *IEEE Transactions on Visualization and Computer Graphics*, *26*(5), 1860–1870. DOI: 10.1109/TVCG.2020.2973474 PMID: 32070981

Yang, W., & Zhong, R. (2024). Internationalization of Curriculum: Developing Cross-Cultural Competence in Teacher Education Programs through Service Learning. Eurasian Journal of Educational Research (EJER), (111).

Yin, R. K. (2018). *Case study research and applications: Design and methods* (6th ed.). SAGE.

Keywords and Definitions

Cultural Diversity:

The multiplicity of national: ethnic, linguistic, and socio-cultural backgrounds within a group of learners, which influences communication, collaboration, and leadership styles in educational contexts.

Gamified Learning:

An instructional approach incorporating elements of gameplay: such as competition, point systems, or badges, into non-game settings to enhance motivation, engagement, and skill development.

Business Simulation:

A high-fidelity: interactive learning environment that replicates real-world market and organizational conditions, allowing learners to apply theoretical concepts and make strategic decisions under authentic constraints.

Intercultural Competence:

The combination of attitudes: skills, and knowledge enabling individuals to communicate, collaborate, and resolve conflicts effectively with people from diverse cultural backgrounds.

Experiential Learning Cycle:

Kolb's model describing how learners progress through concrete experience: reflective observation, abstract conceptualization, and active experimentation to construct and refine knowledge.

High- vs. Low-Context Communication:

A continuum proposed by Edward Hall describing how some cultures rely on indirect cues and contextual understanding (high context): whereas others prioritize explicit, direct communication (low context).

Power Distance:

A cultural dimension identified by Geert Hofstede referring to how comfortably a culture or organization accepts unequal distributions of power: affecting leadership preferences and team hierarchy.

Compilation of References

Abend, G. (2023). Words and distinctions for the common good: Practical reason in the logic of social science.

Abu-Shawish, R. K., & Ghamrawi, N. (2025). Sense-making and middle leaders: Analyzing perceptions of role in the development of teacher leadership. *Management in Education*, •••, 08920206251315629. DOI: 10.1177/08920206251315629

Adelakun, N. O. (2024). Exploring the impact of artificial intelligence on information retrieval systems. *SSRN*, *4*(5), 1–5. DOI: 10.2139/ssrn.4834942

Adeleye, I. O. (2023). The AI effect: Rethinking design workflows for enhanced productivity and creativity. *International Journal of Science and Technology Innovation*, *2*(1), 1–19. DOI: 10.70560/c9m3kd97

Agrawal, A., McIntyre, B. B., Agg, C., & Zou, Y.-X. (2025). Diverse and Inclusive Learning and Working Environments. *Lecture Notes in Networks and Systems*, *1097*, 333–352. DOI: 10.1007/978-3-031-68282-7_18

Aguayo, A. J. M., & Aros, P. A. V. (2023). Financial inclusion, microfinance, and financial education in Latin America. In *Handbook of Microfinance, Financial Inclusion and Development*. Edward Elgar Publishing Ltd. DOI: 10.4337/9781789903874.00026

Ahuja, V. (2024). Simulations in business education: Unlocking experiential learning. Practices and implementation of gamification in higher education, 1-21. DOI: 10.4018/979-8-3693-0716-8.ch001

Aibar-Almazán, A., Castellote-Caballero, Y., Carcelén-Fraile, M. C., Rivas-Campo, Y., & González-Martín, A. M. (2024). Gamification in the classroom: Kahoot! as a tool for university teaching innovation. *Frontiers in Psychology*, *15*, 1370084. Advance online publication. DOI: 10.3389/fpsyg.2024.1370084 PMID: 38646120

Aidoune, Y., Nordin, N. R., Kaur, M., & Singh, P. S. (2022). Effect of online English learning game 'Kahoot' on L2 undergraduate learners in a Malaysian university. *Journal of Intercultural Communication, 22*(3), 13–18. DOI: 10.36923/jicc.v22i3.66

Aila, A. (2024). Developing an End-to-End Scenario Simulation Tool for Strategic Decision-Making in a Large Cap OEM - Simulating Multiple Futures to Understand Business Implications of Key Strategic Variables.

Akazawa, S. (2025). Women's Comprehensive Outpatient Clinic and Antiaging. In *Anti-Aging Medicine: Basics and Clinical Practice*. Springer Science+Business Media. DOI: 10.1007/978-981-97-8514-8_162

Alasadi, E. A., & Baiz, C. R. (2024). Multimodal generative artificial intelligence tackles visual problems in chemistry. *Journal of Chemical Education, 101*(7), 2716–2729. DOI: 10.1021/acs.jchemed.4c00138

Alene, A. A., Tsegaye, M. A., & Wolle, G. S. (2025). Secondary school principals' adaptive leadership practices amid the quality education crisis in Amhara regional state, Ethiopia. *Social Sciences & Humanities Open, 11*, 101349. DOI: 10.1016/j.ssaho.2025.101349

Alenezi, W. (2024). Potentiality and Apprehensions of Artificial Intelligence in Education: Perspectives of Education Staff. *International Journal of Education in Mathematics. Science and Technology, 12*(4), 942–956.

Alfawzan, N., & Christen, M. (2023). The future of FemTech ethics & privacy – a global perspective. *BMC Medical Ethics, 24*(1), 88. Advance online publication. DOI: 10.1186/s12910-023-00976-z PMID: 37891591

Alhojailan, M. I. (2012, October). Thematic analysis: a critical review ofits process and evaluation. In *WEI international European academic conference proceedings*, Zagreb, Croatia.

Ali, Z. (2020). Artificial intelligence (AI): A review of its uses in language teaching and learning. *IOP Conference Series. Materials Science and Engineering*.

Allen, K. A., Gray, D. L., Baumeister, R. F., & Leary, M. R. (2022). The need to belong: A deep dive into the origins, implications, and future of a foundational construct. *Educational Psychology Review, 34*(2), 1133–1156. DOI: 10.1007/s10648-021-09633-6

Almaktary, H. (2024). Reflections on translating poetry through ChatGPT: Insights from Arabic, English, and French. *Journal of English Studies in Arabia Felix, 4*(1), 1–12. DOI: 10.56540/jesaf.v4i1.108

Almusharraf, N. (2023). Incorporation of a game-based approach into the EFL online classrooms: Students' perceptions. *Interactive Learning Environments, 31*(7), 4440–4453. DOI: 10.1080/10494820.2021.1969953

Alsajri, A., Salman, H. A., & Steiti, A. (2024). Generative Models in Natural Language Processing: A Comparative Study of ChatGPT and Gemini. *Deleted Journal, 2024*, 134–145. DOI: 10.58496/BJAI/2024/015

Alzate, C. (2024). Learning from femtech to inform the design of healthcare technologies. In *Digital Transformation in Design: Processes and Practices*. Transcript-Verlag. DOI: 10.1515/9783839471425-008

Ameloot, E., Rotsaert, T., Ameloot, T., Rienties, B., & Schellens, T. (2024). Supporting students' basic psychological needs and satisfaction in a blended learning environment through learning analytics. *Computers & Education, 209*, 104949. DOI: 10.1016/j.compedu.2023.104949

Amo, R., Matias, S., Yamanaka, A., Tanaka, K. F., Uchida, N., & Watabe-Uchida, M. (2022). A gradual temporal shift of dopamine responses mirrors the progression of temporal difference error in machine learning. *Nature Neuroscience, 25*(8), 1082–1092. DOI: 10.1038/s41593-022-01109-2

Anane, C. (2024). Impact of a game-based tool on student engagement in a foreign language course: A three-term analysis. *Frontiers in Education, 9*, 1430729. Advance online publication. DOI: 10.3389/feduc.2024.1430729

Ang, S., & Van Dyne, L. (2015). *Handbook of cultural intelligence: Theory, measurement, and applications*. Routledge., DOI: 10.4324/9781315703855

Antony, V. N., & Huang, C. M. (2025). ID. 8: Co-creating visual stories with generative AI. *ACM Transactions on Interactive Intelligent Systems, 14*(3), 1–29. DOI: 10.1145/3672277

Aparicio, M., Bacao, F., & Oliveira, T. (2016). Cultural impacts on e-learning systems' success. *The Internet and Higher Education, 92*, 95–110. DOI: 10.1016/j.iheduc.2016.06.003

Ardila, A. D. A., & Hernández, A. H. H. (2024). Impact of the development of skills in resilience and financial education in the professional development of military personnel: To face VUCA environments. In *Organizational Management Sustainability in VUCA Contexts*. IGI Global., DOI: 10.4018/979-8-3693-0720-5.ch010

Artopoulos, A. (2023). Labyrinths of platformization of education in the Global South (and beyond). In *The new digital education policy landscape* (pp. 147–164). Routledge. DOI: 10.4324/9781003373018-11

Babazade, Y. (2024). Proverbs in Pedagogy: Their Role in Language Teaching and Cultural Transmission. *Global Spectrum of Research and Humanities*, *1*(1), 69–82. DOI: 10.69760/gsrh.0101202407

Baker-Bell, A. (2020). *Linguistic justice: Black language, literacy, identity, and pedagogy*. Routledge. DOI: 10.4324/9781315147383

Balfour, L. (2023a). FemTech: Intersectional Interventions in Women's Digital Health. In *FemTech: Intersectional Interventions in Women's Digital Health*. Springer Singapore. DOI: 10.1007/978-981-99-5605-0

Balfour, L. (2023b). Introduction: Who Is FemTech For? In *FemTech: Intersectional Interventions in Women's Digital Health*. Springer Singapore. DOI: 10.1007/978-981-99-5605-0_1

Baltzer, C., & Bonancina, S. (2023). Enhancing Women's Health: An Assessment of Data Privacy and Security of Menopause FemTech Applications. *Studies in Health Technology and Informatics*, *309*, 155–159. DOI: 10.3233/SHTI230765 PMID: 37869830

Bansal, G., Nawal, A., Chamola, V., & Herencsar, N. (2024). Revolutionizing visuals: The role of generative AI in modern image generation. *ACM Transactions on Multimedia Computing Communications and Applications*, *20*(11), 1–22. DOI: 10.1145/3689641

BECKWITH, S. L. (2024). CHAPTER TWO AI–AGENCY AND INNOVATION–. Advancing Honors Education for Today and Tomorrow, 35.

Benjamin, R. (2019). *Race after technology: Abolitionist tools for the New Jim Code*. Polity Press.

Bergreen, G. (2023). *Revolutionary Technologies: Educational Perspectives of Technology History*. Rowman & Littlefield. DOI: 10.5771/9781475870664

Bernedo-Moreira, D. H., Almirón-Cuentas, J. A., Espiritu-Martinez, A. P., Ochoa-Tataje, F. A., & Romero-Carazas, R. (2024). Financial education from elementary school, a perspective to today. *Periodicals of Engineering and Natural Sciences*, *12*(1), 123–134. DOI: 10.21533/pen.v12.i1.25

Bertão, R. A., Yeoun, M. H., & Joo, J. (2025). A blind spot in AI-powered logo makers: Visual design principles. *Visual Communication*, *24*(1), 222–250. DOI: 10.1177/14703572231155593

Bhuana, G. P. (2022). The benefits and drawbacks of Kahoot: Students' perspective. *Journal on English Language Teaching and Learning Linguistics and Literature, 10*(2), 2224–2232. DOI: 10.24256/ideas.v10i2.3508

Binagwaho, A., Bonciani Nader, H., Brown Burkins, M., Davies, A., Hessen, D. O., Mbow, C., & Tong, S. (2022). *Knowledge-driven actions: transforming higher education for global sustainability: independent expert group on the universities and the 2030 agenda.* UNESCO Publishing.

Binhammad, M. H. Y., Othman, A., Abuljadayel, L., Al Mheiri, H., Alkaabi, M., & Almarri, M. (2024). Investigating how generative AI can create personalized learning materials tailored to individual student needs. *Creative Education, 15*(7), 1499–1523. DOI: 10.4236/ce.2024.157091

Bisht, P., & Pujari, J. P. (2025). Translating Subh-e-Azadi: ChatGPT, Gemini, and the Cultural Complexity of 1947 Partition Poetry. In Al Aqad, M. (Ed.), *Role of AI in Translation and Interpretation* (pp. 267–292). IGI Global Scientific Publishing., DOI: 10.4018/979-8-3373-0060-3.ch010

Blodgett, S. L., Barocas, S., Daumé, H., III, & Wallach, H. (2020). Language (technology) is power: A critical survey of "bias" in NLP. *arXiv*. https://doi.org//arXiv.2005.14050DOI: 10.18653/v1/2020.acl-main.485

Bonde, L., & Dembele, S. (2024, August). A unified generative artificial intelligence approach for converting social media content. In *2024 International Conference on Artificial Intelligence, Big Data, Computing and Data Communication Systems (icABCD)* (pp. 1-5). IEEE. https://doi:DOI: 10.1109/icABCD62167.2024.10645267

Bono, G. (2024). Text-to-building: Experiments with AI-generated 3D geometry for building design and structure generation. *Architectural Intelligence, 3*(1), 1–24. DOI: 10.1007/s44223-024-00060-5

Boyd, C. M., & Díez-Amigo, S. (2023). Effectiveness of free financial education provided by for-profit financial institutions: Experimental evidence from rural peru. *Economics of Education Review, 97*, 102462. Advance online publication. DOI: 10.1016/j.econedurev.2023.102462

Bo, Z., & Ruihai, D. (2022). Natural language processing technology empowers the development of educational intelligence: The perspective of artificial intelligence scientists. [Educational Science Edition]. *Journal of East China Normal University, 40*(9), 19.

Braun, V., & Clarke, V. (2006). Using thematic analysis in psychology. *Qualitative Research in Psychology, 3*(2), 77–101. DOI: 10.1191/1478088706qp063oa

Bromham, L., Dinnage, R., Skirgård, H., Ritchie, A., Cardillo, M., Meakins, F., Greenhill, S., & Hua, X. (2022). Global predictors of language endangerment and the future of linguistic diversity. *Nature Ecology & Evolution, 6*(2), 163–173. DOI: 10.1038/s41559-021-01604-y PMID: 34916621

Bulathwela, S., Pérez-Ortiz, M., Holloway, C., Cukurova, M., & Shawe-Taylor, J. (2024). Artificial intelligence alone will not democratise education: On educational inequality, techno-solutionism and inclusive tools. *Sustainability (Basel), 16*(2), 781. DOI: 10.3390/su16020781

Buley, L., & Natoli, J. (2024). *The user experience team of one: A research and design survival guide*. Rosenfeld Media.

Buratti, G., & D'Ignazio, A. (2024). Improving the effectiveness of financial education programs. A targeting approach. *The Journal of Consumer Affairs, 58*(2), 451–485. DOI: 10.1111/joca.12577

Burns, M. A. R. Y. (2023). Technology in education. Paper commissioned for the.

Caires, C. S., Estadieu, G., & Olga Ng Ka Man, S. (2024). Design Thinking Methodology and Text-To-Image Artificial Intelligence: A Case Study in the Context of Furniture Design Education. In Martins, N., Brandão, D., & Fernandes-Marcos, A. (Eds.), *Perspectives on Design and Digital Communication IV* (Vol. 33, pp. 113–134). Springer Nature Switzerland., DOI: 10.1007/978-3-031-41770-2_7

Caliskan, A., Bryson, J. J., & Narayanan, A. (2017). Semantics derived automatically from language corpora contain human-like biases. *Science, 356*(6334), 183–186. DOI: 10.1126/science.aal4230 PMID: 28408601

Callegari, L. S., Mosley, E. A., Borrero, S., Talabi, M. B., Kazmerski, T. M., Donley, G., & Krishnamurti, T. (2025). Implementing digital sexual and reproductive health tools: Challenges and recommendations post-Dobbs. *Contraception*, 110969. Advance online publication. DOI: 10.1016/j.contraception.2025.110969 PMID: 40412590

Canali, S., & Hesselbein, C. (2023). Using and Interpreting FemTech Data: (Self-) Knowledge, Empowerment, and Sovereignty. In *FemTech: Intersectional Interventions in Women's Digital Health*. Springer Singapore. DOI: 10.1007/978-981-99-5605-0_13

Cannistrà, M., De Beckker, K., Agasisti, T., Amagir, A., Põder, K., Vartiak, L., & De Witte, K. (2024). The impact of an online game-based financial education course: Multi-country experimental evidence. *Journal of Comparative Economics, 52*(4), 825–847. DOI: 10.1016/j.jce.2024.08.001

Canta, C., & Leroux, M.-L. (2024). Financial education as a complement to public pensions: The case of naive individuals. *Journal of Population Economics*, *37*(4), 69. Advance online publication. DOI: 10.1007/s00148-024-01046-3

Cao, Y., Li, S., Liu, Y., Yan, Z., Dai, Y., Yu, P. S., & Sun, L. (2023). A comprehensive survey of AI-generated content (aigc): A history of generative AI from GAN to GhatGPT. *arXiv preprint arXiv:2303.04226*. https://doi.org//arXiv.2303.04226DOI: 10.48550

Carbajal-Carrera, B. (2024). AIsplaining: Generative AI explains linguistic identities to me. *Australian Review of Applied Linguistics*, *47*(3), 340–365. DOI: 10.1075/aral.24077.car

Carre-Skinner, H. (2024). The rise of FemTech and why compliance is key to its success. *Regulatory Rapporteur, 21*(2).

Casanova-Mata, I. (2023). Enhancing English acquisition: Effects of Among Us game-based gamification on language competence, motivation, attention, and attitude towards the English subject. *Education Sciences*, *13*(11), 1094. Advance online publication. DOI: 10.3390/educsci13111094

Caspari-Sadeghi, S. (2022, January). Applying learning analytics in online environments: Measuring learners' engagement unobtrusively. []). Frontiers Media SA.]. *Frontiers in Education*, *7*, 840947. DOI: 10.3389/feduc.2022.840947

Cátia Sofia, S., Silva, M. P., & Martins, M. L. (2022). The impact of Kahoot! on vocabulary acquisition in foreign language education. *Educational Research and Development Journal*, *20*(4), 142–158.

Chabaefe, N. N., & Qutieshat, A. (2024). Financial Literacy, Financial Education and Financial Experience: Conceptual Framework. *International Journal of Economics and Financial Issues*, *14*(4), 44–55. DOI: 10.32479/ijefi.15627

Channi, H. K., Kaur, A., & Kaur, S. (2025). AI-Driven Generative Design Redefines the Engineering Process. In Chelliah, P. R., Dutta, P. K., Kumar, A., Gonzalez, E. D. R. S., Mittal, M., & Gupta, S. (Eds.), *Generative Artificial Intelligence in Finance* (1st ed., pp. 327–359). Wiley., DOI: 10.1002/9781394271078.ch17

Chen, J., Wang, M., & Hsia, C.-H. (2025). *Artificial Intelligence and Machine Learning in Sensing and Image Processing* (Vol. 25). MDPI.

Chen, T. (2025). The new patriarchal digitality? Understanding gendered power dynamics through a systematic review of femtech apps in China. *Gender, Technology and Development*, *29*(2), 263–286. Advance online publication. DOI: 10.1080/09718524.2025.2503561

Chew, Y. W. (2022). Performing presence with the teaching-body via videoconferencing: A postdigital study of the teacher's face and voice. *Postdigital Science and Education, 4*(2), 394–421. DOI: 10.1007/s42438-022-00288-2 PMID: 40477497

Choi, H. M. (2024). To What Extent Does the Cultural Diversity within Organizations Impact and Contribute to Creative Problem-Solving Capabilities and Innovation? (Master's thesis, UIS).

Choi, A., Stoutland, D., & Blanco, L. (2024). An evaluation of a digital financial education program and the impact of COVID-19 on financial well-being among college students. *Journal of American College Health, 72*(9), 3690–3702. DOI: 10.1080/07448481.2023.2191142 PMID: 37084244

Chu, I.-T., & Lin, H.-H. (2024). Transformation of the imagery of Taiwan's unique cultural elements into styling design. *Innovation on Design and Culture, 3*(1), 13–21. DOI: 10.35745/idc2024v03.01.0002

Cobian, K. P., Hurtado, S., Romero, A. L., & Gutzwa, J. A. (2024). Enacting inclusive science: Culturally responsive higher education practices in science, technology, engineering, mathematics, and medicine (STEMM). *PLoS One, 19*(1), e0293953. DOI: 10.1371/journal.pone.0293953 PMID: 38232083

Cook, S., Mehrnezhad, M., & Toreini, E. (2024). Bluetooth security analysis of general and intimate health IoT devices and apps: The case of FemTech. *International Journal of Information Security, 23*(6), 3547–3567. DOI: 10.1007/s10207-024-00883-3

Cordova, J. C. (2024). Creating a Digital House of Knowledge: Ensuring the Continuation and Integrity of Indigenous Knowledge Transfers in the Digital Era (Master's thesis, University of Alaska Fairbanks).

Corso, S. (2023). ON FEMALE TECHNOLOGY OR FEMTECH. ARTIFICIAL INTELLIGENCE, WOMEN'S HEALTH AND THE WILL OF THE INDIVIDUAL; [Sulla female technology o Femtech. Intelligenza artificiale, salute della donna e volontà della persona]. *BioLaw Journal, 3*, 81 – 112. DOI: 10.15168/2284-4503-2755

Couto, R. F., Maracajá, K. F. B., & de Araújo Machado, P. (2023). Analysis of the Path of Studies on Financial Education and Sustainability. In *The Route Towards Global Sustainability: Challenges and Management Practices*. Springer International Publishing., DOI: 10.1007/978-3-031-10437-4_7

Cramton, C. D., & Webber, S. S. (2005). Relationships among geographic dispersion, team processes, and effectiveness in software development work teams. *Journal of Business Research, 58*(6), 758–765. DOI: 10.1016/j.jbusres.2003.10.006

Creswell, J. W., & Poth, C. N. (2018). *Qualitative inquiry and research design: Choosing among five approaches* (4th ed.). SAGE.

Cromack, S. C., & Walter, J. R. (2024). Consumer wearables and personal devices for tracking the fertile window. *American Journal of Obstetrics and Gynecology, 231*(5), 516–523. DOI: 10.1016/j.ajog.2024.05.028 PMID: 38768799

Cukurova, M., Miao, X., & Brooker, R. (2023). Adoption of artificial intelligence in schools: Unveiling factors influencing teachers' engagement. International conference on artificial intelligence in education.

Dahlman, S., Just, S. N., Pedersen, L. M., Lantz, P. M. V., & Kristiansen, N. W. (2023). Datafied female health Sociotechnical imaginaries of femtech in Danish public discourse. *MedieKultur, 39*(74), 105–126. DOI: 10.7146/mk.v39i74.133900

Danaher, J. (2022). Techno-optimism: An analysis, an evaluation and a modest defence. *Philosophy & Technology, 35*(2), 54. DOI: 10.1007/s13347-022-00550-2 PMID: 35378903

Davidavičienė, V., & Al-Majzoub, K. (2022). The effect of cultural intelligence, conflict, and transformational leadership on decision-making processes in virtual teams. *Social Sciences (Basel, Switzerland), 11*(2), 64. DOI: 10.3390/socsci11020064

Davis, F. D. (1989). Perceived usefulness, perceived ease of use, and user acceptance of information technology. *Management Information Systems Quarterly*, •••, 319–340.

De Bie, A., Marquis, E., Cook-Sather, A., & Luqueño, L. (2023). *Promoting equity and justice through pedagogical partnership*. Taylor & Francis.

Deardorff, D. K. (2009). Implementing intercultural competence assessment. In Deardorff, D. K. (Ed.), *The Sage handbook of intercultural competence* (pp. 477–491). SAGE., DOI: 10.4135/9781071872987.n28

Deci, E. L., & Ryan, R. M. (2000). The "what" and "why" of goal pursuits: Human needs and the self-determination of behavior. *Psychological Inquiry, 11*(4), 227–268. DOI: 10.1207/S15327965PLI1104_01

Dhadphale, T. (2024). A FRAMEWORK FOR CULTURALLY ORIENTED PRODUCT DESIGN. *Proceedings of the International Conference on Engineering and Product Design Education, EPDE 2024*, 681–686. DOI: 10.35199/EPDE.2024.115

Di Franco, G., & Santurro, M. (2021). Machine learning, artificial neural networks and social research. *Quality & Quantity, 55*(3), 1007–1025. DOI: 10.1007/s11135-020-01037-y

Dichek, N. P., Kopotun, I. M., Shevchenko, S. M., Antonets, N. B., & Pohribna, D. V. (2021). Implementation of the cross-cultural approach in the modern school. International Journal of Learning. *Teaching and Educational Research, 20*(4), 210–244.

DigitalOcean. (2025). *14 AI design tools for creative professionals*. DigitalOcean. Retrieved April 6, 2025, from https://www.digitalocean.com/resources/articles/ai-design-tools

Ding, L. (2022). Application of information technology in teaching Chinese as a second language. MATEC Web of Conferences

Djafarova, E., & Foots, S. (2022). Exploring ethical consumption of generation Z: Theory of planned behaviour. *Young Consumers, 23*(3), 413–431. DOI: 10.1108/YC-10-2021-1405

Doshi, A. V. (2024). The loss in AI translation. *ResearchGate*. https://www.researchgate.net/publication/383037053_The_Loss_in_AI_Translation

Doshi, A. R., & Hauser, O. P. (2024). Generative AI enhances individual creativity but reduces the collective diversity of novel content. *Science Advances, 10*(28), 1–17. DOI: 10.1126/sciadv.adn5290

Doudou, W., & Faizi, H. (2024). Enhancing Poetry Translation via ChatGPT 3.5: A Comparative Contrastive Study on Translated versions Qabbani's Poem Belqees & Fortune Teller by Kevin Moore [MA Dissertation, Kasdi Merbah Ouargla University]. https:// dspace. univ - ouargla. dz/ jspui/ bitstream/ 123456789/ 36859/ 1/ Enhancing %20Poetry %20Translation %20Via %20ChatGPT %203. 5. pdf

Dron, J. (2022). Educational technology: What it is and how it works. *AI & Society, 37*(1), 155–166. DOI: 10.1007/s00146-021-01195-z

Duan, H., & Zhao, W. (2024). The effects of educational artificial intelligence-powered applications on teachers' perceived autonomy, professional development for online teaching, and digital burnout. *International Review of Research in Open and Distance Learning, 25*(3), 57–76.

Duncan-Andrade, J. M. (2022). *Equality or equity: Toward a model of community-responsive education*. Harvard Education Press.

Du, Z., Wang, F., Wang, S., & Xiao, X. (2022). Enhancing Learner Participation in online discussion forums in Massive Open Online Courses: The role of mandatory participation. *Frontiers in Psychology, 13*, 819640. DOI: 10.3389/fpsyg.2022.819640 PMID: 35496232

Ebadi, S., Rasouli, R., & Mohamadi, M. (2023). Exploring EFL learners' perspectives on using Kahoot as a game-based student response system. *Interactive Learning Environments, 31*(4), 2338–2350. DOI: 10.1080/10494820.2021.1881798

Ebert, J. W., Williams, T. N., Major, A. K., Pitts, K., Yohman, D., Levit, J., & Anderson, T. (2025). University Student Organizations: Influence on Leadership Skills in the Workforce. *The Guardianship Journal, 1*(1), 3. DOI: 10.7771/3066-8468.1007

Eppard, J., Kaviani, A., Bowles, M., & Johnson, J. (2021). EdTech Culturation: Integrating a Culturally Relevant Pedagogy into Educational Technology. *Electronic Journal of e-Learning, 19*(6), 516–530. DOI: 10.34190/ejel.19.6.2065

Erbo, A., Amentie, C., & Kant, S. (2025). Does Organizational Learning Affect Organizational Performance with Innovation Practice as a Mediating Role in the Case of Ethiopia?. *International Journal of Organizational Leadership, 14.*

Espíndola, L. N., Grisolia, A. M. M., & de Oliveira, G. M. M. (2025). Digital Health – A Tool of Empowerment and Gender Equality? *Arquivos Brasileiros de Cardiologia, 121*(12), e20240739. Advance online publication. DOI: 10.36660/abc.20240739i PMID: 39813462

Estelami, H., & Estelami, N. N. (2024). The differential impact of cognitive style on the relationship between financial education and financial literacy. *Journal of Financial Services Marketing, 29*(2), 242–256. DOI: 10.1057/s41264-022-00204-6

Eva, K., Adnyani, K., Adnyana, W., & Murniasih, N. N. (2020). Teacher and students' perception on using Kahoot! for English learning. In *Proceedings of the 3rd International Conference on Innovative Research Across Disciplines (ICIRAD 2019)*. Atlantis Press.

Evurulobi, C. I., Dagunduro, A. O., & Ajuwon, O. A. (2024). Language learning technologies: A review of trends in the USA and globally. *World Journal of Advanced Research and Reviews, 23*(03), 2697–2707. DOI: 10.30574/wjarr.2024.23.3.2851

Fan, H., Chen, G., Wang, X., & Peng, Z. (2024). LessonPlanner: Assisting novice teachers to prepare pedagogy-driven lesson plans with large language models. *Proceedings of the 37th Annual ACM Symposium on User Interface Software and Technology*

Farahani, N. Z., Faubion, S., Sundsbak, J., Bethke, S., & Enayati, M. (2025). FEMTECH SOLUTIONS AND DEVICES: TECHNOLOGICAL INNOVATIONS AND THEIR IMPACT ON WOMEN'S HEALTH OUTCOMES. *Proceedings of the 2025 Design of Medical Devices Conference, DMD 2025.* DOI: 10.1115/DMD2025-1107

Faubion, S. S. (2021). Femtech and midlife women's health: Good, bad, or ugly? *Menopause (New York, N.Y.)*, *28*(4), 347–348. DOI: 10.1097/GME.0000000000001742 PMID: 33534432

FaXing, L., & Loang, O. K.FaXing. (2024). Green Investing and Financial Education: The Case of China's A-Share Market. *Studies in Systems. Decision and Control*, *223*, 29–41. DOI: 10.1007/978-3-031-51997-0_3

Feiyu, S. (2024). Employing Technologies to Apply Ethnic Motifs into Contemporary Product Design (Master's thesis).

Fishman, B., & Herrenkohl, L. R. (2022). Equitable learning. The Foundational Handbook on Improvement Research in Education, 47.

Fitas, R. (2025). Inclusive Education with AI: Supporting Special Needs and Tackling Language Barriers. arXiv preprint arXiv:2504.14120.

Flores-Camacho, F., & Gallegos-Cázares, L. (2024). Representational Pluralism in Science Education: A Point of View from the Inferential-Pragmatical Approach of Scientific Representations. *Science & Education*, •••, 1–21.

Foronda, C. L., Baptiste, D.-L., Pfaff, T., Velez, R., Reinholdt, M., & Hudson, K. W. (2018). Cultural competency and cultural humility in simulation-based education: An integrative review. *Clinical Simulation in Nursing*, *15*, 42–60. DOI: 10.1016/j.ecns.2017.09.006

Frascara, J., Gardien, P., Noël, G., Rosenberg, D., Stappers, P., & Wilde, D. (2023, November 29). Towards strengthening Methods in Design Education and Practice. *LearnXDesign 2023. LearnXDesign, 2023.* Advance online publication. DOI: 10.21606/drslxd.2024.029

Fraser-Barbour, E., Robinson, S., Gendera, S., Burton-Clark, I., Fisher, K. R., Alexander, J., & Howe, K. (2025). Shifting power to people with disability in co-designed research. *Disability & Society*, *40*(2), 259–280. DOI: 10.1080/09687599.2023.2279932

Fu, Y., Shi, K., & Xi, L. (2025). Artificial intelligence and machine learning in the preservation and innovation of intangible cultural heritage: Ethical considerations and design frameworks. *Digital Scholarship in the Humanities*, fqaf034. DOI: 10.1093/llc/fqaf034

Fu, L., Zeng, Y., & Kang, X. (2023). Bridging the urban–rural gap: A qualitative examination of perceived access, barriers, risks and opportunities of children's digital learning during the COVID-19 pandemic. *Child & Family Social Work*, *28*(4), 1023–1035. DOI: 10.1111/cfs.13045

Gajendran, T., Tucker, C., Ware, S., & Tose, H. S. (2022). Integrating Indigenous, Western and Inclusive Pedagogies for Work-Integrated Learning Partnerships in Architecture and Design Disciplines. *International Journal of Work-Integrated Learning, 23*(2), 259–277.

Gao, B., Zhang, Y., Xiang, G., & Jiang, Y. (2024). DLM: A Decoupled Learning Model for Long-tailed Polyphone Disambiguation in Mandarin. *Proceedings of the 2024 Conference of the North American Chapter of the Association for Computational Linguistics: Human Language Technologies* (Volume 1: Long Papers)

Gao, Y., Fang, W., Gao, Y., & Lin, R. (2018). Conceptual Framework and Case Study of China's Womanese scripts Used in Culture Product Design. *Journal of Arts and Humanities, 7*(3), 57. DOI: 10.18533/journal.v7i3.1363

Garcia, M. B. (2024). The paradox of artificial creativity: Challenges and opportunities of generative AI artistry. *Creativity Research Journal*, •••, 1–14. DOI: 10.1080/10400419.2024.2354622

Garrido, R., & Homa, A. I. R. (2024). Digital educational game for family financial education in primary school. *Acta Scientiae, 26*(3). Advance online publication. DOI: 10.17648/acta.scientiae.6122

Ge, J., Smyth, R. E., Searle, M., Kirkpatrick, L., Evans, R., Elder, A., & Brown, H. (2021). Perspectives from students: How to tame the chaos and harness the power of technology for learning. *Brock Education Journal, 30*(1), 74–74. DOI: 10.26522/brocked.v30i1.850

Gigerenzer, G. (2022). *How to stay smart in a smart world: Why human intelligence still beats algorithms*. MIT Press.

Gilbert, C., & Pasque, P. A. (2023). Defining culturally responsive research: Learnings and tensions in minoritized researcher perspectives. *Journal of Diversity in Higher Education*.

Goldfarb, A. (2024). Pause artificial intelligence research? Understanding AI policy challenges. *The Canadian Journal of Economics. Revue Canadienne d'Economique, 57*(2), 363–377. DOI: 10.1111/caje.12705

Gomes, M., Provaggi, E., Pembe, A. B., Olaitan, A., & Gentry-Maharaj, A. (2025). Advancing Cervical Cancer Prevention Equity: Innovations in Self-Sampling and Digital Health Technologies Across Healthcare Settings. *Diagnostics (Basel), 15*(9), 1176. Advance online publication. DOI: 10.3390/diagnostics15091176 PMID: 40361993

González, E. L. M. (2023). Factors that influence the financial education of young people in Celaya, Guanajuato, México [Factores que influyen en la educación financiera de los jóvenes de Celaya, Guanajuato, México]. *Revista Mexicana de Economia y Finanzas Nueva Epoca, 18*(3). Advance online publication. DOI: 10.21919/v18i3.890

Goodfellow, I. J., Pouget-Abadie, J., Mirza, M., Xu, B., Warde-Farley, D., Ozair, S., & Bengio, Y. (2014). Generative adversarial nets. *Advances in Neural Information Processing Systems, 27*, 2672–2680.

Gordon-Tapiero, A., Wood, A., & Ligett, K. (2022, November). The case for establishing a collective perspective to address the harms of platform personalization. In *Proceedings of the 2022 Symposium on Computer Science and Law* (pp. 119-130). DOI: 10.1145/3511265.3550450

Gorton, I. (2022). *Foundations of scalable systems*. O'Reilly Media, Inc.

Gove, D., Nielsen, T. R., Smits, C., Plejert, C., Rauf, M. A., Parveen, S., Jaakson, S., Golan-Shemesh, D., Lahav, D., Kaur, R., Herz, M. K., Monsees, J., Thyrian, J. R., & Georges, J. (2021). The challenges of achieving timely diagnosis and culturally appropriate care of people with dementia from minority ethnic groups in Europe. *International Journal of Geriatric Psychiatry, 36*(12), 1823–1828. DOI: 10.1002/gps.5614

Grill, G. (2022). Constructing Certainty in Machine Learning: On the performativity of testing and its hold on the future.

Grimme, S., Spoerl, S. M., Jung, F., & Koelle, M. (2025). Hidden in Plain Sight: a Structured Analysis of Privacy Policies in the Context of Body-worn "FemTech" Technologies. *Conference on Human Factors in Computing Systems - Proceedings*. DOI: 10.1145/3706598.3713702

Guo, C., Lu, Y., Dou, Y., & Wang, F. Y. (2023). Can ChatGPT boost artistic creation: The need of imaginative intelligence for parallel art. *IEEE/CAA Journal of Automatica Sinica, 10*(4), 835-838. https://doi:.DOI: 10.1109/JAS.2023.123555

Gupta, R., Srivastava, D., Sahu, M., Tiwari, S., Ambasta, R. K., & Kumar, P. (2021). Artificial intelligence to deep learning: Machine intelligence approach for drug discovery. *Molecular Diversity, 25*(3), 1315–1360. DOI: 10.1007/s11030-021-10217-3 PMID: 33844136

Gwin, R. W. (2021). *Investigating Cultural Values and Educational Technology Adoption in Central Asia: A Case Study*. Boise State University. DOI: 10.18122/td/1883/boisestate

Hajkova, A., & Doyle, T. A. (2024). Hacking the Cycle: Femtech, Internalized Surveillance, and Productivity. *Philosophy & Technology, 37*(4), 123. Advance online publication. DOI: 10.1007/s13347-024-00801-4

Hall, E. T. (1976). *Beyond culture*. Doubleday.

Han, B. A., Varshney, K. R., LaDeau, S., Subramaniam, A., Weathers, K. C., & Zwart, J. (2023). A synergistic future for AI and ecology. *Proceedings of the National Academy of Sciences of the United States of America, 120*(38), e2220283120. DOI: 10.1073/pnas.2220283120 PMID: 37695904

Hang, N. T. (2024). The Role of Adoption, Ease of Use and Teachers' Experience of Artificial Intelligence on Teaching Effectiveness: Moderating Role of Student Interest. *Journal of Pedagogical Research, 8*(4), 16–29.

Harsch, C., Mueller-Karabil, A., & Buchminskaia, E. (2021). Addressing the challenges of interaction in online language courses. *System, 103*, 102673. DOI: 10.1016/j.system.2021.102673

Harvey, M., & Urban, C. (2023). Does financial education affect retirement savings? *The Journal of the Economics of Ageing, 24*, 100446. Advance online publication. DOI: 10.1016/j.jeoa.2023.100446

Harzing, A.-W., & Pudelko, M. (2016). Do we need to distance ourselves from the distance concept? Why home and host country context might matter more than (cultural) distance. *MIR. Management International Review, 56*(1), 1–34. DOI: 10.1007/s11575-015-0265-4

Hashinaga, M. (2023). Financial education and financial behavior. In *A Research Agenda for Consumer Financial Behavior*. Edward Elgar Publishing Ltd., DOI: 10.4337/9781803922652.00011

Hattie, K. (2021). Building a language of learning: The harvest home learner. *Connect*, (248), 7–10.

Hendl, T., & Jansky, B. (2022). Tales of self-empowerment through digital health technologies: A closer look at 'Femtech.'. *Review of Social Economy, 80*(1), 29–57. DOI: 10.1080/00346764.2021.2018027

He, R., Cao, J., & Tan, T. (2025). Generative artificial intelligence: A historical perspective. *National Science Review, 12*(5), nwaf050. Advance online publication. DOI: 10.1093/nsr/nwaf050 PMID: 40191253

Hersh, W. (2024). Search still matters: Information retrieval in the era of generative AI. *Journal of the American Medical Informatics Association : JAMIA*, *31*(9), 2159–2161. DOI: 10.1093/jamia/ocae014

Heutte, J., Fenouillet, F., Martin-Krumm, C., Gute, G., Raes, A., Gute, D., Bachelet, R., & Csikszentmihalyi, M. (2021). Optimal experience in adult learning: Conception and validation of the flow in education scale (EduFlow-2). *Frontiers in Psychology*, *12*, 828027. Advance online publication. DOI: 10.3389/fpsyg.2021.828027 PMID: 35069401

Hishamudin, M. Z., Kamarudin, N. S., Hadi, N. A., & Ahmad, A. (2025). Intention to Use Digital Platforms for Islamic Financial Education in Malaysia: Structural Equation Model. *Journal of Advanced Research in Applied Sciences and Engineering Technology*, *49*(1), 298–311. DOI: 10.37934/araset.49.1.298311

Hod, M., Divakar, H., Kihara, A. B., & Geary, M. (2023). The femtech revolution—A new approach to pregnancy management: Digital transformation of maternity care—The hybrid e-health perinatal clinic addressing the unmet needs of low- and middle-income countries. *International Journal of Gynaecology and Obstetrics: the Official Organ of the International Federation of Gynaecology and Obstetrics*, *163*(1), 4–10. DOI: 10.1002/ijgo.15032 PMID: 37554042

Hofmann, D. (2024). FemTech: Empowering reproductive rights or FEM-TRAP for surveillance? *Medical Law Review*, *32*(4), 468–485. DOI: 10.1093/medlaw/fwae035 PMID: 39361867

Hofstede, G., Hofstede, G. J., & Minkov, M. (2010). *Cultures and organizations: Software of the mind* (3rd ed.). McGraw-Hill.

Hogue, M. S., & Bell, D. P. (2022). Interreligious Resilience.

Holmes, W., Bialik, M., & Fadel, C. (2019). *Artificial intelligence in education promises and implications for teaching and learning*. Center for Curriculum Redesign.

Holstein, K., & Doroudi, S. (2021). Equity and artificial intelligence in education: will" aied" amplify or alleviate inequities in education? arXiv preprint arXiv:2104.12920.

House, R. J., Hanges, P. J., Javidan, M., Dorfman, P. W., & Gupta, V. (Eds.). (2004). *Culture, leadership, and organizations: The GLOBE study of 62 societies*. SAGE., DOI: 10.5465/ame.2005.16965495

Howard, B., Ilyashenko, N., & Jacobs, L. (2023). Cross-cultural collaboration through virtual teaming in higher education. *Perspectives in Education*, *41*(1), 74–87. DOI: 10.38140/pie.v41i1.6319

Howes-Mischel, R., & Tracy, M. (2025). Interembodiment beyond kin: Leveraging partibility within microbial FemTech. *Social Science & Medicine, 376*, 117742. Advance online publication. DOI: 10.1016/j.socscimed.2025.117742 PMID: 40279782

Hsu, C.-H., Lin, C.-L., & Lin, R. (2011). A Study of Framework and Process Development for Cultural Product Design. In Rau, P. L. P. (Ed.), *Internationalization, Design and Global Development* (Vol. 6775, pp. 55–64). Springer Berlin Heidelberg., DOI: 10.1007/978-3-642-21660-2_7

Huang, S. (2020). Research on the application of artificial intelligence in teaching Chinese as a foreign language. *2020 International Conference on Social Sciences and Big Data Application (ICSSBDA 2020)*

Huang, Y., Lv, S., Tseng, K. K., Tseng, P. J., Xie, X., & Lin, R. F. Y. (2023). Recent advances in artificial intelligence for video production system. *Enterprise Information Systems, 17*(11), 2246188. DOI: 10.1080/17517575.2023.2246188

Iannotta, G., Cannistrà, M., & Agasisti, T. (2024). It's never too late to be financially literate: Evaluating a financial education intervention for adults in Italy. *The Journal of Consumer Affairs, 58*(2), 397–431. DOI: 10.1111/joca.12592

Ingham, M. (2021). *Agents*. Agency, & Agencies in Assembling Liminal Learning Spaces.

Işık, V. (2024). Exploring artistic frontiers in the era of artificial intelligence. *Sanat ve Tasarım Dergisi, 14*(2), 577–603. DOI: 10.20488/sanattasarim.1603119

Iskhakova, M., & Ott, D. L. (2020). Working in culturally diverse teams: Team-level cultural intelligence (CQ) development and team performance. *Journal of International Education in Business, 13*(1), 37–54. DOI: 10.1108/JIEB-11-2019-0052

Jafarov, S. (2024). Internationalisation and Cultural Aspects of Online Learning, Training, and Research. *Pakistan Journal of Life and Social Sciences, 22*(2), 6437–6452. DOI: 10.57239/PJLSS-2024-22.2.00486

Jain, T., & Mudliar, P. (2024). Platforming PCOS Treatment Online: FemTech Logics of Care. *Conference on Human Factors in Computing Systems - Proceedings*. DOI: 10.1145/3613904.3642882

Jariwala, H. V. (2023). Do financial education workshops enhance parent–adolescent communication about money? *Managerial Finance, 49*(5), 829–846. DOI: 10.1108/MF-09-2021-0469

Jaton, F. (2021). *The constitution of algorithms: Ground-truthing, programming, formulating*. MIT Press. DOI: 10.7551/mitpress/12517.001.0001

Jayanthi, K., Priya, M. S., Saranya, S., Gomathi, R., & Sam, D. (2023). E-Learning as a Desirable Form of Education in the Era of Society 5.0. In *Advances in Distance Learning in Times of Pandemic* (pp. 23–51). Chapman and Hall/CRC. DOI: 10.1201/9781003322252-2

Jeswani, N., Jain, N., Sharma, A., & Roychowdhury, S. (2023). Comprehensive Fem-Tech Solution for Feminine Health. *Proceedings of 2023 International Conference on Signal Processing, Computation, Electronics, Power and Telecommunication, IConSCEPT 2023*. DOI: 10.1109/IConSCEPT57958.2023.10170571

Jia, K., Kang, R., Wang, Y., Ma, L., & Liu, X. (2025). Constructing an empathy education system: Values, principles, and approaches. *Journal of Moral Education*, •••, 1–29.

Jin, J., Yang, M., Hu, H., Guo, X., Luo, J., & Liu, Y. (2025). Empowering design innovation using AI-generated content. *Journal of Engineering Design*, *36*(1), 1–18. DOI: 10.1080/09544828.2024.2401751

Jio, W., Kant, S., & Lemi, K. (2025). Ethical Leadership: Effect on Future of Organizational Citizenship Behavior by Mediation of Organizational Culture in Ethiopia. In *Generation Alpha and Next Generation Leadership for Greener Futures* (pp. 41-62). IGI Global Scientific Publishing.

Jio, W., Kant, S., & Lemi, K. (2025). The Influence of Ethical Leadership on Organizational Citizenship Behavior by the Mediating Role of Organizational Commitment in Ethiopia. In *Humanizing the Hyperconnected Workplace* (pp. 221–248). IGI Global Scientific Publishing. DOI: 10.4018/979-8-3693-8171-7.ch008

Jonker, N., & Kosse, A. (2022). The interplay of financial education, financial inclusion and financial stability and the role of Big Tech. *Contemporary Economic Policy*, *40*(4), 612–635. DOI: 10.1111/coep.12578

Jony, A. I., & Hamim, S. A. (2024). Empowering virtual collaboration: Harnessing AI for enhanced teamwork in higher education. *Educational Technology Quarterly*, *2024*(3), 337–359. DOI: 10.55056/etq.746

Kahila, J., Vartiainen, H., Tedre, M., Arkko, E., Lin, A., Pope, N., Jormanainen, I., & Valtonen, T. (2024). Pedagogical framework for cultivating children's data agency and creative abilities in the age of AI. *Informatics in Education*, *23*(2), 323–360. DOI: 10.15388/infedu.2024.15

Kaiser, T., Lusardi, A., Menkhoff, L., & Urban, C. (2022). Financial education affects financial knowledge and downstream behaviors. *Journal of Financial Economics*, *145*(2), 255–272. DOI: 10.1016/j.jfineco.2021.09.022

Kalantzis, M., & Cope, B. (2025). Literacy in the time of Artificial Intelligence. *Reading Research Quarterly*, *60*(1), e591. DOI: 10.1002/rrq.591

Kalleny, N. K. (2020). Advantages of Kahoot! game-based formative assessments along with methods of its use and application during the COVID-19 pandemic in various live learning sessions. *Journal of Microscopy and Ultrastructure*, *8*(4), 175–185. DOI: 10.4103/JMAU.JMAU_61_20 PMID: 33623744

Kalota, F. (2024). A primer on generative artificial intelligence. *Education Sciences*, *14*(2), 172. DOI: 10.3390/educsci14020172

Kamalov, F., Santandreu Calonge, D., & Gurrib, I. (2023). New era of artificial intelligence in education: Towards a sustainable multifaceted revolution. *Sustainability (Basel)*, *15*(16), 12451. DOI: 10.3390/su151612451

Kang, S. H. K., Eglington, L. G., Schuetze, B. A., Lu, X., Hinterstoisser, T. M., & Huaco, J. (2023). Using Cognitive Science and Technology to Enhance Financial Education: The Effect of Spaced Retrieval Practice. *Financial Counseling and Planning*, *34*(1), 20–31. DOI: 10.1891/JFCP-2021-0032

KANİ, Z. G. (2021). How (un) critically oriented is english language teaching?: Perspectives from the turkish efl context1. Research & reviews in educational sciences, 87.

Kant, S., Adula, M., Debebe, T. S., & Kumari, M. (2025). Managerial Motivation Effect on Employee Share Ownership With Mediation of Corporate Governance in Ethiopia. In *Organizational Models, Cultural Dynamics, and CSR Applications in Employee-Owned Enterprises* (pp. 119-146). IGI Global Scientific Publishing. DOI: 10.4018/979-8-3373-1762-5.ch005

Kant, S., Toma, F., Niguse, T., & Adula, M. (2025). Transnational Higher Education Landscape Effect on Building a Global Vision for Staff Development by Navigating Cultural Diversity in Africa. In *Training and Development in Transnational Higher Education* (pp. 1–20). IGI Global Scientific Publishing. DOI: 10.4018/979-8-3373-1897-4.ch001

Karakas, A. (2023). Breaking down barriers with artificial intelligence (AI): cross-cultural communication in foreign language education. In *Transforming the language teaching experience in the age of AI* (pp. 215–233). IGI Global.

Karlsen, E. H., & Nazar, M. (2024). How cultural diversity affects communication and collaboration within global high-performance project teams? *Procedia Computer Science*, *239*, 491–497. DOI: 10.1016/j.procs.2024.06.197

Kaur, G. (2020). Enhancing classroom engagement with Kahoot! in language education. *Asian Journal of Educational Technology*, *5*(1), 34–47.

Kaur, P., & Nadarajan, R. (2020). Language learning and teaching using Kahoot! *International Journal of Medical Education*, *2*(5), 19–28. DOI: 10.35631/IJMOE.25003

Kayyali, M. (2025 a). AI and Gamification: Engaging EFL Learners With Language Games. In Application of AI in the Teaching and Learning of English as a Foreign Language (EFL) (pp. 33-64). IGI Global Scientific Publishing.

Kayyali, M. (2025 b). Impact of AI on Student Learning Outcomes: Measuring Success and Identifying Challenges. In Transforming Education With AI-Powered Personalized Learning (pp. 81-122). IGI Global Scientific Publishing.

Kayyali, M. (2025 c). Classroom Management: Techniques for Creating a Positive, Friendly Learning Environment. In Exploration of K-12 Teaching and Learning for Teacher Educators (pp. 53-78). IGI Global Scientific Publishing.

Kayyali, M. (2025 d). Ethical Implications of Generative AI in Education: Privacy, Bias, and Integrity. In Transformative AI Practices for Personalized Learning Strategies (pp. 185-218). IGI Global Scientific Publishing.

Kayyali, M. (2025a). E-Learning Platforms and Their Influence on Lifelong Learning. In Impact of Digitalization on Education and Social Sustainability (pp. 155-176). IGI Global.

Kayyali, M. (2025b). Digital Literacy for Sustainability: Preparing Students for the AI-Driven World. In Rethinking the Pedagogy of Sustainable Development in the AI Era (pp. 197-224). IGI Global Scientific Publishing.

Kayyali, M. (2026 a). Strategies for Engaging Generation Z Students in Higher Education. In Developing Student Engagement Opportunities in Higher Education (pp. 199-230). IGI Global Scientific Publishing.

Kayyali, M. (2026 b). AI in Higher Education: The Risk of Excluding Vulnerable Learners. In AI and New Forms of Exclusion (pp. 57-82). IGI Global Scientific Publishing.

Kayyali, M. (2026a). Online and Blended Learning in Doctoral Studies: Opportunities and Challenges. Improving Doctoral Education and Research Development for Sustainability, 103-138.

Kayyali, M. (2026a). The Role of Digital Platforms in Shaping Competitive Intelligence Strategies. In Competitive Intelligence in the Digital Age: Strategies for Business and Technology Leadership (pp. 241-264). IGI Global Scientific Publishing.

Kayyali, M. (2026b). The Digital Transformation of Education: Opportunities and Challenges for Communication. Effects of Education Communication in Digital Learning Environments, 433-472.

Kayyali, M. (2026b). The Role of Digital Platforms in Shaping Competitive Intelligence Strategies. In Competitive Intelligence in the Digital Age: Strategies for Business and Technology Leadership (pp. 241-264). IGI Global Scientific Publishing.

Kayyali, M. (2026c). The Digital Transformation of Education: Opportunities and Challenges for Communication. Effects of Education Communication in Digital Learning Environments, 433-472.

Kayyali, M. (Ed.). (2024b). Building Resiliency in Higher Education: Globalization, Digital Skills, and Student Wellness: Globalization, Digital Skills, and Student Wellness. IGI Global.

Kayyali, M. (2022). Equity, Equality, Diversity, and Inclusion as Key Performance Indicators in Higher Education. *Online Submission*, *3*(5), 1–3.

Kayyali, M. (2024). Digital literacy in higher education: Preparing students for the workforce of the future. *International Journal of Information Science and Computing*, *11*(1). Advance online publication. DOI: 10.30954/2348-7437.1.2024.6

Kayyali, M. (2024a). Quality Assurance in Online and Blended Learning Environments. In *Quality Assurance and Accreditation in Higher Education: Issues, Models, and Best Practices* (pp. 227–292). Springer Nature Switzerland. DOI: 10.1007/978-3-031-66623-0_5

Kayyali, M. (2026 c). Case Studies of E-Learning Programs Focused on Sustainability. In *Harnessing E-Learning to Create a Sustainable Future* (pp. 1–22). IGI Global Scientific Publishing.

Kelly, B. G., Junchaya, O., Min, J., & Burdan, M. (2025). Safeguarding autonomy: Examining the complexities and implications of under-regulated period-tracking apps and paired devices in a post-Roe landscape. *Contraception*, 110981. Advance online publication. DOI: 10.1016/j.contraception.2025.110981 PMID: 40513932

Key, K., Healy, M., & Mulligan, E. (2022). Closing the cultural intelligence skills gap in accounting students: An action research approach to cross-cultural teamwork. *The British Accounting Review*, *54*(6), 101034. DOI: 10.1016/j.bar.2021.101034

Khan, K. L., & Azhar, F. (2023). FemTech and Taboo Topics: Raaji as a Tool for Educating Women in Pakistan. In *FemTech: Intersectional Interventions in Women's Digital Health*. Springer Singapore. DOI: 10.1007/978-981-99-5605-0_9

Khan, N. (2025). Deep acting attraction: Predation, masculinity and erotic labour in algorithmic romance. *New Media & Society*, •••, 14614448251336419. DOI: 10.1177/14614448251336419

Khan, S. (2024). *Brave New Words: How AI Will Revolutionize Education (and why That's a Good Thing)*. Penguin.

Khanuja, S., Ramamoorthy, S., Song, Y., & Neubig, G. (2024). An image speaks a thousand words, but can everyone listen? On image transcreation for cultural relevance. arXiv preprint arXiv:2404.01247. DOI: 10.18653/v1/2024.emnlp-main.573

Kılınç, A. Ç., & Özdemir, N. (2025). Does distributed leadership matter for student achievement? Evidence from a centralised education system. *Educational Studies*, *51*(1), 1–21. DOI: 10.1080/03055698.2022.2117543

Kim, D., & Li, M. (2021). Digital storytelling: Facilitating learning and identity development. *Journal of Computers in Education*, *8*(1), 33–61. DOI: 10.1007/s40692-020-00170-9

Kim, G., & Spear, S. J. (2023). *Wiring the winning organization: liberating our collective greatness through slowification, simplification, and amplification*. IT Revolution.

Köbis, N., & Mossink, L. D. (2020). Artificial intelligence versus Maya Angelou: Experimental evidence that people cannot differentiate AI-generated from human-written poetry. *PLoS One*, *15*(12), e0243863. DOI: 10.1016/j.chb.2020.106553 PMID: 33320864

Koehl, S. (2025). Designing AI Software for Large Classroom Engagement (Doctoral dissertation).

Kolb, D. A. (2015). *Experiential learning: Experience as the source of learning and development* (2nd ed.). Pearson.

Kölemen, E. B., & Yıldırım, B. (2025). A new era in early childhood education (ECE): Teachers' opinions on the application of artificial intelligence. *Education and Information Technologies*, *30*(12), 1–42. DOI: 10.1007/s10639-025-13478-9

Koole, M., Smith, M., Traxler, J., Adam, T., & Footring, S. (2024). Decolonising educational technology. *Education Sciences*, *14*(10), 1070. DOI: 10.3390/educsci14101070

Korinek, A. (2024). *Generative AI for economic research: LLMs learn to collaborate and reason (No. w33198)*. National Bureau of Economic Research. DOI: 10.3386/w33198

Kourgiantakis, T., Bogo, M., & Sewell, K. M. (2019). Practice Fridays: Using simulation to develop holistic competence. *Journal of Social Work Education, 55*(3), 551–564. DOI: 10.1080/10437797.2018.1548989

Kovács, L., & Terták, E. (2024). Thematic review of financial education and financial literacy in the digital age. *Acta Oeconomica, 74*(4), 483–506. DOI: 10.1556/032.2024.00023

Krishnamurti, T., Talabi, M. B., Callegari, L. S., Kazmerski, T. M., & Borrero, S. (2022). A Framework for Femtech: Guiding Principles for Developing Digital Reproductive Health Tools in the United States. *Journal of Medical Internet Research, 24*(4), e36338. Advance online publication. DOI: 10.2196/36338 PMID: 35482371

Kukreti, M., Sehajpal, S., Tiwari, R., & Sood, K. (2024). Driving global health and sustainable development goals with smart technology. In *Driving Global Health and Sustainable Development Goals With Smart Technology*. IGI Global., DOI: 10.4018/979-8-3373-0240-9

Kumar, V., & Tissenbaum, M. (2022). Supporting collaborative classroom networks through technology: An actor network theory approach to understanding social behaviours and design. *British Journal of Educational Technology, 53*(6), 1549–1570. DOI: 10.1111/bjet.13274

Lachney, M., Bennett, A. G., Eglash, R., Yadav, A., & Moudgalya, S. (2021). Teaching in an open village: A case study on culturally responsive computing in compulsory education. *Computer Science Education, 31*(4), 462–488. DOI: 10.1080/08993408.2021.1874228

Lai, Y., Chen, H.-J., & Yang, C. (2023). *Exploring the Impact of Generative Artificial Intelligence on the Design Process: Opportunities, Challenges, and Insights* (9). AHFE 2023 Hawaii Edition. DOI: 10.54941/ahfe1004178

Lameras, P., Arnab, S., Dunwell, I., Stewart, C., Clarke, S., & Petridis, P. (2017). Essential features of serious games design in higher education: Linking learning attributes to game mechanics. *British Journal of Educational Technology, 48*(4), 972–994. DOI: 10.1111/bjet.12467

Lanzing, M. (2025). Our Bodies, Our Data, Our Choices: The Value of Privacy for Female* Self- Determination in a Post- Roe Era. In *Beyond Privacy: People, Practices, Politics*. Bristol University Press., DOI: 10.2307/jj.12348234.7

Lauring, J., & Selmer, J. (2018). Person-environment fit and emotional control: Assigned expatriates vs. self-initiated expatriates. *International Business Review, 27*(5), 982–992. DOI: 10.1016/j.ibusrev.2018.02.010

Leask, B. (2015). *Internationalizing the curriculum.* Routledge., DOI: 10.4324/9781315716954

LeCun, Y., Bengio, Y., & Hinton, G. (2015). Deep learning. *nature, 521*(7553), 436-444. https://doi.org/DOI: 10.1038/nature14539

Lee, S. J., & Kwon, K. (2024). A systematic review of AI education in K-12 classrooms from 2018 to 2023: Topics, strategies, and learning outcomes. *Computers and Education: Artificial Intelligence, 6*, 100211. DOI: 10.1016/j.caeai.2024.100211

Lee, S. Y., Law, M., & Hoffman, G. (2025). When and how to use AI in the design process? Implications for human-AI design collaboration. *International Journal of Human-Computer Interaction, 41*(2), 1569–1584. DOI: 10.1080/10447318.2024.2353451

Lemi, K., Kant, S., & Jio, W. (2025). Greener Hospital Future in the Horn of Africa by Transactional Leadership: Outcome on Altruism Through Adaptability. In *Generation Alpha and Next Generation Leadership for Greener Futures* (pp. 1-22). IGI Global Scientific Publishing.

Li, M., Yu, Y., Yang, Y., Ren, G., & Wang, J. (2023). Stroke extraction of Chinese character based on deep structure deformable image registration. *Proceedings of the AAAI Conference on Artificial Intelligence*

Lim, S. (2023). Junior high school teachers' perspectives on integrating computers in lessons. *JALT Post Conference Publication, 2022*(1), 1. DOI: 10.37546/JALTPCP2022-03

Lincoln, Y. S., & Guba, E. G. (1985). Naturalistic inquiry. *Sage (Atlanta, Ga.).*

Lin, R.-T. (2007). *Transforming Taiwan Aboriginal Cultural Features into Modern Product Design:* Moalosi, R., Popovic, V., & Hickling-Hudson, A. (2010). Culture-orientated product design. *International Journal of Technology and Design Education, 20*(2), 175–190. DOI: 10.1007/s10798-008-9069-1

Litterscheidt, R., & Streich, D. J. (2020). Financial education and digital asset management: What's in the black box? *Journal of Behavioral and Experimental Economics, 87*, 101573. Advance online publication. DOI: 10.1016/j.socec.2020.101573

Liu, Q., Zhou, Y., Huang, J., & Li, G. (2024). When ChatGPT is gone: Creativity reverts and homogeneity persists. *arXiv preprint arXiv:2401.06816.*

Liu, X. (2025). Bridging Cultures in Virtual Workplaces: A Communication-Focused Review of Global Virtual Teams. *Business and Professional Communication Quarterly*, 23294906251327747. Advance online publication. DOI: 10.1177/23294906251327747

Li, Y. (2024). Application and Effectiveness Evaluation of Artificial Intelligence Technology in the Guangdong-Hong Kong-Macao. *International Conference on Artificial Intelligence and Communication Technology*

Li, Y., Chen, H., Yu, P., & Yang, L. (2025). A review of artificial intelligence in enhancing architectural design efficiency. *Applied Sciences (Basel, Switzerland)*, *15*(3), 1476. DOI: 10.3390/app15031476

Li, Y., Zhou, X., & Chiu, T. K. (2024). Systematics review on artificial intelligence chatbots and ChatGPT for language learning and research from self-determination theory (SDT): What are the roles of teachers? *Interactive Learning Environments*, •••, 1–15. DOI: 10.1609/aaai.v37i1.25220

Li, Z. (2020). The Application of Intelligent Technology in Chinese Language Teaching. *Innovative Computing*, *IC*, 2020.

Loewen, S., Isbell, D. R., & Sporn, Z. (2020). The effectiveness of app-based language instruction for developing receptive linguistic knowledge and oral communicative ability. *Foreign Language Annals*, *53*(2), 209–233.

Lopez-Agudo, L. A., & Marcenaro-Gutierrez, O. D. (2023). Financial Education in Secondary Education: A Cross-Country Analysis. *CESifo Economic Studies*, *69*(1), 21–60. DOI: 10.1093/cesifo/ifad002

Lorde, A. (1984). *Sister outsider: Essays and speeches.* Crossing Press.

Low, D. H., & Yamat, H. (2022). The use of Kahoot and its role in improving irregular verbs learning among primary ESL learners. *International Journal of Academic Research in Progressive Education and Development*, *11*(2). Advance online publication. DOI: 10.6007/IJARPED/v11-i2/13358

Lu, A. J., Marcu, G., Ackerman, M. S., & Dillahunt, T. R. (2021, June). Coding bias in the use of behavior management technologies: Uncovering socio-technical consequences of data-driven surveillance in classrooms. In *Proceedings of the 2021 ACM Designing Interactive Systems Conference* (pp. 508-522). DOI: 10.1145/3461778.3462084

Luckin, R., & Holmes, W. (2016). Intelligence unleashed: An argument for AI in education.

Luckin, R., Cukurova, M., Kent, C., & Du Boulay, B. (2022). Empowering educators to be AI-ready. *Computers and Education: Artificial Intelligence*, *3*, 100076.

Lukan, E. (2025). *The 50 best AI tools for 2025*. Synthesia. Retrieved April 6, 2025, from https://www.synthesia.io/post/ai-tools

Lu, S. H., & Chen, C. C. (2025). Principals' distributed leadership and the effectiveness of school innovation management: The mediating role of school organisational culture. *Journal of Educational Administration*, *63*(2), 129–143. DOI: 10.1108/JEA-04-2024-0109

Luzón, M. J., & Pérez-Llantada, C. (2022). Digital genres in academic knowledge production and communication: Perspectives and practices.

Lyu, J. J.-C. (2024). The New Horizon of Financial Education. *Review of Pacific Basin Financial Markets and Policies*, *27*(3), 2450024. Advance online publication. DOI: 10.1142/S0219091524500243

Ma, B. (2024). The Impact of Artificial Intelligence Tools on Bilingual Students in US Education: A Study on Academic Language-learning, Cultural Sensitivity and Inclusiveness (Master's thesis, University of Washington).

Machmud, M. T., Wattanachai, S., & Samat, C. (2023). Constructivist gamification environment model designing framework to improve ill-structured problem solving in learning sciences. *Educational Technology Research and Development*, *71*(6), 2413–2429. DOI: 10.1007/s11423-023-10279-0

Machuca-Vílchez, J. A., Ramos-Cavero, M. J., & Cordova-Buiza, F. (2023). Knowledge management in financial education in Peruvian government programs focused on women: Progress and challenges. *Knowledge and Performance Management*, *7*(1), 1–14. DOI: 10.21511/kpm.07(1).2023.01

Madsen, T. (2022). Autonomy, Economy, and Colony: Practicing Human Identity in a State of Algorithmic Transition. Western Tributaries, 8.

Mahat, D. (2023). Technology Adoption and Teaching performance:"A Moderating Role for Age". *International Journal of Contemporary Sciences*, *1*(1), 45–58.

Malik, S., Singh, K. N., & Ehigiamusoe, G. (2024). Fintech for MSME and the Role of Financial Education for MSMEs in Optimizing their Return as Investors. In *Applications of Artificial Intelligence in Business and Finance 5.0*. Apple Academic Press. DOI: 10.1201/9781003535133-9

Maman, D., & Rosenhek, Z. (2023). Governing individuals' imaginaries and conduct in personal finance: The mobilization of emotions in financial education. *Journal of Consumer Culture, 23*(1), 188–208. DOI: 10.1177/14695405211069952

Mansour, S. (2023). Intelligent graphic design: The effectiveness of Midjourney as a participant in a creative brainstorming session. *International Design Journal, 13*(5), 501–512. DOI: 10.21608/idj.2023.231684.1090

Manuel, M., Gottlieb, J., Svarovsky, G., & Hite, R. (2022). The intersection of culturally responsive pedagogy and engineering design in secondary STEM. Journal of Pre-College Engineering Education Research (J-PEER), 12(2), 11.

Marandi, S. S. (2024). Virtual supremacy and electronic imperialism: The hegemonies of e-learning and computer assisted language learning (CALL). *Learning, Media and Technology, 49*(4), 527–543. DOI: 10.1080/17439884.2023.2207832

Marcovitz, D. M. (2022). The intersection of social justice and educational technology: The educational technology social justice matrix. *Education and Information Technologies, 27*(4), 5129–5151. DOI: 10.1007/s10639-021-10828-1

Martins, H. F. (2012). The Use of a Business Simulation Game in a Management Course. In Cruz-Cunha, M. (Ed.), *Handbook of Research on Serious Games as Educational, Business and Research Tools* (pp. 693–707). IGI Global Scientific Publishing., DOI: 10.4018/978-1-4666-0149-9.ch035

Martins, H. F. (2023). *Mastering the Game: A Reference Handbook On Business Simulations*. LABS - Information and Communication Sciences.

Martins, H. F. (2024). The Impact and Future of AI-Enhanced Teaching Methods in the Use of Business Simulations. In Ahmed, Z., Hassan, A., & Saeed, R. (Eds.), *AI-Enhanced Teaching Methods* (pp. 305–321). IGI Global Scientific Publishing., DOI: 10.4018/979-8-3693-2728-9.ch014

Mathiason, J. L. (2023). Femtech: The "Smart" Business of Menstruation, Hormone Tracking, and the Corporate Construction of Risk. *Feminist Studies, 49*(1), 118–149. DOI: 10.1353/fem.2023.a901596

Matzner, T. (2024). Algorithms as complementary abstractions. *New Media & Society, 26*(4), 1799–1815. DOI: 10.1177/14614448221078604

Mazhabi, Z. (2025). Investigating leadership attributes and strategies during times of crisis and educational change: A story of public primary school principals in Lombok, Indonesia. *Educational Management Administration & Leadership*, •••, 17411432241300280. DOI: 10.1177/17411432241300280

McHaney, R. (2023). *The new digital shoreline: How Web 2.0 and millennials are revolutionizing higher education*. Taylor & Francis. DOI: 10.4324/9781003447979

McMillan, C. (2022). MONITORING FEMALE FERTILITY THROUGH 'FEM-TECH': THE NEED FOR A WHOLE-SYSTEM APPROACH TO REGULATION. *Medical Law Review*, *30*(3), 410–433. DOI: 10.1093/medlaw/fwac006 PMID: 35482289

McMillan, C. (2024). Gender, health and technology: The rise of femtech - periods, profit and power. In *A Research Agenda for Gender and Health*. Edward Elgar Publishing Ltd., DOI: 10.4337/9781802209228.00010

Mehrnezhad, M., Shipp, L., Almeida, T., & Toreini, E. (2022). Vision: Too Little too Late? Do the Risks of FemTech already Outweigh the Benefits? *ACM International Conference Proceeding Series*, 145 – 150. DOI: 10.1145/3549015.3554204

Mengesha, Z., Heldreth, C., Lahav, M., Sublewski, J., & Tuennerman, E. (2021). "I don't think these devices are very culturally sensitive."—Impact of automated speech recognition errors on African Americans. *Frontiers in Artificial Intelligence*, *4*, 725911. DOI: 10.3389/frai.2021.725911 PMID: 34901836

Ministry of Education. Culture, Sports, Science and Technology (MEXT). (2018). *Shin gakusyuu shidouyourou ni tsuite: Manabi no naiyou-henkaku ni tsuite* [New Courses of Study: enrichment and transformation of learning content]. https://www.mext.go.jp/b_menu/shingi/chousa/shisetu/044/shiryo/__icsFiles/afieldfile/2018/07/09/1405957_003.pdf

Ministry of Education. Culture, Sports, Science and Technology (MEXT). (2020). *Gaikokugo no shidou niokeru ICT no katsuyou nitsuite* [The use of ICT in teaching foreign languages]. https://www.mext.go.jp/content/20200911-mxt_jogai01-000009772_13.pdf

Ministry of Education. Culture, Sports, Science and Technology (MEXY). (2022). *GIGA sukuuru no saishin no jyoukyou nituite* [Update on the GIGA School initiative]. https://www.mext.go.jp/kaigisiryo/content/20210319-mxt_syoto01-000013552_02.pdf

Mishra, P., Kaur, R., Vikram, S., & Sharma, P. (2024). Femtech apps and quantification of the reproductive body in India: Issues and concerns. *Current Sociology*, *72*(7), 1340–1359. DOI: 10.1177/00113921231206491

Mishra, P., & Suresh, Y. (2021). Datafied body projects in India: Femtech and the rise of reproductive surveillance in the digital era. *Asian Journal of Women's Studies*, *27*(4), 597–606. DOI: 10.1080/12259276.2021.2002010

Mollick, E. (2024). *Co-intelligence: Living and working with AI.* Penguin.

Morton, D., Bird-Naytowhow, K., & Hatala, A. R. (2021). Silent voices, absent bodies, and quiet methods: Revisiting the processes and outcomes of personal knowledge production through Body-Mapping methodologies among Indigenous youth. *International Journal of Qualitative Methods*, *20*, 1609406920987934. DOI: 10.1177/1609406920987934

Mukherjee, S. (2022). Teaching Shakespeare in the Indian (Google) Classroom: The Digital Promise and the Digital Divide. In *Digital Shakespeares from the Global South* (pp. 73–92). Springer International Publishing. DOI: 10.1007/978-3-031-04787-9_5

Mukherjee, S., Thakur, D., Chandel, P. K., Chandra, S., & Karia, A. (2025). Cultivating sustainable growth and well-being in digital financial education. In *Exploring Psychology, Social Innovation and Advanced Applications of Machine Learning*. IGI Global., DOI: 10.4018/979-8-3693-6910-4.ch014

Munshi, D. (2024). Enhancing Digital Transformation Project Success through Design Thinking-Driven Agile Project Management.

Nadeem, M., Oroszlanyova, M., & Farag, W. (2023). Effect of digital game-based learning on student engagement and motivation. *Computers*, *12*(9), 177. DOI: 10.3390/computers12090177

Nasution, D. K. (2024). Culturally responsive teaching approach by using Kahoot in teaching English. *INSIS Journal*, *4*(1), 903–912.

Nazaretsky, T., Bar, C., Walter, M., & Alexandron, G. (2022, March). Empowering teachers with AI: Co-designing a learning analytics tool for personalized instruction in the science classroom. In LAK22: 12th international learning analytics and knowledge conference (pp. 1-12).

Neiman, E., Bornstein, M., Turner, A. N., Kavanaugh, M. L., & Gallo, M. F. (2025). Use of period- or fertility-tracking technologies pre- and post-Dobbs. *Contraception*, 110812. Advance online publication. DOI: 10.1016/j.contraception.2025.110812 PMID: 39800282

Nellore, N., Mishra, T., & Zimmer, M. (2024). Unveiling User Perspectives: Exploring Themes in Femtech Mobile App Reviews for Enhanced Usability and Privacy. *Proceedings of the ACM on Human-Computer Interaction*, *8*(MHCI). DOI: 10.1145/3676530

Netemeyer, R. G., Lynch, J. G.Jr, Lichtenstein, D. R., & Dobolyi, D. (2024). Financial Education Effects on Financial Behavior and Well-Being: The Mediating Roles of Improved Objective and Subjective Financial Knowledge and Parallels in Physical Health. *Journal of Public Policy & Marketing, 43*(4), 254–275. DOI: 10.1177/07439156241228197

Neureiter, D., Klieser, E., Neumayer, B., Winkelmann, P., Urbas, R., & Kiesslich, T. (2020). Feasibility of Kahoot! as a real-time assessment tool in (Histo-)pathology classroom teaching. *Advances in Medical Education and Practice, 11*, 695–705. DOI: 10.2147/AMEP.S264821 PMID: 33117039

Nguyen, H. P., Vo, D. K., Do, T. L., Nguyen, H. D., Nguyen, T. C., Nguyen, V. T., . . . Le, T. N. (2024, December). EPEdit: Redefining image editing with generative AI and user-centric design. In *International Symposium on Information and Communication Technology* (pp. 272-283). Singapore: Springer Nature Singapore. https://doi.org/DOI: 10.1007/978-981-96-4288-5_22

Ng, W. Y., Lau, N. Y., Lee, V. V., Vijayakumar, S., Leong, Q. Y., Ooi, S. Q. D., Su, L. L., Lee, Y. S., Chan, S.-Y., Blasiak, A., & Ho, D. (2024). Shaping Adoption and Sustained Use Across the Maternal Journey: Qualitative Study on Perceived Usability and Credibility in Digital Health Tools. *JMIR Human Factors, 11*, e59269. Advance online publication. DOI: 10.2196/59269 PMID: 39352732

Niguse, T., Kant, S., & Kebede, K. (2025). Relationship Between Organization Alignment and Co-Creation: The Role of Technology Innovation in the Case of Eco Hotels, Ethiopia. In *Empowering Value Co-Creation in the Digital Era* (pp. 229-256). IGI Global Scientific Publishing.

Nikolić, J., Nikolić, J., Gajić, T., & Gagić, A. (2022). The use of Kahoot! in foreign language teaching. In *Sinteza 2022 – International Scientific Conference on Information Technology and Data Related Research* (pp. 347–352). DOI: 10.15308/Sinteza-2022-347-352

Nishi, T., Aikawa, Y., Kato, K., Kaneko, M., & Kiyono, K. (2025). Menstruation-Related Physical Condition Management for Women Using an Underwear-Type Wearable Biosensor †. *Engineering Proceedings, 92*(1), 5. Advance online publication. DOI: 10.3390/engproc2025092005

Noble, S. U. (2018). *Algorithms of oppression: How search engines reinforce racism*. NYU Press. DOI: 10.18574/nyu/9781479833641.001.0001

Nowell, L. S., Norris, J. M., White, D. E., & Moules, N. J. (2017). Thematic analysis: Striving to meet the trustworthiness criteria. *International Journal of Qualitative Methods, 16*(1), 1–13. DOI: 10.1177/1609406917733847

O'Brien, B., & Iriarte, E. G. (2025). Periods, technology and identity: The experience of period-tracking app users. *Irish Journal of Sociology*, 07916035251338808. Advance online publication. DOI: 10.1177/07916035251338808

O'Donnell, A. (2022). Sharing the world without losing oneself: Education in a pluralistic universe. *Discourse (Abingdon), 43*(5), 666–685. DOI: 10.1080/01596306.2022.2045072

Oberrauch, L., & Kaiser, T. (2024). Financial Education or Incentivizing Learning-By-Doing? Evidence from an RCT with Undergraduate Students. *Journal of Behavioral and Experimental Finance*, *43*, 100954. Advance online publication. DOI: 10.1016/j.jbef.2024.100954

Okiri, P. O., & Hercz, M. (2025). The tenets of distributed pedagogical leadership in educational contexts—A systematic literature review on perception and practice. *Educational Management Administration & Leadership, 53*(1), 47–64. DOI: 10.1177/17411432231154444

Ooi, K. B., Tan, G. W. H., Al-Emran, M., Al-Sharafi, M. A., Capatina, A., Chakraborty, A., Dwivedi, Y. K., Huang, T.-L., Kar, A. K., Lee, V.-H., Loh, X.-M., Micu, A., Mikalef, P., Mogaji, E., Pandey, N., Raman, R., Rana, N. P., Sarker, P., Sharma, A., & Wong, L. W. (2025). The potential of generative artificial intelligence across disciplines: Perspectives and future directions. *Journal of Computer Information Systems*, *65*(1), 76–107. DOI: 10.1080/08874417.2023.2261010

Organization for Economic Co-operation and Development (OECD). (2019). *TALIS 2018 results (Volume I): Teachers and school leaders as lifelong learners*. OECD publishing. DOI: 10.1787/1d0bc92a-en

Ortiz, N. R., Torres, J. V., & Rodríguez, V. H. P. (2024). Digital Financial Education for Economic and Financial Inclusion in Vulnerable Sectors of Peru. *Theoretical and Practical Research in the Economic Fields, 15*(4), 928–938. DOI: 10.14505/tpref.v15.4(32).11

Oubibi, M., Zhao, W., Wang, Y., Zhou, Y., Jiang, Q., Li, Y., Xu, X., & Qiao, L. (2022). Advances in research on technological, pedagogical, didactical, and social competencies of preservice TCFL teachers. *Sustainability (Basel), 14*(4), 2045. DOI: 10.3390/su14042045

Owens, A., Zeek, H., & Oye, E. (2024). The Role of Cultural Identity in Shaping Educational Experiences.

Özdemir, O. (2024). Kahoot! game-based digital learning platform: A comprehensive meta-analysis. *Journal of Computer Assisted Learning*, *41*(1), 118–141. DOI: 10.1111/jcal.13084

Page, A., Mavropoulou, S., & Harrington, I. (2022). Culturally responsive inclusive education: The value of the local context. *International Journal of Disability Development and Education*, *69*(4), 1313–1326. DOI: 10.1080/1034912X.2020.1757627

Parameswaran, U. D., Molloy, J., & Kuttner, P. (2024). Healing schools: A framework for joining trauma-informed care, restorative justice, and multicultural education for whole school reform. *The Urban Review*, *56*(1), 186–209. DOI: 10.1007/s11256-023-00666-5

Park, S., Chun, S., Cha, J., Lee, B., & Shim, H. (2021). Multiple heads are better than one: Few-shot font generation with multiple localized experts. In Proceedings of the IEEE/CVF international conference on computer vision (pp. 13900-13909).

Park, J. Y., Hsueh, S., Woytuk, N. C., Huang, X., Felice, M. C., & Balaam, M. (2024). Critiquing Menstrual Pain Technologies through the Lens of Feminist Disability Studies. *Conference on Human Factors in Computing Systems - Proceedings*. DOI: 10.1145/3613904.3642691

Paul, P. K., Bommali, T., Kayyali, M., Chakraborty, S., Debnath, D., Gupta, S. K., & Sharma, S. K. (2025). Demystifying Issues and Concerns of AI and Allied Technologies in Digital Education and Learning: A Scientific Study. In AI-Enabled Sustainable Innovations in Education and Business (pp. 1-32). IGI Global Scientific Publishing. DOI: 10.4018/979-8-3373-3952-8.ch001

Paulus, T., Bichelmeyer, B., Malopinsky, L., Pereira-Leon, M., & Rastogi, P. (2005). Power distance and group dynamics of an international project team: A case study. *Teaching in Higher Education*, *10*(1), 43–55. Advance online publication. DOI: 10.1080/1356251052000305525

Peñarreta-Quezada, M.-Á., Salas-Tenesaca, E.-E., Álvarez-García, J., & de la Cruz del Río-Rama, M. (2023). Socio-demographic variables and levels of financial education among young university students in Ecuador. *Revista Mexicana de Economia y Finanzas Nueva Epoca*, *19*(19). Advance online publication. DOI: 10.21919/remef.v19i1.920

Peter-Spiess, M.-H., & Hofmann, D. (2025). Navigating FemTech app regulation in Switzerland: Challenges and opportunities from a public health perspective. *Contraception*, 110975. Advance online publication. DOI: 10.1016/j.contraception.2025.110975 PMID: 40412592

Pettalongi, S. S., Londol, M. M., & Umboh, S. E. (2024). Disparities in digital education: Socioeconomic barriers to accessing online learning resources. *International Journal of Social and Human Sciences*, *5*(2), 145–162. DOI: 10.59613/be6gdv98

Piacentini, T. (2024). Critical Pedagogy and Pedagogic Discomfort. In *Developing a Critical Pedagogy of Migration Studies* (pp. 1–23). Bristol University Press.

Piaget, J. (1970). *Science of education and the psychology of the child.* Viking.

Pimentel, J., Arias, A., Ramírez, D., Molina, A., Cockcroft, A., Chomat, A. M., & Andersson, N. (2020). Game-based learning interventions to foster cross-cultural care training: A scoping review. *Games for Health Journal*, *9*(3), 1–18. DOI: 10.1089/g4h.2019.0078 PMID: 32027184

Pinhanez, C., Cavalin, P., Storto, L., Finbow, T., Cobbinah, A., Nogima, J., . . . Gonçalves, I. (2024). Harnessing the Power of Artificial Intelligence to Vitalize Endangered Indigenous Languages: Technologies and Experiences. arXiv preprint arXiv:2407.12620.

Plump, C. M., & LaRosa, J. (2017). Using Kahoot! in the classroom to create engagement and active learning: A game-based technology solution for eLearning novices. *Management Teaching Review*, *2*(2), 151–158. DOI: 10.1177/2379298116689783

Polydorou, E. (2025). The Effect of Simulation Games in Entrepreneurship Education. In *Integrating Simulation Tools Into Entrepreneurship Education* (pp. 445–468). IGI Global Scientific Publishing., DOI: 10.4018/979-8-3693-9040-5.ch020

Porter, B., & Machery, E. (2024). AI-generated poetry is indistinguishable from human-written poetry and rated more favorably. *Scientific Reports*, *14*(1), 26133. DOI: 10.1038/s41598-024-76900-1

Poth, R. D. (2024). *How to Teach AI: Weaving Strategies and Activities Into Any Content Area.* International Society for Technology in Education.

Potnis, D., Tahamtan, I., & McDonald, L. (2025). Negative consequences of information gatekeeping through algorithmic technologies: An Annual Review of Information Science and Technology (ARIST) paper. *Journal of the Association for Information Science and Technology*, *76*(1), 262–288. DOI: 10.1002/asi.24955

Prathyusha, N. (2020). Role of gamification in language learning. *International Journal of Research and Analytical Reviews*, *7*(2), 577–583.

Presley, T. (2022). *Assertive communication: Develop your assertive communication skills and instantly learn how to stand up for yourself, communicate effectively, and boost your confidence while winning the respect.* Timothy Presley.

Price, J., & Fox, A. (2023). Transformative Praxis: A Critical Design Framework for Belonging and Inclusion in Technology-Rich Learning Spaces. *Journal of Teaching and Learning with Technology, 12*(1), 55–71. DOI: 10.14434/jotlt.v12i1.36425

Prieto, C. A. G., Santa, J. S. S., & Álvarez, L. C. V. (2024). Financial education as a mediator between financial planning and financial performance in microentrepreneurs of the solidarity sector. *Cuadernos de Economia (Colombia), 43*(91), 265–295. DOI: 10.15446/cuadernos.v43n91.104375

Pronzato, R. (2023). Reproducing hegemony, returning to critical pedagogy. The relationships of youth with digital platforms.

Puentedura, R. R. (2014). SAMR: A contextualized introduction. *Lecture at Pine Cobble School. Retrieved*, (March), 13.

Puetate Medina, E. E., Castillo Martínez, C. P., & Méndez Ortega, M. G. (2025). *Kahoot para la enseñanza del idioma inglés* [Use of Kahoot for teaching the English language]. SATHIRI., DOI: 10.32645/13906925.1363

Pybus, J., & Mir, M. (2025). Tracking menopause: An SDK Data Audit for intimate infrastructures of datafication with ChatGPT4o. *New Media & Society, 27*(4), 1888–1908. DOI: 10.1177/14614448251314401

Qiao, H., & Zhao, A. (2023). Artificial intelligence-based language learning: Illuminating the impact on speaking skills and self-regulation in Chinese EFL context. *Frontiers in Psychology, 14*, 1255594. DOI: 10.3389/fpsyg.2023.1255594 PMID: 38022973

Radford, A., Kim, J. W., Hallacy, C., Ramesh, A., Goh, G., Agarwal, S., & Sutskever, I. (2021, July). Learning transferable visual models from natural language supervision. In *International conference on machine learning* (pp. 8748-8763). PMLR.

Raji, I. D., Scheuerman, M. K., & Amironesei, R. (2021, March). You can't sit with us: Exclusionary pedagogy in ai ethics education. In *Proceedings of the 2021 ACM conference on fairness, accountability, and transparency* (pp. 515-525). DOI: 10.1145/3442188.3445914

Ramírez Ruiz, J. J., Vargas Sanchez, A. D., & Boude Figueredo, O. R. (2024). Impact of gamification on school engagement: A systematic review. *Frontiers in Education, 9*, 1466926. Advance online publication. DOI: 10.3389/feduc.2024.1466926

Rane, N., Choudhary, S., & Rane, J. (2024). Gemini Versus ChatGPT: Applications, Performance, Architecture, Capabilities, and Implementation. SSRN Electronic Journal. DOI: DOI: 10.2139/ssrn.4723687

Ranta, S., Heiskanen, H., & Kahila, S. (2025). Team leadership profiles in Finnish early childhood education centres–Teachers' experiences of team leadership. *Educational Management Administration & Leadership*, *53*(2), 298–317. DOI: 10.1177/17411432231168234

Ravichandran, K., Virgin, B. A., Edwin, M. R., Morris, V. S., & Milton, B. J. (2024). Moving towards a Blended Tomorrow: The Evolution of EdTech in Education. Library of Progress-Library Science, Information Technology & Computer, 44(3).

Razo, R., & Blankenship-Knox, A. E. (2022). The Internet Isn't a Luxury Anymore: How Educational Leaders Can Promote Equitable Digital Access for All Students. *Educational Leadership and Administration: Teaching and Program Development*, *34*, 55–68.

REMOVED HYPERLINK FIELDWadinambiarachchi, S., Kelly, R. M., Pareek, S., Zhou, Q., & Velloso, E. [REMOVED HYPERLINK FIELD]Wadinambiarachchi, S., Kelly, R. M., Pareek, S., Zhou, Q., & Velloso, E. (2024). The effects of generative AI on design fixation and divergent thinking. *Proceedings of the 2024 CHI Conference on Human Factors in Computing Systems*, 1–18. https://doi.org/DOI: 10.1145/3613904.3642919

Resende, N., & Hadley, J. (2024). The Translator's Canvas: Using LLMs to enhance Poetry translation. In *Proceedings of the 16th Conference of the Association for Machine Translation in the Americas* (Vol. 1). https:// aclanthology .org/ 2024 .amta - research .16 .pdf

Reus-Smit, C. (2021). The end of global pluralism? *European Journal of International Relations*, *27*(4), 1249–1273. DOI: 10.1177/13540661211017273

Richardson, N., Kothapalli, S., Onteddu, A. R., Kundavaram, R. R., & Talla, R. R. (2023). AI-Driven Optimization Techniques for Evolving Software Architecture in Complex Systems. *ABC Journal of Advanced Research*, *12*(2), 71–84. DOI: 10.18034/abcjar.v12i2.783

Roberts, G. M. (2023). Providing Care When There Is No Cure: How FemTech Can Help Destigmatize Autoimmune Diseases. In *FemTech: Intersectional Interventions in Women's Digital Health*. Springer Singapore. DOI: 10.1007/978-981-99-5605-0_6

Røe, Y., Wojniusz, S., & Bjerke, A. H. (2022, January). The digital transformation of higher education teaching: Four pedagogical prescriptions to move active learning pedagogy forward. [). Frontiers Media SA.]. *Frontiers in Education*, *6*, 784701. DOI: 10.3389/feduc.2021.784701

Ruckenstein, M. (2023). *The feel of algorithms*. Univ of California Press.

Ruiz, T. A., Benito, L., & Penabad, M. C. L. (2023). Influence of behavioral biases on investment decisions. The importance of financial education during an economic crisis [Influencia de los sesgos del comportamiento en las decisiones de inversión. La importancia de la educación financiera en tiempos de crisis]. *Revista Galega de Economia, 32*(1). Advance online publication. DOI: 10.15304/rge.32.1.8190

Sailer, M., & Homner, L. (2019). The gamification of learning: A meta-analysis. *Educational Psychology Review, 31*(4), 1191–1220. DOI: 10.1007/s10648-019-09498-w

Salas-Velasco, M. (2022). Causal Effects of Financial Education Intervention Aimed at University Students on Financial Knowledge and Financial Self-Efficacy. *Journal of Risk and Financial Management, 15*(7), 284. Advance online publication. DOI: 10.3390/jrfm15070284

Salas-Velasco, M. (2023). Economic and financial education for investment and financing decision-making in a graduate degree: Experimental evaluation of the effectiveness of two delivery methods. *The Journal of Economic Education, 54*(3), 225–242. DOI: 10.1080/00220485.2023.2191594

Salas-Velasco, M. (2024). Attitudes of college seniors toward graduate student loan debt: The role of financial education. *Journal of Financial Economic Policy, 16*(4), 442–462. DOI: 10.1108/JFEP-09-2023-0259

Saltman, K. J. (2022). *The alienation of fact: Digital educational privatization, AI, and the false promise of bodies and numbers*. MIT Press. DOI: 10.7551/mitpress/14387.001.0001

Sandhaus, H., Gu, Q., Parreira, M. T., & Ju, W. (2025). *Co-Designing with Algorithms: Unpacking the Complex Role of GenAI in Interactive System Design Education.*

Sato, N. (2003). *Inside Japanese classrooms: The heart of education.* Routledge., DOI: 10.4324/9780203465707

Schiff, D. (2022). Education for AI, not AI for education: The role of education and ethics in national AI policy strategies. *International Journal of Artificial Intelligence in Education, 32*(3), 527–563. DOI: 10.1007/s40593-021-00270-2

Schwidtal, J. A. N. (2022). Comprehensive Evaluation of Electricity Market Design Elements for the Strategic Integration of Renewable Energies.

Sconti, A. (2022). Digital vs. in-person financial education: What works best for Generation Z? *Journal of Economic Behavior & Organization, 194*, 300–318. DOI: 10.1016/j.jebo.2021.12.001

Sconti, A., Caserta, M., & Ferrante, L. (2024). Gen Z and financial education: Evidence from a randomized control trial in the South of Italy. *Journal of Behavioral and Experimental Economics, 112*, 102256. Advance online publication. DOI: 10.1016/j.socec.2024.102256

Sefton-Green, J. (2022). Towards platform pedagogies: Why thinking about digital platforms as pedagogic devices might be useful. *Discourse (Abingdon), 43*(6), 899–911. DOI: 10.1080/01596306.2021.1919999

Sekhar, A. (2024). How transformation from traditional to participatory learning and teaching pedagogy helps build confidence and communication skills in international students-a reflective analysis. *Journal of Global Business & Technology, 20*(2).

Sekimoto, S. (2023). Rhythmic bodies: Sensorial multimodality, entrainment, and intercultural communication. In *Multimodal communication in intercultural interaction* (pp. 41–57). Routledge. DOI: 10.4324/9781003227281-4

Senduk, F. F. W., Djatmika, E. T., Wahyono, H., Churiyah, M., Mahasneh, O., & Arjanto, P. (2024). Fostering financially savvy generations: The intersection of financial education, digital financial misconception and parental wellbeing. *Frontiers in Education, 9*, 1460374. Advance online publication. DOI: 10.3389/feduc.2024.1460374

Serido, J., McGee, D., Zhang, Y., Li, L., Quinones, M., & Ramos, G. (2024). Transformational Learning Within African American Culture: What Does Financial Education That Addresses Systemic Inequalities Look Like? *Financial Counseling and Planning, 35*(3), 307–322. DOI: 10.1891/JFCP-2023-0020

Shah, P. (2023). *AI and the Future of Education: Teaching in the Age of Artificial Intelligence*. John Wiley & Sons.

Sharadgah, T. A., & Sa'di, R. A. (2022). A systematic review of research on the use of artificial intelligence in English language teaching and learning (2015-2021): What are the current effects? *Journal of Information Technology Education*, •••, 21.

Shedlock, K., & Hudson, P. (2022). Kaupapa Māori concept modelling for the creation of Māori IT Artefacts. Journal of the Royal Society of New Zealand, 52(sup1), 18-32.

Sheikh Salavat, S., Smaeil, K. G. K., & Amani, M. (2025). The mediating role of purposeful organizational forgetting in the relationship between distributed leadership and organizational development of elementary teachers. *Mental Health in School, 3*(1), 102–113.

Shen, V. (2025). TEACHING FOREIGN LANGUAGES IN THE AGE OF AI: EXPERIMENTS IN AN ADVANCED CHINESE LANGUAGE CLASS. INTED2025 Proceedings, Shiming, Y. (2019). *Investigation and analysis of polyphonetic word acquisition by primary international students and teaching suggestions* Nanjing Normal University].

Shonfeld, M., Cotnam-Kappel, M., Judge, M., Ng, C. Y., Ntebutse, J. G., Williamson-Leadley, S., & Yildiz, M. N. (2021). Learning in digital environments: A model for cross-cultural alignment. *Educational Technology Research and Development, 69*(4), 1–20. DOI: 10.1007/s11423-021-09967-6 PMID: 33654347

Shu, L., & Liu, M. (2019). Student engagement in game-based learning: A literature review from 2008 to 2018. *Journal of Educational Multimedia and Hypermedia, 28*(2), 193–215. DOI: 10.3102/1442816

Sianturi, A. D., & Hung, R. (2022). The challenges of using Kahoot! in teaching and learning in higher education: A systematic review. In *Proceedings of the 6th International Conference on Digital Technology in Education (ICDTE '22)* (pp. 72–77). ACM. DOI: 10.1145/3568739.3568753

Siapka, A., Tzanou, M., & Nelson, A. (2024). Re-imagining data protection: Femtech and gendered risks in the GDPR. In *Critical Reflections on the EU's Data Protection Regime: GDPR in the Machine.* Bloomsbury Publishing Plc. DOI: 10.5040/9781509977871.ch-005

Siddiqui, F. (2024). The birth of femtech lays fertile grounds for pregnancy discrimination in the workplace. *Family Court Review, 62*(2), 413–427. DOI: 10.1111/fcre.12787

Sillence, E., Osborne, A. K., Kemp, E., & McKellar, K. (2025). Menopause apps: Personal health tracking, empowerment and epistemic injustice. *Digital Health, 11*, 20552076251330782. Advance online publication. DOI: 10.1177/20552076251330782 PMID: 40297381

imandan, R., Leu tean, B., & Dobrescu, R. M. (2022). An Uphill Battle: Financial Education in Romania in the Midst of Societal Transformation. *Journal of Risk and Financial Management, 15*(11), 494. Advance online publication. DOI: 10.3390/jrfm15110494

Singh, K. N., & Misra, G. (2023). Victimisation of investors from fraudulent investment schemes and their protection through financial education. *Journal of Financial Crime, 30*(5), 1305–1322. DOI: 10.1108/JFC-07-2022-0167

Sitzmann, T. (2011). A meta-analytic examination of the instructional effectiveness of computer-based simulation games. *Personnel Psychology*, *64*(2), 489–528. DOI: 10.1111/j.1744-6570.2011.01190.x

Smith, C. H., & Lundström, F. (2024, July). Hyperhumanism in the age of generative AI: The impact on human creativity and identity. In *Proceedings of EVA London 2024* (pp. 154-159). BCS Learning & Development. http://dx.doi.org/DOI: 10.14236/ewic/EVA2024.27

Smitherman, G. (1977). *Talkin and testifyin: The language of Black America*. Wayne State University Press.

Spennemann, D. H. R. (2024). Generative Artificial Intelligence, Human Agency and the Future of Cultural Heritage. *Heritage*, *7*(7), 3597–3609. DOI: 10.3390/heritage7070170

Spillers, H. J. (1987). Mama's baby, papa's maybe: An American grammar book. *Diacritics*, *17*(2), 65–81. DOI: 10.2307/464747

Spivak, G. C. (1988). Can the subaltern speak? In C. Nelson & L. Grossberg (Eds.), Marxism and the interpretation of culture (pp. 271–313). University of Illinois Press.

Spivak, G. C. (1993). The politics of translation. In *Outside in the teaching machine* (pp. 179–200). Routledge.

Starkey, H. (2021). Classroom counternarratives as transformative multicultural citizenship education. *Multicultural Education Review*, *13*(3), 229–244. DOI: 10.1080/2005615X.2021.1964266

Stein, H. F. (2021). *Listening deeply: An approach to understanding and consulting in organizational culture*. Routledge. DOI: 10.4324/9780429034190

Striuk, O., & Kondratenko, Y. (2023). Implementation of generative adversarial networks in mobile applications for image data enhancement. *Journal of Mobile Multimedia*, *19*(3), 823–838. DOI: 10.13052/jmm1550-4646.1938

Sun, J., Pae, H. K., & Ai, H. (2021). The recognition of coordinative compound words by learners of Chinese as a foreign language: A mixed methods study. *Foreign Language Annals*, *54*(4), 923–951. DOI: 10.1111/flan.12586

Suryadevara, C. K. (2020). Generating free images with OpenAI's generative models. *International Journal of Innovations in Engineering Research and Technology*, *7*(3), 49–56. DOI: 10.26662/ijiert.v8i3.pp74-80

Svensson, I., & von Knorring, M. (2025). Connecting Distributed Leadership and Leadership-as-Practice to Increase Understanding of Leadership as Distributed in Healthcare Practice. *Journal of Change Management, 25*(1), 1–20. DOI: 10.1080/14697017.2025.2453136

Tan, D. A. L., Lee, B. C., Ganapathy, M., & Kasuma, S. A. A. (2022). Language learning in the 21st century: Malaysian ESL students' perceptions of Kahoot! In *Research anthology on developments in gamification and game-based learning* (pp. 802–820). IGI Global., DOI: 10.4018/978-1-6684-3710-0.ch036

Tan, L., & Luhrs, M. (2024). Using generative AI Midjourney to enhance divergent and convergent thinking in an architect's creative design process. *The Design Journal, 27*(4), 677–699. DOI: 10.1080/14606925.2024.2353479

Tan, T. Y., Wachsmuth, L., & Tugade, M. M. (2022). Emotional nuance: Examining positive emotional granularity and well-being. *Frontiers in Psychology, 13*, 715966. DOI: 10.3389/fpsyg.2022.715966 PMID: 35273535

Taras, V., Steel, P., & Kirkman, B. L. (2016). Does country equate with culture? Beyond geography in the search for cultural boundaries. *MIR. Management International Review, 56*(4), 455–487. DOI: 10.1007/s11575-016-0283-x

Tartaglione, E., Barbano, C. A., & Grangetto, M. (2021). End: Entangling and disentangling deep representations for bias correction. In Proceedings of the IEEE/CVF conference on computer vision and pattern recognition (pp. 13508-13517).

Taylor, J., El Ardeliya, V., & Wolfson, J. (2024). Exploration of artificial intelligence in creative fields: Generative art, music, and design. *International Journal of Cyber and IT Service Management, 4*(1), 39–45. DOI: 10.34306/ijcitsm.v4i1.149

Tegon, R. (2024). An updated systematic review on the impact of gamification in education: Insights from early 2024. In Martínez-Roig, R., Pulido-Montes, C., & Mateu-Luján, B. (Eds.), *Nuevas investigaciones educativas para definir la enseñanza y el aprendizaje* (pp. 318–330). Octaedro.

Ten Holter, C. (2022). Participatory design: Lessons and directions for responsible research and innovation. *Journal of Responsible Innovation, 9*(2), 275–290. DOI: 10.1080/23299460.2022.2041801

Tham, J., Howard, T., & Verhulsdonck, G. (2022). Extending design thinking, content strategy, and artificial intelligence into technical communication and user experience design programs: Further pedagogical implications. *Journal of Technical Writing and Communication, 52*(4), 428–459. DOI: 10.1177/00472816211072533

Tharayil, A. (2024). Examining the Association Between Financial Education and Financial Risk Tolerance. *The American Economist, 69*(1), 59–79. DOI: 10.1177/05694345231186082

Tiribelli, S., Pansoni, S., Frontoni, E., & Giovanola, B. (2024). Ethics of Artificial Intelligence for Cultural Heritage: Opportunities and Challenges. *IEEE Transactions on Technology and Society, 5*(3), 293–305. DOI: 10.1109/TTS.2024.3432407

Tiwari, S. V. (2023). Review of the Research on Design Education and Practices. In Suman, R. S., Moccia, S., Chinnusamy, K., Singh, B., & Regin, R. (Eds.), (pp. 230–240). Advances in Educational Technologies and Instructional Design. IGI Global., DOI: 10.4018/978-1-6684-6682-7.ch018

Tjandraprawira, K. D., Armawan, E., Aziz, M. A., & Djuwantono, T. (2025). A Study on the Quality of Patient-Centred Endometriosis Mobile Applications: Analysis and Future Prospects. *Obstetrics and Gynecology International, 2025*(1). DOI: 10.1155/ogi/5582127

Torma, J., Barbić, D., & Ivanov, M. (2023). Analyzing the Effects of Financial Education on Financial Literacy and Financial Behaviour: A Randomized Field Experiment in Croatia. *South East European Journal of Economics and Business, 18*(2), 63–86. DOI: 10.2478/jeb-2023-0019

Trompenaars, F., & Hampden-Turner, C. (2012). *Riding the waves of culture: Understanding diversity in global business* (3rd ed.). McGraw-Hill.

Tuktamyshova, A., Ayre, M. E. A., & Coombe, C. (2025). Lived Experiences on Mentoring and its Role in Leadership Development with Multilingual TESOL Professionals. In *Multilingual Leadership in TESOL* (pp. 17–30). Routledge.

Udoewa, V. (2022). An introduction to radical participatory design: Decolonising participatory design processes. *Design Science, 8*, e31. DOI: 10.1017/dsj.2022.24

Urban, C. (2023). Does state-mandated financial education reduce high school graduation rates? *Economics of Education Review, 95*, 102427. Advance online publication. DOI: 10.1016/j.econedurev.2023.102427

Varghese, J., & Crawford, S. S. (2021). A cultural framework for Indigenous, Local, and Science knowledge systems in ecology and natural resource management. *Ecological Monographs, 91*(1), e01431. DOI: 10.1002/ecm.1431

Verma, S. (2024). Weaving Cultural Threads Through Virtual Exchange: A Case Study on Task-Based Language Teaching use in European Secondary Schools (Master's thesis).

Volpe, D. (2024). Educators Reimagining the Experiences of Multilingual Learners in the Classroom a Practitioner Action Research Study (Doctoral dissertation, Montclair State University).

Vreuls, J., Koeslag-Kreunen, M., van der Klink, M., Nieuwenhuis, L., & Boshuizen, H. (2022). Responsive curriculum development for professional education: Different teams, different tales. *Curriculum Journal, 33*(4), 636–659. DOI: 10.1002/curj.155

Wakkary, R. (2021). *Things we could design: For more than human-centered worlds.* MIT press. DOI: 10.7551/mitpress/13649.001.0001

Walls, J. (2021). Tensions in care and control in the middle school classroom: Lessons for equitable social-emotional learning. *Middle School Journal, 52*(3), 25–34. DOI: 10.1080/00940771.2021.1893591

Walstad, W. B., & Wagner, J. (2023). Required or voluntary financial education and saving behaviors. *The Journal of Economic Education, 54*(1), 17–37. DOI: 10.1080/00220485.2022.2144573

Wang, A. I., & Tahir, R. (2020). The effect of using Kahoot! for learning – A literature review. *Computers & Education, 149*, 103818. Advance online publication. DOI: 10.1016/j.compedu.2020.103818

Wang, J., Cheng, G. H. L., Chen, T., & Leung, K. (2019). Team creativity/innovation in culturally diverse teams: A meta-analysis. *Journal of Organizational Behavior, 40*(6), 693–708. DOI: 10.1002/job.2362

Wang, L., Zhao, Z., Liu, H., Pang, J., Qin, Y., & Wu, Q. (2024). A review of intelligent music generation systems. *Neural Computing & Applications, 36*(12), 6381–6401. DOI: 10.1007/s00521-024-09418-2

Wang, Y. (2021). Artificial intelligence in educational leadership: A symbiotic role of human-artificial intelligence decision-making. *Journal of Educational Administration, 59*(3), 256–270. DOI: 10.1108/JEA-10-2020-0216

Wanxiang, C., Zhicheng, D., Yansong, F., Tao, G., Xianpei, H., Baotian, H., Minlie, H., Xuanjing, H., Kang, L., & Ting, L. (2023). Natural Language Processing in the Era of Big Models: Challenges, Opportunities, and Developments. *Chinese Science: Information Science, 53*(9), 1645–1687.

Weger, K., Matsuyama, L., Zimmermann, R., Mesmer, B., Van Bossuyt, D., Semmens, R., & Eaton, C. (2023). Insight into user acceptance and adoption of autonomous systems in mission critical environments. *International Journal of Human-Computer Interaction, 39*(7), 1423–1437. DOI: 10.1080/10447318.2022.2086033

Weissker, T., Bimberg, P., & Froehlich, B. (2020). Getting there together: Group navigation in distributed virtual environments. *IEEE Transactions on Visualization and Computer Graphics, 26*(5), 1860–1870. DOI: 10.1109/TVCG.2020.2973474 PMID: 32070981

Weisz, J. D., He, J., Muller, M., Hoefer, G., Miles, R., & Geyer, W. (2024). Design Principles for Generative AI Applications. *Proceedings of the CHI Conference on Human Factors in Computing Systems*, 1–22. DOI: 10.1145/3613904.3642466

Weller, M. (2022). Metaphors of ed tech. Athabasca University Press.

Westwood, H. L. (2023). Reinventing the Beauty Myth? FemTech's Cost to the Consumer. In *FemTech: Intersectional Interventions in Women's Digital Health.* Springer Singapore. DOI: 10.1007/978-981-99-5605-0_3

Weuffen, S., & Willis, K. (2023). The fallacy of cultural inclusion in mainstream education discourses. In *Inclusion, equity, diversity, and social justice in education: A critical exploration of the sustainable development goals* (pp. 91–106). Springer Nature Singapore. DOI: 10.1007/978-981-19-5008-7_7

White, K., Olajide, O., Watkins, K., Reiter, M., Johnson, P., & McCoy, M. (2024). Financial Education and Financial Anxiety: Do Quality and Quantity Differ? *Financial Counseling and Planning, 35*(2), 276–291. DOI: 10.1891/JFCP-2023-0022

Williams, D. P. (2022). Belief, Values, Bias, and Agency: Development of and Entanglement with "Artificial Intelligence" (Doctoral dissertation, Virginia Polytechnic Institute and State University).

Worku, M. Y. (2025). Access-equity tensions in education: Examining Ethiopia's educational reforms through a distributive social justice lens. *Social Sciences & Humanities Open, 11*, 101443. DOI: 10.1016/j.ssaho.2025.101443

Wu, X.-J., Ao, X., Zhang, R.-S., & Liu, C.-L. (2023). Structural Recognition of Handwritten Chinese Characters Using a Modified Part Capsule Auto-encoder. *CAAI International Conference on Artificial Intelligence*

Xia, J., Ge, Y., Shen, Z., & Rahman Najar, M. (2024). The Auxiliary Role of Artificial Intelligence Applications in Mitigating the Linguistic, Psychological, and Educational Challenges of Teaching and Learning Chinese Language by non-Chinese Students. *International Review of Research in Open and Distance Learning, 25*(3), 116–133.

Xi, C., & Chung, J. (2023). A study on character design using [Midjourney] application. *International Journal of Advanced Culture Technology, 11*(2), 409–414. DOI: 10.17703/IJACT.2023.11.2.409

Yang, W., & Zhong, R. (2024). Internationalization of Curriculum: Developing Cross-Cultural Competence in Teacher Education Programs through Service Learning. Eurasian Journal of Educational Research (EJER), (111).

Yeh, C. Y., & Tsai, C. C. (2022). Massive distance education: Barriers and challenges in shifting to a complete online learning environment. *Frontiers in Psychology*, *13*, 928717. DOI: 10.3389/fpsyg.2022.928717 PMID: 35859848

Yi, C. Q., Sin, S. H., & Sam, T. L. (2024). A Bibliometric Analysis of Female Technology (Femtech) Research: Trends and Gaps from 2013 to 2023. *Journal of Technology Management & Innovation*, *19*(4), 127–144. DOI: 10.4067/S0718-27242024000400127

Yin, H., Zhang, Z., & Liu, Y. (2023). The exploration of integrating the Midjourney artificial intelligence generated content tool into design systems to direct designers towards future-oriented innovation. *Systems*, *11*(12), 566. DOI: 10.3390/systems11120566

Yin, R. K. (2018). *Case study research and applications: Design and methods* (6th ed.). SAGE.

Yi, P., & Xia, Y. (2025). Irony detection, reasoning and understanding in zero-shot learning. *arXiv*. https://arxiv.org/abs/2501.16884

Yoshioka, S. (2024, February 16). FOCUS: Digitalization drive proving tough for Japanese school teachers. *Kyodo News*.

Yuming, L. (2001). The establishment of general language norms and standards - Experience in studying the "Law of the People's Republic of China on the General Language and Writing System". *Language and character application*(2), 17-24.

Yuning, T. (2023). A conceptual framework for financial education. *Citizenship. Social and Economics Education*, *22*(2), 65–84. DOI: 10.1177/14788047231180851

Yu, Y. (2024). Research on Design Concept and Cultural Inheritance System of Tourism Cultural and Creative Products in the Context of Deep Learning. *Applied Mathematics and Nonlinear Sciences*, *9*(1), 20231252. DOI: 10.2478/amns.2023.2.01252

Zallio, M., & Clarkson, P. J. (2022). Designing the metaverse: A study on inclusion, diversity, equity, accessibility and safety for digital immersive environments. *Telematics and Informatics*, *75*, 101909. DOI: 10.1016/j.tele.2022.101909

Zawacki-Richter, O., Marín, V. I., Bond, M., & Gouverneur, F. (2019). Systematic review of research on artificial intelligence applications in higher education–where are the educators? *International Journal of Educational Technology in Higher Education, 16*(1), 1–27. DOI: 10.1186/s41239-019-0171-0

Zgrzywa-Ziemak, A. H., Walecka-Jankowska, K. A., & Zimmer, J. (2025). The effect of organizational learning on business sustainability–the role of distributed leadership. *The Learning Organization, 32*(1), 7–34. DOI: 10.1108/TLO-11-2022-0135

Zhan, F., Yu, Y., Wu, R., Zhang, J., Lu, S., Liu, L., Kortylewski, A., Theobalt, C., & Xing, E. (2023). Multimodal image synthesis and editing: The generative AI era. *IEEE Transactions on Pattern Analysis and Machine Intelligence, 45*(12), 15098–15119. DOI: 10.1109/TPAMI.2023.3305243

Zhang, J., & Zhang, Z. (2024). AI in teacher education: Unlocking new dimensions in teaching support, inclusive learning, and digital literacy. *Journal of Computer Assisted Learning, 40*(4), 1871–1885. DOI: 10.1111/jcal.12988

Zhang, L., & Xing, H. (2023). The interaction of orthography, phonology and semantics in the process of second language learners' Chinese character production. *Frontiers in Psychology, 14*, 1076810. DOI: 10.3389/fpsyg.2023.1076810 PMID: 36935946

Zhang, R. (2024). The impact of artificial intelligence represented by ChatGPT on UI design. *Applied and Computational Engineering, 77*(1), 56–62. DOI: 10.54254/2755-2721/77/20240651

Zhang, Y., & Liu, C. (2024). Unlocking the potential of artificial intelligence in fashion design and e-commerce applications: The case of midjourney. *Journal of Theoretical and Applied Electronic Commerce Research, 19*(1), 654–670. DOI: 10.3390/jtaer19010035

Zhang, Y., Lu, X., & Xiao, J. J. (2023). Does financial education help to improve the return on stock investment? Evidence from China. *Pacific-Basin Finance Journal, 78*, 101940. Advance online publication. DOI: 10.1016/j.pacfin.2023.101940

Zhou, X., & Marslen-Wilson, W. (1999). Sublexical processing in reading Chinese. In *Reading chinese script* (pp. 49-76). Psychology Press. UNESC0. 2023. Global Education Monitoring Report 2023: Technology in education-A tool on whose terms? Paris, UNESCO. DOI: DOI: 10.54676/UZQV8501

Zhou, E., & Lee, D. (2024). Generative artificial intelligence, human creativity, and art. *PNAS Nexus, 3*(3), 1–8. DOI: 10.1093/pnasnexus/pgae052

Zhu, T., & Xiao, J. J. (2022). Consumer financial education and risky financial asset holding in China. *International Journal of Consumer Studies*, *46*(1), 56–74. DOI: 10.1111/ijcs.12643

Zindulka, T., Sekowski, J. M., Lehmann, F., & Buschek, D. (2025, April). Exploring Mobile Touch Interaction with Large Language Models. In *Proceedings of the 2025 CHI Conference on Human Factors in Computing Systems* (pp. 1-21). DOI: 10.1145/3706598.3713554

Zokaityte, A. (2025). FemTech Assets. *Feminist Legal Studies*. Advance online publication. DOI: 10.1007/s10691-025-09570-7

About the Contributors

Shaoxu Du is a Ph.D. candidate at the Centre for Instructional Technology and Multimedia, Universiti Sains Malaysia. His research interests include virtual reality, augmented reality, human-computer interaction, and cultural creativity.

Mageswaran Sanmugam acquired his B.Sc. (Hons) in Electrical Engineering from Universiti Teknologi Tun Hussein Onn in 2005 and Master's degree in Educational Management in 2012 from Universiti Utara Malaysia and Ph. D in Educational Technology in 2017 from Universiti Teknologi Malaysia. He worked as an Educator in both Primary and Secondary schools from 2008-2018, before being appointed as a Senior Lecturer in the Centre for Instructional Technology and Multimedia, Universiti Sains Malaysia, Pulau Pinang, Malaysia (from 2018- till 2021). Currently he is the Deputy Director of Research, Innovation and Networking in the Centre for Instructional Technology and Multimedia, Universiti Sains Malaysia, Pulau Pinang, Malaysia (from 2022- till now). His research interests encompass educational technology, ludology, game-based learning, gamification and game theory. He also serves as an exco-member in the Malaysian Educational Technology Association (META), and as a Senior Member under the Institute of Electrical and Electronics Engineers (IEEE).

Nurul Maziah Mohd Barkhaya acquired her B.IT. (Hons) in Software Engineering from Universiti Malaysia Terengganu in 2011 and Master's Degree in Education (TVET) in 2013 from Universiti Tun Hussein Onn Malaysia and Ph.D in Educational Technology in 2023 from Universiti Teknologi Malaysia. She worked as an educator in International Secondary schools from 2019 – 2023, before being appointed as a Senior Lecturer in the Centre for Instructional Technology and Multimedia, Universiti Sains Malaysia, Pulau Pinang, Malaysia started on 2024. Her research interests include the educational technology, creative multimedia, and e-Learning.

Chuang Chen is an Associate Professor at Zhengzhou University of Industrial Technology. He is also a Ph.D. graduate from the Centre for Instructional Technology and Multimedia, Universiti Sains Malaysia. His research focuses on virtual reality, augmented reality and instructional technology

Jia Wang obtained her Master's degree in Art Design from Peking University in 2014. She worked as a lecturer specializing in Digital Media at Nanyang Normal University, Henan, China, from 2016 to 2023. During this time, she published over ten academic papers on art education and research, guided students to win more than 30 awards in competitions, and received over ten awards in professional competitions herself. In 2023, she was awarded the Chinese Government Scholarship and began pursuing her Ph.D. in Cultural and Arts Management at Chung-Ang University, South Korea. Her research interests include art education, digital media, and cultural management.

***

Siti Nazleen Abdul Rabu is a senior lecturer at the Centre for Instructional Technology and Multimedia (CITM), Universiti Sains Malaysia (USM), Penang. Her research interests include instructional strategies in online learning, specifically looking into online learning discourse analysis, computer-supported collaborative learning (CSCL), including game-based learning and gamification.

Aditi Dirghangi is an Assistant Professor from the Department of English and Cultural Studies, Christ University, Delhi-NCR, India. Her Ph.D. thesis revolved around the retelling of Hindu mythology from a feminist point of view, exploring the misunderstood, devoiced, and disregarded female characters from the Mahabharata and the Ramayana. Her research interests are in the field of Mythology studies, Indian Writing in English, Post-colonial studies and Digital Cultures.

Hélder Fanha Martins currently holds the position of Full Professor at the Lisbon Accounting and Business School, part of the Polytechnic University of Lisbon (LABS-ISCAL). He is an Integrated Researcher affiliated with CETAPS at NOVA University of Lisbon. With a doctoral degree conferred by Nova University (UNL), Professor Martins has dedicated his research endeavours to the fields of Business Simulation Studies, Languages for Specific Purposes, and Computer-Assisted Language Learning. He serves on the editorial boards of multiple academic journals. Within LABS-ISCAL, he is responsible for overseeing the Department of Information and Communication Sciences and spearheads the International Business Simulation course.

Shinji Okumura holds a Ph.D. in Applied Linguistics from Monash University, Australia, and is an Associate Professor in the Faculty of Information and Communications at Bunkyo University, Japan. His research focuses on technology-mediated task-based language teaching, virtual exchange, and intercultural education. Dr. Okumura has authored a book chapter titled "Enhancing Intercultural Language Learning Through Virtual Exchange and Technology-Mediated Task-Based Language Teaching," which will be included in R. Vurdien & W. Chambers (Eds.), Technology-Mediated Language Learning and Teaching (IGI Global). He is currently leading virtual exchange projects that introduce Japanese subcultures to students in different countries in higher education, promoting global community engagement and enhancing additional language learning and intercultural competence.

Jyoti Prakash Pujari is an Assistant Professor in the Department of English and Cultural Studies at Christ University, Delhi NCR. His research interests include postcolonial studies, intellectual history, and digital pedagogy. His Ph.D., awarded by NIT Rourkela, focused on British women's writing in colonial India. A former Jawaharlal Nehru Memorial Fund scholar, he has published on AI and pedagogical implications, and surveillance cultures. He currently teaches American and World Literatures and is involved in curriculum design, creative writing pedagogy, and interdisciplinary course development.

Index

A

B

C

D

www.ingramcontent.com/pod-product-compliance
Lightning Source LLC
LaVergne TN
LVHW062325300926
849161LV00007B/1569